PENGUIN BOOKS

DREAMS OF LOVE AND FATEFUL ENCOUNTERS

Ethel S. Person, M.D., is Professor of Clinical Psychiatry at Columbia University, and the Director of the Columbia Psychoanalytic Center for Training and Research, where she is a Training and Supervisory Analyst. Dr. Person is also in private practice. She lives in Manhattan with her husband and two sons.

Dreams of Love and Fateful Encounters

THE POWER OF
ROMANTIC PASSION

Ethel S. Person

PENGUIN BOOKS

PENGUIN BOOKS
Published by the Penguin Group
Viking Penguin, a division of Penguin Books USA Inc.,
40 West 23rd Street, New York, New York 10010, U.S.A.
Penguin Books Ltd, 27 Wrights Lane,
London W8 5TZ, England
Penguin Books Australia Ltd, Ringwood,
Victoria, Australia
Penguin Books Canada Ltd, 2801 John Street,
Markham, Ontario, Canada L3R 1B4
Penguin Books (N.Z.) Ltd, 182-190 Wairau Road,
Auckland 10, New Zealand

Penguin Books Ltd, Registered Offices,
Harmondsworth, Middlesex, England

First published in the United States of America by
W.W. Norton & Company, Inc., 1988
Published in Penguin Books 1989

10 9 8 7 6 5 4 3 2

Credits for borrowed material:
    Pages 33, 165, 322: W. H. Auden, *The Collected Poems*, edited by Edward Mendelson. © 1976
by Edward Mendelson, William Meredith, and Monroe K. Spears, executors of the Estate of W. H.
Auden. Reprinted by permission of Random House, Inc.
    Page 173: "Paper Doll" (John S. Black). Used by permission of Edward B. Marks Music
Company.
    Page 213: From *The Divine Comedy* by Dante Alighieri, translated by John Ciardi. Copyright
© 1970 by John Ciardi. Reprinted by permission of W. W. Norton & Company, Inc.

LIBRARY OF CONGRESS CATALOGING IN PUBLICATION DATA
Person, Ethel Spector.
    Dreams of love and fateful encounters: the power of romantic
    passion/Ethel Spector Person.
        p.   cm.
    Bibliography: p.
    Includes index.
    ISBN 0 14 01.2055 6
    1. Love.   I. Title.
    [BF575.L8P43   1989]
    152.4—dc19   88-32403

Printed in the United States of America
Set in Avanta

Contents

5

THE FATE OF LOVE

Acknowledgments

THIS BOOK is written for those who, like me, have struggled to understand the importance and power of romantic love. My efforts have been informed and enriched throughout by the generosity of friends and colleagues who have read and critiqued parts of the manuscript, suggested references, or shared anecdotes. In particular I want to thank Shana Alexander, Susannah Bianchi, Jessica Diamond, Nancy Diamond, Richard G. Druss, Ilene Lefcourt, Nadine MacKinnon, Roger MacKinnon, Steven Marcus, Lucas Matthiessen, Robert Michels, Regina Ovesey, Lucy Simon, Caroline Stoessinger, Gladys Topkis, and Milton Viederman. Sandy Kadet has been ever willing to play devil's advocate and force me to clarify my thinking. Beth Rashbaum has helped me think through some important distinctions, and follow them to their logical conclusions. My thanks also go to Doris Parker, who with the help of Delmina Price and Jacob Clark typed and retyped the manuscript, and to Elizabeth Olds, who checked the bibliography and the quotations. Joan Jackson, has, as usual, monitored my schedule and preserved my writing time, and assisted in countless other ways.

My debts to the psychoanalytic literature and to the work of Freud are self-evident. Of recent contributors to the psychoanalytic literature on love, I have been most influenced by the contributions of Otto Kernberg and by Eva Lester's paper on the erotic transference. But I have relied on many sources from different disciplines, from literature, and from films. The notes to be found at the end of the text detail my intellectual indebtedness.

I am especially grateful to my agent, Rhoda Weyr, who has been consistently kind and supportive, and to my editor, Linda Healey, who has tactfully and effectively shaped this manuscript. My sons Louis and Lloyd Sherman have been patient and loving. And beyond generosity, my husband has been my mainstay.

Introduction

LOVE HAS BEEN one of the most profound interests of my life since I was no more than twelve. I never feel that I know people well without knowing something of the narrative of their loves, nor do I feel that anyone can truly know me without knowing something of that part of my life. And, as a practicing psychoanalyst, I have found that romantic love appears to be just as important to many people—though not to all—as it is to me. In Scott Spencer's novel *Endless Love* the young lover David has this insight, "If endless love was a dream, then it was a dream we all shared, even more than we all shared the dream of never dying or of traveling through time." While I don't agree with David that the longing for love is unanimous, I think the longing for love, and the experience itself, open us to some of the most enriching and liberating possibilities that life can offer.

There are many people, however, who are either dismissive of love, or fearful of it. Love has always had its enthusiasts as well as its naysayers, and each group can provide ample evidence for its own viewpoint—that love is a self-transforming and self-transcending experience or, alternately, that it is a self-deluding and often self-destructive one. But this very split in the valuation of romantic love, and the fervor with which people declare themselves to be adherents of one view or the other, tells us something about the power of love. Few other aspects of our emotional lives are capable of evoking such strong and conflicting feelings. When lovers are in the opening phases of love, they revel in it and believe it will last forever. When love ends, as alas it very often does, they curse it and feel that they were victimized by a storm in the blood or by a capricious Cupid whom they swear to evade the next time he aims his poisonous arrows at them. Those who have never felt those darts may long for them, fear them, or make light of them. But for anyone who has been struck, there is no denying that love, though seldom endless and never perfect, is an extremely powerful force, filled with joy as well as sorrow. Moreover, it is a force capable of changing the lover in profound ways—both good and bad—and these changes often endure even when the love that engendered them does not.

Passionate romantic love is the subject of this book—its sources in our early lives, its relationship to imagination and creativity, its capacity to transform the lover and enable the lover to transcend the self. In exploring the subject of romantic love, I have been influenced by William James's admonition that to study religion one ought to look at the most religious man in his most energetically religious mood. To describe the experience of love I have relied on the testimony of lovers, and their observers, which is found in novels, films, autobiographies, biographies, and letters. I have also made plentiful use of the stories of people I know. Those that are retold here without alteration are used with the express, written consent of the protagonists. Others have been altered and sometimes combined in such a way that the facts are no longer exact to each instance, but the basic outlines are true to the central emotional content of the experience.

Though what I know about love is surely based in part on my experience as an analyst, there is no patient material from my clinical practice in these pages, and this for two reasons. First and foremost, that material is confidential. Less important, though relevant, is the fact that many people dismiss patient material as distorted and neurotic. I am not moved by this common criticism of theories that evolve out of clinical practice, for I generally find patients to be as "normal" as anyone else; but perhaps testimony on love from people not in treatment will better convince nonbelievers that passionate love is a normal—and often desirable—human occurrence. Be that as it may, I have not hesitated to make use of particularly interesting case histories from other therapists' practices if they have already appeared in published form.

Psychoanalysis has much to say about love and its relationship to sex, psychological development, bonding and attachment, identification and ego ideal. Yet psychoanalysis cannot be the only tool with which to examine the subject. Love cannot be conveyed or understood through the language of any single discipline. In order to understand the existential dilemmas inherent in love, one must view it from a philosophical perspective; in order to understand its cultural variability, one must utilize a cultural perspective. I have brought what I know of both into this book.

I also want to address a common misperception: the belief that women are more liable (or able) to fall in love and are more influenced by it than men, who pursue their lives more in accord with the dictates of what we think of as reason. The capacity for romantic love is inherent in human nature. Men and women both seek it. Love may or may not be realized in any given individual, it may receive a higher valuation in some cultures than in others, and it may take different forms according to sex. While men and women may be more interested in love at different times in the life cycle or may be more vulnerable to different distortions of love, the power of love does not by nature affect one sex more than the other. Love is a uniquely human experience, and it does not discriminate between the sexes.

Above all else, lovers want to be together. Barring that, they most enjoy two other pastimes: thinking, daydreaming, or brooding over the beloved; and confiding, confessing, or speaking obsessively about the love to an intimate friend (or therapist). Consequently, most love affairs, even secret ones, are almost always subjected to the scrutiny of outside observers. The lovers and the observers, from their different vantage points, will almost inevitably disagree as to the seriousness, appropriateness, and value of the love affair.

For the lover, two aspects of his subjective experience are paramount. First is the centrality of his passion. The lover is lost in contemplation of the Other, and obsessed with the minute shifts, the ups and downs, of their relationship; love intrudes upon every moment of waking life (and many of sleep). Second is the "fact" of the superiority of the beloved. The loved one is usually idealized, endowed with almost supernatural powers and attributes, felt to be the most wonderful creature in the world. The lover basks in the reflected glory of the love object, and believes (or fears) that life would not be worth living if the beloved were to leave. The lover's *raison d'être* and self-worth are inextricably bound up with the continued reciprocation of love.

The lovers savor the secret knowledge that is theirs. In their experience, never has there been such rapture, such transport, such transcendence and bliss. The flesh of a peach, the luminosity of early morning, the sound of distant churchbells—the pleasure the lover takes in all these small experiences is heightened by love, suffused with special meaning. The lovers believe their friends could never understand, for they alone (or in company with perhaps a few legendary couples from the past) have been initiated into the divine mysteries of true love.

But friends are often dubious. Hers say (though usually not in her presence), "He isn't worth it. What does she see in him? He will only hurt her, he is not to be relied upon." His remark, "She's not great looking, not so smart. I wonder what he sees in her. She must be good in bed." If the beloved has a little fame or money, then friends may grant, though derisively, "Well, for her he's a star." Friends may even think the lovers mad or obsessed.

Sometimes, of course, parents or friends may be as thrilled as the lover, idealizing the love relationship along with the lovers. But generally there is a marked difference between the subjective experience—rich, resonant, filled with promise—and the "objective" observation on the part of friends—calibrated, calm, and judging. This difference in perception is rationalized by both sides. The confidantes to the love affair invoke the cliché "love is blind," while the lovers tell themselves and each other that their friends are just jealous. There is some truth to both claims, but the perceptual dissonance between lovers and observers goes beyond this, straight to the very essence of the experience of love.

It is precisely the lovers' leap out of objectivity and into subjectivity that signals the liberation of love. If it is true that the greatest breach in nature is between two minds (as William James suggested), then we must acknowledge the magnitude of the emotion that allows us to bridge such a chasm. Once we lose the psychological sense of oneness with mother, which prevails (if ever) only during infancy, we become increasingly isolated beings. Sometimes that isolation is so profound as to be painful, raising the awful spectre that one may exist as a consciousness all alone in the universe. Only by sharing in each other's subjective realities can we mitigate that isolation. While empathy, intuition, and identification all help, romantic love goes much further: it denies the barriers separating us, offering hope for a concordance of two souls; or at least for a free flow between them—what has been called "emotional telepathy."

Romantic love, subjectively experienced, is an emotion of extraordinary intensity. The experience of love can make time stop, therefore giving one the rare opportunity to live in the present and to escape momentarily the nagging abstractions of past and future. Love may confer a sense of inner rightness, peace, and richness; or it may be a mode of transforming the self. Beyond enlarging and changing the self, love may also enable the lovers to break through the stifling limits of self. Hence, it is a mode of transcendence, frequently designated as a religion of two.

While it is true that love can be an agent for personal growth and change, it is also a loose cannon on the deck of human affairs. Because of its intensity, love has the capacity to disrupt social norms and conventions, giving lovers both cause and sanction to escape the established order. In this sense romantic passion is the expression of individuality (or of two individualities joined), sometimes played out against the restraints of convention. Romantic love is the celebration of the individual and the pair, not of larger social units, and so it is that romantic love may come in direct conflict with ordered society. No wonder, then, that it is regarded with awe and suspicion by those not in its thrall.

Lovers, too, may have reason to fear love. Passion can devour them. In unrequited love (and even in mutual love, when its fulfillment threatens to destroy already existing commitments), the lover is tormented. In such instances, love is experienced as involuntary, not subject to conscious control and, therefore, an affront to honor, will, and reason, if not an outright curse of madness. Even in love that is fulfilled under the most favorable of circumstances, there is risk for the lovers. Mutual love can end slowly, seeming simply to disappear, or it can turn sour. Most horribly of all it can end in ennui and the sense of emptiness.

But in defense of love as the glue that holds society together rather than the explosive that blows it apart, it must be pointed out that while love may begin as a religion of two lovers set apart from the rest of the world, it evolves into a socially integrating force that more often than not is co-opted to the perpetuation of the generations. Love may separate the couple from the group, thereby threatening it, but it is also the agent of the group's survival.

And even if romantic love is often short-lived, how mistaken it is to think that its transience disqualifies it from significance. Such a point of view bespeaks a miserly and reductive way of thinking, as though love were a thing to be acquired and retained if it is to be of value. To think this way is to glorify possession over experience. Love is not an object, it is a feeling and an intention (of the heart, the senses, the imagination). Whether or not romantic love is necessarily doomed, it is the experience itself and the difference it renders to a life that makes it valuable.

The divergence in the valuation of romantic love by lovers and observers is exactly duplicated in the way romantic love is regarded in popular culture as opposed to intellectual and scientific discourse: love is typically celebrated by the former and deplored by the latter. This reflects a deep rift in our culture between feeling and knowing. Our contemporary valuation of passionate love is split between two coexistent and contradictory traditions—the romantic and the rational.

"Rationalists" regard romantic love as a foolish if not downright dangerous illusion which creates impossible expectations in people and makes them unable to just accept the good that *is* possible in relationships. They associate passionate love with "consumptive heroines, heroes wasting away with feverish desire, and deathbed farewells; with the overwrought, unhealthy music of Wagner, Strauss and Puccini." Romantic lovers are faulted for their insecure insistence on monogamy and exclusivity, their encouragement of mutual dependency, their confusion of love and possession, their jealousy and need to control the other, their self-destructiveness.

Most academic disciplines either ignore love or treat it in accordance with the rationalist tradition. Many people feel that to treat love seriously would be to betray one's naiveté—longing for love being considered the adult version of believing in Santa Claus. To the extent that love receives attention from them at all, the predilection of the rationalists is to discredit it as foolish at best, called into being by personal weakness and neurosis. The debunkers of love view it as a temporary giddiness, an affliction, or even a kind of illness or madness. The rationalist mode of thinking about romantic love prevails in our professional literature, whether of psychology, sociology, or philosophy. It has been said that the three great languages of contemporary Western culture—Christian, psychoanalytic, and Marxist—all conspire to devalue love. A more recent view, that of neuroscience, contributes to the negative valuation by reducing love to no more than a biochemical excitation.

Literary criticism is the only form of intellectual discourse likely to give serious and respectful attention to love, and then only because literary critics deal with fiction. In fiction, if the novelist is successful, the reader is enabled to feel *with* the character. In fiction, as in love, there is the possibility of entering into another's subjectivity. Hence in fiction, where the mandate of the writer is to convey the emotional content of experience, love is a natural subject and is given its due. In most other modern forms of discourse, however, it is description and analysis of experience (often by means of a quantification) which are the goal, not the imaginative apprehension and recreation of experience. Intellect must then preempt imagination as the means to the end. But without the warm light of imagination to temper the cool linearities of reason, intellect is doomed to the reductivist, if not out-and-out hostile, view of love.

Consequently, love remains for the most part the province of poets, lyricists, novelists, and filmmakers. It is in works of the imagination that romantic love is dwelt upon and celebrated. They may treat it reverentially or fearfully, but there is no mistaking its centrality. And it is because they do acknowledge love's power that they are so popular. As Emerson observed: "What books in the circulating libraries circulate? How we glow over these novels of passion, when the story is told with any spark of truth and nature!"

There is disagreement about whether romantic love is a basic predisposition of human nature or merely a culturally induced phenomenon. Morton Hunt even goes so far as to suggest that it is fictional: "Believed in but not practiced." Others feel that it is indeed practiced, but as the enactment of an almost exclusively female disease. The feminist critique, beginning with Simone de Beauvoir, often characterizes romantic love as a rationalization for female subordination and dependency, as the glamorous trap that camouflages the prison to which marriage condemns women.

As an antidote to the disease, whatever its etiology, the rationalists— including armies of psychotherapists, marriage counselors, and family therapists, aided and abetted by the sexual liberationists and advocates of "open" marriage—counsel a cool approach to the creation of stable, affectionate relationships. Insofar as contemporary psychoanalysts, and particularly some so-called revisionist analysts, address the question of love at all, they attempt to distinguish "mature" love from romantic love, loving from being in love: the former being healthy, the latter neurotic (perhaps worse) or inconsequential, or just an adolescent phase. Most mental health treatments of love are stale, antiseptic, and preachy; they generally denigrate the experience of falling in love. In essence they downgrade romantic love and endorse some version of nonpassionate "love" which is based on a rational decision to commit oneself to a person or situation. They counsel a kind of love stripped of "excess"—mature, as it were—and based on mutual respect, shared values, and common interests. Duty and responsibility are valued above emotional pleasure and sexual passion. Their hope is that tamed, mutual love will be less disorderly than romantic love.

"Romantics," on the other hand, see the rationalist view as love with the heart cut out. They tend to regard the rationalists as emotionally shallow or inhibited, fearful of their passions and imprisoned in caution.

But, ironically enough, rationalists and romantics often cross over into one another's camps. A realist can be taken off guard by a grand passion. And often enough a romantic comes to understand the treacheries of romantic passion, if not intellectually, then experientially.

So it is, whether for reasons of ideology or experience, that many of us regard love with a split or alternating consciousness: we argue that most love is a form of self-deception or even self-destruction, but nonetheless we long for it and seek it out. We may denigrate love with our words, but we consecrate it with our hearts. Thus it happens that, despite the polarity of their values, the romantic and rationalist viewpoints can often be observed in a single consciousness, either simultaneously or sequentially.

The protagonist of James Salter's novel, *Light Years*, remembers passionate love as "that sumptuous love which made one drunk, which one longed for, envied, believed in. . . . Gone from her completely was the knowledge she once was sure she would keep forever: the taste, the exaltation of days made luminous by love—with it, one had everything. 'That's an illusion,' she said." Consider also the related sentiment as expressed by Lily Briscoe in Virginia Woolf's *To the Lighthouse:* "Yet, she said to herself, from the dawn of time odes have been sung to love; wreaths heaped and roses; and if you asked nine people out of ten they would say they wanted nothing but this—love; while the women, judging from her own experience, would all the time be feeling, This is not what we want; there is nothing more tedious, puerile, and inhumane than this; yet it is also beautiful and necessary. Well then, well then?"

Of course, such ambivalence in the valuation of love is no accident. As already suggested, its cause lies within the very nature of love. It is precisely because love is so powerful, so close to our deepest longings and dreams that it may prove glorious and even transform and enlarge the self. But for the very same reason, the pain to which the lover is made vulnerable by love may make love a suspect, even a dreaded experience.

The conflict between "romantic" and "rational" appraisals in contemporary culture is not new. It corresponds to a long-standing bifurcation in Western attitudes about love. Both attitudes may in fact be traced at least as far back as Plato's time. Plato bequeathed to us the original Western conception of love, that through love one seeks the other half of one's soul, in order to form a union that will make one whole again. But it is also in Plato that we encounter Socrates' cautionary admonition: "As wolves love lambs, so lovers love their loves." Ambivalence about love has ancient and honorable roots.

What is unique about our century is not its dual valuation of love; rather, it is the extent to which love is no longer even deemed worthy of intellectual analysis. Discourses on love have virtually disappeared from our major intellectual enterprises. The interest in love has been relegated almost exclusively to private concerns and popular culture. This distinguishes our century from the several centuries that have preceded it.

The decline in the amount of serious attention paid to love may be attributed in part to the fact that many of the great discourses on love belong to religious literature, and ours is a secular age. In part, it is because philosophy—the last great sanctuary of questions relating to the "soul" and the one discipline where love was addressed seriously—has itself largely been transformed and now addresses analytic and linguistic questions rather than metaphysical and transcendental concerns. And perhaps the twentieth-century response to love as a fit subject for discussion and thought has also to do with our rejection of what we see as the nineteenth century's sentimentality and its animosity to sexuality. In fact, we have come to think of passionate love as symptomatic of the nineteenth century and the sentimental corollary of its repressive attitude towards sexuality. Hence, as we celebrate our own permissive sexuality we downplay the importance of love, demonstrating once more what is so evident in our own culture: the tendency to isolate sexuality, to reduce its contextual importance, even as we acknowledge our fascination with it.

The main reason for the virtual disappearance of discourse on love, though, is the enormous prestige of science in our age, and science's propensity to value only that which it can explain. But that dismissal of what does not seem amenable to testing, quantification, verification, and replication, of what is judged to be sentimental or based on feeling, is itself often pseudoscientific, irrational. It denies what we *know* of the limits of reason, and of reason's easy corruptibility by unconscious forces; and it ignores the finiteness of what we now "know" or can ever know. Even so, the pseudoscientific point of view remains very powerful, and it tends to discredit the immense importance of all passions and feelings in our lives.

This tendency of the scientific attitude may be related to another predisposition of the human spirit. "Humankind cannot bear very much reality," T. S. Eliot remarks in *Four Quartets,* and it is common knowledge that the search for the private "truth" of any individual's psychic life evokes resistance. We are all too easily seduced away from the truth, the reality, of our own inward experience, which may often seem beyond communication and hence beyond respect or value. Too easily, in the name of the good, or the rational, or the moral, or the Christian, or the democratic, or even the merely socially acceptable, we blink away the actualities of our condition—the feelings, drives, dreams, and desires that express, with painful accuracy, the depths at which we really *live.* Not where we think or imagine we should live, or where society advises us to live, but where our lives are fueled and our deepest satisfactions experienced—this is what we disregard. We allow ourselves too often to live lives that are secondhand and largely theoretical, devoted to goods we do not truly desire, to gods in whom we do not truly believe.

Our need for authenticity is not, of course, to deny another and opposing need: that of believing in and belonging to some reality larger than the self or our subjective world of experience. We must, in fact, reconcile these apparently conflicting needs, and in some measure, and for some people, I shall argue, this is precisely what is accomplished through passionate love. But for all of us it is necessary to recognize the existence of these contrary realms and to find some way of living—and of feeling—within them both.

To do so we may have to reconsider some of the discarded wisdom of the nineteenth-century Romantics. That century's impulse to romanticism was meant to counter the one-sided legacy of the Enlightenment—the overwhelming regard for reason. Victor Hugo expressed the Romantics' impatience with the strait jacket of reason alone: "How strange that after eighteen centuries of progress, the freedom of thought is proclaimed, the freedom of the heart is denied."

In the romantic tradition, the fact of a feeling's existence is sufficient justification for and validation of it. Keats, writing to a friend about his belief in the authenticity of the imagination, spoke with equal fervor about the value of love, and about the essential correspondence between love and imagination: "I am certain of nothing but of the holiness of the Heart's affections and the truth of Imagination. What the Imagination seizes as Beauty must be truth—whether it existed before or not, for I have the same Idea of all our passions as of Love—they are all, in their sublime, creative of essential Beauty." And he goes on to anatomize the failure of reason and imagination to find any common ground: "I have never yet been able to perceive how any thing can be known for truth by consequitive reasoning."

Love is an act of the imagination. For some of us, it will be the great creative triumph of our lives. In its very nature as an act of the imagination lies the source of its power for both good and ill, for it can indeed exploit the lover's illusions or delusions, but alternately can lead the lover to transcending truths.

Perhaps the enormous appeal of fiction, film, and psychotherapy in our time is that they are almost the only permissible cultural channels of unrestrained subjectivity and feelings. They accept, endorse, and validate the immense importance of that which science dismisses with a condescending wave of a hand. They emphasize the importance of the inner experience, of subjectivity. They have in common the ability to serve as windows into another's subjectivity.

Psychoanalysis, like fiction, ought to be well suited to depicting love, drawing as it does upon both the unconscious and the imagination. Despite the long-standing hesitancy of analysts to deal with love theoretically, psychoanalysis, among all the human sciences, is perhaps uniquely well equipped to do so. It is its professional duty, of course, insofar as it claims human desires as its area of special study. But more important, psychoanalysis is characterized precisely by that dialectic between the subjective and objective which would make understanding of love possible, and communicable, by discursive methods.

The importance of romantic love could hardly escape an analyst's notice. It is the primary focus in many psychoanalytic therapies. Sometimes the patient focuses on his quest for romantic love as the search for a soul mate, sometimes, less grandly, as the search for a committed, deep relationship. Many patients come into treatment specifically for problems related to love. But even when they come to treatment for other reasons, sooner or later most spend a great deal of time talking about love. Problems of love are very different depending on the patient's history and situation. Patients talk about the waning of passion and the loss of real intimacy (or the fear of it), the torture of unremitting jealousy, the inability to fall in love, or the impossibility of finding an appropriate partner, the mourning and depression accompanying the breakup of a love affair or marriage, the tendency to linger too long in intense but idealized love attachments, and to feel stuck in hopeless unrequited love affairs, or the longing for love when the prospect for it does not appear anywhere on the horizon. And often the patient's erotic feelings towards the analyst also eventually become part of the ongoing analytic dialogue.

Strangely enough, however, although discussions of love comprise a large portion of the psychoanalytic (therapeutic) dialogue, theoretical discussions of love are notoriously absent from the psychoanalytic literature. (There are a very few exceptions, and they all begin by pointing out the paucity of the psychoanalytic studies of love.) Psychoanalysis does give a nod in the direction of love insofar as mental health is defined as the ability to love and work, but what is meant is generally the "mature" form of committed love. Many analysts, like others, have regarded romantic love, with its idealization of the love object, as an expression of neurosis, a maladaptive effort to solve a dependency problem, or an adolescent fixation.

It is both strange and disheartening that the subject of love in psychoanalytic discourse has been relegated to the periphery. This neglect is especially striking when the paucity of material about love is compared with the abundance (possibly overabundance) of work on issues of sexuality—inhibited, aberrant, or driven.

Some of the reluctance to theorize on love may go back to the origins of psychoanalysis. While trying to establish psychoanalysis as a reputable science, Freud insisted on presenting his theories in the guise of "objective" science in order to render them acceptable and palatable. Freud, in attempting to achieve a science of mind, was very much a "biologist of the mind." He focused on forces rather than on feelings as the mediators of behavior. Although there is in fact a complex psychological theory of love scattered throughout his writings, most analysts have subscribed to his most schematic formulation of love, which depicted it merely as sublimated libido—sexual energy. In classical psychoanalytic formulations, libido rather than passion is viewed as the central force in personality formation. And libido theory is better suited to explaining sex than love.

Then, too, analysts have been most comfortable theorizing in areas they thought were fundamental to human nature, and not so culturally variable as romantic love. Clearly romantic love does not have the same priority or value in all cultures. While love draws on fundamental human propensities—in particular the longing for some form of transcendence as a means of ameliorating the basic isolation of the human condition— different cultures promote different means to transcendence. Socialization to the values of a particular culture plays an enormous role in determining whether or not romantic love will be sought as the route to self-affirmation and transcendence. Socialization also promotes different strategies for the gratification of sex and tender nurturance. Some cultures, for example, sanction the separation of passionate friendship and sex. Moreover, in any given culture, men and women are often socialized to different roles, values, and modes of transcendence. The experience of love, then, surely varies according to epoch, culture, class and caste, and even gender. But as psychoanalysts have come to acknowledge, sometimes to their chagrin, very little of fundamental interest to analysts is ahistorical—not even the behavioral expressions of sex. It is important to reclaim romantic love as a fit subject for psychoanalytic scrutiny and theorizing.

However, even if that is granted, part of the psychoanalytic reservation about addressing the topic of love has to do with love itself, not with the difficulty of theorizing it adequately. Romantic love has been as problematic to therapists as to lovers themselves. Some psychoanalysts have developed reservations about romantic love, not on theoretical grounds or out of any adherence to a scientific ethos, but because of their clinical experience. Passionate attachments reported by patients are often permeated with pathological elements. Some therapists see the clinical problems as evidence of the limitations in all romantic love.

But, in fact, passionate attachments range from healthy to unhealthy. By and large, passionate attachments belong to the realm of normal psychology, though a certain minority are permeated with derivatives of intrapsychic conflict. But those unencumbered by personal pathology are nonetheless subject to the existential problems inherent in all passionate attachments. It does not follow, though, that love is not worth the pain, any more than one would suggest that life's existential limitations make life not worth living. Such a valuation neglects the good that can come of romantic love, and also fails to take into account those fundamental impulses through which love becomes so important for our patients and ourselves.

This book breaks with the contemporary intellectual and philosophic assumptions about romantic love. Instead of echoing the negative, dismissive point of view now dominant in academia, I will side with the evaluation of popular culture, which acknowledges love's vital importance and its power. While it has been proposed that love is no more than the combination of "physical gratification with a happy relationship," the subjective experience of passionate love belies such an oversimplified definition. Such reductionism merely exposes the naive, over-rationalized modern understanding of love. It ignores love's magnetic pull, its peremptoriness and imaginative power.

It is my central thesis that love serves an important function not only for the individual but also for the culture. It is the narrative thread not just in novels, but in lives. Love determines one's sense of obligations and time, or transforms them. Romantic love offers not just the excitement of the moment but the possibility for dramatic change in the self. It is, in fact, an agent of change.

Romantic love often demands a significant reordering of values and priorities, and it presents the content and conditions requisite to such change. Love creates a situation in which the self is exposed to new risks and enlarged possibilities; it is one of the most significant crucibles for growth. Romantic love takes on meaning and provides a subjective sense of liberation only insofar as it creates a flexibility in personality that allows a break-through of internal psychological barriers and taboos, and sometimes external ones as well. It creates a flux in personality, the possibility for change, and the impetus to begin new phases of life and undertake new endeavors. As such, it can be seen as a paradigm for any significant realignment of personality and values; in this way it resembles the great religious conversion experiences.

Yet it is not my purpose simply to extol romantic love and point to its value as an agent of self-transformation and transcendence. I will address not only the aims or projects of love and its power to unlock the soul, but also its inherent paradoxes and conflicts and its propensity to disintegrate and cause harm.

There is an inevitable crisis or struggle in mutual love, one that will test love and either strengthen or break it. Consequently, the fate of love is diverse: it may be unrequited or the lover rejected; it may wane and die, or it may modulate into affection. Not often, but sometimes, the intensity and passion of the initial phase can persist and find a place within a committed, sustained love. Despite its glories, romantic love is notorious for its brevity, and—often because of that brevity—for the pain and suffering that may accompany it. But even in failed love, the lover may still benefit and retain those benefits long after love has ended. However, though the lover may be redeemed in love, it is also true that he may be destroyed by it.

All these outcomes are natural by-products of the aims of love, which are not only complex and diverse, but also paradoxical, and, at times, downright contradictory. Love is an affirmation of what one already is, yet at the same time one uses it to escape to a new self. (In the same way, the child uses his mother's affirmation as a springboard for change.) Moreover, love can unleash destructive forces. Love may be devouring or self-abnegating. Love is often coupled with domination or slavishness. There is undoubtedly a potential for treachery to the self and to others inherent in romantic love. The question that haunts all who desire love and seek it is how to reconcile its contradictory aims, how to enable its life-enhancing qualities to triumph.

In addition to the existential problems inherent in it, romantic love may also be disrupted or disfigured by individual neuroses. Because love draws upon so much of our personality, it is subject to distortion by our pasts, the histories of all our relationships, and the other passions that inhabit us.

Nonetheless, romantic love remains one of the most worthwhile and transcendent human experiences, its inherent dilemmas and the fact that it serves as a magnet for psychopathology notwithstanding. Despite the general cautions of traditional wisdom and psychoanalytic theory, I am certain that romantic love is generally more enriching than it is depleting. It is a magnificently human condition, and yet not everyone will experience it. Despite its (usually) transient nature, it offers access to the unconscious, lights up the emotional life, and brings internal change in a way that often far outlives the experience itself. Romantic love is the preserve of hope and imaginative longing; it is one of the passions that move us, that initiate the great quests and adventures of our lives. Like so many other human gifts, romantic love has the potential for both good and evil, but should not be judged by its corrupted forms or dismissed on account of its transience.

A Note

Though clearly the lover may be of either sex, and the beloved too, it has proved too cumbersome to refer to them always as "he or she." Consequently I have felt forced to declare my pronouns, and after much back and forth, to and fro, have settled on the lover as "he" and the beloved as "her," albeit with a few inconsistencies depending on context. I have done so for two reasons. First (though less important), this usage is the convention in works on love. Second, there seems to be a current prejudice that *he* no longer falls in love, moved as he is by reason or by sentiments nobler than mere romantic love. My designation of the lover as "he" is a vote of confidence that the male remains as much a lover as ever. But I surely do not mean to imply that "she" is not, or that "he" as the lover is active and "she" as the beloved is passive. "He" may be the lover and may love her—or him; "she" may be the lover and may love him—or her. And in any of these permutations, the fate of love depends not only upon the activity of the lover but upon the beloved's activity as well. Moreover, it could be argued that insofar as there is a "passive" party, it is the lover, requiring as he does so much affirmation from the beloved. The lover is the one who feels overcome and ravished, in need of nourishment from the beloved.

1

THE EXPERIENCE OF
ROMANTIC LOVE

CHAPTER ONE

Falling in Love

N THE novel *Endless Love*, Arthur, preparing his son David to meet the woman he loves, explains how he became disenchanted with David's mother (Rose) and how he came to fall in love again.

"You were my inspiration—Seeing you in love reminded me."

"Of what?"

"Of how I once felt about Rose and how she never ever felt about me, until I didn't feel that way about her either. But you reminded me of how it feels. A lot of people never have it, that feeling, not even once. You know that, don't you? But you had it—"

"With Jade."

"And you reminded me that I once had it and that I never felt so large and important as I did when being in love was *everything*. I saw you walking a foot above the earth and I remembered that was where *I* used to walk, for a few months."

Although Rose was not in love with him, Arthur had adjusted to his marriage and accepted his lot in life, up until the time his son fell in love and reminded him of what he was missing.

"I'd forgotten. You made me remember and then Barbara showed me I hadn't missed my chance. It was like waking up twenty years younger . . ."

Many of us who are not in love long to be. We know only too well the glories we are missing. We may enjoy full, rich lives and be proud of our accomplishments, but still feel lonely and isolated. Friends and family are no protection against such aloneness. When she was advanced in age Helene Deutsch observed that loneliness was the result of not being first for someone else. Aside from brief moments in infancy and childhood (when we may not even be aware of it), we hardly ever come first. But love restores that blissful state to us. Being the most important person in someone else's life is one of the defining premises of passionate love.

Sometimes we are brought up short by the realization that friendship, no matter how deep and intimate, cannot supply us with the priority of place we long for. A woman once told me of a poignant incident that had occurred many years earlier, when she was a college freshman. She was at that time involved in a passionate friendship with her college roommate, the first such relationship of her life because it was the first to combine intellectual depth with emotional resonance. Coming home one night, she saw her roommate embracing a boyfriend. At that moment, suddenly she realized that she did not—and could not ever—come first with her friend. Devoid of any homosexual urges then or now, she was amazed at the depth of her pain and sense of betrayal. From that time on, in an effort to shield herself from further hurt, to ward off the knowledge that she could never achieve priority in such relationships, she devalued friendships with women.

We long for intimacy, for priority, for the exultation of love. Yet however well we may learn to wall ourselves off from love (in any of its manifold forms) we cannot do the reverse and will ourselves into love. It is said that it is as easy to fall in love with a rich man as with a poor one. This means that one can and should marry a rich man—but one either loves or does not. While following such advice (marrying a rich man) may prove advantageous under certain circumstances, injunctions to fall in love are impossible to obey. So Lady Capulet discovers in the wake of her advice to Juliet, who declares herself willing to follow that advice but proves unable to do so. In one of the early scenes in *Romeo and Juliet* Lady Capulet urges her daughter to love "the valiant Paris," telling her, "So shall you share all that he doth possess" and demanding of her "Speak briefly, can you like of Paris' love?" The obedient Juliet replies: "I'll look to like, if looking liking move." But Juliet, like everyone who has ever uttered the words "I wish I could love him," fails because the emotion of love cannot be willed into existence. Paradoxically, it is love's very immunity to social pressure and legislation that makes it free, albeit involuntary. Expediency may dictate, but love does not obey. Love is free from expediency and so is free itself.

Even when the would-be lover himself, without pressure from an outside advisor, longs to fall in love with a particular person, it is not within his control. Lillian Hellman, writing about her friend Arthur Cowan, who had declared her too old for him, finally divined what she thought was his true reticence in relation to her: "I was what he wanted to want, could not ever want, and that must have put an end to an old dream about the kind of life that he would now have because he didn't really want it." In fact, he seemed to prefer fashion models. It is for good reason that Cupid is known to be willful, mischievous, and sometimes even perverse.

Love comes when it does. Rather than *willing* it, we are *struck* by it as though by lightning. Lovers experience love as completely spontaneous, autonomous, independent of need—a gift, a feeling altogether inspired by the virtues of the beloved, not by any internal quest or need (though sometimes the *unhappy* lover may feel driven). The lover's belief mirrors his subjective experience. He begins to fall in love shortly after meeting the beloved: thus he attributes his feelings to an external agency—the overwhelming charms of the beloved. Love has always been experienced as a response provoked by something outside of us—if not the qualities of the beloved, as we tend to believe today, then thunderbolts, Cupid's arrows, or love potions.

But the actual dynamics of love run counter to our subjective experience. It is neither Cupid's arrows nor the perfection of the beloved that calls forth love. Love arises from within ourselves as an imaginative act, a creative synthesis, that aims to fulfill our deepest longings and our oldest dreams, that allows us both to renew and transform ourselves. There are two great unsolved mysteries about falling in love (love itself is filled with mystery). The first is why we fall in love when we do, the second why we "choose" whom we do.

We do have a few hints about the timing of love. Sometimes, particularly in adolescence, but later on as well, one can be infatuated with two different people almost simultaneously. Here the would-be lover admires two prospective candidates for his affection and fantasizes that one or the other relationship might evolve into love given the right circumstances. This capacity for simultaneous or sequential infatuation speaks to the question of when we fall in love, suggesting that there are psychological moments at which one is ripe, regardless of whether there is an appropriate love object at hand. Though such a lover appears at first glance to be fickle, it may only be his longing for a beloved who will reciprocate that makes him seem so. Romeo is the quintessential example. Although he died for love of Juliet, only five days before meeting her he had been sick with love for Rosaline. Rosaline, however, did not return his love. This may be why, within seconds of glimpsing Juliet for the first time, he forsakes his old love for a new: "Did my heart love till now? forswear it, sight! For I ne'er saw true beauty till this night." When Juliet returns his love, he is transformed into the truest of true lovers.

Indeed, special moments in one's individual development and particular kinds of life circumstances do appear likely to foster love. Falling in love often follows closely on the heels of anticipated or actual separation and loss, hence the love affairs and marriages that occur toward the end of the college years or when soldiers are mobilizing to go off to war, or even toward the end of an analysis. In one very close family where the mother died in her mid-forties, leaving behind not only her loving husband but four children in their late teens and early twenties, three of the children were involved in serious love affairs within six months of her death, and her husband within the year. The readiness with which some widows and widowers fall in love after the death of a spouse speaks not to their callousness, but to the very magnitude of their loss. The belief held by some families that it is a deep tribute to the dead spouse for the survivor to remarry is an acknowledgment of the longing for reconnection that grows out of the loss of someone who was deeply loved.

Sometimes being away from home acts as a stimulus to love not so much by causing a sense of loss as by loosening internal inhibitions. Consequently, separation may promote new possibilities. It is as though an unbearable weight of conscience and rectitude is lifted, and part of the personality freed. And so it is that shipboard romances abound; widows, spinsters, and lonely middle-aged women seek their Roman Springs; and love affairs flourish on movie sets and at business conventions. One thinks also of the ease with which students or professors fall in love during a year abroad, cut off both from the comforts and the constraints of home. As we shall see later, separation from the constraints of "real" life facilitates love in myriad other ways. For example, when a relationship appears of necessity to be time-limited, the fear of free-fall self-abandon can be assuaged by the convenient external limits rather than any internal braking.

The frequent love affairs between soldiers stationed abroad and the women they meet on foreign soil offer solutions to fundamentally different problems: for the soldier, cut off as he is from the world he knows, there is solace against the pain of loneliness; for the woman, the hope for a new beginning in a world she dreams is better than the one she knows only too well. But such love affairs are often extremely complex, invoking such diverse elements as the excitement of breaking taboos, the freedom of making counter-Oedipal selections, the glamor of the exotic, the bittersweet joys of a romance played out against the threat of death, and so on. The prevalence of this kind of love affair is obvious from its enduring popularity as a theme in books and movies: one thinks of men and their "war brides"—Lieutenant Frederick Henry and Catherine Barclay in Ernest Hemingway's A Farewell to Arms; of Dirk Struan and May-May in James Clavell's *Tai-Pan;* of Michael Corleone (Al Pacino) hiding out in Sicily and the beautiful Italian girl he falls in love with and marries in Francis Ford Coppola's film of *The Godfather.* Something of this dynamic is also at work in the ambivalent relationship between Charlie and her Israeli control in John Le Carré's *The Little Drummer Girl.*

In many other instances, falling in love appears to be triggered not by any real or threatened loss or danger, but by the reverse: when there is a situation experienced as stultifying, static, and all too enduring. Just as first love facilitates the separation of adolescents and young adults from their families (and any potential incestual threats), falling in love later in life can provide unhappily married spouses with either solace or escape.

Often, however, the psychological circumstances that prompt a lover to fall in love are unknown—perhaps unknowable—both to the lover and the observer. In his twenties and thirties, W. H. Auden is said to have despaired of ever finding love. He wrote of it in a tone both humorous and poignant:

> When it comes, will it come without warning
> > Just as I'm picking my nose?
> Will it knock at my door in the morning,
> > Or tread in the bus on my toes?
> Will it come like a change in the weather?
> > Will its greeting be courteous or rough?
> Will it alter my life altogether?
> > O tell me the truth about love.

And indeed love did come into Auden's life rather haphazardly when it finally made its longed-for appearance. An account of Auden's meeting with his lover and lifelong companion, Chester Kallman, suggests the way circumstances can conspire—when the moment is right and one or more possible candidates are available—to promote the magic synthesis of love. Auden was giving a reading to a group of college students. "For a long time now he had been seeking the mythical beloved in many love objects, but he had been disappointed. Then, suddenly, during his first month in America, he found what he had been looking for, sitting in the front row of a stuffy lecture hall." Yes and no. He was attracted to someone in the audience, but it wasn't Kallman. He was drawn to another young man: "Miller, tall, blonde, Anglo-Saxon, and heterosexual, probably reminded Auden of the schoolboy chums of his youth with whom he had been infatuated during boarding school years." Auden agreed to an interview with Kallman, believing Miller would accompany him. But Kallman came

alone. Christopher Isherwood, who let Kallman in, reportedly said to
Auden "It's the wrong blond." After a slow conversational start, Kallman
and Auden discovered a mutual interest in a Renaissance poet and Auden
"recognized a kindred spirit." And so "if at first Chester was perceived
to be the wrong blond, by the end of the afternoon he became the only
right one."

While it is often difficult to judge when someone is ready to fall in
love, except after the fact, it's even harder to account for the "choice"
of the beloved. Toward the end of his life, struggling to understand what
had been one of his lifelong preoccupations, H. G. Wells wrote an analysis
of the longing for love which each of us feels (in varying degrees) and tried
to come to grips with the question of why we love whom we love:

> I think that in every human mind, possibly from an extremely early age, there
> exists a continually growing and continually more subtle complex of expectation
> and hope; an aggregation of lovely and exciting thoughts; conceptions of encoun-
> ter and reaction picked up from observation, descriptions, drama; reveries of
> sensuous delights and ecstasies; reveries of understanding and reciprocity; which
> I will call the Lover-Shadow. . . . I think it is almost as essential in our lives as
> our self consciousness. It is *other* consciousness. . . . It is the inseparable correla-
> tive to the *persona*, in the direction of our lives. . . .
>
> When we make love, we are trying to make another human being concentrate
> for us as an impersonation or at least a symbol of the Lover-Shadow in our minds;
> and when we are in love it means that we have found in someone the presentation
> of the promise of some, at least, of the main qualities of our Lover-Shadow. The
> beloved person is for a time identified with the dream—attains a vividness that
> captures the role, and seems to leave anything outside it unilluminated.

Wells is clear in his own mind that our choice of lovers has to do with
our internal psychic processes—with imagination, in short. First we create
within our minds the complex of qualities that seems to us to constitute
the ideal love. But we each have different priorities, generally unconscious,
for those qualities essential to our images of the Lover-Shadow. Whatever
the shape of the Lover-Shadow we have created, we then, by another
imaginative act, transform some living creature into the embodiment of
this product of our minds. (We "try . . . to make another human being
[into] an impersonation . . . of the Lover-Shadow. . . .") Wells does not
explain, because no one can, how the imagination performs its alchemy.

In extreme cases, the lover may fall in love at first sight; what this
means is that he finds someone who appears to correspond to an already
well developed image of the Lover-Shadow. (And so one falls in love across

a dinner table or a crowded room.) Though some relationships born of love at first sight evolve and endure, many others prove vulnerable in the extreme to disillusionment—on both sides. The lover becomes horrified at the beloved's slightest deviation from his template, the beloved more and more aghast at how little the love showered on her seems to have anything to do with who she is. Rita Hayworth, who became world renowned as "Gilda," complained to many an interviewer that men went to bed with Gilda only to wake up disappointed with Rita, inevitably wounding her. Perhaps it is fortunate that for most of us falling in love does not occur at first sight, but is a more gradual process taking place in fits and starts as the Lover-Shadow and the real person are brought into approximate alignment.

Sometimes the very opposite of love at first sight transpires: a lover falls in love with someone he has long known. The classic story of love at second sight is perhaps that which takes place between two old friends when their situation changes remarkably, for example, when one or the other (or both) is widowed or divorced, and the context of life creates either the need or psychic space for a new love. Such was the background of the relationship between Aldous Huxley and his second wife, Laura Archera. Huxley and his first wife, Maria, had had a six-year, warm though casual friendship with Laura; among other things they were interested in her psychotherapeutic techniques. Laura wrote Huxley after Maria's death, and began to visit him frequently. According to Huxley's biographer, the second wife "was not one of the candidates resolved to enter upon a life of service;" in fact she was something of a reluctant bride being fearful of losing her hardwon freedom, but what she brought Huxley was youth, drive, and renewal.

More dramatic, though, are those instances in which there is no dramatic change in context, but some change from within. For example, one bachelor, approaching middle age, had had a long but uninspired courtship with a woman who wanted to marry him. He broke off the relationship because he was not in love with her; but, a year later, he called her again, saying he had made a terrible mistake and now realized how much he loved her. He feared only that she might be otherwise engaged. She was not, and they married, and are still, years later, living quite happily, he still tremulous when he thinks back on how close he came to losing her.

In those instances when a lover falls in love with someone well known to him long before then he must concede that some internal psychological change has occurred which finally permits him to appreciate the beloved's charms, previously obscured to him by virtue of his own limitations. "I wasn't ready," "I was too immature," we hear such a lover say by way of explanation. This lover intuits that love is related to an internal psychological state, bounded by readiness and need, as well as the availability of someone who approximates his idealized image of the Lover-Shadow.

But the process by which we shape the image of our Lover-Shadow and "select" a particular love object is elusive. Even once we "choose," we may sometimes feel the choice is not right. We may be puzzled, objectively, by the inappropriateness of those with whom we fall in love, though usually our puzzlement is tinged with wonder. For outsiders, however, the astonishment at our choice of the beloved may be tinged more with humor or horror than with wonder. The choice sometimes appears so odd as to stagger the imagination of the "observers" of love. Carson McCullers wrote from the point of view of such an objective observer of love: "The most outlandish people can be the stimulus for love. A man may be a doddering great-grandfather and still love only a strange girl he saw in the streets of Cheehaw one afternoon two decades past. The preacher may love a fallen woman. The beloved may be treacherous, greasy-headed, and given to evil habits. Yes, and the lover may see this as clearly as anyone else—but that does not affect the evolution of his love one whit. A most mediocre person can be the object of a love which is wild, extravagant, and beautiful as the poison lilies of the swamp. A good man may be the stimulus for a love both violent and debased, or a jabbering madman may bring about in the soul of someone a tender and simple idyll."

In the Hebrew Bible, man does not choose whether or not to love, only what he shall love. However, the implicit assumption is that the object of our love determines the direction of our actions. Therefore, the choice of what to love is crucial in a man's life; it determines what he will do and what he will become. This emphasizes something we certainly know about romantic love, that our "choice" in love becomes a large part of our destiny. (It is this insight to which I will return when attempting to confront the problems in understanding unhappy or masochistic love.)

One comes to see that choice is intimately connected to the very stuff of the self. The beloved is the right screen for the projection of something internal. For some, the beloved must be someone who is envied and can be exalted, for others, someone who needs rescuing or someone who is viewed as nurturer. Or the beloved has something we don't have and unconsciously desire. Often enough, buried in the unconscious, the Lover-Shadow evokes the dim memory of our earliest love—a kind of re-finding;

but for some the resemblance is to a bad or problematic parent. And sometimes, it appears as though the Lover-Shadow represents a buried or unexpressed part of the self rather than an earlier significant Other.

Sometimes the dynamics of choice are partly in evidence. If we return to Aldous Huxley's life story, we discover that though he made two excellent marriages, his most passionate experience of "falling in love"— during his first marriage—was directed towards another woman, Nancy Cunard, of whom he disapproved. Here his biographer describes the intense episode of lovesickness Huxley experienced:

Nancy went through a good many lovers; she had the kind of bad reputation, that aura of casual lasciviousness, that can be an added bait. To Aldous it was the ultimate of the pendulum swing of his flight from puritanism. . . . But if Nancy was promiscuous she was also capricious, and she was choosy. What she wanted were men who were more than a match for her, strong men, brutes. Aldous simply was not her type. He was far too gentle, too unexcessive and, with her, too hang-dog, too love-sick. Unfortunately for him she happened to like him and enjoy his company. If she did not strictly lead him on, she did not let him go.

Nevertheless, Huxley went on wanting Nancy, as he had said, against his principles, ideals, and reason, even against his own feelings.

For it appears he did not even like her.

The dynamics of choice, like those of timing, illuminate something of the nature of love as a process born of internal psychic need, culminating in an act of the imagination. Yet because love is an imaginative act, our understanding must remain incomplete. In the end, the lover is left with the explanation Montaigne gave of his love for his dear friend: "Because it was he, because it was I."

The Experience and Process of Falling in Love

However unique and specific the details of our individual experience of falling in love, certain general characteristics pertain to it. Falling in love is often accompanied by physical sensations—loss of appetite, breathlessness, and sleeplessness. Lovers feel the growth of love in their pounding hearts and in less traditional (or less poetic) sites as well—their stomachs, arms, groins, and lungs. Love becomes a delirium and is spoken of as a fever. These are the physical counterparts of the excitement and the fear that accompany falling in love. And it is no wonder that we are frightened. To fall in love is to risk opening up, revealing one's true self, and then being rejected. The most loquacious lover finds himself tongue-tied at the side of the beloved, embarrassed and yet eager to please. The lover, preparing to meet the beloved, worries about his smell, his clothes, his hair, his plans for the evening, and ultimately, his worthiness. Falling in love is an agitation, a mixture of hope, anxiety, and excitement.

Lovers always fear they might not *really* be in love or that they are not truly loved in return. The lover alternates between extolling the loved one and wondering if he has made the right choice. The lover is frightened at giving himself over to love and that fear may take the form of second-guessing his own choice, his own feelings.

When not doubting his own judgment, the lover doubts the beloved's feelings. The question of whether or not one is loved in return consumes the mind. "Does she love me? If not, why not? And how can I make her love me?" For very young lovers, the half-joking, half-serious ritual of plucking petals from a daisy gives voice to the longing for certainty: "He loves me . . . he loves me not." When a lover asks, "What are you thinking?" he generally wants to be assured that the beloved is thinking of him and of her love for him. But even when the beloved loves in return, it is no guarantee that she will continue to do so. Just as one may fall into love, so, too, may one fall out of love. Lovers constantly alternate between fears and yearnings, torment and hope.

As the lover begins to fall in love, his thoughts and fantasies drift involuntarily toward the beloved. In the beginning, and as long as the courtship prospers, this preoccupation is most often experienced as a high, a liberation, the greatest pleasure. The lover feels caught up in a great emotion, literally swept away, and he rides the crest of that wave of emotion with a feeling of exultation as long as there is either hope of reciprocity, or a clear signal of love from the beloved. When things are going well, the exultation of love seems to offer a kind of freedom; nor is this sense of freedom wholly illusory. Falling in love confers one of the greatest of freedoms—freedom from the confines of the self. Momentarily one exchanges one's preoccupation with oneself for a consuming interest in the Other. The lover is bound to the beloved, but paradoxically he is freed from himself. He has the sense that someone has entered his subjective world, and he hers.

Falling in love is a grand obsession, and the repetitive thinking about the beloved is an integral part of the experience, just as distinctive as its feeling state. In part, falling in love is gratifying precisely because it is both mentally and emotionally so all-consuming. Thus, in *As You Like It*, Rosalind, in the first flush of her love for Orlando, speaks in the voice of all lovers when she asks her friend Celia to describe every detail of her

recent meeting with Orlando: "What did he when thou saw'st him?
What said he? Did he ask for me? How parted he with thee? and when
shalt thou see him again? Answer me in one word." Though in other
passages she's able to mock love, the sophisticated Rosalind is just as
preoccupied with it as a simple shepherdess. Thinking about the beloved
often may interfere with life's other activities, but these are seen as
intruding upon the really important business at hand—the strategies and
attempts to realize mutual love. (There are, of course, exceptions. Some
lovers find themselves able to give themselves to work with an unprece-
dented abandon.)

The passion of love comes to rank as the most important thing in the
lover's world. He has found his passionate quest, and though it may
sometimes torment, it also comforts. Love eradicates all uncertainties
except the uncertainty about whether one could be, is, or will continue
to be loved by the beloved. Love gives purpose to living, meaning to life.

Because of both its all-consuming fervent nature and its instant ability
to confer meaning, love has been likened to a religion of two. In love as
in religion, there is an object of worship, a means of communion, a route
to transcendence. Perhaps the most eloquent expression of the uncertain
boundaries between love and religion and the longing for union common
to both of them is to be found in the sacred and the profane poems of
John Donne. In the love poetry, the beloved is worshipped as divine, the
lovers are canonized, and the tokens of their love transformed into saints'
relics. So it is perhaps inevitable that, in a religious poem that began
"Batter my heart, three-personed God," the deity should be addressed as
a passionate lover: "Take me to you, imprison me, for I,/ Except you
enthrall me, never shall be free,/ Nor ever chaste, except you ravish me."
The paradox of freedom in bondage is as true in love as in religion if not
more so.

Retrospectively, one remembers falling in love as all of a piece—pure
ecstasy, pure bliss. But, in fact, the experience progresses in fits and starts.
(This erratic quality may well have to do with the unconscious work of
aligning the image of the Lover-Shadow with the reality of the beloved.)
The state of falling in love is characterized by bursts of desire and exultation followed by feelings of withdrawal and boredom, doubts about the
loved one's worth and loyalty, then a reawakening of longing in tandem
with abject fear that the beloved will have grown tired of all the waiting
and indecision. All of this vacillation occurs and recurs until the lovers
pledge their love (or until one or the other finally gives up hope).

Realized love—after the lovers have pledged themselves to one another—is itself not a continuous feeling state; it is a series of blissful

moments. Even when the desired merger seems, in magical moments of union, to be achieved, the sense of joining is unstable and delicate. Like water, love can vaporize and seem to disappear, but then it condenses and is again visible.

Love as Crystallization

Among the theorists of love, Stendhal (1783–1842) is its major enthusiast. He was aware of its detractors, nonbelievers in love, and he despaired of conveying to someone who had never had it what the experience of love was like. How can one describe color to someone who is color-blind? As Stendhal put it, "Imagine a moderately complicated geometrical figure traced with white chalk on a blackboard: well! I am going to explain this geometrical figure; but in order for me to do so, it is essential that the figure should already exist on the slate; I cannot trace it myself." Stendhal required certain experience in amorous affairs from his readers. As one small example of what it might suffice a reader to know, he suggested that a man ought to be able "on entering the room where the woman is with whom he thinks he is in love, to have no thought but that of reading in her eyes what she is thinking of him at that moment, without any idea of putting any love into his own glances."

Unlike other theorists of love, Stendhal focused on the anatomy of love, not on its reasons but on its components, its emotional center, and its course. Many questions—when one falls in love, with whom one falls in love, even why one falls in love—he does not address. His task, as he saw it, was to describe "simply, rationally, mathematically, as it were, the different emotions which follow one after the other and which taken all together are called the passion of Love."

The metaphor on which Stendhal models his conception of the birth of love is that of a branch or bough stripped of its leaves in winter and thrown into an abandoned salt mine. Months later, the branch is pulled out and is covered with brilliant crystals. It is, so to speak, crystallized. Even the tiniest twigs are spangled over with sparkling, shimmering diamonds, and the bare bough is no longer recognizable.

For Stendhal, love is an act of the imagination. The fever of the imagination does for the loved one what the salt did for the bough; the loved one, like the bough, is transformed into an object of great beauty. "Crystallization" in love is that process by which the mind idealizes the beloved and discovers fresh perfections in her. This process of imaginative crystallization in love follows laws and has a sequence.

Stendhal discussed the process of crystallization in some detail. Initially, one feels only admiration for some quality of the prospective beloved. Next one muses on or fleetingly imagines the possibility of some mutuality. Such an auspicious beginning eventuates in love only if hope exists, and hope requires some sign from the admired one that mutuality is possible. With hope, love is born and the first crystallization begins. The lover now views the beloved in a different way from that in which others see her. For the lover, her beauty, her soul, and her character are unblemished. But in order for full crystallization to take place, some doubt about whether she is his must intercede. As the lover fluctuates between hope and doubt, the second stage of crystallization occurs and the lover is simultaneously or sequentially exulted or tormented by several alternatives: that the loved one is (or is not) perfect, that the loved one does (or does not) love in return, and that some proof should be (should not be) demanded. This is a time of oscillating hope and hopelessness, sweet torment and boundless yearning.

According to Stendhal, to fall in love, to feel the full force of passion, one must first admire, then fantasize, then be given at least a shred of hope which must be followed by a dollop of doubt. If one is lucky, mutual love will ensue.

Naturally, there are exceptions to Stendhal's description of the process. Two people may meet and from the moment of their meeting never be parted. For them, love at first sight is a reality. They seem to fulfill each other's pre-existing fantasies in the flesh, and no doubts about reciprocity need intercede in order for "crystallization" to take place. But they represent only the few. For the many, falling in love is a process such as Stendhal describes, both for those who initiate love and those who are reciprocally drawn into it.

However, if we are to scrutinize the metaphor of "crystallization" we must note an obvious discrepancy between the bough and the beloved. The bough is actually covered with crystals; the beloved, however, no matter how he or she is transformed by the power of love, can never appear as perfect to others as to the lover. "Idealization" is contemporary psychology's word for that phenomenon which Stendhal called "crystallization."

Idealization

To the lover, the experience of falling in love is a direct response to the special qualities of the beloved. By insisting that it is this special man or that unique woman who has elicited the love, the lover rejects any notion that individuals are interchangeable. It is the uniqueness of the loved one that is cherished. In this way, love becomes a celebration of individuality. Because of its insistence on the uniqueness of the beloved, romantic love is antithetical to sexual promiscuity in which it is the interchangeability of "sex objects" that is stressed.

The lover thinks his love is aroused solely by the virtues of the loved one. It will not help to tell him that this is an illusion, that it is he who has endowed the beloved with so much value. Outsiders say that beauty is in the eye of the beholder, that love is a projection, but the lover feels enthralled by what he believes to be the actual attributes of the beloved. The lover (knowing nothing of the concept of the Lover-Shadow) invariably attributes his love to the loved one's specialness, not to the creative powers of his imagination. But Shakespeare, for one, saw through the illusion with great lucidity: "The lunatic, the lover, and the poet/ Are of imagination all compact." In saying so, his Duke Theseus both celebrates and mocks the act of the imagination we call falling in love. There are some famous loves that reveal the extent of the role of the imagination in their genesis. One extreme case is that of Dante, who never attempted to realize his love in any earth-bound way. Dante immortalized his love for Beatrice in the *Vita Nuova* and *The Divine Comedy,* but he actually saw her only three times in his life—the first time when they were both nine—and he never met her. We know little of his life, but we do know that he grieved her early death and that her memory became his life's inspiration. (Nonetheless, his idealized and rapturous love did not prevent him from subsequently marrying someone else and having children.) But all lovers, including those intent on the realization of their erotic yearning, infuse their images of the beloved with imaginative colorations and dramatizations, even though their appraisals will be admixed with realistic perceptions as well. (And as has already been suggested, love may well fare better on a long-term basis if it is interlaced with substantial realistic perceptions.)

The lover generally comes to value *all* of the characteristics of the beloved. This does not necessarily mean that love is blind, as some claim, but it does often mean that the lover's appraisal of the beloved will differ significantly from that of "objective" acquaintances. Others may be more beautiful, yes, but the beloved has a more interesting face, hers reveals her soul. Others may be smarter, but he is more sensitive, which is what counts. And so forth. Loving may in fact feel so good because it is so creative.

Often it is some apparently insignificant detail that triggers the initial romantic reverie. It may be the way someone lights a cigarette in the wind, tosses her hair back, or talks on the phone (I personally think such gestures "tell" much, if not all, about the personality and aspirations of the person who is so observed). They are signals to those who read them about the way the person sees himself, and, particularly for men, these triggers tend to be visual. Very often, one remembers the gesture or the detail as the beginning of the process of falling in love only after love has been realized, much as Borges claims an author creates his literary "predecessors" by the fact of what he has written, after he has written it. The emotional meaning of the present determines the emotional significance attached to memories of the past.

However, idealization alone cannot account for the genesis of love. Idealization in romantic love is much like that in other forms of worship. The atheist desiring to be a devout Catholic is a soul in search of idealization, transcendence, romance. Some people have the gift of idealizing even the simplest moments of daily life. I always envied an old German friend of mine. Whenever we walked down the street together, he managed to find beauty where I saw plainness. He took pleasure in the clientele of the restaurant where we had lunch; to him they were always a fine, cultured, and distinguished group. I lived in an ordinary world and had lunch in a restaurant on Madison Avenue frequented by well-dressed, upper-middle-class patrons and a sprinkling of art dealers. My friend carried with him an idealized Rue St. Honoré that he so dearly loved. Though we ate together, his lunches were always far more glamorous and elegant than mine. (Retrospectively, now that he is dead, I share his experience.)

The difference between the experience of falling in love and mere admiration or idealization is this: in love something further is urgently desired and sought. Something more is required. The would-be lover senses the potential power the beloved has over him; he senses she can touch him, fulfill him, gratify him in some unique way. The loved one elicits some yearning, some need in the lover, which he believes that *only* she will be able to fulfill.

In Stendhal's account, too, idealization is crucial to the initiation of love, but by itself is not sufficient. Though love begins with admiration and idealization, it develops only when there is hope for reciprocity and, eventually, the demand for it. The next stage requires that the beloved respond to the lover's warmth and admiration. Only then may the lover's deepest fantasies come to some kind of fulfillment and his wishes be realized.

As Sartre put it, the purpose in loving must be to be loved in return.

The lover, through his love, *demands* to be loved. Though the lover insists that he loves only because of the specialness of the beloved, nonetheless he ultimately insists on the satisfaction of his own desires. Otherwise, without hope for reciprocation, he remains merely an admirer, not a lover. Simone Weil states the matter rather starkly:

Instead of loving a human being for his hunger, we love him as food for ourselves. We love like cannibals. To love purely is to love the hunger in a human being. . . . But the way we actually do love is very different. Thanks to their companionship, their words, or their letters, we get comfort, energy, and stimulation from the people we love. They affect us in the same way as a good meal after a hard day's work. So we love them like food. It is indeed an anthropophagous love.

In love, the lover concentrates all his desire on the single object of his passion. He desires her with his soul and with his body. It is his singleness of purpose, the sheer intensity of his desire, its power and apparent fixation which alarm his friends. He has symbolically destroyed the rest of his world. His single-mindedness is like that of the child who wails for its mother, who will have none other. And like the child, the lover may feel that the sheer strength of his desire must be enough to achieve its demand.

It is for this reason that the beloved may resist; she feels the consuming nature of the lover's desire and fears his voracity. The lover is trying to own the beloved, to claim any and all relations with her, irrespective of the effect on her. The beloved senses that despite the awe with which the lover regards her, she is no more than love fodder to him.

The Vulnerable Period of "Opening-Up"

The progression from admiration to the hope and demand for reciprocation and, finally, the fruition of love is a journey fraught with uncertainty, particularly in its very early stages. The language of courtship is tentative yet intermittently insistent, teasing and hopeful. Just as long gazes herald the exulted stage of realized mutual love, so the emblem of courtship is the sidelong glance, the fan its ideal prop.

Falling in love is, by its nature, predicated on risk-taking. In order to achieve mutual love, one must gamble on opening up psychically to achieve real intimacy and mutuality. But by revealing oneself to the Other, one becomes vulnerable. Therefore, falling in love—and the ultimate achievement of genuine love—requires an ability to trust oneself as well as the Other, to reveal one's weaknesses and foibles and risk becoming the object of fear and hatred, of condescension, humiliation, or rejection.

In the very beginning of love, when it is still characterized by titillation or infatuation, in the first moments of hope but not later, passion may be nipped in the bud. This happens if hope is undercut by the lover's knowledge that the beloved is bad, her reputation dangerous, because without trust there is no real hope for true reciprocation. (There are, of course, those few lovers who require some evil of the beloved.) The lover may also renounce the possibility of love if he has been badly wounded in love before. Or he may renounce adulterous love if he completely identifies with his children (or the beloved's) and remembers the hurt of his own mother or father abandoning him.

At first, when the lover is just beginning to fall in love, he may be frightened that his love will not be reciprocated. Consequently, he tries to seize the initiative and persuade or coerce the beloved to his way of feeling; he is very vulnerable because he is unilaterally needy and wanting. Such a lover bends all his powers of seduction to the task. This is why courtship is so often referred to as a "campaign" (waged with flowers or gourmet dinners, special kindnesses, and promises). The frightened or self-protective lover attempts to persuade the beloved to love him *first*, before he risks opening up. He may be motivated by fear, usually stemming from feelings of worthlessness and inferiority. But whatever his motives, by resorting to manipulation, the lover is attempting to control the Other. The lover's manipulations may be successful in securing love. But those who employ them impair their own chances of falling in love. Insofar as the lover feels himself to be subordinate and powerless vis-à-vis the Other, even as he attempts to manipulate the relationship, he cannot totally experience love himself. Riding a wave of emotion and manipulating that emotion tend to be mutually exclusive. When asked if he would prefer to be in love or be loved, the timid or insecure lover answers that he would choose the latter.

The beloved, in turn, may also be frightened, fearing the lover's omnivorous needs. Even if ready to risk being consumed, she may distrust the words of the lover, perhaps having learned through past experience that the suitor may not be sincere. The beloved fears that the lover may only be simulating intimacy and caring to camouflage other needs. Men are often accused of feigning affection and admiration in order to achieve their sexual aims, but both sexes indulge in this duplicity in order to gain their ends: companionship, short-term advantage, the gratification of vanity or lust.

And the lover may be pursuing even baser ends. The lover may be a Don Juan cloaked as Romeo or a Jezebel in the garb of Juliet. For these "lovers," the primary goal is a hostile one, to seduce and abandon or control and humiliate. For whatever reason, they are emotional gangsters, driven not just by the desire for love but by power, hatred, even sadism. Trapped by their need to dominate, these seducers are endlessly hungry and rapacious, incapable of experiencing lasting satisfaction. Of course, their pre-emptory needs seriously compromise their ability to open up. For them, exposure of the self is a charade, an impersonation; they may have, as Clement Greenberg said of James Agee, "the ability to be sincere without being honest." Their openness is ultimately inauthentic and used only as a means to an end. Seduction is a base version, or perversion, of courtship. (Perhaps one might say that domination, seduction, and courtship form a continuum of sorts.)

But even the would-be seducer may become a lover. One Latin American husband deeply estranged from his beautiful but over-fastidious wife fell in love with his secretary. Distraught by his wife's vindictiveness and refusal to give him a divorce, he felt hemmed in, and he alternately fantasized hiring someone to kill his wife or paying someone to seduce her into falling in love. Given the circles in which he traveled, a world of high rollers and con men, both fantasies were potentially realizable—the murder fantasy more apparently foolproof. But the husband, motivated either by strictures of conscience or residual feelings for his wife, or through the accident of meeting a locally famed Lothario, opted for the altogether unlikely plan of hiring someone to seduce his wife, with the intent that *she* would then press for a divorce. A large amount of money changed hands, and the local Lothario went off to his appointed task. Strange though it might seem, the seducer saw in the discarded wife the woman he had always been looking for, and did his job in earnest. (Aside from issues of guilt and redemption that are sometimes present in the genesis of romances of this genre, I have always thought this particular Lothario was playing out an unconscious scenario perhaps as much connected to the husband's distinction as to the wife's undoubted merits.) In this "inspirational" tale it is perhaps fitting that the husband, recovered from his infatuation, wanted to reconcile, but it was by then too late. Lothario and the wife married, and, over the years, fared as well as most. The story of falling in love in a relationship initially embarked upon for merely utilitarian reasons is, of course, an enduring imaginative theme; it is the plot line of *Ninotchka* and of innumerable films in which a spy defects for love. Such stories portray the actuality of a handful of real-life romances; more importantly they appear to fulfill the widely dispersed wishful fantasy that each of us may inspire love even against the prospective lover's self-interest or intended purpose.

In real life, Don Juans—more often than cons—may be surprised into love. In Milan Kundera's *The Unbearable Lightness of Being*, the characterization of Tomas as a latent Tristan, living as a Don Juan, is compelling. Feeling liberated and celebratory following his divorce, Tomas spent ten years knowing many women, but never committing himself to any one of them even to the extent of staying overnight. Shocked to discover he had fallen in love with Tereza, he eventually became so wedded to her that he followed her back to a restricted impoverished life in Czechoslovakia, rather than stay in Switzerland without her. Sometimes a Don Juan figure is merely someone who was himself wounded in love, and whose retreat to a defensive posture is masked by his assumption of an aggressive womanizing role—until the time when he falls in love again.

Some self-protective people cannot allow themselves to begin to fall in love until the lover has already declared himself. They appear distanced from the normal emotionality of the experience of falling in love but may find a release once the words "I love you" are uttered. In *The Two Mrs. Grenvilles*, Junior Grenville and Alice Arden are having a passionate sexual affair and she remarks that he never expresses his feelings and wonders if he is waiting for her to go first.

> Enraptured, he stared at her and said nothing.
> "I love you," she said.
> He felt unleashed. Torrents of blocked feelings flowed from him, a lifetime of withheld emotion. "I love you," he whispered to her, and repeated and repeated and repeated the words. He could not stop saying them.

Sometimes, the love is not pre-existent. But, nonetheless, feeling oneself the object of a lover's idealization may gradually awaken new possibilities. Contemplating them, the loved one can be drawn into a reciprocal imaginative process. Just as other emotions are contagious, so love can elicit love. As the recipient of love, or the object of crystallization, the beloved begins by basking in the admiration of the lover. The flattery of seeing oneself as the object of a passion can itself be the inducement one needs to fall in love. But being loved ultimately confers warmth and confirms worth only if the beloved comes to idealize the lover in turn, because being idealized has value only if one's admirer is deemed valuable. Therefore, the beloved's real joy in being idealized awaits her own awakening to love.

If one waits to be loved, the risk of rejection appears to be diminished. But such security is false. Even when one's lover is sincere and honorable in intention, guarantees of security can never be achieved in love. What's more, some men (and some women, too) are experts in eliciting love, but are notoriously unreliable in their ability to sustain it at their own end. In *My Life*, Isadora Duncan writes of one of the legendary masters of invoking love:

Perhaps one of the most wonderful personalities of our time is Gabriel d'Annunzio, and yet he is small and, except when his face lights up, can hardly be called beautiful. But when he talks to one he loves, he is transformed to the likeness of Phoebus Apollo himself, and he has won the love of some of the greatest and most beautiful women of the day. When D'Annunzio loves a woman, he lifts her spirit from this earth to the divine region where Beatrice moves and shines. In turn he transforms each woman to a part of the divine essence, he carries her aloft until she believes herself really with Beatrice, of whom Dante has sung in immortal strophes. . . . At that time he flung over each favourite in turn a shining veil. She rose above the heads of ordinary mortals and walked surrounded by a strange radiance. But when the caprice of the poet ended, this veil vanished, the radiance was eclipsed, and the woman turned again to common clay.

D'Annunzio's lovers were inspired initially only by his flattery, but eventually they felt themselves to be in love. Isadora Duncan goes on to describe their fate, one common to the rejected lover: "She herself did not know what had happened to her, but she was conscious of a sudden descent to earth, and looking back to the transformation of herself when adored by D'Annunzio, she realised that in all her life she would never again find this genius of love." Falling in love for these women was the *response* to being loved, the imaginative response to someone else's creative act.

How can one ever know whether one's suitor is sincere? There is, for some, a perfect fantasy of what the ardent lover might do to allay the beloved's insecurity. The lover would declare his love and put himself totally at the disposition of the beloved. This would give the beloved the freedom to set the tempo of the relationship with the ultimate assurance of his full committment. In the original film version of *The Postman Always Rings Twice*, Cora puts her lover to the test. She and her lover swim out so far that she becomes exhausted and knows she can never get back to shore without his help. She can now test her lover's sincerity (he has no scruples against murder; he has already murdered). If he loves her, he will save her life. If he doesn't, she is willing to die, because there would be nothing more to live for.

Most of us do not find it necessary or relevant to put our lovers to such a dramatic test. But even in less dire circumstances, courtships often do involve a series of tests of love, one lover asking the other to prove his sincerity. In mythology the hero must prove his worth by surmounting an obstacle before he can claim the heroine. His worth will be gauged in combat or contest, his sincerity in his commitment to performing the Herculean task.

In extreme cases, fear of rejection can inhibit the full experience of loving until after the death of the beloved—when one finally feels oneself to be safe from the possibility, however remote, of abandonment and humiliation. One woman who always spoke of her husband somewhat disparagingly and was inclined to ridicule him, secretly feared he was going to leave her for his off-and-on-again mistress. When he died, his wife experienced a profound change in her feelings towards him. She found herself heartbroken, but relieved that her husband had stayed the course. She suddenly valued his virtues and idealized him, mourned him profusely, and thereafter carried a silver framed photograph of him with her wherever she went. A somewhat tepid and tenuous relationship was converted retroactively into a passionate love.

Some lovers, frightened not of false seduction but of the true reward of love, *mutuality*, which they view as cannibalism, or as an enthrallment to which they might succumb, restrict their interests to courtship. Of them it is often said that they prefer the chase to the quarry. Excitement is everything, realization nothing; they may become love addicts, whose lives are parsed out in rapid alternations of erotic excitement and disappointment.

Given the almost universal self-protectiveness and instinctive distrust that would-be lovers bring to courtship, it is no wonder that many courtships end abortively or issue in marriages that have nothing to do with real openness and mutuality. Yet some lovers intuitively grope their way to the freedom of mutual love, and to the transcendence and transformation it may catalyze. To the degree that reciprocity is achieved, love will be realized and its idyllic phase ensue.

CHAPTER TWO

Love Realized: The Idyllic Phase

S OME OF what passes as love amounts to much less, hence the common preoccupation with deciding if an attachment is "true" love or a passing fancy, the "real thing" or a mere fling. There are varieties of incomplete or stunted kinds of love. In fact, the truncated versions are much more common, having been called into being as the answer to myriad needs. Whether one seeks relief from boredom, the palliation afforded by love on the rebound, gratification of the ego, social validation, or the pleasures of the flesh, the name of love is invoked to rationalize and idealize need. Most of all, it is used to deny the existence of the pains and problems that in fact precipitated the relationship, and to glorify the result as a positive choice. Consequently, many people who find themselves in relationships of a certain intensity simply assume they must be in love.

Love has been subdivided into its various forms, the religious separated from romantic love, brotherly love from patriotism, and so forth, but "romantic love" is still too broad a category. Its purest form, passionate love, needs to be distinguished from three other forms with which it may be confused (and with which it may overlap): carnal love, affectionate bonding, and self-aggrandizing love. And, as we shall see, each of these other forms of love has its own advocates, those who tout it as the preferential one.

Mutual passionate love is the most complete form of romantic love. The direction of this form of love is clear: one seeks union with the Other. What distinguishes passionate love is its intensity, the strong mutual identifications the lovers feel, and their longing for union with its attendant transcendental aims. I consider it the most complete form of love because it is the one, above all, that allows for self-transformation and self-transcendence. (While most observers would think that affectionate bonding was a necessary constituent of passionate love, they would be far from the mark. Sometimes passionate love appears to be based on bonds of mutual destructiveness.)

In contrast, carnal (or sexual) love, though quite authentic, is founded on the often short-lived passion of physical attraction, which is experienced as the urgent need to possess the Other sexually. Occasionally even a single night of sexual passion suffices to convince someone that he is in love; but generally when we speak of carnal love we mean something of longer duration and deeper meaning. Sometimes soaring into what Salter has called "great carnal duets," this is the kind of love most likely to be confused with passionate love. Novels and movies afford glimpses of many such intense but short-lived duets, for example, the ship-wrecked couple in Lina Wertmuller's *Swept Away*, whose love does not survive their rescue, or the steamy lovers in the movie *Last Tango in Paris*.

At its height, sexual passion is an almost insatiable bodily appetite centered exclusively on the Other, a fixation of erotic intensity on one person. Often it is like a summer squall that disappears as rapidly as it first appeared. But while it lasts, the hunger is for more than sex alone, otherwise no one object would be so compelling. The lover often becomes physically and mentally obsessed by the beloved, who seems to disappear even as she is possessed; holding her, the lover still finds her elusive. Desire is perpetuated by the elusiveness of its object. The lover becomes obsessed with breaking through the barriers of Otherness. Yet, paradoxically, in lust unconnected to love, the lover does not seek to know the beloved's subjective self, predominantly only her sexual self. And it is this that distinguishes carnal passion from passionate love; in the former, one aims exclusively for sexual possession, whereas in the latter one aims to know and embrace the Other, body *and* soul. When experienced outside of passionate love, carnal love, however intense it appears to be, is ultimately self-limiting, destined to fade when a feeling of possession—of total carnal knowledge—is achieved. Nevertheless, carnal passion is the type of love most highly prized by those for whom sexual liberation represents the major step forward in the relations between the sexes. In our culture while carnal passion may often exist in its own right, it almost always forms part of passionate mutual love.

In affectionate bonding, the form of love generally most highly touted by mental health professionals, a couple gradually develops deep and reliable ties of mutual caring, interests, and loyalty. They come to believe in one another and to feel assured of the on-going sustaining nature of their relationship. Not Romeo and Juliet, but Ma and Pa Kettle are the exemplary pair. This kind of love may or may not have intense sexuality connected to it; sometimes it may exist without any sexual congress whatsoever. It may be the end product of what began as passionate love; or, it may have developed as affectionate bonding from the start, without any intense emotional preamble. But it is praised for its reliability, predictability, safety, and warmth, and for the lovers' realistic appraisals of one another as contrasted with the mutual idealization of passionate lovers.

In self-aggrandizing love (or vanity-love), the lover forms an attachment in large part as a means to an end, either to achieve some specific gain like money, a less tangible one like social advantage, or to prop up his vanity or ego. Vanity-love is a very common form of attachment and in some settings it seems to predominate. Writing in the nineteenth century, Stendhal described the sensibility that informed such a milieu then: "The Duchesse de Chaulnes used to say that a duchess is never more than thirty years old to a snob; and people who frequented the court of that upright man, King Louis of Holland, still recall with amusement a pretty woman at the Hague who could never bring herself to think a man anything but charming if he was a Duke or a Prince."

However, self-aggrandizing love is as common today as it was in more aristocratic times. It was certainly evident in my high school in Kentucky, which was situated as much in the basketball belt as in the Bible belt. And sometimes its lures may even topple a pre-existing love, as it did in my class. We had in our midst a lovely couple, famous within the school, doted on and envied as certain high school lovers sometimes are. "He" was a gifted basketball player, and in my high school that made him a great hero. Every Friday morning, at assembly, the lights were dimmed and members of the current team—football or basketball or whatever was seasonal—marched down the aisle to applause or some other show of acknowledgment. "She" was friendly and warm and modest. And, as was the custom for class couples, he visited her in homeroom every morning to talk with her for a few minutes before school started. They lunched together, walked hand in hand, and their relationship seemed the very prototype of warmth and intimacy. They seemed destined to be one of those couples who fall in love early and live out their lives together.

But it was not to be. During the basketball season, as the basketball player's exploits waxed, he drew the concentrated attention of one of the premiere cheerleaders. Now cheerleaders were the only girls to be accorded prestige and adoration comparable to that accorded to (male) athletes. The basketball player wavered in his allegiance; one could chart the course of his internal struggle by the pattern of early morning home room visits he paid. In the end, his girlfriend gave him an ultimatum, and he balked, choosing the cheerleader. The new couple lasted but two seasons; moreover, to this observer, the basketball player never achieved the kind of closeness with the cheerleader that he had had with his former girlfriend, their public preening appearing more integral to the relationship than any personal intimacy. (Some of the people I went to high school with seemed to peak *then,* on the playing fields, and it is *my* fantasy that the basketball player, like one of John O'Hara's failed men, remembers best his scoring basket that made our high school the city champion, *and* his early, abandoned love.)

A typical example of vanity-love is the liaison unattractive or insecure wealthy men seek with beautiful women. The woman is sought not for her qualities but for the pride of manhood she confers; she is more a prized possession than a soul mate. However crass the motivations, such attachments can indeed result in a form of love. The ugly rich man using the beautiful woman as a means to the end of personal enhancement, may nonetheless feel something intense which *he* experiences as love, can be hurt as a consequence, and can feel great pleasure or passion. (Likewise, the beautiful woman using the rich man as a means to her ends may feel she is in love.) The lines separating the kinds of love are blurry and wavering.

Trying to get ahead in turn-of-the-century New York society, Lily Bart, the heroine of Edith Wharton's *The House of Mirth,* finds herself intrigued with Selden and muses on her buoyancy of spirit: "Was it love, she wondered, or a more fortuitous combination of happy thoughts and sensations? . . . She had several times been in love with fortunes or careers, but only once with a man." Lily is perceptive enough to know that there are several different kinds of love and to see in retrospect that she's experienced at least two, but she's not sure which kind the current love is. Her dilemma conveys how hard it is to make those distinctions about love when we are *in* it, and how intense it may be no matter what its source.

In addition to the four major categories of love just described, there are a few additional ones worth noting. There is a love more tepid than any of the preceding, with little authentic passion, affection, or even lust. Stendhal named it sympathy-love (or mannered love), and its main attribute is its conventionality. While it may appear to the lovers and their social set as constituting an authentic emotional attachment, it lacks the substance of one, being essentially conformist or convenient. This love might have been Lady Violet Effingham's fate had she followed through on her sardonic words: "I shall take the first that comes after I have quite made up my mind. You'll think it very horrible, but that is really what I shall do. After all, a husband is very much like a house or a horse. You don't take your house because it's the best house in the world, but because just then you want a house. You go and see a house, and if it's very nasty you don't take it. But if you think it will suit pretty well, and if you are tired of looking about for houses, you do take it. That's the way one buys one's horses, and one's husbands." Of course few are as self-aware as Lady Violet (which may be why, in fact, she married for love after all, and fared very well). Many of those whose intimate relationships are limited to the essentially conventional are not conscious of how much they are missing, and certainly did not set out in a calculating fashion to arrive at a merely serviceable relationship.

There is one category that some observers would cite as extremely common: neurotic love. Neurotic love, analogous to vanity-love, seeks to satisfy a real need, but not the same kind of need that is met by mutual, reciprocal love. Many neurotic attachments are based on dependency needs or the fear of being alone. I was amazed when one acquaintance, who always seemed to be at some point on the trajectory of love, confessed she never felt the high, because she was too intent on preserving emotional security and preoccupied with the fear of rejection. When not in an intense relationship with a man, she felt empty and experienced a low-grade depression.

Mary McCarthy offers an example of neurotic love in her novel *The Company She Keeps.* Enslaved by love, the heroine looks to an analyst to help her understand what has transpired and comes to the following astonishing discovery.

Now for the first time she saw her own extremity, saw that it was some failure in self-love that obliged her to snatch blindly at the love of others, hoping to love herself through them, borrowing their feelings, as the moon borrowed light. She herself was a dead planet.

McCarthy sees love in this instance as stemming from a defect in the integration of the self. Insofar as one might generalize from this example, perpetual lovesickness appears to be a misguided remedy for a deficiency in self-love.

When categorizing love, one must also allow that these various forms of love are hardly ever pure. One sees mixtures of all the types described, and one type can evolve into another. For example, vanity-love can sometimes evolve into passionate love, and sadly enough, passion-love may fade into conventional love. Nor do these categories by any means exhaust the subject. There are still other ways to classify love's myriad, truncated forms. Mutual love depends upon both need satisfaction and idealization, but one sees abortive forms of love that are unbalanced in these areas. Appetitive love seeks nourishment only for itself; the lover may demand that the beloved service him and yet he may feel no real interest in her. Conversely, idealization can exist in the form of admiration without any attendant attachment. And love that is merely a kind of admiration is no more than a variant of vanity-love. This must have been what the Katharine Hepburn character in *The Philadelphia Story* intuited when she rejected the adoring Jimmy Stewart, who saw her as a goddess to put on a pedestal, in favor of Cary Grant, who liked to recall one of the few moments when she had fallen off the pedestal—specifically a drunken night when she climbed on the roof, and, stark naked, bayed at the moon.

Love addicts, those individuals who fall in love with great frequency, regularity, and intensity, are usually involved in one or another of the truncated forms of love. The "fool for love" is most often deceiving himself as to his true motives. Very often he requires the intense excitement of repeated episodes of "falling in love" (as another might use a drug to counter depression or emptiness), but is as a consequence inhibited from achieving the pleasure of stable mutual love. The self-deceit of the love addict can be contagious, enticing the person with whom he appears to be falling in love into reciprocating that love. The disappointed lovers who are the love addict's victims would say, in the words of the song lyric, "You were only fooling, while I was falling in love."

Many of the truncated forms of love are experienced for a time as true love, and they do have purpose and meaning. They shouldn't be dismissed or taken lightly, but ultimately they do not have the same intensity, depth, or capacity for expanding and transforming the self as genuine passion-love.

The Experience of Mutual Love

Love may or may not last. It may be as relatively unencumbered as first love, or it may be entangled with the history of past lives—children, husbands, wives, and lovers. But when love is mutual, for a moment or a lifetime, annual or perennial, it blooms with a shape, a smell, and a color that makes it at once particular and general, impossible to convey fully yet amenable to precise characterization. Lovers often feel their love as unique, but that very feeling of uniqueness is one of love's universal defining characteristics.

Regardless of its duration, passionate love is not only exultant but also transcendent and transformative. It changes thinking, feeling, perception, even the very sense of self.

OBSESSION AND POSSESSION. In mutual love the lovers have an urgent, ceaseless need to make each other feel—and confirm—the fullness of their love. When they are together, they search each other's faces for the effect of a word, a thought, an idea, a glance. If they are apart, they can think of nothing but one another, and wish to know at all times what the other is doing. The lovers' obsessive rumination feels almost like possession—as though thinking of one another were tantamount to embracing.

If separated, the lovers live by two clocks—their own and each other's. She notes the hour when he usually rises and when he goes to sleep. If she imagines they are eating a meal or going to bed or looking out at the night sky at the same time, she is delighted. With friends, each guides the conversation (subtly, they think) to a discussion of the beloved. They are bored and impatient when talking about anything else. When apart, the lovers feel incomplete and unnatural. They find it hard to breathe, lose their appetite, and feel an emptiness in the chest. Each has a dread of something going wrong, imagining the worst when they are not in each other's company. There is panic when the letters don't arrive, the call is cut short, the weekend cancelled. The lovers alternate between feeling a need to be cared for and a wish to protect the Other.

Pledges are made to establish the covenant of love. The covenant is a guaranty of safety; by promising continuity, it makes the risk of opening up seem smaller. Tokens are exchanged as the concrete expressions of the promise that the lovers belong to each other, now and forever. The ring and the pin are the material evidence of good faith and the promise of eternal union. Sometimes items of clothing may be exchanged: she will wear an old sweater of his, he will hang her robe where he can gaze at it from his bed. These are the fetishes of love, the totems of the beloved. They are adult lovers' transitional objects, akin to the child's blanket or teddy bear in that they, too, ward off the anxiety of separation and provide a temporary substitute for the flesh, the person of the beloved.

In love, there is a desire to generate endless time. The lovers luxuriate in the freedom to linger, and nothing else seems so valuable. One retrieves the present tense in love. Only the present matters, past and future are dispensable, irrelevant. Love is valuable for the feeling it evokes in the present, not for its use in generating future yields. Time is reckoned by love's calendar, where there is only *before* and *ever since*.

Moments when the lovers are together are experienced as timeless, but in separation they seem endless. One is willing to wish one's life away (if time would only pass!) in order to be reunited. As Shakespeare's Cleopatra pleads:

> Give me to drink mandragora
> That I might sleep out the great gap of time
> My Antony is away.

Even when the lovers come together, there is an obsession not only with each other but with time. Promises are cast in terms of future assurances that the love will last forever. The spectre overshadowing love is the fear that it will end.

When love is interrupted by death, the surviving lover may fear the very passage of time that friends look to as balm for the pain. Time may indeed heal, but to the lover time is like a terrible train, rushing the lover away from the last moment with the beloved. Time becomes space and inexorably separates.

Perhaps it is in letters that an outsider can best sense the lovers' desires to possess and be possessed. Even the pronouns reflect that urgency. In one of his letters to Milena, Kafka signs off—as lovers are wont to do— "Thine," and then adds a parenthetical gloss on the word: "(now I've lost even my name; it has been growing shorter all the time and now it is: Thine)."

It is of course love's very hallmark—its obsessiveness—that makes outsiders so judgmental about love, ready to declare it a kind of insanity. And who can blame them? The lover is utterly consumed, oblivious to outside influences and obligations. But the obsessiveness is no mere appendage to love, it is the very heart of love; it is that which permits love to act as an agent of change. The working and reworking of the same ideational content is similar to the "working through" that occurs in psychoanalytic therapies. The lover is written in, as it were, into every conceiveable experience and dream. Such "obsessions" are signs that a major psychic shift is occurring, with changes in allegiances, values, perceptions, goals, and the sense of self.

EXULTATION. In the arms of the beloved, the boundaries of the lover's world expands, and his life is suffused with a sense of drama. Excitement transforms—and expels—the mundane, charges each moment with meaning, enraptures the body, and enlarges the spirit. Love catalyzes a kind of organic high—the feeling that the true, most spirited, most alive part of the self, long slumbering, has been awakened.

The lover feels like a king in loving; now he has his own domain.

Lovers, reveling in their exulted feelings, know that the real saints are those who have gone beyond exercises of the intellect and returned to faith through feeling. Only feelings lead to truth; the body does not lie. In love, the most ordinary moments can seem extraordinary: "Sometimes, seeing Elgin walk across the room unclothed would make all the breath leave Caroline's body, and she would not even be conscious of her gasp or that he heard her."

The lovers feel that their love is the beginning of a wondrous journey: they are only setting out, and they anticipate all that is yet to come, the life that is to be lived in tandem. Although the lovers may feel periodic letdowns, they believe that their exultation will not dim, that their love will not die prematurely but will live out its life in fullness and joy.

The lovers feel a deep sense of affinity (known to the Romantics as "elective affinities"), sometimes spiritual, sometimes "flesh of my flesh," often both. Their desires coincide; they believe that the way their wishes and rhythms match must be unique. Nothing the Other wants feels like an obligation or imposition. To be alone together and to feel as one is to experience a harmony more perfect than either thought possible. The surprised lover exclaims, "You never bore me." And even more amazing, "I do not find myself boring in your company." Together the lovers delight in discovering their shared responses to experiences and their common tastes. So intrinsic to love is this feeling of harmony that the lovers want it to be experienced exclusively in the context of their love.

Though Simone de Beauvoir and Jean-Paul Sartre committed themselves to a credo of sexual freedom, and by and large she remained unthreatened by his affairs, there came a time when de Beauvoir feared that another woman was more important than she, not just a romantic adventure. Her fear had nothing to do with the other woman's charms, or insecurity about her own. It arose when Sartre described to her just such a perfect harmony as that alluded to above. "The way he [Sartre] described Dolores, she shared completely all his emotions, his irritations and his desires. When they went out together she always wanted to stop or go at the same instant as he, and Simone wondered if this meant Dolores and Sartre were together at a depth she had never achieved with him." De Beauvoir understood perfectly well—exultation and ease are indeed the emotional hallmarks of passionate love.

SELF-VALIDATION AND JOINT NARRATIVES. In mutual love, the lovers validate one another's uniqueness and worth. They literally confirm the existence and worth of each other's subjectivity. In love, there is a chance for the lovers to be fully known, accepted without judgment, and loved despite all shortcomings. The lover thinks: "I never thought anyone could know me completely and still love me."

Here is Malraux's Kyo contemplating the love he shares with May: "A partnership consented, conquered, chosen. . . . Men are not my kind, they are those who look at me and judge me; my kind are those who love me and do not look at me, who love me in spite of everything, degradation, baseness, treason—*me* and not what I have done or shall do—who would love me as long as I would love myself . . . with her alone I have this love in common."

In love, one desires to know and be known to the beloved. For some, love is the first occasion for a deep interest in the inwardness of another. Not just the major milestones of the Other's life, but the most insignificant idiosyncrasies of habit and taste take on importance and meaning. Whether or not she wears perfume, and what kind, may matter as much to her lover as who her other lovers have been. Both are part of what makes her who she is—her unique and indefinable essence, which it is the lover's ceaseless desire and ambition to try to define. Even one's own idiosyncrasies take on meaning because of the lover's attitude toward them. Her preference for red becomes interesting to her because *he* notices it. He becomes aware of his mannerisms only because she regards them with affection. The otherwise insignificant in both oneself and one's beloved is treasured and assumes importance. There is validation in love, because all of one's attributes are noticed and are of concern to the beloved. Our insecurities are healed, our importance guaranteed, only when we become the object of love.

Lovers seek not only to share the present, but also their pasts. They are jealous of each other's pasts because they were not there. Each wants to know the other's memories, to recast their lives in such a way that their separate histories were clearly destined to lead only to the present moment. If their meeting was truly random, they mythicize all the contingencies that led up to it, marvel at how close they came to missing each other. All that has gone before serves as prehistory and the lovers attempt to void it of meaning except as preface. They need to own each other's pasts. Sometimes she tells of an incident from his past as though it happened to her, not to him; or he says to her about some event in her life: "That's not the way it happened." Real, profound life is felt to have begun only with this love. Couples begin friendships with other couples by exchanging stories of how they met and courted. In this way they present their joint narrative, their personal epic.

The construction of joint narratives is an important source of self-validation, and not just in romantic love. One of the touching scenes to be observed between mother and child occurs when the two are sitting side by side, talking about the family's history, perhaps poring over old family mementoes. The mother reminisces about what was happening to the child at a particular time and relates it to the family chronicle, analogizing what the child did to something she or the father or the uncle or aunt did at the same time in their lives, or talking about what her own childhood was like compared to the child's. The rapt expression on the child's face is clear evidence that he revels in the importance accorded to him by his mother. He interrupts with his own reminiscences. He and his mother are constructing the narrative of his life and of their lives together. (In an extreme version of this scenario, Thomas Merton's lifelong work on successive volumes of his spiritual autobiography might be seen as in part an attempt to reclaim the feeling of importance he lost when his mother, after the birth of a second child, abandoned the journal in which she had faithfully recorded all the minutiae of Thomas's daily life.)

Most people make instrumental use of us, just as we do of them. We reduce them to objects. We are not truly interested in the waiter; if we are the waiter, we know that we are perceived principally as the instrument by which a glass of water may make its way to the table. We do not feel ourselves validated for our central and unique value until we are central to someone else's narrative. The lovers create a densely interwoven narrative; it signifies the lovers' importance to each other both in the present and in the future.

In order for mutual validation to occur, however, the lovers must tell the truth about who they are. Validation cannot be complete without full disclosure. If a man was homosexual before he married, he will cheat himself if he does not tell his wife (though psychiatrists, who sometimes miss the point of love, may counsel otherwise). There are often dire consequences in telling the truth, but there are always negative consequences in withholding it. In Thomas Hardy's *Tess of the D'Urbervilles*, Tess's husband makes a wedding night confession to her. She, in turn, confesses to him, telling him of her affair, her ensuing pregnancy, and the death of her illegitimate child. Even though she has been wronged while her husband had been a wrong-doer, he abandons her. We empathize deeply with her desire to reveal herself. To lie about those issues that pertain to one's identity is to forfeit whatever slim chance there is of feeling loved for who one is—not who one is more or less successfully pretending to be. (But, as accomplished lovers know, there are stray thoughts of little significance that may be better left unspoken, because they would only serve to wound the beloved.)

Simone de Beauvoir was reluctant to tell Sartre about her sexual craving for him when they were separated, and about the sexual arousal she then experienced in response to accidental contact with others. But reticence was worse: "If I didn't dare confess such things, it was because they were unknowable. By driving me to such secrecy my body becomes a stumbling block rather than a bond between us, and I feel a burning resentment against it." It is through sharing deep confidences with the beloved that we may master our shame over past and present foibles, humiliations, and weaknesses. The necessity for this kind of openness as a prerequisite to love's intimacy, finds its way into popular fiction. Daisy, the heroine of Judith Krantz's novel *Princess Daisy*, frees herself and is enabled to fall in love only after she confesses to Patrick Shannon two dark secrets from her past: the existence of a retarded twin sister and the brief sexual encounter she had had with her half-brother Ram, who raped her when she tried to break away from him.

"WE." Love creates new identifications for the lovers. These are symbolized by the new names they give one another, the terms of endearment they use. Re-naming symbolizes the psychological fact that each lover now has a new identity, special and specific to the relationship. Consequently, the lover cannot bear to hear the beloved use those words with someone else; he feels that they are his alone, and that through them the beloved has created a new identity (a new narrative) for him.

However, in mutual love it is not just the Other who is celebrated, not just the "I" who is enhanced, not just individual identities that are transformed. There is a new being, experienced as "we" and perceived by others as a "couple." In Virginia Woolf's *To the Lighthouse*, Mrs. Ramsay, an observer of a couple's coming together, muses on the occasion: "She knew from the effort, the rise in his voice to surmount a difficult word that it was the first time he had said 'we.' 'We did this, we did that.' They'll say that all their lives, she thought . . . a curious sense rising in her, at once freakish and tender, of celebrating a festival, as if two emotions were called up in her, one profound—for what could be more serious than the love of man for woman, what more commanding, more impressive, bearing in its bosom the seeds of death; at the same time these lovers, these people entering into illusion glittering eyed, must be danced around with mockery, decorated with garlands." (And so musing, Mrs. Ramsay gives voice to thoughts characteristic both of lovers and observers.)

The feeling tone informing the "we" differs from couple to couple. "The world is our oyster" is not the same as "Us against the world." But both are part of the world of coupledom called into being by love. While the "we" is often public, sometimes it is illicit and hidden, as for example, in adulterous affairs or when two young lovers continue a clandestine relationship against the wishes of their parents.

The "couple" is itself the first child of the union. It has a birthday and an anniversary—the day we met, the day we first went out, the day we first slept together, the day we married. The couple—"we"—accumulates its own history. The lovers delight in recounting it to each other, because all of its milestones, however ordinary and inert when described to an outsider—the time they cooked lobsters, the day they saw the giraffe running at the zoo, the night they slept on a public beach—are sacred to them by virtue of the power they have to revivify past emotions. Old familiar places, once visited by lovers, are perceived differently; they take on new meaning and beauty in association with the memory of moments experienced there. New places discovered together are "owned" by the couple. (Thus, the abandoned lover resents it if the beloved takes a new love to one of "their" old places. Even in separation or estrangement, the sacred places must be respected.)

The couple speaks a different language together. Others might think this foolish—the pet names for each other, the baby talk, the made-up nouns and verbs, and the verbal shorthand—but it expresses their feelings for each other as no other language could. The fact of a private language symbolizes the uniqueness of their love. To describe their love to the outside world—no, for that they would need to quote poetry or love songs. No one else could understand. They have the sense that few if any have had their experience, that their love is unique, and that a love such as theirs can only end with death.

Not only do the lovers speak a separate language; they also long to inhabit a separate magical place. They experience themselves joined in an almost virginal pure love. But they sometimes fear that their love might become contaminated if they are immersed in an impoverished physical world or a depressed or hostile interpersonal one. If so, they try to elude that fate by escape to the imaginative world of make-believe. The dream of the picket-fenced, rose-covered cottage is the wishful fantasy of romantic isolation from the corrosive influences of the external world. The lovers are innocents aspiring to return to the Garden of Eden or to enter into the Promised Land. Movies invoke this fantasy in all those stories depicting a pair of lovers isolated on a South Sea Island. The lovers' fantasied world attempts to keep their love pure. Alternately the power of the imagination may be so great that the lovers are able to project their feelings onto their environment; then the world becomes more intense, more beautiful, and less threatening. City streets become glamorous, filled with the lovers' own sense of life and joy, the small town takes on a Thornton Wilderesque aura of intimacy and suspended magic. Whatever the place, it can undergo love's sea change and be seen as wondrous.

Insofar as the "we" constitutes a world unto itself, its boundaries are marked by secrets. If feelings, perceptions, or insights are unshared or unspoken they lose their significance—likewise if they are shared indiscriminately. The creation of mutual secrets and confession of past ones signify the importance not only of the secrets' content but of the lovers' bond as well. Secrets are rooted in intimacy, trust, and commitment. However trivial they may appear to be, confidences play a vital role in our psychic lives—perhaps reversing that childhood ignominy when we were excluded from our parents' conversations and bedrooms. The shared secrets between lovers comprise more than the exchanged confidences of past skeletons; they are made up of private jokes and the knowledge of sexual preferences, hidden antipathies, and concealed ambitions. For lovers, to betray one another's secrets is a major transgression—and some loves have been shattered upon the discovery of such a betrayal. For some lovers, not even sexual infidelity rankles so much as the disclosure of one's sexual idiosyncrasies or hidden fears to a third party. Furthermore, lovers expect the sacred trust engendered by shared secrets to be respected even if love ends. Just as shared secrets affirm love, a solitary secret may signal and symbolize the end of perfect mutual love. In *Light Years* Viri asserts his psychological separation from his wife by having an affair which he keeps hidden from her: "He was empty, at peace . . . He had come in from the sea, from a thrilling voyage. He had straightened his clothes, brushed his hair. He was filled with secrets, deceptions that had made him whole."

THE SENSE OF MERGER AND TRANSCENDENCE. Lovers may go beyond a sense of joint identity, may feel that they have in fact merged. Charles Williams said, "Love you? I *am* you," perhaps echoing Cathy's famous declaration, "Nelly, I *am* Heathcliff." Lovers play on merging their names as a symbol of soulful merging. The Duke and Duchess of Windsor, in their love letters written before their marriage, referred to themselves as WE, the *W* standing for Wallis and the *E* for Edward. I have friends who sign their correspondence "Georgellen."

The impulse to merge is often expressed by homely metaphors of bodily incorporation: "I could eat you up," "He inhaled her presence," "She drank him in with her eyes." The lover feels the Other to be so much a part of him that she has incorporated him, or he her. Each step of intimacy suggests the next: talking becomes like touching, touching like making love, making love a merging of souls. Sex does not simply serve lust, but the transcendent aims of merger. Through the compulsion to merge, the lovers become more aware of their bodies. Each lover lives in his body and is grateful for it, for it is the instrument of his desire for union. Not only does it allow him to make love to his beloved but it offers the possibility of making that love manifest in the form of a child. The body is both metaphor and instrument of the longing to merge. The body has become a tool for the soul.

Sex informed by love results in heightened sexuality. It is in love that one is granted the most compelling sexual experiences of one's life. Every sexual act is informed with wonder, tenderness, and awe. Other women, other men cease to interest the lover. In the phase of idyllic love, the lover is passionately monogamous—even if he in fact sleeps with someone else. (For some, "object constancy" depends on whom they think of when they make love, not whom they are with.)

In the act of making love, in the very act of pleasing both himself and his beloved, the lover comes to feel a unique intimacy with her; then the lovers often feel a sense of merging. Sex is a sacred rite in the religion of mutual love, and like all sacred rites, is an encounter with the mysteries.

At moments of spiritual union—transcendent moments as it were—whether the route to union is sexual or otherwise, time no longer exists. The moment is timeless, eternal, the boundaries of self dissolve though paradoxically the self is neither lost nor diminished. Quite the contrary, the self is affirmed and enriched. The sensory perceptions of that instant are heightened and its emotional resonance enshrined in memory. For such a moment, one will sacrifice the future and the past. The memory of it can be suppressed but never really obliterated; it may return unexpectedly and it can always be recalled at will.

QUARRELS AND TESTS. Most lovers mark the occasion of their first quarrel. In the beginning of the love affair they marvel at the absence of acrimony or argument, assuming this to be the natural result of their perfect harmony. After the first quarrel, however, they breathe a sigh of relief. They have survived the threat of mutual anger, and their love has been proved strong. They reassure one another that fights or the lack of them have nothing to do with harmony; at worst they are counterpoint in the music of love.

The mystique surrounding the first quarrel reveals a good deal about romantic love. Part of love's magic is the freedom it grants from the ambivalence inherent in most relationships. In romantic love, the lovers do not weigh and balance; they feel love without rancor, anger, or ambivalence. Obsessive personalities in particular, because they are by nature more ambivalent than most, feel the freedom from ambivalence that comes with love as an immense liberating force. Their love is like a sparkling mountain stream or a dam breaking open. Such a sweep of emotion is a revolution, a blessing, a release.

Once past the first quarrel, different lovers react differently to successive quarrels. If love is freedom from ambivalence, how bitter it can be when fault-finding and anger enter. For some, it marks the end of the idyllic period. Emotional life goes back to "normal." For others, as long as the quarrels are "passionate," the resolution of the quarrel (more often than not in love-making) symbolically reenacts the expulsion of ambivalence. To them arguments are like periodic Bacchanalia, or Carnival; they give the release that allows the passion to continue. For these lovers, the slippery slope is the risk of unleashing authentic instead of ritualized anger. Sometimes lovers are distraught when they learn that rage runs just below the surface of passion.

For other lovers, spats are a form of coquetry they enjoy, a love dance, in which the ritualization of ambivalence, rather than its expulsion, is itself the desired end. For these lovers, the slippery slope is insipidity.

Still others interpret passionate anger and even violence as the sure signs of love, because only through such palpable intensity does love seem validated to them. Of course, this is most common among lovers with strong streaks of masochism and sadism. For them, raging love rationalizes aggressive tendencies that might otherwise be regarded with suspicion.

Even without quarrels there remain tests to meet, barriers to overcome. The joint institutionalization of their lives together is no easy task. Each has other priorities and commitments, and each has goals separate from the other. It is in this stage that one commonly sees the first great struggle in love.

The lovers are now one, but they have also realized that they maintain separate priorities. Differences crystallize. She believes if he loved her he would agree to her demands. He believes that if she loved him she would not make such impossible requests. Each feels love toward the other, but there are limits—despite each one's belief that there should be no limits. He fears the loss of his autonomy and pulls away. "I've had the experience," he says, by which he implies that nothing further that is new or expansive will take place even if the relationship continues. But he wants to replace her with a duplicate, in order to deny her uniqueness and his need for *her*. He is naive and tries to fall in love with a new woman. Of course, he will usually return to his beloved. He tries to reconsider her point of view, her issue, and to make an accommodation. Then she must decide between pride and love.

If they are to survive as a couple, these issues must be resolved or pushed aside. Their basic goals, with each other or in the world, must coincide or at least overlap. For love to proceed, they must compromise, settle the issues between them, and declare their unity and common purpose. Above all, the couple itself, the "we," must take first priority.

Transformation and Release in Realized Love

With the beloved, the lover discovers a new world of feeling and meaning. But as it turns out, love changes more than the scope of the lover's experience; it changes the lover as well. Both the exultation of love and the obsessive preoccupation with it are so dramatic that they tend to obscure this cardinal feature of passionate love: it changes the lover, most often, but not invariably, for the good. Theorists of love have spent so much time on the lover's perception of the beloved that they tend to minimize the profound internal changes that take place in the psyche of the lover. They focus on the lover's idealization of the beloved and his subsequent de-idealization, when illusion is shattered by the most relentless of all debunkers, the dailiness of life together. And yet, not all love ends in de-idealization of the beloved. But all love *does* eventuate in some change in the lover, whether great or small, for better or for worse.

It has been said that love "like a certain divine rage and enthusiasm, seizes on man at one period and works a revolution in his mind and body; unites him to his race, pledges him to the domestic and civic relations, carries him with new sympathy into nature, enhances the power of the senses, opens the imagination, adds to his character heroic and sacred attributes, establishes marriage and gives permanence to human society." This fact of change in the lover is so obvious that it ought to be a truism about love, but it escapes notice. Just as there is thought to be a ladder of love ascending from the bestial to the celestial, so, too, is there a ladder of successively etheralized changes in the lover, beginning with the merely physical.

Love allows the lover to feel more attractive. The magical transformation of appearance in love is the main plot device of many a popular novel and movie. In the movie *The Enchanted Cottage*, a homely couple fall in love and come to see each other as beautiful, despite the fact that they are objectively unchanged. Similarly, in the movie *Mr. Skeffington*, the heroine Mrs. Skeffington is a ruined beauty who has lost her hair and reconciles herself to her altered state only when she is reconciled with Mr. Skeffington, who still perceives her as beautiful (enabled to do so not only because, like love, he is blind, but because he has never stopped loving her). Lovers confer beauty where it does not, objectively, exist, because both lover and beloved are enabled, through the power of love, to believe in that beauty.

However, it is also true that, even in the eyes of the objective observer, beauty can bloom with love's nurturing. Many girls grow up believing that if they fall in love—and take off their glasses or let down their hair—they will become beautiful, that being a premise in many of the love stories that supply basic life plots to the imagination. And there is some truth to this: love sometimes literally does change the way the lover looks.

Some people claim to be able to diagnose pregnancy in the eyes of the expectant mother; others claim the state of being in love can be discerned in the lover's eyes. One is almost shocked if the bride lacks the radiance we have come to associate with love. Convention has it that the lover becomes more attractive, sometimes because of an inner spiritual change that lends luster to the exterior, sometimes, more practically speaking, because of an increase in confidence and the freedom to experiment with appearance. Women often intuit when a close friend is embarking on an affair—and the first clue may well be her radiance. Love, transcendent sex, and weight loss go together and may all act in the same direction, to improve the lover's appearance.

Conversely, observers sense a crisis if the appearance of one or both of the lovers abruptly deteriorates. If a wife suddenly gains weight, her friends assume that there has been some sexual or emotional disruption in her marital relationship.

When lovers come together to form a "We," there are frequently changes in their situations. Sometimes these changes appear to be merely external, however dramatic they may be. One thinks of all the Cinderella stories: the commoner who marries the king, the au pair who marries the millionaire's son, or, conversely, the prince who gives up his kingdom for the women he loves. But changes in situation create changes in role. In assuming new responsibilities and different roles, one stretches one's potential in ways that are impossible without definitive internal changes.

The complaint is sometimes raised against love that it causes lovers to make vows and to incur a new set of duties. This may sometimes be the undoing of love but it also offers new beginnings.

More fundamentally, there also appears to be changes in the lover's sense of self. Love evokes in us something positive; at its best it gives us a sense of goodness, restoration, harmony, and mutuality. Because of the way in which each lover sees the other as his best self, the worth of each, previously buried or unrealized, is allowed to surface. It is this goodness towards which love strives. The lover feels expanded, conscious of new powers and a newfound goodness within himself. He attempts to be his best self, not in the sense of putting his best foot forward, as he might in courtship, but in the deeper sense of rising to the occasion, of feeling stretched by a new and profound experience. The beloved sees good in the lover, of which the lover was only dimly aware. Often what allows us to fall in love is the lovely picture of ourselves reflected in the lover's eyes. That picture enables us to love ourselves and hence to love another. We often become more lovable as a result of being loved. The new self is richer and fuller.

Sexual inhibitions are often dissolved in love. For Celie, the heroine of Alice Walker's *The Color Purple*, who had been an abused child and then an abused wife, sexual awakening (and spiritual salvation) comes through the idealization and love she conceives for her husband's great love, a blues singer named Shug. The entire novel is written in the form of letters, and in one letter addressed to God, Celie describes her sexual awakening:

My mama die, I tell Shug. My sister Nettie run away. Mr. _____ come git me to take care his rotten children. He never ast me nothing bout myself. He clam on top of me and fuck and fuck, even when my head bandaged. Nobody ever love me, I say.

She say, I love you, Miss Celie. And then she haul off and kiss me on the mouth.

Um, she say, like she surprise. I kiss her back, say, *um*, too. Us kiss and kiss till us can't hardly kiss no more. Then us touch each other.

But sexual inhibitions are not the only kind to be dissolved; restrictions and inhibitions of character can also be undone. One man, romantically passionate in a long-standing marriage, confides that his wife was the first person in his life to say, metaphorically, "Don't stop," undoing not only his inhibitions of sensuality but also of intimacy.

Here is Anna, the protagonist in Sue Miller's novel *The Good Mother*, describing her sexual awakening:

As for me, it was his wildness, his openness which intrigued me. . . . It was the fact that during sex I lost track of the boundaries between us, thought of his cock as a feeling inside me, thought of my cunt as a part of his body, his mouth. And because I became with him, finally, a passionate person.

The Good Mother goes beyond the depiction of Anna's sexual awakening to show us the more basic kind of release that can accompany a love affair (though in her tale the love is ultimately problematic; she may be named Anna for good reason). Anna and her husband had "stopped noticing and valuing the separateness of the other." But in her great awakening love affair with Leo, a free-spirited artist, the same thing could never happen. As Anna muses:

With Leo that didn't happen, couldn't happen, though there were times when I yearned for the unconsciousness, the self-forgetfulness that would have made it possible. From the start, we fought and then made love, both with a passionate intensity that I had thought as lost to me as the possibility of making great music. I felt I'd been traveling all my life to meet him, to be released by him. It was what Babe had promised me, what my Gray grandparents had promised, what music had promised me: another version of myself, another model for being.

One of the most famous "transformations" under the impact of love was that of the poet Elizabeth Barrett, a virtual invalid and recluse following the accidental drowning of her brother, into Elizabeth Barrett Browning, lover and beloved of Robert Browning. Her relationship with him is, of course, one of the most celebrated love stories in recent history. But transformation in love is the rule rather than the exception. Transformations range from a new awareness of previously unobserved parts of the world which can be as slight (or immense) as the appreciation of someone else's point of view, to the wholesale reorganization of one's personality. Of Victor Hugo's love affair with Juliette Drouet and the changes it wrought in him, Matthew Josephson has this to say: "His own life had been formerly a rather respectable and almost insulated affair, and much of what he had written was inspired by books he read or by historic events. But with Juliette he drew closer to life itself, to earthly beauty, and soon, as he realized, to a veritable grand passion. He was undergoing a sea change, whose effects were soon to be seen as a gradual alteration of his attitude toward many questions, a change of his interests, even his subjects." Juliette brought him closer to the "people" of whom she declared herself the daughter.

Even when love turns out to be problematic, lovers feel the profound internal shift love has brought about in them. Maria Callas, speaking of the change in her after she fell in love with Aristotle Onassis, could have been speaking for any number of lovers when she said: "I had the feeling of being kept in a cage for so long . . . that when I met Aristo, so full of life, I became a different woman." "I had become prematurely old and dull. I had got heavy, thinking of nothing but money and position." Meeting him made the difference. "Life for me really began at forty, or at least nearly forty."

A valued and lasting transformation in one or both of the lovers often survives the end of love. In Kundera's *The Unbearable Lightness of Being,* Franz is changed and enriched by his affair with Sabina, despite the fact that she deserts him. Through his relationship with her he was enabled to leave a stultifying marriage and grow emotionally:

Sabina's physical presence was much less important than he had suspected. What was important was the golden footprint, the magic footprint she had left on his life and no one could ever remove. Just before disappearing from his horizon, she had slipped him Hercules' broom, and he had used it to sweep everything he despised out of his life. A sudden happiness, a feeling of bliss, the joy that came of freedom and a new life—these were the gifts she had left him.

Psychic transformation through love, whether or not love endures, is, of course, one of the greatest of love's gifts, one that we intuit and may seek, whether consciously or unconsciously. And it is one of the themes that I will explore later in greater detail. But it must also be said that some passionate love affairs are destructive. In them the lover not only suffers; he may also undergo a loss of self-esteem, a constriction of self, even a negative transformation—one that is usually transient but which may, on occasion, last.

In Francesca Stanfill's novel *Shadows and Light,* the heroine Allegra is transformed in different ways and directions during the course of her ill-fated, ill-advised passionate love affair with a mysterious seductive man named Alexander, a dishonest financier about to be exposed. In the beginning Allegra feels a deep fulfillment and a sexual awakening. But under Alexander's critical tutelage and uncertain affection, Allegra's bearing breaks down. Her friend Emily notices the change, and writes in her journal:

Clearly this is not the same girl as the one I met last September . . . There's *une espece de lassitude,* as the French say, in her eyes—a trapped look. As if the internal radiance has dissolved into grim sparks. . . .

It's not every day that one gets to see this kind of perverted metamorphosis.

As to Allegra's subjective experience, she

had begun to feel tired on her return from Europe. . . .

She had grown self-conscious about her physical self—including her height—and began to imagine, in the presence of every diminutive woman, that Alexander wished that she, too, resembled a small Dresden doll. . . .

At dinner with him, there would be moments when she would be seized by an inner silence, as if something inside her had suddenly frozen. And paradoxically, it was often at such moments that she would reach for his hand, or touch his face, or his hair, as if to reassure herself that he were there, and that whatever it was between them lay intact.

Allegra gradually recovers, demonstrating that what she suffered was reversible. But part of her is forever changed. Though perhaps not so dramatically changed as lovers who are thoroughly transformed by love, she is wiser, and her sexual awakening will never be undone.

What are the mechanisms that effect change in the lover? In part, the beloved's approval offers a kind of redemption to the lover. It has often been remarked that the inner peace and self-confidence of the lover is comparable to that which is felt when one achieves religious certainty. Psychological expansion is reflected in an expansion in the real world. The burst of confidence that the lover feels allows him to take new risks, make new assertions, and initiate new enterprises. The lover's enlarged ego state is reflected in his mood, in his newfound generosity, and in his sense of himself as a better person. He is changed not only in his sense of self but in his adaptive engagement with the world. The lover may doubt whether he is worthy of the beloved, but he no longer doubts his fundamental goodness and his abilities.

What also happens is that the lover incorporates features of the beloved into himself, at the very least some capacity to look at the world with the eyes of the beloved. His interests expand, often to include those of the beloved. He develops new aptitudes and insights. The lover may receive gifts as varied as an interest in old movies, a greater facility in intimacy, a passion for skiing, the ability to trust and to open up the self, the awakening of the capacity for laughter. And, depending on the responsivity and flexibility of the beloved, the lover gives such gifts of the self in return. (These exchanges occur not just between lovers, but between friends as well; however they are more intense and far-reaching with lovers.)

The transformation that takes place in the lover's psyche may be even more extensive. Though love is born in the imagination, it promotes real changes in personality organization. It is through the sense of merger and identification with the beloved that the boundaries of the self are changed. Love not only heals the breach between body and soul, but leaps over the chasm that separates the self from the Other. The lover achieves that almost impossible task: he both possesses the Other and surrenders himself. In the process, he is not obliterated but, paradoxically, enlarged and changed, having incorporated into himself aspects of the Other as well as recovering buried parts of himself.

CHAPTER THREE

Love's Divided Nature: The Pleasure and Pain of Romantic Love

My passions have made me live and my passions have killed me. —*Rousseau*

OVERS may be suffused with feelings of supreme exultation and bliss, but they may also feel consumed by unremitting despair, jealousy, and rage. Certain proverbial stories, inspirational or cautionary, describe the extremes of happy and transcendent love, painful and destructive love; these tales bespeak either the triumph or the tragedy of love. In "Beauty and the Beast," the Beast is restored to his natural state, that of a handsome prince, by virtue of Beauty's consenting to live with him. So, too, with "The Frog Prince." In these tales, love tames the bestial, raises a man beyond his animal nature, releases something of his higher aspirations and spiritual nature.

But one finds the opposite moral in the many cautionary tales of love. Samson, in the Old Testament, blinded and enslaved by his love for the Philistine woman Delilah, revealed to her the secret of his strength. Betrayed by her, his locks shorn, his power destroyed, he was then literally blinded and enslaved by his enemies. Only through fervent prayer was his strength restored so that he could pull down the pillars in his enemies' temple, killing himself along with his enemies. Adam too, felt the bite of love, with what results we all know. In the cautionary convention, love is not a call to a higher state; it is that which entraps man and lures him away from duty and moral responsibility, leading him to betray his true commitments, to descend from the godlike to his mortal and, ultimately, animal nature.

These two opposing notions of love, both expressions of the male point of view, rest on two age-old perceptions of women: that of savior and of temptress. Parallel stories reveal that woman, too, may be blessed or cursed in love. She may be awakened or rescued by love (as were Sleeping Beauty and Cinderella), or destroyed (as were the wives of Bluebeard).

Both versions of love, the cautionary and the inspirational, have a measure of truth. In love, the lover may indeed find redemption, or may be destroyed. How does it happen that one is either delivered or condemned? Is it a destiny preordained by one's psyche, or is it the luck of the draw? I will return to that question in later chapters. The important point to be made here is that even in basically happy love, the relationship of love to pleasure and pain is a complex one.

"Normal" romantic love has its own set of problems, its own heartaches. Despite the enrichment of experience that love can bring, we know that its passionate phase is notoriously short-lived, permanence quite rare. In fact, some would say that the essential feature of passionate love, other than its intensity and the overriding importance attached to it, is this brevity, even when love develops into an ongoing commitment.

As a rule, the almost overwhelming intensity of a passionate attachment lasts longer if there is some barrier to the union—the long courtship of the Victorian period, the enforced separations in clandestine adulterous affairs, or constraints put upon the lovers by their circumstances or their families. But if there is no external barrier to love, lovers often find it difficult to sustain passion, leading both lovers and theorists of love to question the value of something so fragile and transient.

With or without external obstacles love in its passionate phase does not appear to exist without pain as a backdrop to pleasure. There is a lovely song from Purcell's "The Fairy Queen" which sounds this theme:

> If love's a sweet passion, why does it torment?
> If a bitter, oh tell me whence comes my content?
> Since I suffer with pleasure, why should I complain,
> Or grieve at my fate when I know 'tis in vain?
> Yet so pleasing the pain is, so soft is the dart,
> That at once it both wounds me and tickles my heart.

The way in which love is in fact heightened by pain is well described by Emerson: "In the noon and afternoon of life we still throb at the recollection of days when happiness was not happy enough, but must be drugged with the relish of pain and fear; for he touched the secret of the matter who said of love, 'All other pleasures are not worth its pains.' " The pain takes many forms. The lover may experience unrelieved torments of longing when love is unrequited, of frustration when love cannot be sexually consummated. He fears rejection or humiliation in courtship, and even after love is reciprocated his fears persist. He suffers jealousy or is overtaken by such waves of unjustified hostility towards the beloved that guilt quickly joins the throng of torments assailing him. Even in the full bloom of mutual, happy love, the lover intuits that there is something in the nature of his longing that may defy complete fulfillment and he is saddened.

This strange mixture of pleasure and pain derives in part from the fact that love is an extraordinarily complex emotion, fueled by often conflicting motives, directed towards divergent aims. Swift put the matter succinctly: "Love, why do we one Passion Call? When tis a Compound of them All."

But if the pain of happy love is considerable, the pain of a thwarted love is so great that it may sometimes lead even to madness. David, the young protagonist of the novel *Endless Love,* burns down his girlfriend Jade's house after her father bans him for a month, thinking perhaps that he can "discover" the fire, appear to save Jade and her family, and be reinstated. Instead, in the aftermath of a near catastrophe, he begins to comprehend the significance of his behavior:

I was, I knew then, a member of a vast network of condemned men and women: romance had taken a wrong turn within me and led me into mayhem. I was no better than dialers of anonymous phone calls, hounders, berserk pests, ear severers, committers of flamboyant, accusatory suicides, hirers of private detectives, or a medieval king ready to deploy an army of ten thousand souls in order to gain the favor of a distant maiden—and when the fields are scorched and the bodies lie in heaps beneath the sun, the king will clutch his breast and say: I did it all for love.

Despite such insight, not even hospitalization in a mental institute could dampen David's ardor for Jade.

The lover's urge to totally possess the beloved may become a driving force which influences and organizes behavior. In people like David, it brooks no interference, and has within it the capacity to cause harm not only to the self, but to others.

Justifiably fearful and cautious as most of us are about the negative potential of love, we value it highly nonetheless and continue in varying degrees to pursue it, believing that we will be the exception who will revel in its joys and escape its sorrows. We believe that our love is special and will triumph over adversity (or the lack of it, which is sometimes even more dangerous). And if not, we still subscribe to Tennyson's exhortation:

"T'is better to have loved and lost/than never to have loved at all." We intuit that love enriches us, changes and enlarges us in an enduring way, and we are therefore willing to risk the pain and loss that may be entailed.

This becomes particularly apparent when lovers in dire circumstances choose to stay together, knowingly sacrificing all conventional hope of happiness for the sake of their union. It would not be uncommon for a couple to *choose* poverty together rather than riches alone (for example, when young lovers face disinheritance rather than renounce their romantic choices). Some lovers would prefer even to die together than survive apart, and most would make that claim whether or not it were literally true. For some lovers, the defining question is not "Do you love me?" but "Would you choose to die with me or to survive?" It is in this sense (though incorrectly, I think) that Denis de Rougement sees romantic love as the handmaiden to death, not pleasure. Whether we agree with him or not, we must concur with his insight that the wish of lovers to be together may take precedence over anything we normally call happiness and, if need be, over survival itself. It is this priority, whatever the cost, that some observers find so terrible and would label as self-destructive or masochistic. In the judgment of the lovers, though, it is this very priority which is the essence of love.

Love encompasses pleasure, but will endure pain; in fact, sorrow may be part of its essential nature. Whatever the deepest longing in love, it transcends a mere search for pleasure or the routine avoidance of pain, or happiness as conventionally described.

Pleasure and Love

Not only is the quest for love more complex than the pursuit of pleasure, but the nature of pleasure is itself complex and by no means self-evident. Because love does encompass pleasure, even if it is not defined by its pursuit, it is important to understand something of the nature of pleasure.

For Freud, pleasure was a release from tension, particularly a sexual release, while pain was defined as frustration or the inability to release tension. This formulation, designated the "pleasure principle," postulates that people seek pleasure and avoid pain. It has become one of the pivotal concepts of psychoanalysis. In essence, then, early psychoanalytic theory was based on the concept of hedonic regulation though the pursuit of pleasure was acknowledged to be tempered by the "reality principle." In this schema, love is seen largely as a sublimated expression of libido, or the sexual instinct, and therefore the pleasure connected with love is ultimately derived from the sexual instinct.

But pleasure as a relief from tension is too narrow a definition to account for all the different forms of pleasure. C. S. Lewis distinguishes between two kinds of pleasure. He defines the first group of pleasures as those preceded by desire and realized by gratification of that desire. The pleasure that comes from the release of sexual tension would certainly be among this group, as would be the pleasure of drinking a glass of water when one is thirsty. The second group, however, consists of experiences that are pleasurable in their own right, without prior need or tension. As an example, Lewis points to the pleasure we take in the unexpected fragrance of flowers. This pleasure may be great, but it was unsolicited and not desired as a release from tension or the sating of an appetite. Lewis refers to these two separate categories of pleasure as, respectively, "Need-pleasures" and "Pleasures of Appreciation." The pleasures of appreciation do not gratify needs; instead our appreciation comes unbidden, *elicited by the object.*

The pleasures that people give to one another are of both kinds. While the pleasure a child takes in its mother may be regarded as related to the need pleasures, one's subjective impression is that romantic love is related to the pleasure of appreciation, that love is elicited by our delight in the beloved. But, as we shall see, romantic love is characterized by both "need pleasures" and "pleasures of appreciation." It is simultaneously selfish (aimed at satisfying the lover's needs and releasing his tensions) and altruistic (having no aim at all beyond the appreciation of the beloved and the granting of pleasure to her).

But pleasure comprises more than mere relief, or even appreciation. Though it does indeed draw on the sensual and aesthetic, pleasure is embedded in the context of our earliest relationships. As Freud pointed out, the child necessarily learns that his gratifications depend upon permanent access to a benevolent figure. Consequently, although Freud sometimes suggested that affection, like sexuality, was derived from libido, at other times he acknowledged that the need to be loved was a psychological response to the biological limitations of infancy: "The biological factor is the long period of time during which the young of the human species is in a condition of helplessness and dependence. . . . The biological factor, then, establishes the earliest situations of danger and creates the need to be loved which will accompany the child through the rest of its life."

Within this interpersonal context, pleasure is symbolically and imaginatively metamorphosized from a simple sensual experience into something more complex.

Because our earliest sensual pleasures are so intertwined with the Other, our well-being and even our sense of self becomes bound up with the Other. Because we learn who we are in connection to some other person, our sense of self is always tied to our intimate relationships. Ultimately, our capacity for self-validation rests on some concomitant validation from another person. The apparently curious need to exist in the mind of another is poignantly captured by Pascal: "We do not content ourselves with the life we have in ourselves and in our own being; we desire to live an imaginary life in the mind of others, and for this purpose we endeavor to shine. We labor unceasingly to adorn and preserve this imaginary existence, and neglect the real. And if we possess calmness, or generosity, or truthfulness, we are eager to make it known, so as to attach these virtues to that imaginary existence." Our deepest sense of self-worth rests on our interactions with those others whom we designate as significant, and their appraisal of us.

The importance of our relationships may come to supercede simpler pleasures, so that the happiness we seek in mutuality may take priority over pleasures experienced more narrowly. According to Marilyn French, "Mutual pleasures are the sacred core of life: food, body warmth, love, and sex. These things are sacred because they are necessary, because they confer pleasure in the giving and the receiving so that it is impossible to say who is giving and who is receiving. They satisfy the profoundest needs, and in their satisfying, satisfy two." Some of our most profound pleasures are grounded in mutuality and can only be realized in love.

Yet at the same time there are equally cogent pleasures that attach not to mutuality, but to those acts that affirm the self as separate, as autonomous, that enlarge the sense of self or that gratify our aspirations, including the wish to be good. We derive pleasure from mastery, achievement, and from doing good, from all those things which add to self-esteem and an enlarged sense of the self.

Here we come to one of those great divides in human development—our need, at one and the same time, to achieve mutuality and independence, our simultaneous and conflicting tendencies toward communion and toward agency. In the very largest sense, one could argue that this is the underlying, intuitive meaning of Freud's dictum that mental health ought be defined as the ability to love and to work. Put another way, his concept of mature development posits the capacity for the enjoyment of two very different kinds of pleasures: one that derives from the gratification of the need for mutuality and communion (as expressed through love or attachment), the other from the gratification of the need for autonomy and agency (as expressed through work). Unfortunately, these two different kinds of needs may sometimes be in conflict. As an aside, we might note that each sex may have a tendency to gratify one set of longings at the expense of the other set: Many women are preferentially drawn to the pleasures of mutuality, many men to the pleasures of autonomous achievement.

However, all these different varieties of pleasure are often mixed with fear and pain. The pleasure in physical exercise is often linked to pain and the ability to push oneself beyond the pain into that high that only athletes can know. Aspiration has as its dark side failure or the fear of failure. The pleasure of anticipation is frequently a combination of fantasy, performance anxiety, and the fear of disappointment. The joys of creativity are usually inextricable from the pain of suffering and strain, the final vision achieved may be dark and shattering.

Clearly, then, though pleasure and pain are often conceived of as opposites, this is not really the case; to open oneself to the possibility of pleasure is always to risk pain. C. S. Lewis's description of what we aspire to in sexual union can serve as a paradigm for pleasure in all its chiaroscuro richness and paradox.

Pleasure, pushed to its extreme, shatters us like pain. The longing for a union which only the flesh can mediate while the flesh, our mutually excluding bodies, renders it forever unattainable can have the grandeur of a metaphysical pursuit.

This passage is surely one of the most potent descriptions of the way pleasure and pain are inextricably bound in our metaphysical longings, whether expressed through the flesh or in the quest for love.

Love, then, draws on many pleasures—sensual, aesthetic, mutual, and selfish. Only by understanding the complexities of these can we grasp the lovers' willingness to undergo hardships or pain. The resulting happiness or pleasure is of a different order from pleasure as it is commonly defined, one that is experienced as more fundamental, necessary even, to the lover's sense of self and goodness.

Lust and Love

Just as love is related to pleasure but not defined by it, so, too, is love connected to the specific pleasure of sex, but not inextricable from it.

(And so, in the previous chapter, I have distinguished between passionate love and carnal love.) Making love and loving are not the same thing, but for those who love, some sort of sexual longing appears to be present even in the most chaste, idealized loves. Nonetheless, although the lover seeks sexual union, he will tolerate abstinence, just as he tolerates pain. The happiness one seeks in love is greater than either simple pleasure or sexual gratification. Though one wishes love to encompass both, it can survive without either.

In lust, it is sexual union alone that is paramount. Not everyone will do, of course, but there is wide latitude. The relationship with a sex object need not even be personal. The sexual partner may be no more than a suitable convenience, and may be used simply for one's own pleasure. For some, the sexual needs of the partner are not important; she is desired for her physical qualities, but her subjective needs are considered irrelevant. (Many are the innocents who have been wounded when their passionate sexual partners fail to call or, worse still, are unable to remember their names when they happen to meet some months later.)

In contrast, in romantic love, one longs not just for the fulfillment of a concrete physical urge or need, but for the person herself, for the Other. In love, it is only a particular individual who is desired, and she is desired for those qualities that make her unique, rather than those she shares with the rest of her sex. When one is in love, sexual union is desired most of all as a symbol of and a route to the longed-for emotional union.

In the world of subjective experience, lust and love surely may overlap, but one knows the difference: "One deed ascribed to Hercules was 'making love' with fifty virgins in the course of a single night: one might on that account say that Hercules was beloved of Aphrodite, but one would not call him a lover." The aim of sex in pure lust usually is personal pleasure, sometimes power; sex as the soulful expression of love generally requires an understanding of the subjective life of the beloved.

But not everyone who is in love chooses to express it through the act of sex. In Kundera's *The Unbearable Lightness of Being*, Tomas concludes: "Making love with a woman and sleeping with a woman are two separate passions, not merely different but opposite. Love does not make itself felt in the desire for copulation (a desire that extends to an infinite number of women) but in the desire for shared sleep (a desire limited to one woman)."

For Tereza (Tomas's beloved), on the other hand, the distinction between sex and love is also a major preoccupation, but leads her to a different conclusion. Her longing to escape the world her mother had foisted upon her—a world in which all bodies are the same and must march in soulless formation—leads her to an obsessive jealousy over her lover's repeated infidelities. "She had come to him to escape . . . a world where all bodies were equal. She had come to him to make her body unique, irreplaceable. But he . . . had drawn an equal sign between her and the rest of them: he kissed them all alike, stroked them alike, made no, absolutely no distinction between Tereza's body and the other bodies. He had sent her back into the world she tried to escape . . ."—to a world where, from her point of view, she was not acknowledged as special or unique.

Most people seem to be more like Tereza than like Tomas; they find that if sex is fueled by love, the act is transformed, becoming something quite different from the gratification of a merely physical urge, and they treasure sexual faithfulness as the expression of true love. As one streetwise and experienced man expressed the distinction: "All my life I thought I was a pretty good stud, but I never knew what sex was. After I fell in love I knew I had just been masturbating into any old sock."

The simultaneity of emotional and sexual union is one of the truly exhilarating human experiences. When sex is part of love, it converts the body into an instrument of soulful communion. ("So soul into the soul may flow/ Though it to body first repair.") The concordance of sex and love allows a release from the tension between mind and body that we so often feel. Through the act of love the individual transcends the body and escapes, if only momentarily, from his dual nature, and from his aloneness.

And so, while most people would agree that the desire for sex can exist without any corollary desire for love or intimacy, the converse proposition, that the desire for love can exist exclusive of sexual yearning, does not seem viable. We cannot honestly contemplate Eros without Venus, longing for a union of souls without a union of the flesh, at least not in our epoch. In earlier historical periods, however, sexuality and romantic love were considered separate (though frequently intertwined) categories of human behavior and experience. One thinks of the chaste loves of the medieval troubadours, the metaphysical love of Petrarch for Laura, of Dante for Beatrice. One thinks also of Montaigne's often-quoted description of his passionate (nonsexual) friendship with another man, Étienne de la Boétie, in which he states their souls and minds, "mix and blend one into the Other in so perfect a union that the seam which has joined them is effaced and disappears."

Just as love is comprised of more than simple pleasure and pleasure itself is more complex than might at first be apparent, so, too, is sex. Sex is clearly more than the mere discharge of tension which leads to pleasure. In sex, as in love, there is often some attempt at transcendence. This is what Simone Weil meant when she said:

If people were told: what makes carnal desire imperious in you is not its pure carnal element. It is the fact that you put into it the essential part of yourself—the need for Unity, the need for God—they wouldn't believe it. To them it seems obvious that this quality of imperious need belongs to the carnal desire as such. In the same way it seems obvious to the miser that the quality of desirability belongs to gold as such, and not its exchange value.

We should not simplify our understanding of sex any more than our understanding of pleasure. But even considering the complexities inherent in pleasure and sexuality, love is seen to transcend the pursuit of either.

The Longing for Merger

What, then, is the aim of love beyond the pursuit of simple pleasure, sex, or happiness? Beyond pleasure, love seems to aim for release from the self. Love's potential to enrich or deplete, to give joy or sorrow, can only be understood within the context of the lover's desire for merger with the beloved. Ultimately, people do not achieve their deepest joy in solitude, but in the concordance of two souls. The aim of love is nothing less than to overcome separateness and achieve union or merger with the beloved. In that merger (or perhaps I should say in that *imaginative* merger) the lover achieves both an exaltation of feeling and a profound sense of release. The longing for union and for the elusive and complex gratifications it promises is so compelling that the lover willingly foregoes lesser pleasures and endures any pain. The peremptoriness of the wish is such that the lover will sacrifice anything whatsoever to fulfill it—even his reason. So it is that love sometimes appears to be related to madness.

This aim of union is revealed in our very language, in the meaning of the word "love." At first glance, the word may appear too broad to be meaningful, encompassing a family of emotions instead of one. It refers not only to romantic love but also to love of country (patriotism), love of fellows (friendship), love of animals, love of family, and love of God. It can even refer to the love of strawberries and of chocolate. But language is a library of stored cultural wisdom, and we ignore its cumulative insights only at our intellectual hazard.

In Freud's judgment, "language has carried out an entirely justifiable

piece of unification in creating the word 'love' with its numerous uses."
Freud's work reveals the underlying unity in the different phenomena
subsumed under the name of love. Although Freud is popularly misunderstood to have regarded eros as libido (as mere appetite, or sex), he actually
considered sex as just one manifestation of libido. For Freud libido was
a drive that coincided "with the Eros of the poets and philosophers which
holds all living things together." It was "the preserver of all things,"
including the narcissism that preserves the self. Its aim was "to establish
ever greater unities and to preserve them thus—in short, to bind together." He explicitly connected the different forms of love. The heart
of libido may be "sexual love with sexual union as its aim. But we do not
separate from this—what in any case has a share in the name 'love'—on
the one hand, self-love, and on the other, love for parents and children,
friendship and love for humanity in general, and also devotion to concrete
objects and to abstract ideas."

In the Hebrew Bible, we see one of the earliest expressions of the
essential unity of different forms of love. Unlike the Greeks, who had
different words for the diverse forms of love (for example, *eros* and *agape*),
the Hebrew word for love *(ahavah)* is the same whether it is sacred or
profane love being chronicled. As the *word* love unifies apparently dissimi-
lar phenomena, so, too, what it conveys is the unifying aim of love, which
is to bring together the lover and the object of his love.

Whether one derives all the manifestations of love from love of God
or the sexual instinct or some other first cause, it appears that language
does indeed speak the truth, that all these diverse loves have something
in common. Our loves all lead us toward union; they are the centripetal
forces in our lives. The aim of romantic love is union or merger with the
Other, hence the shared cultural wisdom of language in relating romantic
love to love of God, as well as to all the other forms of love of which we
are capable.

The wish for union, which is at the heart of the subjective longing in
love, finds its classic expression in Plato's *Symposium*. There Aristophanes
gives an account of an ancient myth about love which survives in the
modern imagination. According to that myth, primordial man was round,
with four hands and four feet, and a single head with two faces on a single
neck that could turn in all directions. These powerful individuals were
marred by such excessive pride that they dared to challenge the gods.
They were defeated, of course, but Zeus chose to punish rather than
annihilate them, and he did so by cutting them in two. Prior to this
trauma, when each man was complete in and of himself, love had been

unknown. But once man was split, each half yearned for the other half, "and when one of them finds his other half . . . the pair are lost in an amazement of love and friendship and intimacy."

Thereafter, whenever they met, these two halves sought to grow together, but had not the means to do so. Zeus, taking pity on them, moved their reproductive organs in order that they could periodically come together in a sexual embrace. Yet their impulse to merge transcended the sexual: "the intense yearning which each of them has towards the other does not appear to be the desire of intercourse but of something else which the soul desires and cannot tell, and of which she has only a dark and doubtful presentiment." For the diminished creature, "this meeting and melting into one another's arms, this becoming one instead of two, was the very expression of his ancient need. And the reason is that human nature was originally one and we were a whole, and the desire and pursuit of that whole is called love." In more recent times, the same underlying fantasy of mythic reunion finds expression in the romantics' belief in "elective affinities," the conviction that each of us has a preordained lover somewhere in the world.

Aristophanes' myth, as portrayed in the *Symposium*, clearly portrays neediness as the motive for love, and the restoration of wholeness as its achievement. It incorporates sexuality into eros, but only as a means to union and transcendence, not as part of love's essence. The myth also suggests that love has its roots in an earlier state of existence, even though the bisected creature remains unaware of the sources of its longing.

Echoing the Platonic formulation, most subsequent philosophical accounts of the purpose of love begin with the assumption that love is meant to counteract man's neediness, emotional poverty, and loneliness. "Merger" (or "union") then serves the function of making a "whole" out of two incomplete and deficient beings.

The most recent and extreme account relating *inamoramento* (falling in love) to weakness is proposed by Francesco Alberoni:

No one can fall in love if he is even partially satisfied with what he has or who he is. The experience of falling in love originates in an extreme depression, an inability to find something that has value in everyday life. The 'symptom' of the predisposition to fall in love is not the conscious desire to do so, the intense desire to enrich our lives; it is the profound sense of being worthless and of having nothing that is valuable and the shame of not having it.

While there is some truth in Alberoni's argument—and his analysis undoubtedly applies to many people—it appears too narrow and exaggerated, focusing almost exclusively on love as the antidote to personal weakness and neurosis. Alberoni underestimates the magnitude of the loneliness and sense of frailty which is humankind's lot.

Love is an antidote not just to personal neediness, but to those existential anxieties that encompass our sense of the frailty and brevity of our life on earth. Half beast and half god, man has been described by philosophers as a paradoxical creature. We are each condemned not only to death and extinction but—and this is what renders our condition tragic—to knowledge of our mortality. It is the dichotomy we feel between the dross of our bodies and the immortal stuff of our souls that makes us crave transcendence. It is the knowledge of our insignificance in the universe and, ultimately, the awareness of our own death that causes us to seek transcendence in soulful merger with a beloved.

We are not only aware of our soul as separate from our animal nature; we are aware of the isolation of our soul from other souls, and of our mind as separate from other minds. The recognition of the existence of other minds and our isolation from them—"the problem of other minds" as it is alluded to in philosophy—first occurs early in childhood. Our separate inner life gives us "space" and privacy and is important to the growth of our individuality, our imagination, and creativity. The separation shields us from the intrusiveness of others. But, eventually, for some of us the separateness becomes oppressive: it condemns us to solitude. Others treat us as functionaries and accept us in the uniforms of our roles. For them, our inner lives are inessential at best, sometimes obstacles, irksome. In madness, some of us may become fearful that we alone exist as sentient beings. Sometimes we are able to touch one another across the chasms that separate us, but this experience is not given to us often. It is our existential sense of isolation and loneliness then, cut off from direct contact with other souls, able to reach them only through the instrumentality of body, which propels us to leap over our solitude and seek union through love.

Through our isolation, we come to understand the finite limits of selfhood. We then strive to move beyond the boundaries of self for relief from the pain our limitations cause us. By nature, we are frail, our lives are finite, and yet our longings are infinite. Love enables us to transcend our insignificance and our aloneness. Someone cares about us as we subjectively experience ourselves. Despite our knowledge of death and our belief (if we are not religious) that we ultimately count for little in the universe, the reciprocal affirmation from someone we love and hold in esteem lends us warmth against the coldness, loneliness, and vastness of eternity.

Transcendence and Pain

The longing for wholeness, completeness, merger, and transcendence is the sorrowful heart of love—sorrowful because it is a longing that can never be wholly satisfied. There is no ultimate remedy for our existential plight, but love is the search for such a remedy, and transcendence the only means of feeling we have achieved it.

Passionate love seeks a transcendence akin to religious experience. The ideal of merger through love represents a potential solution to the central human problems of estrangement, finiteness, and meaninglessness. Consequently, love is more than a relief from pain or alleviation of anxiety; it is a mode of transcendence as well as transformation.

Love is one of the great transcendent experiences, but by no means the only one. Hans Morgenthau has described man's pursuit of transcendence in "the extension of his self in offspring—the work of his body; in the manufacture of material things—the work of his hands; in philosophy and scholarship—the work of his mind; in art and literature—the work of his imagination; in religion—the work of his pure longing toward transcendence."

Another great passion by which man seeks self-transcendence—though always abortively—is in his longing for power. In *Man's Fate* by André Malraux, Gisors delivers a brilliant meditation on power: "What fascinates them in this idea, you see, is not real power, it's the illusion of being able to do exactly as they please. The King's power is the power to govern, isn't it? But man has no urge to govern; he has an urge to compel. . . . To be more than a man, in a world of men. To escape man's fate. . . . Not powerful: all powerful. The visionary disease, of which the will to power is only the intellectual justification, is the will to god-head: every man dreams of being god."

There are still other modes of attempting self-transcendence. Not just religion but, for the zealot, religious wars, offer a means of transcending the finite meaning of earthly life. Some find transcendence in political doctrines that are essentially secular religions. Others seek transcendence in drugs and lust, what Aldous Huxley has aptly called downward transcendence.

The worth accorded to romantic love from culture to culture varies depending on what kinds of transcendental experiences a particular culture values, and what value it places on personal change and development. The preferred remedy depends on specific cultural directives. As observed in *Man's Fate:* "It is very rare for a man to be able to endure—how shall I say it?—his condition, his fate as a man." "There is always a need for intoxication: this country [China] has opium, Islam has hashish, the West has woman. . . . Perhaps love is above all the means which the Occidental uses to free himself from man's fate."

But despite cultural sanctions for or against romantic love, the potential for it, by virtue of both our common developmental experiences and existential plight, exists in every cultural configuration, and it has been known to occur in the most unlikely of situations.

Passionate love is neither irrational nor a mere hormonal storm, as some would have us believe. While it has roots in our biological nature, it also expresses our highest aspirations, our longing for transcendence through merger. Love is not just of the body but of the soul as well and this duality is what accounts for the moral dispensation we accord it: love is the only "appetite" for which an excess is allowed. While gluttony and other excesses are frowned upon, crimes of passion have their own mystique and, in some cultures, are unpunished, forgiven, and even admired. We link love to madness, but call it divine.

Nonetheless, torment and pain may accompany the quest for love and in fact be part of its nature. Even enthusiasts of love acknowledge its inherent existential problems. The separateness between lovers cannot be totally breached (just as Aristophanes' bisected creatures cannot permanently satisfy their deepest longings). This is the quality in erotic longing that does not allow for complete and permanent fulfillment. Carson McCullers has expressed this inherent sadness in love, the ultimately unbridgeable chasm between lovers: "love is a joint experience between two persons—but the fact that it is a joint experience does not mean that it is a similar experience to the two people involved. There are the lover and the beloved, but these two come from different countries. Often the beloved is only a stimulus for all the stored-up love which has lain quiet within the lover for a long time hitherto. And somehow every lover knows this. He feels in his soul that his love is a solitary thing. He comes to know a new, strange loneliness and it is this knowledge which makes him suffer."

To the extent that the lover's goal is merger, he must fall short of it; and the closer he comes to achieving it, the more he will feel his autonomy threatened. In this dilemma lies both the power and the frailty of love. Moreover, the beloved, like the self, is subject to the laws of decay and extinction and so, even if the lover surrenders to her completely, she cannot ultimately counteract the existential threat of nothingness. This is, of course, the reason that religious people believe that only God can be a true object for transcendence.

However, the perils of love are greater than those of mere disappointment or transient pain. Any transcendent endeavor, fueled by some elemental power and aiming to transform the self, may expose the self to the dangers of fracture, of madness, and of unleashed savagery. There is a demonic quality at the source of love, which when thwarted may turn to destruction. The deep irrational force in love, so necessary to the projects of transcendence and transformation, may sometimes run amok. This is, of course, why love is so often likened to madness. Passionate love, like all the experiences that open up the self, verges on the borders of self-harm and aggression. In fact, such hazards are intrinsic to all the great creative projects. Rare though the descent from passion to madness may be, its very possibility is the main inspiration for the cautionary approach to love, and for the futile attempt to rationalize and tame it, to declare "rational" mature love as the happy alternative to passionate love.

2

THE AIMS OF LOVE

CHAPTER FOUR

How Love Develops: Love Dialogues and the Life Cycle

INCE LOVERS so often experience the onset of love as a complete break with the past, locating its roots in their early lives seems to miss the point. Enthralled with the uniqueness of their feeling, lovers exclaim "I've never been in love before," or "I only thought I was in love before." To them, both the emotions and the relationship seem so different from anything in their past that they experience love as a release from their previous mundane existence, not as an echo of or variation on an old theme. Hence, as far as the lover is concerned, love has no developmental history; it is brand new—otherwise it is not love—and through it the lover is changed and made new.

In contrast to the lovers' insistence on love's novelty, the observers of love are quick to point out that love has regressive and/or restorative aspects that link it very firmly to the past. Whether he is aware of it or not, the lover, in the act of falling in love, be it for the first time or the last, draws upon his past experience. And indeed, sometimes the lover will sense a pre-existing fit or an inner rightness; he may feel as though he has always known his beloved, as though their present love is merely a renewal of some long-lost communication dimly glimpsed in dreams.

For Freud, romantic love and all other adult relationships as well are re-editions of earlier feelings, those experienced first in the relationship of the child with its mother and, later, with the Oedipal parent. From the psychoanalytic perspective, the successful achievement of mature love depends on the lover's having been able to negotiate certain prior experiences successfully; otherwise his capacity to fall in love will be sorely limited.

In ancient myth, love is seen as the quest for one's other half, for lost regions of the self. What the psychoanalytic and the mythic formulations have in common is their view of love as a restoration, the end point of a lifelong quest to gain restitution for what was lost long ago—in personal history, or in the history of our species—as the result of prior separations. The union between two lovers is, symbolically, a restoration of that loss. In assuaging the sorrow of old losses, love can restore buried parts of the self.

Lovers and love's chroniclers (both in myth and psychoanalysis) may seem to be at odds with one another's views, but in fact their views can be reconciled, and should be. Of course, it is not necessary for the lover to know anything of love's developmental history. But for the theorizers of love, the failure to grasp the meaning of the lover's sense that he has broken with the past leads to peculiarly sterile and reductive formulations of love, for example, the suggestion that love should aspire to no more than affectionate bonding. Passionate love is much more. In attempting to explain love, one must heed both the lover's intuition that it is an emergent experience and, as such, a catalyst for change, and the outsider's observation that it is a culmination of past experiences.

Deep love always separates us from what has gone before; one might even say that is part of its function. When the lover commits himself to the beloved, he chooses a new life; he leaves the preordained world of the family into which he was born (or the life he has created for himself, which has since come to feel stifling) and leaps forward into the world he and his beloved will create together. In choosing our lovers then, we select much more than a person. We make a path choice and—if we are young enough—a choice that may shape the future development of self. Writing of the lovers Franz and Sabina, Kundera says: "While people are fairly young and the musical composition of their lives is still in its opening bars, they can go about writing it together and exchange motifs . . . but if they meet when they are older, like Franz and Sabina, their musical compositions are more or less complete, and every motif, every object, every word means something different to each of them." By contrast, Kundera writes of Franz's relationship with a younger woman, "The student-mistress was much younger than Sabina, and the musical composition of her life had scarcely been outlined; she was grateful to Franz for the motifs he gave her to insert." But whatever our age when we fall in love, we always feel the promise of at least a few new motifs, and of some internal change that will follow.

The feeling of newness and change is often so dramatic that it seems inconceivable to the lover that falling in love is an internal process. Rather, he experiences it as a force that strikes him from the outside world; hence love's frequent characterization as a thunderbolt, an arrow from Cupid's quiver, a change wrought by a love potion, or less fantastically, the inevitable impact of the beloved's irresistible charms.

As long as love is perceived as coming from outside, it can be experienced as completely novel. However, we cannot begin to understand that which we call love until we have understood that it is our deepest, oldest longings which find themselves fulfilled in it. It is because the wishes and feelings are from our very depths that the re-edition of them in romantic love is so intense and their fulfillment so profoundly exhilarating.

Love is in some sense a refinding. But it is also—and this is love's ultimate triumph—the creation of a new experience. Love does more than restore; love catalyzes change in the self. Love may be regressive but it is also progressive, giving direction and content to the maturation of the self. Love does indeed have a developmental history, but, finally, it is in its essence a mutative experience.

Idealization and the Family Romance

Because falling in love is a complex psychological act, it should come as no surprise that there are precursors during the process of growing up. Indeed, there is a developmental series of "love dialogues," the apex of which is the mature act of achieving mutual love.

One element paramount in all the precursors of love is idealization; and, as it turns out, idealization plays a critical role in development.

Early in life, the child creates a concept of the good mother who gratifies all his needs. The child's image is based on his mother's ability to gratify many of his needs, but he superimposes upon the real-life mother the fantasy of total bountifulness. This earliest of idealizations is believed by psychoanalysts to be the projection of the infant's (disappointed) omnipotence onto his mother. If he himself is not all-powerful, he can regain command by controlling one who *is*. (Only later in life is the child able to integrate negative features into the image of mother, to give up the absolute dichotomy of the good mother/bad mother, the all-powerful mother/the devalued mother.)

From the very beginning of life, idealization of the beloved and yearning for her are closely intertwined. Similarly, at all developmental levels in the history of our successive loves, from mother figure to the great passion of adult life, the "lover" fashions an image of the idealized beloved, one who is perfect and, at least initially, regarded without ambivalence. At any stage of personal development the story of love has three plot elements in common: the choice of an idealized love object (which of course is not a wide choice in infancy and early childhood), the longing to interact with that object in one way or another, and the consequent alteration of self.

But the story is not always the same because idealization, at different points in life, is linked to very different sorts of yearning. Sometimes idealization, or admiration, is primarily connected to identification, the desire to take on the characteristics of that person who appears as exalted. But idealization can also lead to the wish for union, to be joined to the beloved and seek satisfaction from her. The wish for identification, on the one hand, and complementariness, on the other, are often separate, one or the other predominating at different developmental stages, but they may also interact and overlap as they appear to do in mature love.

In the first years of life, the child's emotional longings are directed primarily toward the parents. Not only do the parents serve as the source of the child's gratifications and safety, but they are the magical, idealized beings through whom the child achieves vicarious strength. The child longs for one or the other parent or both, is happiest in their presence, and dreads separation. In the earliest years the parents are simultaneously the objects of desire (for potential satisfaction) and of identification as well. The young boy hangs onto his father's words, brags that *his* father is bigger and stronger than anyone else's, imitates shaving "like daddy," and altogether adores him. He wishes to be *with* his idealized object, to be gratified *by* him, and he hopes eventually to *become* the paragon of perfection he has created in his mind. But at the same time, he directs his Oedipal strivings to his mother; he may try to monopolize her attentions and assure her that he will be stronger than Daddy when he grows up.

Eventually, in order to achieve autonomy and to be free to love, the young lover must give up his idealization of his parents. But idealization itself is not renounced; it is simply displaced, transferred from the parents and onto a series of surrogates that culminates in the figure of the beloved. Desires and identifications follow along the winding trail of our idealizations. The history of our passionate relationships can be read in the history of our sequential idealizations.

In latency, that is, during the years after the manifest resolution of the Oedipal complex but before puberty (from about six to twelve years of age), children begin to separate desire and idealization from the nuclear family and transfer them to other objects. Piqued by their parents' failure to gratify all their wishes, and increasingly aware of imperfections in the family itself, children create a series of fantasies referred to as "the family romance." Children daydream, for example, that they have been adopted or abducted from their real parents, who are believed to be more elevated in status than the everyday false parents with whom they unhappily find themselves. They feel their real parents, though unknown to them, would love them fully, perfectly, unambivalently, and would satisfy all their desires.

Family romance fantasies are imbued with powerful longings, but as Freud suggests, these are echoes of earlier feelings.

The faithlessness and ingratitude are only apparent. If we examine in detail the commonest of these imaginative romances, the replacement of both parents or of the father alone by grander people, we find that these new and aristocratic parents are equipped with attributes that are derived entirely from real recollections of the actual and humble ones; so that in fact the child is not getting rid of his father but exalting him. Indeed the whole effort of replacing the real father by a superior one is only an expression of the child's longing for the happy, vanished days when his father seemed to him the noblest and strongest of men and his mother the dearest and loveliest of women.

Consciously, though, idealization has been detached from the parents and transferred either to fantasy figures or people whom the child knows. The fantasies serve to preserve the child's narcissism insofar as he elevates his self-worth by identifying with his grander imaginary parents. And the fantasies hold out the hope of rescue, of better times, against the disappointment of the present.

Family romances find wide expression in myth. Many of our legendary heroes—Oedipus, Moses, Superman—were adopted, given up by their true parents to avoid some catastrophe; many fairy tales also embody typical family romance themes. One major motif in fairy tales is that of the heroine who finds herself in unhappy circumstances, but who, because of her goodness and essential merits, is finally rescued and elevated to her rightful place (Snow White and Cinderella are two of the most famous examples). Similarly, the young, disinherited hero, through his unique prowess (he alone may be able to pull the sword from the stone, for example), proves the legitimacy of his right to inherit the kingdom.

Eventually, the child becomes better equipped to find gratification in the real world, and the family romance fantasies then begin to diminish or are subsumed into other fantasies—particularly Oedipal ones. But they can also continue into young adult life and, in modified form, throughout life, often reinvoked in times of stultifying stasis. And the generic name, family romance, suggests the continuity between this fantasy and later fantasies of an amorous nature.

One man, now in his mid-fifties, vividly recalls the passionate family romance of his childhood and can trace derivatives of that fantasy into his adult life. As a young boy of about six, he came to believe that he was the son of a Maharajah, and, unhappy with his parents and their virtual adoration of his older brother, he used to lie awake at night, crying and praying for his true father to rescue him. Why he chose Indian royalty is unknown to him, but he is dark and might even be said to have a faint Oriental cast. Though the Maharajah fantasy receded, it was replaced at about the age of eleven with a related preoccupying fantasy. Feeling more and more an outsider in his own family, enraged to the point of rebellious-ness, he imaginatively identified, in the opening years of World War II, with the Japanese enemy—their values, lifestyle, and their hostility to Americans. Though as an adult this man appears the very paragon of equanimity, that is partly because he has managed to translate his child-hood rebelliousness in a constructive way. Derivatives of those early fanta-sies survive in his profound intellectual and aesthetic interest in Japan. He has traveled there extensively, learned Japanese, embraced one of the Oriental religions, and is sexually attracted to Orientals. As for his failure to feel nurtured as a child, he appears to have compensated by means of his passionate nurturance of his lovers (a not uncommon reversal and one on which I will elaborate later).

We have all indulged in one form or another of the family romance. One young woman remembers elaborate fantasies, beginning at around the age of thirteen, that her mysterious bachelor uncle who lived in another state would send for her and rescue her, exposing her to the better things of the world. Her fantasies about him seemed to be triggered by a fifty-dollar gift he gave her for her junior high school graduation, and his telling her to buy something frivolous with it. This was in marked contrast to the advice she was generally given by her practical, academ-ically striving parents. She saw her uncle as the embodiment of the possibility of pleasure. Her fantasies took off from the point of thinking about what she would buy with the money—maybe a good leather purse—and how she would write him a clever and moving letter telling him about it. He would be impressed with her taste and suggest she buy shoes to match, and then a traveling outfit. Eventually it would occur to him to invite her for a visit, and so forth. Her fantasies, compounded of both family romance and Oedipal yearnings, allowed her to elaborate a world that embodied different ideals from those of her parents, and, in small increments, her ideas about the scope of the world enlarged. (Family romances can attach to the actual parents if they are absent, for example divorced or merely inattentive parents. The irony of the child's idealizing such a parent is, of course, not lost on the struggling parent who is left to raise the child.)

Family romances are adaptive fantasies, offering hope for the future and sometimes evolving into life plans. Essentially they are fantasies of being adopted by better parents. (It is extraordinary over the course of many years of a psychiatric practice to see how many people from devastating backgrounds have been able to save themselves by getting someone, whether teacher, employer, relative, or parent of a friend, to actually step in as a kind of surrogate parent.) It is not hard to see the connection between this kind of fantasy and the fantasy of amorous rescue. Family romances are often cannibalized by their successor romantic fantasies, and rescue and nurturance remain one subtext of these latter fantasies. But for many an adult, some version of the family romance persists outside of romantic fantasies; take, for example, the young professional man's wish to find in his boss the hoped-for loving father who will elevate him and rescue him from obscurity and defeat, eventually designating him as a successor.

Even in these early family romances, we can begin to see elements that will distinguish mature love: the "object" who feeds (or loves) us must be idealized in order for him to validate our own worthiness, to gratify, by our identification with him, our longing for omnipotence. In the early romances, this takes the concrete form of our being related to the royal, rich, and famous. We are rescued from situations in which we feel unloved or unappreciated. And by virtue of our association with the exalted personages of our imaginary relationships, we find our true identities and are released from the careworn, shoddy lot that only appears to be our own. How like mutual love in which we at last find our true selves! From earliest life, the validation of our true (desired) identity is confirmed by our joining the object of our desire and beginning a new life.

Concomitant with family romance fantasies, many children have fearful fantasies, what we might call family terrors. In these, usually expressed in daydreams or nightmares, the parents (or parent surrogates) are evil or threatening. The scenarios of these fantasies are extremely varied. One woman remembers that, as a girl, just before going to sleep she was overcome with the fantasy that her mother was not her mother at all, but an Indian disguised as her mother who was going to sneak up in the night and scalp her. A little boy I knew had frequent nightmares about reptiles who, disguised as his parents, would do him harm. These fantasies are partly expressions of castration fears related to Oedipal strivings, but they are also the result of the rage the child feels when he intuits that his many longings will not, cannot, be fulfilled. The rage-filled, destructive fantasies he directs at the disappointing objects of his wishful longing make him fear the possibility of violent revenge from them. So, for example, the bad mother whom the child hates is imaginatively transformed into the witch who may destroy him. Family romances and family terrors presage two prominent reactions to unhappy love affairs: respectively, the search for a new love object and the rage directed at a disappointing one. (And so it is that great love can turn into great hate rather than merely coldness or detachment.)

Rehearsals for Love: Crushes, Infatuations, Flirtations, and Fantasies

As children continue to disengage from their parents, they idealize them less. But naturally their own self-worth shrinks in proportion to the devaluation of their parents, just as their earlier self-esteem swelled with identification with their then-esteemed parents. Ultimately, though, family romances are not an adequate substitute for the lost idealization of parents; as they grow older, children come to fantasize themselves as the principals, not as mere dependents in need of better parents. They strive to live up to the dictates of their own internalized ego ideal (that mental agency that is heir to the infantile wishes for perfection and that serves as a compass to ongoing aspirations). Then, too, they want their imaginative preoccupations to be capable of translation into everyday life, and so reality is set against the continuation of the family romance. Since nature abhors a vacuum, children come to people their world with new heroes and heroines, people who represent projections of their own ego ideals. These heroes are not substitutes for good parents, but are models for what the protagonists themselves hope to become. Preadolescent children transfer their longings to the larger world and begin to idealize teenagers or adults of the same sex, most often people they know and can relate to, however marginally. (But in some cases, the romance of the imaginary continues, in a preoccupation with fictional characters or famous people. We constitute ourselves of others, some real, some imaginary.) They often develop crushes on these newly exalted personages, falling in love with those whose lives they hope to emulate and whose paths they hope to follow. Although these same-sex crushes may be sexual, more often they are not. At this stage of life, the goal of idealization is identification alone, rather than any form of union. But throughout the life cycle, idealization may exist merely as a stimulus for envy and emulation or it may attach to an object then chosen as the object of our love. In psychoanalytic parlance, idealization is the prelude to both identificatory love and object love.

For example, a young boy may hang out with the sports coach, mimicking his speech and adopting his diet. One woman remembers that as a young girl, about eleven, she idealized the young married woman next door and involved herself with the whole family by becoming the baby sitter. (How many mothers lament the fact that their au pairs wish to become daughters, rather than mother's helpers!) Less exalted than the subject of the usual family romance, the neighbor's family had the advantage of affording real interactions and intimacy. It was a wonderful relationship until the outbreak of a polio epidemic (pre–polio vaccination) when the neighbors saw the girl playing with her friends and consequently forbade her any contact with the baby, thereby cutting off her lifeline to the beloved young mother. The woman still remembers her profound grief at what she experienced as a betrayal, clear evidence that she was of no real emotional significance to her idealized friend, worse than second fiddle to the baby. Generally the longing in these crushes is to be like the "beloved" rather than to achieve union, though in the example just cited the girl surely sought nurturance, intimacy, and affection as well.

Sometimes the object of the crush is not anyone known personally; rock stars seem to be the icons of choice in modern times. Here the only function the crush serves is that of identification, not of intimacy. But sometimes the crush does provide real bonds with those peers who share in it. The process of communal idealization is, of course, evident in the eruption of group crushes, for example Beatlemania. The bonding (and identification) with peers can be as important as the admiration for the icon, providing the intimacy that would otherwise be lacking in idealization at such a remove. Something comparable to this sometimes occurs later in life, as for example, when two women who love one man become friends instead of or as well as rivals. In essence, they share the intimacy of a common idealization, not the convoluted homosexual attachment that is so often assumed to have drawn them together. I know of one instance in which two such women became each other's major source of emotional sustenance after their lover's death.

Though they may find a range of satisfactions in one-sided crushes, adolescents hunger even more for intense relationships and those that, because they are reciprocal, may yield real experience and intimacy. These are the years of progressively forming new identifications outside the nuclear family, and one major means of doing so is by taking one's measure in intense friendships. Adolescents idealize their friends and imitate their dress and mannerisms, their swagger and "cool." Parents are sometimes saddened because they feel the loss of their children's idealization and see the admiration and authority that had been vested in them transferred to their children's peers group. In these idealized attachments, the adolescent's goal is to participate in the qualities they admire; they imitate, identify, and feel enhanced.

The adolescent (and preadolescent, too) begins to develop crushes on the opposite sex, derivatives of Oedipal urges now coming to the fore. The passage from nonsexual crushes to the next stage, when the urgency to be *with* appears to take final priority over the wish to be *like*, has never been completely explicated. This process recapitulates the process leading up to the Oedipal complex. (In an Oedipal child, the consolidation of its identification with the same-sex parent leads the child to desire the opposite-sex parent.) For the heterosexual adolescent, the shift from same-sex to opposite-sex crushes occurs when hormonal change makes sexuality more urgent, and when the sense of self reaches the point that continued growth can come via *complementary* rather than *identificatory* relationships, object love rather than identificatory love. (A girl can learn to be a woman by identifying with a woman—or being with a man.)

In the normal course of development, then, the yearning that attaches to idealization is transformed from the wish *to be like* (or to replace) to the wish *to be with*. Once the sense of self is largely consolidated, desire shifts toward complementariness. But identification remains a powerful theme in development; hence the adolescent's "desire" is often for the girlfriend of his best friend. As during the Oedipal stage, desire is triggered through identification, wanting for ourselves the *same* as that which our revered idol has. Some people remain fixated, perpetually poised at this critical bifurcation point between longing to be like someone and longing to be with someone, forever torn, hovering between worship of a friend and lust for his beloved. Here are the perpetual hangers-on, the young man equally in love with both husband and wife, the young woman who dotes on her woman mentor and lusts for her mentor's husband. But sometimes, the desire is to replace altogether the object of one's idealization. In the movie *All About Eve*, Eve (Anne Baxter) is so admiring and envious of Margo (Bette Davis) that she not only wants Margo's career

for herself, but also Margo's husband (Gary Merrill). However, complementariness and identification as modes of relating are never entirely
separate categories. In complementary choices the lover continues,
though to a lesser degree, to identify with the idealized beloved and
generally internalizes some of the beloved's characteristics.

Adolescents, when they do come to form opposite-sex crushes, often
pick as the objects of their affection family friends or relatives halfway
between their age and that of their parents. Then they experience poignant episodes of puppy love, with its attendant fears and yearnings. They
experience longing but are not yet impelled to translate it into sexual
terms. Thrown into contact with the "beloved," the young teenager may
blush, stammer, and appear awkward, all the while feeling possessive of
the beloved and jealous of anyone else the beloved favors with her attention. The age difference between the young lover and his beloved suggests
the link with incestual Oedipal fantasies, but it also protects against the
possibility of a real sexual encounter. And here we see that just as the
family romance reveals (and conceals) a continuity between its dramatis
personae and the beloved parents of one's earliest years, so, too, do romantic fantasies reveal (and conceal) a continuity between the object of desire
and the Oedipal parent.

The narrator in Isaac Babel's short story "First Love" tells of the crush
he had on his neighbor Galina when he was ten years old and of his
reaction when he spied on her with her husband, who had just returned
from the Russo-Japanese war.

Galina would hold her husband's hand all day long. She stared at him
incessantly, for she had not seen him in a year and a half. But her gaze frightened
me, and I would turn away and shiver, glimpsing that obscure and shameful side
of human existence. . . . Galina would bruise herself, pull her robe above her knee,
and say to her husband: "Kiss baby better." The officer would bend his long legs
in their narrow dragoon's trousers, in their smooth, taut leather boots with spurs,
and crawling across the littered floor on his knees, smile and kiss the bruised flesh,
just where a little bulge rose above the garter.

I saw those kisses from my window, and they caused me agony. Unbounded
fantasies tormented me.

But the preoccupation in crushes is not restricted to infatuation with the
Other or obsession about being excluded in a manner reminiscent of
Oedipal exclusion; crushes are often highly self-absorbing, offering adolescents a stage on which to practice new roles for themselves, to experiment
with their own power as the object of another's yearnings and admiration.

Thus, the art of flirtation is learned. (This is part of the mechanism of complementariness, another way, besides identification, that the self is enlarged in relationships.)

In *The Genius and the Goddess,* Aldous Huxley captures the wonderfully intense nature of crushes, their play-acting quality and meandering aim, coursing from preoccupation with the beloved to preoccupation with one's self in a new role. Fourteen-year-old Ruth is in love with her father's colleague, John Rivers, who is himself infatuated with Ruth's mother. The mother is away nursing *her* mother and Ruth uses her newfound freedom to alter her appearance and establish a new identity, a process described by John Rivers, the narrator:

Ruth didn't seem to feel the need of *acting* her new part; it was enough merely to *look* it. She was satisfied with the signs and emblems of the grand passion. Scenting her cotton underclothes, looking at the image of that preposterously raddled little face, she would see and smell herself as another Lola Montez, without having to establish her claim by doing anything at all. And it was not merely the mirror that told her who she had become; it was also public opinion— her amazed and envious and derisive school fellows, her scandalized teacher. She was not the only one to know it; even other people recognized the fact that she had now become the *grand amoureuse,* the *femme fatale.* It was all so novel and exciting and absorbing that for a time, thank heaven, I was almost forgotten.

But then Ruth learns that her mother is to come home:

It was as though she had suddenly remembered who I was—her slave and her predestined Bluebeard, the only reason for her assumption of the double role of fatal temptress and sacrificial victim.

These passages from Huxley dramatize that half-way moment between self-absorption (where the goal is often to be *like* another—in Ruth's case, like the *grande amoureuse* she had most recently read about) and absorption with the Other (where the goal is gratification from that Other). Ruth hovers at the precipice, sometimes retreating so far into the regressiveness of self-absorption that she actually *forgets* her beloved. Huxley catches this pivotal moment for us, freezes Ruth in that moment when she is still balancing on the verge of some very final kind of change—an internal consolidation of identity—that would allow her to love the Other in all his subjectivity, not solely as one of the dramatis personae in *her* play.

Teenagers are endlessly imaginative in playing at love, "practicing" separate components of the love relationship before they gamble on the full involvement of first love, before they are ready to bring idealization of the beloved, yearning, sexuality, and intimacy together. One cautious fourteen-year-old girl, longing to have an adventure and a romance, concocted a minor triumph. Using a pseudonym and pretending to be a reporter for a school paper, she called the local football hero (seventeen and too old for her in real life) for an "interview." She was able to transform that interview into a telephone romance of a year's duration, in which she called him at specified times but would never give him her phone number. The romance flowered. They chose their song and achieved a kind of verbal intimacy that lasted until she met him face to face after one of his football games. After seeing the look of shock on his face (no doubt she was very different from *his* fantasized lover) she never called him again. Some kind of partial romance can suffice for some people throughout their lives, serving as an end in and of itself. One thinks, for example, of George Bernard Shaw's celebrated epistolary romances, in which he eschewed an actual meeting with the object of his affection; or of Kafka's, which suffered serious, ultimately fatal, damage when Kafka gave way to the inevitable insistence upon an occasional meeting in person. For others, partial romance is a transitional phase, serving as a slow induction into love itself.

The developmental sequence of love is variable. Although crushes are particularly common in adolescence and young adulthood, they occur throughout life, and at whatever age they are experienced, they can serve as very valuable imaginative rehearsals for an experience that one is not quite ready to enter into in full. They attach derivatives of Oedipal fantasies to the object of idealization. In a sense they combine elements of the Oedipal drama and the family romance.

Following is an account of an adult crush. The woman who told it to me had had an unhappy love affair and was wary of men for a long time afterwards. This infatuation came in the context of a lifting of her mourning (or depression) for her lost love. It was the first evidence of an emotional thaw and a restored emotional availability. From the vantage point of the observer rather than the lover, it is often possible to see how a crush can act as a harbinger, indeed an agent or catalyst, of change in the lover.

It's actually very exciting to fantasize about a stranger. You become a sculptress, making him into your perfect man. In Kevin Kline's case, I don't think I was too far off. I remember it started when I saw him in *Sophie's Choice*. It was the scene in the bedroom when he's conducting the make-believe orchestra. He was shirtless, and as his arms went up and down, you could see the definition all along his back. I recall mentally running my index finger along each vertebra, tracing all the strength. His energy really hit me right through the screen. You remember him in *The Pirates of Penzance?* He's startling. You have no choice but to respond. Then came *Henry V* at the Delacorte. I missed him in *Richard III.* I was too busy being depressed that summer to go to the theater.

I have a clear recollection of the first time I saw *Henry V.* (I saw it three times.) It was in preview. Very few people showed up because it was overcast and the reviews weren't out yet. I was sitting on the aisle, third row center, praying it wouldn't storm. It didn't.

The first act began with Henry coming out in his red velvet robe to address his subjects. Well, I cannot begin to do justice to what I felt. His presence on that stage made my heart jump into my throat. He was amazing. His hair is heavy black (like cashmere), with streaks of gray that look like tinsel. He could have been a king in another life. At some point he did a monologue at center stage, and if I leaned over, I could have touched him. Now that was like a religious experience. No other person has ever moved me like that. My heart pounded. I was sure he could hear it. But the pedestal I put him on was the real fascination. He became an icon: "Hari Kevin."

I recall how crushed I was when I read in Liz Smith's column that he was seeing Phoebe Cates. I mean, Patti LuPone, Glenn Close, Mary Beth Hurt, Linda Ronstadt, his dresser in *Richard III,* all those others didn't bother me. But Phoebe Cates was like a more perfect version of me. I got depressed.

I sent him a candy jar filled with chocolate for *Arms and the Man,* because he played the chocolate soldier. A few days later his secretary sent me a thank-you note on his stationery and my despondency worsened. I thought he would call me himself; I moped for days, feeling slighted, and inferior.

My friend made good use of her infatuation. It allowed her to awaken emotionally, yet because it was "imaginary," it spared her any sexual exposure as well as the threat of rejection to which she was then, in the wake of her failed love affair, particularly vulnerable. When Kevin Kline failed to respond it was not really *she* who was rejected. "He probably thought I was a fat girl from Queens." She then went on to have a realized love affair, no, not with the boy next door, but with someone of even greater public distinction than Kline. In her infatuation, one is able to observe the intense longing (in her case the reawakening of longing) and the imaginative idealization of the beloved that characterize love in all its developmental stages, and, at the same time, the self-protectiveness and insulation from sexual demands that are features of crushes. In striving for love, of course, we must be willing to run risks, but sometimes a crush is as much as we feel ready for, even as adults.

Crushes are important rehearsals for love. And whether we are uninitiated and fearful of the unknown, or battle-scarred (like my friend) and fearful of what we have known only too well, we can make fruitful use of these rehearsals.

The opening phase of any love affair always bears a resemblance to a crush, characterized as it is by the imaginative fantasy, the mentally elaborated possibilities of what may come to be—trial action without the threat of harm. This opening phase corresponds to Stendhal's description of the first crystallization in love. In it one explores the whole rich panoply of potentiality. During the interval between the first meeting and the re-encounter with the beloved, the lover is primed by his own imaginative play. Sometimes the imagination runs wild: one woman was so horrified by the elaborateness of the scenario she had concocted between the phone call asking her out and the evening of the date with her new admirer that, by the time he actually arrived at her door, she was embarrassed even to look him in the eye.

Intuitively we all recognize the role of fantasy in love, which is why we respond to romantic stories that highlight love's imaginative component, even if the stories seem on the surface to be farfetched, for example, stories in which the lover falls in love with someone even before he meets her, or narratives of one-sided love or of love that can never be realized. In the 1944 movie *Laura*, a detective (Dana Andrews) investigating the murder of a young woman believes that the victim is Laura (Gene Tierney). During the course of his investigation, the detective falls in love with Laura, whose portrait hangs in her apartment. Viewers do not find it madness that the detective should love a dead girl, one he has never known; in fact, they seem to identify with the detective. *Laura* is a deeply romantic film which has found enduring success; the fact that generations of movie-goers have been able to identify with a detective in such an implausible situation must mean that they have an intuitive or unconscious appreciation of the role the imagination plays in their own affairs of the heart. The happy ending provided by the movie—the discovery that the victim is not Laura at all, and that Laura herself is still alive—celebrates and frees the lover's imagination by affirming its ultimate wisdom. Rather than administering the cautions customary to love's critics, the movie gives license to the impulse to love imaginatively, fearlessly, and unreservedly, even against the dictates of what would appear to be common sense. The deep appeal of this film resides in its success at converting dream love to real love.

Somewhere in Time is another movie on a related theme. A writer (Christopher Reeve), allowed back into the past, falls in love with a young actress (Jane Seymour) and decides to stay in the past rather than return to a present without her. For most people versed in psychoanalysis, the underlying fantasy from which *Laura* and *Somewhere in Time* draw their strength would seem to be that of impossible love which is magically realized—a derivative of Oedipal love. The tragedy of the child's longing for his mother is that he is separated from her not only by the incest barrier, but by time. The time of her time is not the same as the time of his time. In a certain sense, both stories might be considered as fantasies in which seemingly impenetrable barriers are penetrated—fantasies, in short, of Oedipal fulfillment, imaginative elaborations of old longings.

Fantasies like these seem to be fairly widely dispersed; that is why they can be relied upon to elicit a popular response. One often sees a related theme in the imaginative lives of girls whose mothers were widowed early (either the mother's first husband died and the girl is the product of the second marriage or the girl's own father died early in her infancy). Romanticizing and idealizing the fallen husbands of their mothers, the girls exalt the love between them. Though not in love with her mother's husband, the girl is nonetheless imaginatively engaged with him. These fantasies, too, are conscious derivatives of unconscious Oedipal fantasies and are closely related to crushes.

In a sense, all the crushes of childhood and adolescence are neither more nor less than phase-appropriate episodes of imaginative love. The "lover" is content with—in fact protected by—the ideality of his love. However, once past adolescence, most of us give way to the yearnings for impossible love only while watching movies or reading novels, for example, or in bouts of nostalgia for past love. Or we enjoy such crushes for what they are, namely imaginative excursions.

But in our real lives we eventually attempt to blend the imaginative with quite tangible gratifications, in the context of an intimate relationship. If we are to enjoy the intimacy, affection, and sexuality of "real" love, and not just the lesser pleasures of the crush, we must put our feelings to the test in the real world, converting longing into action, attempting to bring about some kind of reciprocity between ourselves and the one whom we idealize and for whom we long. We make this a possibility when we allow ourselves to feel passion for someone who might actually be available to us.

First Love

Idealization is an essential ingredient of love throughout the life cycle, but it is only one prerequisite. Old longings reinvoked, reworked, and

directed towards new objects—objects that, at least potentially, offer a
better chance of gratifying those longings for union—are the real fuel of
love. Just as mature sexuality is known to integrate different developmental components, and absorb many pregenital sexual impulses, so, too, does
love serve as the organizer of many different wishes and longings originating at previous stages. In so doing, love becomes something new, more
than the sum of its parts or the culmination of a developmental line.

Perhaps nowhere are the transformative qualities of first love better
expressed in Turgenev's *Spring Torrents:*

Sanin and Gemma were in love for the first time, all the miracles of first love
were happening for them. First love is exactly like a revolution: the regular and
established order of life is in an instant smashed to fragments; youth stands at
the barricade, its bright banner raised high in the air, and sends ecstatic greetings
to the future, whatever it may hold—death or a new life, no matter.

The lover commits to a new life project, a new path, to be undertaken
with his beloved. Consequently, for union with a new object to be a
possibility, the old love objects must be given up. In this, as in many other
respects, the story of Romeo and Juliet is a profoundly accurate depiction
of romantic love is general, and first love in particular. The play dramatizes
the role of romantic love in separating us from our past, creating a new
present and future course, and thereby acting as an agent of change. In
love, just as in the earliest family romances, one frees oneself from what
has gone before and forms a new bond, one at odds, to various degrees,
with previous ties. First love is an especially dramatic turning point in our
lives, because it is often the means by which we achieve "final" psychological separation from our parents.

For every lover, his new love must take priority over his previous
allegiances, but this is particularly true of first love. In *Romeo and Juliet,*
the need for *internal* psychological separation is metaphorically expressed
and fueled by the *external* conflict between the lovers' warring families,
the Capulets and Montagues, whose enmity turns young love into a
matter of life and death. As the action of the play progresses, Juliet
successively disengages from each of her childhood ties—her parents, her
nurse, the Friar—till in the end she stands free of the past, committed
only to her lover and their love. Romeo, too, becomes estranged from
friends and family. Both shed the ties that fetter them and keep them
apart.

The theme of the role of first love in separating the lover from his
family finds its way into many popular novels, too. For example, in *The
Two Mrs. Grenvilles,* Junior (William Grenville, Jr.) falls in love with Ann

Arden because she is free of the stifling conventions of his (upper) class, from which he needs help in disengaging. Unfortunately, she falls in love with him—to the degree that she does—because he is the step up she's been looking for. Each naturally is doomed to disappointment since their aims are ultimately at cross purposes.

However, love, even first love, is not about disengagement alone. First love effects separation from the past, but replaces discarded ties with new ones. Love is not only the instrument of separation, but of reparation and healing, as well. Love overcomes separation just as surely as it separates; it de-idealizes past objects of love and idealizes new ones. Love confers a sense of rightness, of achieving at last one's rightful identity. Joined to the idealized beloved, the lover regains a sense of importance and central-ity. First love, which sometimes endures, and sometimes does not, is an important milestone in maturation, the first in what is usually a series of adult love dialogues in which the consolidation of many partial wishes, impulses, and feelings take place.

First love is surely regarded as one of the great glories of one's life. And consequently it is often accorded a privileged place in memory. Liv Ull-mann, remembering her early marriage, which lasted five years, said, "I can never be so young again with anyone else."

Love throughout the Life Cycle

The sequence of love dialogues does not generally end with first love. The capacity—and the need—to fall in love continues throughout the life cycle, though the factors that predispose to it are not always the same. Love confers many blessings: intimacy and affection combined with sexu-ality, reinforcement of self-esteem and worth, and so on. But viewed from the perspective of catalyzing movement in one's life, the function of love appears to be twofold. Love can give surcease to the disappointments that precede it, but it can also be invoked to catalyze change when the self lacks stimulation, when one feels oneself drowning in a sea of sameness. In the earlier part of life, certainly through young adulthood, the self is hungry for experience—for the motifs of life, to reinvoke Kundera's meta-phor. Consequently the young are notorious in their propensity to fall in love; the prototypical lovesick young man or woman is such a common figure as to have become a staple of certain genres of fiction.

Later in life, when the self is more clearly defined, the traditional assumption has usually been that the personality manifests less fluidity in behaviors and choices, more stability and strength in realistically confront-

ing loss, crisis, and so on—and is therefore relatively immune to storms of passion. This may be true for some, and, for some, one love lasts a lifetime. But for others—perhaps particularly for men—mid-life stability is necessary as a base from which they feel safe in pursuing those long half-buried wishes that can culminate in passionate love. Consequently, some individuals first achieve passionate love only in middle life, or even later.

C. S. Lewis, though an eminent authority on love, fell in love for the first time late in mid-life. His former student and then colleague Peter Bayley recalled Lewis's remark about his idyllically happy marriage: "Do you know, I am experiencing what I thought would never be mine. I never thought to have at sixty what passed me by in my twenties." An apparently committed bachelor, living with his brother at Oxford where both were dons, Lewis had begun to correspond with an American woman, Joy Gresham, who was interested in his work. A year later he met her when she came to England for a "sabbatical." She told Lewis his books had been helpful to her on her spiritual journey, which had taken her from Judaism to Marxism and then to a true spiritual discovery of God. Gradually, Lewis and Gresham became friends, sharing as they did the same interests, even the same publisher. During her stay in England, Gresham received a letter from her alcoholic husband advising her that he had fallen in love with someone else. She went back to the United States, divorced, and returned to England where she resumed her friendship with Lewis, clearly no more than a platonic friendship at that time. Nonetheless Lewis married her when she was unable to renew her visa, offering a marriage of convenience so that she and her boys might obtain British citizenship. But shortly after their civil ceremony, Gresham, then in her early forties, broke her hip and was diagnosed as having breast cancer that had already spread to her bones. Her illness galvanized a passion in Lewis, taking him completely unawares. Only then did he commit himself to a true marriage and therefore arranged for a sacramental ceremony (for him, the symbol of a real marriage in contrast to the earlier civil one), which took place at her hospital bedside. Both Gresham and Lewis found themselves deeply in love and had three glorious years together before she died—years described by all who knew them as radiant and filled with unbounded happiness.

What allows an emotional breakthrough of that magnitude so late in life for a man such as Lewis? There are no more than a few hints in the biographical material that has been published thus far. Perhaps the move from Oxford to Cambridge left him more open, or more needy. (Or

perhaps the move was merely the harbinger, not the cause, of change.) Both the deep mutual interests he shared with Joy and her illness appear to have been important ingredients in the process that allowed him to fall in love. I would guess that Gresham's illness released some old feeling in him (in the television show "Shadowlands," it was suggested that her illness reverberated with his mother's early death), and that it also some-how changed his image of Gresham, probably in the direction of purifying her in his eyes (she was a strange choice for a deeply Christian man, Jewish by birth *and* divorced). But this, of course, is merely conjectural.

Occasionally, through the lives of one's friends or acquaintances, one is allowed a deeper understanding of those specific events that serve to catalyze love. One widower in his early *eighties* married a woman with whom he had been living for fifteen years, but he only fell in love with her *after* the ceremony. For him (and for some others too) love could only be experienced after a commitment had been made. But, of course, the decision to marry, given that he had actively avoided remarriage for so many years, needs to be explained. It seemed to have been triggered by two events: the death of a very close relative and—as with Lewis—the illness of the woman with whom he lived. The death left him unanchored; and, as we know, loss may create the impetus to love. But the role his girlfriend's illness played in his emotional life was quite specific; she, like Gresham, had breast cancer and underwent a mastectomy, though with a much better prognosis than Gresham's. What is so striking is that the widower's first wife had died of the very same disease some thirty years before, having refused to have a mastectomy. Only after his first wife's death did he develop any intensity of feeling about *her*, and he blamed himself for allowing her to disregard medical advice and for failing to be what he considered a "good husband." In fact, he appeared so devoted to the memory of his first wife, that his hypertrophied loyalty seemed to preclude any remarriage. (His friends and relatives were somewhat amazed that the love with which he remembered his wife exceeded by far what he had seemed to feel towards her during her lifetime.) But in the second relationship, when he had the chance to redeem himself, to nurse a woman through cancer, he was able to rise to the occasion, and to fall in love as well. After his second marriage took place, he declared himself happier than he had ever been before; among other reasons, he clearly regarded himself as a more giving, loving, and better man. Successful and affluent, he had never before had much pride in his goodness, though that was the characteristic he most revered in others.

There are many different kinds of situations that facilitate the experi-

ence of falling in love, both in mid-life and later. The mid-life sense of
too much sameness or constricting horizons may precipitate a longing for
change, one that may well take the form of "seeking" passionate love.
And, of course, the loss of an important relationship, or any crisis that
threatens self-esteem or self-identity, may also create a readiness to fall in
love. Sometimes the loss is the actual death of a parent; there are those
who fall in love only after an elderly parent has died.

Sometimes the impetus to a later-life love affair appears fairly obvious.
The lover, overwhelmed and unsupported in the midst of crises, reaches
out for sustenance. Herbert Henry Asquith, the British Prime Minister,
even before his love affair with Venetia Stanley, had long had the capacity
and taste for seeking solace from young women, but the friendships he
undertook seemed without much intensity, conviction, or exclusivity.
However his relationship with Stanley was an intense love affair, at least
on his part (though probably one that was never consummated sexually),
lasting from 1912 until her marriage to Edwin Montagu in 1915. (In the
beginning of their relationship, Asquith was just short of sixty, Stanley in
her mid-twenties.) On March 8, 1915, he wrote her:

My love for you has grown day by day & month by month and [now] year by
year: till it absorbs and inspires all my life. I could not if I would, and I would
not if I could, arrest its flow, or limit its extent, or lower by a single degree its
intensity, or make it a less sovereign & dominating factor in my thoughts and
purposes & hopes. *It has rescued me* (little as anyone but you knows it) from
sterility, impotence, despair. It enables me in the daily stress of almost intolerable
burdens & anxieties to see visions & dream dreams.

Asquith's love for Venetia emerged at a crisis point in his life. Not only
was it born amidst a severe political crisis; but Asquith's second marriage
(entered into after the death of his first wife) though a love match on his
part, had proved disappointing and even debilitating. His wife was in
chronic poor health, was said to have lacked the tact expected of one in
her position, and worst of all, had developed strained relationships with
all Asquith's children by his first marriage, particularly with Violet (whose
good friend was none other than Venetia). Apparently Asquith and Montagu both began to admire Venetia after they saw the help and kindness
she bestowed on Violet, whose fiancé had been killed in an accident, and
both fell in love with her after a trip they made to Sicily with her and
Violet. According to one commentator, the intense love Asquith felt for
Venetia benefitted him; it improved his spirits and helped him contain
his drinking, which had shown signs of getting out of hand. After Ven-

etia's sudden marriage to Montagu, Asquith was unable to continue to write her. But he resumed some relationship with her after Montagu's death and the last outing he made before his death was to visit her.

There are still other factors that predispose one to falling in love in mid-life. Least acknowledged, though possibly the most common factor, is the impetus to love invoked by the envy parents come to feel vis-à-vis the burgeoning sexuality, eroticism, and love they witness in their own offspring. They may feel a revival of intense Oedipal furies when their children fall in love and leave them to lead lives of their own. To the extent that their own Oedipal feelings were either intense or unresolved, so, too, are they more susceptible to Oedipal envy and jealousy in the later phases of their lives. It is not at all uncommon for the love affair or marriage of a beloved child to trigger a massive crisis in the lives of the parents.

Sometimes of course, the opposite can happen. The marriage of children—or just their absence from the parental home—lends enough solitude so that middle-aged couples can resume a blissful dyad freed from all the triadic complications that come with raising children. One of the most pleasing things about mid-life love is that it can be rekindled between long-married lovers whose ardor had apparently dampened.

As we have recently come to see, with the advent of changed social mores and the condoning of amatory impulses throughout the life cycle, many of the elderly form the same intense attachments as the very young. It is one of the strengths of Muriel Spark's novel *Memento Mori* that she so vividly depicts the continuity of our wishful fantasies and dearest preoccupations even into our seventies and eighties. Moreover, the imaginative component—the mental facility for fantasizing love—remains important in its own right, even when it does not serve as a dress rehearsal for (or prelude to) love. It brings solace, lends variety, serves as wish fulfillment, and allows an imaginative identification with others. I think, for example, of a vigorous professional woman in her mid-seventies, one of those vital and remarkable souls who has kept her work life and social life intact through twenty-four years of widowhood and never obsessed about remarrying; yet who is fond of remarking to her younger male colleagues, "I wish I had met you when I was only seventy," thereby sharing her playful "if only" fantasies. The men are, of course, enchanted with her coquetry and charm, and remain doting admirers.

For the lover to be able to participate in mutual love, each of the preceding love dialogues of his life must have been successfully negotiated without his suffering too much hurt or responding with too much fear. Otherwise the would-be lover becomes stuck in one or another developmental phase of love, or altogether inhibited in his capacity to love. The lover who in childhood succeeded in integrating negative features into his image of mother will, once the first flush of romantic love has subsided, likewise be able to integrate negative features into his overall sense of the goodness of his beloved. He must be able to accept her with all her flaws, knowing that she cannot gratify him completely. If he is unable to do so, his recognition of her imperfections will result in his radically de-idealizing the beloved, and his love affairs will as a consequence be extremely short-lived. Or, in another typical scenario, the young woman who continues to idealize her father—for whatever mixture of real and fantasized qualities—will almost certainly have difficulty finding a lover who measures up to her inflated view of her father.

Idealization is merely a prerequisite or preliminary step to love; by itself it is not love. Idealization may lead nowhere, provoking feelings of admiration or emulation—or even envy—but remaining unconnected to any yearning for union. Only those relationships that tap into that early yearning can flower into romantic love. But, the lover must not *feel* the connection between his primal longings, his infantile cravings, and the yearnings he experiences in love. For only when love's humble origins are obscured from consciousness by that mysterious creative process that makes the very old seem entirely new, can one overcome the old taboos and give in to love's power.

CHAPTER FIVE

The Creative Synthesis in Love

L OVE IS often depicted as a nucleus of physical passion surrounded by an array of other feelings—admiration, respect, affection, intimacy, and commitment. However, the real core of passionate love is the lover's longing for the Other, and it is *this* nucleus that draws to itself the aggregation of other feelings.

The lover's longing for the Other is so intense that it supplants all his previous preoccupations and seems to be a distillate of all the previous longings of his life. It becomes a force that draws on his very essence. Here is how Francesco Alberoni describes passionate love: ". . . a terrible force is born that leads to our fusion and makes each of us irreplaceable and unique for the other. The other, the beloved, becomes what only she can be, that absolutely special one. And this happens even against our will, even though we continue for a long time to believe that we can do without the one we love and can find that same happiness in another person." One thinks again of Aristophanes' account of love: each of the two parts of primordial spherical man, now split in half, yearned for the other half, "and when one of them finds his other half . . . the pair are lost in an amazement of love and friendship and intimacy."

Despite the general agreement that the defining feature of passionate love is the lovers' urgency to be together, the source of that intense force remained wholly obscure until Freud intuited that love is a re-finding. Freud's great insight into love was to demonstrate the continuity, despite appearances to the contrary, of the lover's emotional life, and to flesh out the Platonic insight that the union in love is truly a re-union. It was Freud's genius to see that all the lover's unfulfilled yearnings are transferred to the beloved, who is as a consequence experienced as the reincarnated source of all that is potentially good. The enormous power the beloved seems to exert on the lover can in part be explained by the love object having been invested with the mystique of all the lost objects from the past.

In love, even while seeking renewal, lovers hark back to the past, to ongoing, often unconscious, wishes and fantasies. Love seeks to undo many disappointments of early life. Just as the "motive forces of phantasies are unsatisfied wishes, and every single phantasy is the fulfillment of a wish, a correction of unsatisfying reality," so it is that love seeks (unconsciously) to undo the losses of early life, to gratify unfulfilled and forbidden childhood wishes. In love the lover regains his lost omnipotence, takes total possession of the beloved and achieves Oedipal victory. In achieving a union with the beloved, he undoes the defects, losses, and humiliations of his past. In doing so, he identifies with the victorious rivals of his childhood and assuages his wounded narcissism.

Why does the quest for "re-finding" the lost object take the form of passionate longing? One can only long for something of which one already has some glimmer of awareness. Theodor Reik gives us an important clue to the motor force in love when he reminds us that *longing* cannot depend simply upon the memory of love but upon the feelings of loss accruing to that memory: once we felt ourselves to be the objects of unconditional love, but no longer. "The zeal to regain paradise springs from the memory that men once possessed it and lost it."

Longing in love is a longing for the surcease of unfulfilled desire, but it is also longing for the confirmation that, because of one's infinite value, one will never again be abandoned and left to do without. (One longs for unconditional love, yet, paradoxically, one also longs to be loved for one's particularity. The only satisfying answer to the question, "Would you love me if I weren't pretty?" is yes *and* no.) Each of our successive love dialogues gives us a new chance to undo previous frustrations and to find both fulfillment and self-validation. In love is born anew the dream of fulfilling the half-forgotten, inevitably frustrated wishes for perfect harmony and complete mutuality—wishes that are re-editions of the buried fantasy of obtaining the perfect mother who would love unerringly and unceasingly.

But it is not just the general material of old fantasies that is reinvoked in romantic love: the loved one ("object," in psychoanalytic parlance) is herself chosen after the model of the original love objects. In love, we reincarnate all the lost objects of our life in the person of the beloved. The new objects "attract to themselves the affection that was tied to the earlier ones," to the parents. And here we come to a source of potential inner conflict, the first of many of those that serve to confound love. *"In any love relationship, the new love object must recall the old, but for this recall to result in happy love, it must not reawaken incestuous guilt."* In other words, the excitement of love generally depends on the evocation of some

Oedipal reverberations, but if this approaches consciousness it can lead to paralyzing inhibitions. Successful love both reinvokes the past and moves us out of it, separating us from too much smell of mother's milk. (Of course, re-finding a lost object is not the only factor in "selecting" the beloved. I have already suggested that one's love object may also embody some buried aspiration of the self.)

How are we so sure that in forward-looking love, the lover is also looking back? Searching for and re-finding the lost "object" is a process which oftimes leaves visible residues in the series of adult love dialogues. The subjective experience of re-finding is part of happy love; it is revealed in the lover's words: "I feel as though I've always known you." The sense of re-finding is probably the unconscious source of the lover's belief in elective affinities, marriages preordained in heaven, destiny fulfilled. "We were made for each other" is how it's usually expressed.

The element of re-finding sometimes emerges in odd ways. A married woman friend had had an incandescent love affair with a married man, one who had claimed to be utterly devoid of any but negative feelings for his emotionally isolated and eccentric wife. But he could not or would not leave his children, still very young, and she, who had left her husband, finally disavowed him in a fury. They parted on the worst of terms. Nonetheless, they were in the same profession and, therefore, might have been expected to meet by chance from time to time. However, he stayed away from meetings where she might be present and their paths would have crossed.

Over the years, however, he came to establish an interesting pattern with her (at least according to her interpretation). Having stayed in his "miserable" marriage, consoling himself with a series of affairs, he always managed to "accidently" meet my friend whenever he "fell in love" again, and would always be sure to tell her of his new passionate interest. At first she thought he was gloating. As time passed, she hypothesized he had come to tell her that he was okay too (she had successfully remarried), and that she needn't feel sorry for him or despise him. But finally an event occurred that shed light on his curious pattern. Once again he had sought her out at a public meeting, this time to tell her that he was truly in love for the *first* time in his life (the hostility in his remark was certainly not lost on her). After the meeting and reception, where they had spent a good deal of time talking, he made to put her into a cab and was helping her on with her coat. Looking at her coat, he let out a spontaneous squeal of delight—his new beloved had exactly the same coat as she. Witnessing his extraordinary pleasure at the coincidence, she thought she finally understood why he had always sought her out whenever he fell in love: he had come to compare his new love with the old, with her, not competitively but as a touchstone, to reassure himself of some emotional correspondence or continuity between the old and the new. He appeared quite moved that his new love had picked the same coat as she.

She remembered then how much store he had set on her clothes as reflecting her true essence; early in their affair, he had fantasized that she would take his wife shopping, would dress her and mold his wife in her own image. He seemed to want the wife to *be* her, so that he would not be confronted with the dilemma of wanting her and loathing the prospect of divorce. (But even the coincidence of the coat was not enough to convince him of the rightness of his new choice. By then his children were grown, but he lived on and on with the same wife.)

The refinding of the same object is frequently noted by the observers of love: "She's exactly like his first wife. I wonder if he sees it!" "She keeps making the same mistake. You would think she'd pick someone totally different." (And, of course, some people cling to what appear—even to them—to be inappropriate, limiting, or self-destructive choices because they believe they would only make the same mistake again. Sometimes this may be a valid fear based on the intuition that their neurotic needs would still prevail; sometimes it is no more than a rationalization covering the dread of separation.) The theme of re-finding, and its dangers, is, of course, a powerful one in myth, the paradigmatic story being that of Oedipus, literally destined to "re-find" his mother Jocasta, with tragic results.

But tragedy is not the norm, which is fortunate because to the degree that love is profound, the beloved always—though sometimes in indirect ways—evokes resonances from the past. Love serves to assuage the sorrows and wounds of some old developmental conundrums by binding the present to the past. It repairs the lingering humiliations of early life, melds the sensual to the tender, the body to the soul, and provides continuity at the same time that it separates the lover from the past.

The Mutual Identifications between Lovers

However, the aims of love are more complex than simply the gratification of half-buried wishes or the refinding of a lost object. Lovers by definition participate in a double identity; that is part of the power of their experience. Therefore the lover wants to gratify the beloved as much as he wants to be gratified by her. This is readily apparent in the lover's impassioned desire to provide for the beloved; he wants to please her, care for her, and give her pleasure of the soul and body. In *Endless Love*, David, speaking of his love for Jade, recalls:

Of course when you love someone it is a tireless passion to experience their pleasure, especially sexual pleasure. Of all the many perversions, the one I found myself most capable of succumbing to was voyeurism—as long as the object of my voyeurism was Jade. I never failed to be moved by her expressions of sexual pleasure.

Reciprocity, above all, distinguishes adult love from the love dialogues of childhood. In realized love, through union with the Other, the lovers energize, indeed create, a new complex set of identifications, new yet echoing the past. The lovers identify imaginatively with each other, each according the Other's subjectivity equal weight with his own.

The lovers in O. Henry's story "The Gift of the Magi," a couple in reduced circumstances, are appealing because each sells his most precious possession in order to buy a Christmas gift for the other, a gift intimately tied to the other's most treasured possession. Della cuts off her long beautiful hair—hair that would put a Queen to shame—and sells it so as to buy a platinum fob chain for Jim's gold watch. Jim meanwhile has sold the precious watch that was his father's and grandfather's before him in order to buy Della the tortoise shell combs with which she longed to adorn her beautiful hair. Nonetheless, O. Henry regards the two not as foolish children but as Magi, the wisest of men, because their gifts were those of the heart.

The importance to the lover of ministering to the beloved can be viewed in its purest form in those love stories that celebrate love's power by depicting lovers who renounce love's rewards. In such tales, the lover sacrifices his personal gratification to preserve the welfare of the beloved and, sometimes, the social good as well. He may go so far as to renounce his very right to possess the beloved, to be with her. In so doing, he asserts his altruism, his goodness, and his capacity for self-sacrifice on behalf of the beloved. He achieves a kind of moral superiority and one of the "purer" forms of love: the ability to put the beloved first.

Rick (Humphrey Bogart) in the movie *Casablanca*, reunited with his lost love, Ilsa Lazlo (Ingrid Bergman), renounces her out of his sense of honor, relinquishing her to her husband, one of the leaders of the underground. Ennobled by his love, Rick gives up the glamorous role of the worldly cafe owner, and goes off to fight with the Free French. It is not at all surprising that this role is said to have established Bogart as one of Hollywood's great romantic leads.

In *A Tale of Two Cities,* Charles Darnay and Sidney Carton are virtually indistinguishable look-alikes, and both are in love with Lucie Manette. Lucie loves Darnay. Sidney Carton, in many ways an unrealized man, never declares his love for Lucie but goes to the guillotine in place of Darnay for her sake. Every former school child recognizes Carton's ringing declaration, "It is a far, far better thing that I do, than I have ever done; it is a far, far better rest that I go to than I have ever known."

For me, the most moving of these tales of renunciation is portrayed in Chaplin's *City Lights.* The tramp (Chaplin) scrapes together the money for the operation that will restore the sight of the poor little blind girl. Her sight regained, she never knows it is he who is her savior, but she is freed to begin a normal life and to find love. This movie always moves at least part of its audience to tears, no doubt because the audience participates in a double identification, with the self-sacrificing and nurturant little tramp as well as with the beloved little flower girl whom he saves.

The fictional examples of noble renunciation that come to mind most readily are of men. But there are stories of women, too, of whom the prototypical example may well be Camille. The lady of the camellias, Dumas' tragic heroine, was a beautiful courtesan who renounced her one true love so as not to destroy his life and was only reunited with him as she lay dying.

Self-sacrifice, of course, may take one of two different forms: the lover may renounce the beloved for her own good, or for some worthy cause, or he may stay in the relationship, sacrificing his own self-realization in favor of the beloved. To the extent that there is a sex difference, men are more likely to renounce the relationship, women more likely to make self-sacrifices within it.

The magnitude of the capacity for self-sacrifice demonstrates that the lover has moved beyond any wish for purely personal pleasure. In realized love, the lovers' mutual concern, commitment, intimacy, and capacity for self-sacrifice all point to a strong two-way process of identification transpiring between them. Reciprocity and deep intimacy ultimately depend on mutual identification between the lovers. Each has an authentic sense of the subjectivity of the Other, a knowledge of the Other's point of view that assumes equal importance with his own.

While Freud located the origins of the need to be loved in the child's dependence on its parents, he was less explicit in deriving the developmental history of the need to love, to be active in loving. Whence comes the need to minister to the beloved? One can, of course, attempt to view reciprocity merely as a functional agreement between two parties. But the lover's willingness to sacrifice unilaterally testifies to some deeper cause. And for that we must again look to the child's earliest emotional ties and the identifications engendered by them.

Many different commentators on romantic love have noted the exaggerated idealization of the beloved that is an invariable prerequisite for passionate love. But it is not just the physical or spiritual person *per se* who is idealized; it is the potential ability of the beloved, as imagined by the lover, to gratify him. After all, the original model for his image of the beloved is, in part, that of either the actual or the imagined good mother, the all-giving ever-bountiful person of one's dreams. Such an image is ultimately based on her real (or hoped for) ministration to the child's needs, not on any of her other virtues. Very early in life the child internalizes the image of the good loving person and begins to identify with it. The child plays with dolls, cares for pets, learns to cuddle others as he wishes to be cuddled. Such an identification with the internalized image of a giving person insures that the lover will have the capacity—and desire—to take the active role, and not just the passive one, in love. Just as the child is imaginatively involved in identifying with his mother (or with the longed-for "nurturer"), so, too, does the lover identify with the beloved.

I am at pains to emphasize that such an identification with a bountiful, nurturing figure is not necessarily predicated on having had such a parent (or any such person) in one's real life. In fact, some of the most nurturant lovers are making up for what they did *not* have. One might say that the wishful fantasy of a loving figure may be all the stronger for having had to be imagined. And, in fact, it may be precisely because each and every one of us was frustrated in reality that we imaginatively conjured up fantasies of the all-giving mother, fantasies that subsequently become incorporated into our own conceptions of who we aspire to be, and sometimes become.

So it is that a woman (Bette Davis) in *Now, Voyager* can do for her lover's child what her own mother never did for her. *Now, Voyager* is a wonderful story of self-transformation first through psychotherapy and then through love, and finally a tale of noble renunciation. Despite its campy aspects, the movie retains a certain power and has a cult following, perhaps because it condenses many of the themes central to love. Bette

Davis's character is first introduced as an extremely unattractive woman, past her first youth, dominated by a very social, rich, unloving, and selfish mother. In a flashback we are led to understand that the mother had crushed her daughter's first experience of love and systematically put down all her efforts to be attractive. About to suffer a mental breakdown the daughter is sent to Cascades, a sanitarium where a psychiatrist (Claude Rains) helps her to achieve freedom from her mother's dictatorial and destructive demands, and to pursue her own goals. His therapeutic endeavor issues forth in a miraculous change in the woman's appearance. Discharged from Cascades, she goes on a cruise to South America. There, she has a transcendent love affair with an attractive man (Paul Henreid), who unhappily is married. Neither can sanction his leaving his wife and thus they are parted. However, there's an ingenious resolution to this authentic tearjerker: the beloved man's daughter, like the Bette Davis character, is an unwanted child, and displays many of the same problems. Finally, she, too is sent to Cascades as a patient. The Bette Davis character, who has gone back briefly, meets the girl and dedicates herself to nurturing and rescuing this child of her beloved. Through her action she and her beloved are able to preserve their transcendent connection, though they are destined never to be together.

In becoming the ministering, nurturant one, the lover is able to transcend raw infantile need; he becomes the full rich giver *and* (through his identification with his beloved) he shares vicariously in the pleasure of being ministered to. Ultimately, it is not just the beloved who is idealized, but the love relationship itself and the reciprocity inherent in it. The lover combines two profound pleasures: his own gratification (supplied by the magical person of the beloved), and the assurance that he is a magical person himself because of his ability to gratify.

To gratify and be gratified simultaneously is a heady combination. The lover can be cared for without feeling infantile because he is also a caretaker. His caretaking impulses are heightened by his intuition that his own gratification is guaranteed by his ability to continue to satisfy the beloved. The result is a kind of perpetual dynamic. Once set in motion, this dynamic generates rewards aplenty to keep itself going, though the system does break down often enough.

Insofar as love mobilizes the individual to act for another rather than directly for the self, it serves as an agent of individual change. The lover is enabled to move out of the solipsism of his own consciousness and to embrace another consciousness as a separate and equal center to the universe. One lover bestows on the other an importance commensurate with his own. He thereby achieves a sort of shift in the center of personal gravity. Many people can do for others what they cannot do for themselves, and what they can thus do often represents a "higher" moral value, as in self-sacrifice, generosity of various kinds, thoughtfulness, and so on. Love, being directed outward, toward an Other, gives one, quite literally, a sense of direction, hence, a purpose and value which are lacking in isolated individuality. This sense of direction and meaning further alters the sense of self, enabling one to feel capable of becoming something even more.

Having transcended the boundaries of self by identifying with the Other, the lover is empowered beyond the usual, and no longer bound by old patterns, habits, and other rigidities of character. This is one of the reasons that falling in love and achieving mutual love are often accompanied by spurts of energy, growth, and change and by a sense of richness and abundance.

In mutual love, the lover is impelled by opposite but not necessarily conflicting or exclusive motives: to love and be loved. However, one or the other impulse may predominate, in which case, one sees, at one extreme, tales of noble renunciation such as those just recounted, or, at the other extreme, heart-chilling stories of a preemptory insistence on personal gratification at any cost (for example, when a husband insists on a child even though bearing one may kill his wife). In idyllic love, the lovers achieve an oscillating balance between giving and receiving, active and passive roles, pleasing and being pleased, enacting the role now of the child, now of the parent. In moving back and forth between these two roles, the lover experiences the vital interests of the beloved as his own, and he values her pleasure and happiness as much as his own. His identification with her is so complete that she assumes an importance commensurate with his own.

The "We" and the Parental Couple

In addition to their reciprocal identifications, lovers form still another new identification as part of a couple. They relinquish the usual insistence on the boundaries of the self and come to believe in the autonomous life of a new entity—the "we" created by love. Their new identity as part of a couple reverberates with all their memories of the important couples of their developmental lives, particularly their parents.

It is not only the fantasized magical giver with whom the lover identified, nor just the beloved. The couple lovers form becomes part of their identity; the "we" takes on a significance of its own. But here is the paradox that needs explaining: in mutual identification the self is not obliterated, but, strangely enough, enlarged. Lewis Hyde in *The Gift* catches the psychological trick we have of incorporating another's identity, expanding, and yet maintaining our separate identities:

> I find it useful to think of the ego complex as a thing that keeps expanding, not as something to be overcome or done away with. An ego is formed and hardened by the time most of us reach adolescence, but it is small, an ego-of-one. Then, if we fall in love, for example, the constellation of identity expands and the ego-of-one becomes an ego-of-two. The young lover, often to his own amazement, finds himself saying "we" instead of "me."

Here Hyde catches the sense in which a joint identification with the Other becomes, of necessity, part and parcel of self-identity.

The lover identifies the new couple he forms with the powerful parental couple of his childhood and thus it has a resonance and meaning, which, like other aspects of the experience of love, relate to his earliest experiences. While we know that the Oedipal child longs to enter into the parental sexual and romantic drama in the place of one of his parents, the replacement of that parent is not all that he seeks. Just as importantly, he seeks to recreate the envied couple. The lover forms a new identification as part of a couple, and through this new identification, formed in union with his beloved, he identifies with his parents (as a couple).

Becoming part of a couple is one step on the way to taking one's place in the march of generations. Falling in love, and becoming part of a couple, while it separates us from our parents, is also a kind of validation of them, and of their parenting. It means that we have been given enough love from them to enable us to move forward from the hurt and rejection we suffered as part of the necessary separation of child from parent. It is a sign of trust in the basic goodness of life, of ourselves, of other people, that we can once more open ourselves to love and the risks of rejection we run in love. We validate our parents' choice (their coming together as a couple) by imitating it. And thus in the very act of separating from them via romantic love, we signal our identification and unity not only with the beloved, but with them as well. We, too, are joining the dance of life, having chosen our own partners.

Love is an instrument of healing and reparation not just in one's relationship with the beloved, but indirectly (as described) with one's parents as well. (They may not see it that way of course, nor may we.) It is only when we are "grown up" ourselves that we come to understand our parents better—partially through recreating their experience—and to forgive them what we perceived as their transgressions against us. In this sense the integration of the negative into our fantasy of the perfect parent is a long process—for some a process never completed, admittedly—and romantic love, itself a developmental process, is a part of the even more basic process of separation and individuation, at the same time that it serves as a compensation for our previous losses. (Both separation and reparation are symbolized in marriage ceremonies, for example, when the father of the bride gives her to the groom. The mother of the bride cries and offers the clichéd explanation "I'm so happy." In fact, she cries because she intuits her fundamental loss. If she cries from happiness, it is of a very complex kind. She may be crying because she intuits that her daughter will be experiencing what she herself has experienced, both its sorrows and its joys, and will thereby be enabled to identify with her. She further intuits that for her and her daughter fully to understand one another, to become closer, they must undergo this separation. But how bittersweet this knowledge is.)

The ambition to reduplicate the powerful parental couple is the ambition of succession, of strength. The ability to form this new identification is partly regressive but ultimately serves progressive aims. It is one source of adult strength—the strength of the couple—and the longing for it coalesces with the childhood belief that strength lies in symbiosis with the mother. Mutuality is thus integrated at a new level in romantic love.

There is good reason for the lover to experience love as progressive rather than regressive. In love, the lover creatively synthesizes aims and gratifications which did indeed originate in different developmental periods of his life, but he does so in ways that are so indirect, allusive, and complex that the original aims are transformed by their realization. The lover takes both the active and passive role. Psychologically, he is able to condense and to identify with two powerful images, that of mother and child (the lover now playing both roles), and further to identify with the image of the Oedipal couple. He simultaneously participates in all these individual and dual identifications and, in so doing, integrates many partial and contradictory identifications. The achievement of love is to incorporate many diverse aims, among them restoration of the oceanic sense of the mother-child dyad, satisfaction of the transgressive wishes of the Oedipal child, and duplication of the power of the parental couple. The lover has created a wonderful synthesis and has transcended the traumas and insufficiencies of his childhood.

Merger

Love serves not only psychological needs but transcendental ones as well. Passionate love attempts to overcome the pain of separation, separateness, and the felt inadequacies of the solitary self through merger with the Other. If sufficiently extensive, the lovers' profound mutual identification may be understood as the psychological counterpart of the philosopher's concept of merging.

The longing at the heart of love is almost literally the longing for merger, as portrayed in the Aristophanes myth. But what is merger? Singer, in contrasting the idealist and realist notions of love, helps us to understand the distinction between merging and mere bonding:

According to the realist, people come together for the sake of individual benefit: men and women live with one another as a convenient way of satisfying their needs. This kind of community, whether in society or in the love of man and women, the realist interprets as an overlapping or wedding of interests rather than a merging of personalities. Yet it is merging through love that the idealist tradition often seeks to glorify. For things only conjoined can be readily separated; they may fit together but they cannot become an essential part of one another; and to the extent the overcoming of separateness remains incomplete. What is merged, on the other hand, contains a common element, an identity that defines the nature of both participants equally well. In finding the beloved, each lover discovers the hidden reality which is himself.

Love, as Singer says, is more than the simply functional or expedient relationship that the realists propose. The advantages the realist sees in union are indeed part of love, but they are almost always incidental to the true heart of of love, which the lovers feel as more *real* than any other form of reality, "more real than any other world, more real than time, more real than death, more real even, than she and I."

This larger-than-life reality that lovers discover is the experience of merger. If union is the commitment between lovers to be together, to be joined, then merger goes much further; it connotes an interpenetration of selves. These are not simple identifications to understand. There is a quality, simultaneously, both of mingling with the beloved *and* expansion of the self.

The testimony to the experience of merger in love is overwhelming, not to be discounted as mere rhetoric, coming as it does from so many disparate sources—both lovers and observers of love—and describing the same subjective phenomena. In Shelley's *Epipsychidion:*

I am not thine: I am a part of *thee.*

In *Wuthering Heights,* Catherine of her love for Heathcliff:

". . . because he's more myself than I am. Whatever our souls are made of, his and mine are the same. . . .

"I cannot express it; but surely you and everybody have a notion that there is or should be an existence of yours beyond you. What were the use of my creation, if I were entirely contained here? My great miseries in this world have been Heathcliff's miseries, and I watched and felt each from the beginning: my great thought in living is himself. If all else perished and *he* remained, I should still continue to be and if all else remained, and he were annihilated, the universe would turn to a mighty stranger. I should not seem part of it. . . . Nelly, I *am* Heathcliff. He's always, always in my mind—not as a pleasure, anymore than I am always a pleasure to myself—but as my own being."

The lovers in Ernest Hemingway's *For Whom the Bell Tolls:*

"Afterwards we will be as one animal of the forest and be so close that neither one can tell that one of us is one and not the other. Can you not feel my heart be your heart?"

"Yes. There is no difference."

The behavioral correlates of merger are revealed in the lover's willingness to act on behalf of the beloved as he would for himself, and to do so automatically, naturally and not out of any sense of duty or sacrifice. Montaigne's description of his love in friendship for Etienne Boitie comes close to describing the merger, even beyond the exercise of reciprocity, that one sees in romantic love (and it suggests the close kinship between passionate friendship and passionate love):

Our souls traveled so unitedly together, they felt so strong an affection for one another, and with this same affection saw into the very depths of each other's hearts, that not only did I know his as well as my own, but I should certainly have trusted myself more freely to him than to myself.

Let no one put other, everyday friendships in the same rank as this.

There is no distinction between the one friend's interests and the other's. They are as one.

Successful lovers establish a union, characterized by ongoing warmth, commitment, intimacy, reciprocity, and some degree of mutual identification. But although the lovers may strive for complete merger (what we might then describe as fusion) they cannot sustain it. Instead, if they are lucky enough to enjoy a *passionate* love, their feelings of union will be interspersed with ecstatic moments of merger. These magical moments are experienced as epiphanies. At such times, there is, if not a loss of ego boundaries, at least a permeability of ego boundaries. During those moments, the lovers experience a sense of timelessness, bliss, and transcendence. Their intermittent experience of merger is completely unlike the obliteration of the sense of self that one sees in psychotic states and which leads to terror. Rather, the self is preserved, the spirit exalted.

Passionate love cannot be sustained without those moments in which the lovers feel they have achieved merger, that they are one. Part of the ongoing intensity in love is the insistent hunger to re-experience such epiphanies. For many, sex is the principal channel for the mystical urge toward transcendence through merger, though it is by no means the only route. Epiphanies can occur in moments of extreme intimacy in which the sense of merger is marked by no more physical an exchange than a gaze, the touching of fingertips, one lover's arm around the other's shoulders. Perhaps these moments evoke something of that oceanic sense of oneness that floods mother and infant in their early days together. Roland Barthes gives a beautiful description of the counterpart of such a state in romantic love: "Besides intercourse . . . there is that other embrace, which is a motionless cradling: we are enchanted, bewitched: we are in the realm of sleep, without sleeping; we are within the voluptuous infantilism of *sleepiness:* this is the moment for telling stories, the moment of the voice which takes me, . . . this is the return to the mother. . . . In this companionable incest, everything is suspended: time, law, prohibition: nothing is exhausted, nothing is wanted: all desires are abolished, for they seem definitively fulfilled." Yet this state cannot be indefinitely sustained. Nonetheless, unless these moments prove too threatening, they can be reinvoked, time and again.

Merger may most readily be expressed through physical means, but its actual locus is within the psyche. It is there that the fluidity of ego enables the kind of interpenetration of selves that constitutes merger. The repository of meaning is located in the merger itself, in the lover's internal psychic process. Merger is in part surrender to a person, but primarily it is surrender to love's powers. Merger enables the lover not only to cross the personal boundary separating the self from the beloved, but also, in the act of losing the limited, mundane self, to refind an earlier self. The earlier self, lost as a consequence of age and experience (and of the differentiation of the personality) is the creature Wordsworth describes as coming to earth (being born) "trailing clouds of glory." Wordsworth evokes both the freshness with which that self experiences the world, and the inevitable loss of "the visionary gleam."

> There was a time when meadow, grove, and stream,
> The Earth, and every common sight,
>   To me did seem
>   Appareled in celestial light.
> The glory and the freshness of a dream.
> It is not now as it hath been of yore;
>   Turn whereso'er I may,
>   By night or day,
> The things which I have seen I now can see no more.

In merger, the lover momentarily recaptures a state of de-differentiated personality. It is as though the lover's ego and superego were dissolved or suspended and he has greater access to the unconscious and to buried emotions. This is similar to what Otto Kernberg has described as crossing the boundaries of the self; and I believe it is the "wholeness" that the lovers in Aristophanes' myth seek. The transported lover regains a primordial tensionless state of consciousness. It is the oceanic feeling sometimes recovered in meditation or religious ecstasy. Wordsworth found it in contemplating nature. But most of us find it, if we find it at all, in passionate love.

Paradoxically, the self-realization possible in adult love demands that the lover have the ability and the strength, the sureness of his own autonomy to let go enough to achieve the sense of merger. One finds oneself only by losing oneself. When the lover transcends the limits of self, his sense of self expands, his spirit soars, and the result is a feeling of exultation.

The deep intoxicating pleasure of love can only be described as an exultation. It is so remarkable a feeling as to be regarded as an altered ego state, a sense of being so extraordinary that it has always served as one of the greatest inspirations of poetry. The illusion of achieving merger is made real and reinforced by the feeling of exultation. What appears as illusion to the outside world has an inner reality to the lovers, one of feeling and affective involvement. Love may be born in illusion and imagination, but it is in the achievement of the exulted state that love becomes real and tangible. And it is the exultation of love that appears to be connected to the ability of love to transform the lover.

It has been said that "the sense of bliss associated with falling in love has its origins in a state of longing" however dimly remembered "of the feeling state of the symbiotic phase." This refers to the oceanic sense of oneness that is presumed to exist between mother and child. Yes and no. The exultation may well be in a clear line of descent from one's earliest feelings towards mother, but the glory of love is that it also moves us through the past and out of it, in the end separating us from what has gone before.

Love, then, is more than a mere echo of an earlier bliss. The exultation the lover feels is, in part, due to the gratification, at last, of unfulfilled longings of childhood; in part, the thrill experienced in the pursuit of the unknown and the forbidden; in part, the ability simultaneously to care and to be cared for, and so finally to transcend the taint of infantilism with which our longing to be loved has been imbued. But the exultation of love is most of all attributable to the new expanded sense of self that results when two separate beings come together as one. In large measure, exultation is made possible by the lovers' periodic achievement of "merger," with its sense of release from the burdens of self, the immersion in something larger than self. In the pursuit of his goals the lover is indeed in the grips of a true passion, an intense feeling state, which becomes the major organizing force in his life.

In the exalted ego state that accompanies the realization of love, the usual ego defenses are less rigidly maintained. Furthermore, the influence of earlier experiences may be mitigated or changed and new resolutions to old conflicts achieved so that the lover has less of a stake in maintaining those defenses. This overall lessening of defensiveness allows for a flux in personality that permits a creative synthesis, a rediscovery of buried parts of the self, and these may in turn be incorporated with newly developed parts of the self, and new identifications. The range of possibilities is thus enlarged.

Even if love ends, these changes persist and the exulted state is often remembered as a magical interlude. Because of the intensity of the feelings associated with the memories of mutual love, a realized love affair always has a privileged status in memory. The fantasy or memory of the intense love affair—something like a tape of an old movie reel and which I call the "lover's reel"—is stored away in the mind. It is replayed at intervals, sometimes involuntarily. It can also be cut, spliced, and edited, all depending on cues to memory and current need. In the end, whether or not mutual love is sustained in external reality, the memory of it is preserved and continues to enrich the lover.

Self-Will and Self-Transformation in Love

Creative writers and biographers, as well as lovers themselves, sense the catalytic effect of love in changing the lover and intuit that the resultant change sometimes takes priority of importance over the love itself. From them we get a glimmer that the power of love is an internal one, its magic ultimately residing in the lover's internal creative flux, not in the worth of the beloved (however worthy the beloved may be), not in possession, not in reciprocity. Even the most transported lovers sometimes retain an awareness that love is often brief, the beloved fickle, while all the time still revelling in their love. Rosalind, in *As You Like It*, knows love's limits, and her beloved Orlando's too, but that never stops her from glorying in the very tumult of her own emotions—in the recklessness, the excess, and the freedom of letting go. That freedom seems to be the joyousness that runs throughout the play, bubbling up and overcoming her in the midst of her witty commentary on love. She may mock her lover's oath that he'll love Rosalind "Forever and a day." ("Say a day, without the ever.") But she's as prone to tears and fainting and mooning as any country wench, as downright lovesick as the simple shepherd Silvius. Indeed, it is Rosalind herself who tells us so: "Jove, Jove! this shepherd's passion/Is much upon my fashion." And yet she's as high spirited a lover as can be found anywhere in the Forest of Arden. Realism cannot quench her ardor, and seems if anything to enhance the pleasure she feels in her own recklessness.

Perhaps it requires an artist's temperament to revel so purely in the internal freedom that is both the cause and effect of love, to intuit that while being loved can satisfy one's vanity and provide a host of other benefits too, it is loving, not being loved, which is the greater pleasure. A large part of the pleasure resides in the fact that love is, as Carson McCullers put it, no honey-coated accident, but "a creative experience." Many poets seem to have understood that it is the lover, not the beloved, who is the chief beneficiary of love's joys. As W. H. Auden pleads in his succinct couplet: "If equal affection cannot be/ Let the more loving one be me." The Duc de la Rochefoucauld voices much the same sentiment when he remarks that "the pleasure of love is in loving, and one is happier in the passion one feels than in the passions one arouses in another." More extreme, perhaps is the remark made by one of Goethe's characters: "When I love you, what does that concern you?"

Being in love with love—as all of the above might be said to be—is often about being in need of change. The poets themselves I cannot speak for. But Rosalind is again a case study in point. At the beginning of the play, she is unhappy and, when her cousin Celia urges her to be merry, she sets out to obey. "From hence forth I will, coz, and devise sports. Let me see, what think you of falling in love?" No sooner does she propose it than she does it, for it is only minutes before she's met and fallen in love with Orlando. And within minutes of that, her life is in every respect changed. Love does not always have such dramatic effects, but love does always change the lover, because through love he achieves a newly en-larged, or changed, sense of self.

This change in the sense of self, experienced by the lover as the novelty and orginality of love, is at the core of love. It is in large part the result of the multiple identifications in which the lover participates when he falls in love. Love propels the lover's move to new commitments, and away from old ones. That is what stag parties acknowledge. The man on the eve of his marriage says farewell to his old buddies, whose central place in his life is about to be usurped. And that is why the father gives the bride away, acknowledging that her place is now beside her husband. But whether it is one's parents one forsakes, as in first love, or an old love for a new one, or the sterility of a loveless life for the richness of a love-filled life, love is always an agent of change. Its dialectic is that of separation and union, disengagement and re-engagement. And the lover's innermost self is the primary beneficiary of that change.

Growth of the self occurs through desire and the self-will (assertion) that seeks to gratify desire. The self grows through its desire for the Other, through its longing to be joined to the idealized object of yearning, and through the new identification (and the consolidation of old ones) that take place by virtue of the union between the lover and his beloved.

The succession of love dialogues depends upon our self-assertion in separating from the old and recommitting to the new. In separating, a gulf between us and the past is created, one that leads to a chasm in our emotional lives. Love permits (perhaps demands) a leap over this chasm. The paradox romantic love solves is how to reassert one's separateness and yet not be alone. It does so by allowing us to separate from one object (or set of allegiances) and unite with another. Such a sequence of separation and re-merger is the story of the child's developmental growth and of mature love as well. It is the dramatic plot that Margaret Mahler tells in her story of the infant's separation and individuation from its mother. It is the story that is retold in the second individuation of adolescence, and again when we fall in love.

Because of its neccessary links with self-assertion romantic love cannot be so important in cultures that value conformity as it is in those that value differentiation and autonomy. In Japan, where conformity and identification with the group are valued above all, romantic love does not have a high priority. However, the Japanese do celebrate one highly romantic convention: lovers who cannot be together in life join each other in death—by suicide. For the Japanese, self-will (and its potential for disharmony with the mores and dictates of the group) cannot exist within the cultural framework. Consequently, the only acceptable outlet for love (which is dependent on self-will) is doomed love, in which the lovers, by dying for their love, simultaneously assert and extinguish the self, thus insuring that the group is undamaged by the individualism of the lover. Stories of doomed love are sanctioned by the Japanese as a means of channeling illicit desires in a way consonant with the cultural demand for conformity and duty. The Japanese weep at stories of doomed lovers' suicides, and thereby vicariously indulge, romanticize, and exorcise those impulses within themselves. This kind of dynamic sheds a little light on why doomed love has been celebrated at moments in the West, during those periods of time when the valuation of autonomy was coming into its ascendancy but the individual's behavior was still bound by strict laws of fealty and obligation, for example, in the Middle Ages. In such times the outcome of pre-emptory love must of necessity be the Liebestod.

Without self-will, there is no capacity for psychological separation from a pre-existing tie and therefore no possibility for a new love relationship. Without self-will, there can be no psychological separation. But neither is there any highly individuated self. The self is delineated only through separation, but the sense of being separated proves impossible to bear. The solitary self feels cut off, alone, without resources. The solitary self feels impelled to merge with a new object, and it does so in love.

The changes wrought by love become part of the new and expanded self and they may last even when love does not. Love is a product of need and of the imagination, but once called into being, love asserts its reality by virtue of the sheer intensity of the feelings it arouses, and the resulting changes in the self. It is this inner reality that sustains our fundamental belief in love as life-enhancing and when we are without it stirs our hopes for achieving it once again.

Love is a creative achievement, synthesizing as it were real and illusory gratifications of wishes and desires from all developmental levels and, through the new identifications the lovers form, expanding and enriching the self. Although love is illusory in its insistence that possession of the beloved will magically lead to eternal bliss, love *is* in fact magical. It becomes the organizing scheme of mental life. By virtue of the real relationship it engenders, the exultation it creates, and the changes in the self that it facilitates, love is vindicated as change-agent and creative endeavor. In its achievement there is a release from the constraints of the self, a state that goes far beyond the fulfillment of narrow needs or desires. The transcendence and transfiguration that one can experience in love suggest that it may be the secular correlative of the transports and transformations one hears described as accompanying mystical religious experiences. This may be why we perceive love as grace, as a gift, as being connected to the body but spiritual or soulful in its nature.

There is a deep psychological reality that accounts for the perpetuation of Aristophanes' myth of the separated halves that come together in love. In love we recover parts of the self. But we buried them only because they had brought us too much pain; either they led us to strive for the unattainable or belonged to the deep undifferentiated self. For example, the early wish that seeks satisfaction in the ecstatic oceanic sense of oneness with another must be buried if we are to differentiate and thrive as autonomous beings. It can come to the surface again—oh so tentatively—only in love or perhaps in religious transports. And when wishes as deep as this one find fulfillment, the exultation we feel is extraordinary. The energy released when at last we feel loved and loving enough to admit our deepest needs, to allow those long buried parts of the self to surface, is what fuels the sheer exhilaration of love. The sense of relief and, ultimately, the peace with ourselves and with the universe that we feel, is a result of coming to terms with our deepest feelings, finding in our beloved our "better half," that which we have previously repressed in ourselves. Ultimately, it isn't just the beloved with whom the lover identifies or the earlier images of the all-giving person or the "we"; the real discovery in love is the self. What is most extraordinary about this recovery (and crucial to it) is that it can only occur when the lover makes all those other identifications so completely that he loses his usual inhibitions and forgets his narrow sense of self, and thus is enabled, ultimately, to find the larger self. This is the essential and defining paradox of love.

3

THE PARADOXES AND STRUGGLES INHERENT IN LOVE

CHAPTER SIX

Self-Surrender: Transcendence versus Enslavement

T HE FIRST of love's inevitable paradoxes inheres in one of its fundamental aims—the longing for merger with the Other. In merger, the lover seeks to dissolve the barrier between the self and the beloved. Since the barrier is the self's boundary, what is sought is a form of self-transcendence. Thus there is a striking overlap between the language of love and that of religion, particularly that of religious mysticism. Some degree of self-surrender in the service of self-purification and self-transformation is a necessary component of merger, of those epiphanies intrinsic to passionate love.

But here is the problem. Unfortunately, the impulse to merge is fundamentally at odds with another of the aims of love. One may seek merger, but one seeks it with an Other. If one were successful in achieving complete and total merger (what we would then call fusion), there would be no Other. The concrete fulfillment of fantasies of merger carries with it the threat of the symbolic annihilation of the self *and* of the Other. Love, by its nature committed to the preservation of the beloved as well as the self, cannot press through to its goal. Here is the dilemma as presented by the political theorist, Hans Morgenthau:

> . . . if love is a reunion of two human beings who belong together, that reunion can never be complete for any length of time. For, except in the *Liebestod,* which destroys the lovers by uniting them, it stops short of the complete merger of the individualities of the lovers. It is the paradox of love that it seeks the reunion of two individuals while leaving their individualities intact. *A* and *B* want to be one, yet they must want to preserve each other's individuality for the sake of their love for each other. So it is their very love that stands in the way of their love's consummation.

This conflict is one of the existential dilemmas that destabilizes love and leads to its frequent corruption by the lover's insistence on merger, either through self-surrender (as I will discuss in this chapter), or by recourse to colonization of the Other through domination (as I will discuss in the next chapter). When the pursuit of merger is unchecked, the lover becomes either a slave or a tyrant.

Consequently, experiences of merger must be fleeting. While the impulse to self-surrender—as part of the impulse to merge—must be regarded as an essential component of passionate love, it can only be realized for brief moments. In such epiphanies the lovers experience their separate selves as mingled, enriched without compromise of the essential autonomy and integrity of either. The transcending of ego boundaries enlarges and enhances the self rather than obliterating it. Paradoxically, then, intermittent self-surrender can be a form of self-assertion, a kind of giving of oneself that is the ultimate expression of one's will as a free agent. Rather than being demeaning, self-surrender is experienced as an empowering act. This may be because the lover is surrendering more to the power of love than to the power of the Other.

Whereas in moments of intermittent merger, the lover seeks a new and expanded joint identity, the impulse to merge may be debased into a different kind of surrender—one in which the lover seeks to submerge his identity into that of the Other. Such surrender is extended in time rather than intermittent, one-sided rather than mutual. Perhaps the relevant distinction is between joint merging in mutual surrender to love as opposed to *sub*merging in unilateral surrender to the Other. In the latter case, the lover is seeking not so much to transcend the self as he is to bolster the self, to make up for what he experiences as lacunae in his own personality.

Some of the more extensive—or even debased—kinds of self-surrender are sometimes still adaptive insofar as the lover achieves self-worth through his sense of devotion to the beloved. Though he has surrended part of his autonomous identity, he may still preserve a central self-identity and pride in himself as the full nurturant giver. In between merger on the one hand, and enslavement, on the other, one sees different kinds of self-surrender, more sustained than moments of merger, but where the purpose is not masochistic degradation of the self but elevation of the self—where the self finds its meaning in connection to the Other.

However, in its most extreme forms, surrender results in an impoverishment of the self rather than in any enrichment. The lover may lose the pride in himself as a nurturer and life-giver, devoted to a worthy person and cause and become no more than an appendage to the beloved.

Even in love uncontaminated by neurosis, the impulse to self-surrender often conflicts with the impulse to self-assertion. Everything we know of the deepest sources of human longing points to a need for self-transcendence but also to a competing urge for self-assertion. These paradoxical, contradictory aims that are both so deeply entrenched in our human nature find eloquent expression in Aldous Huxley:

Men desire to intensify their consciousness of being what they have come to regard as "themselves" but they also desire—and desire, very often, with irresistible violence—the consciousness of being someone else. In a word, they long to get out of themselves, to pass beyond the limits of that tiny island universe, within which every individual finds himself confined.

This is the profound sense in which I understand Freud to mean that we are motivated by both Eros and Thanatos.

It is commonly believed that, in the area of love, women are more inclined to surrender than are men. The objection might be raised then that in proposing the *capacity* for surrender as integral to both self-liberation and the ability to fall in love I might inadvertently be legitimizing an unfortunate female propensity for surrender. However, I would have to disagree. In highlighting the capacity for self-surrender as prerequisite to passionate love I distinguish it from both the psychological need for unilateral surrender to the Other and the impulse to enslavement. There may well be a gender difference in the common neurotic distortions of the capacity for surrender: men are often inhibited in that capacity, women only too proficient at it. As a consequence, men may be relatively inhibited in their ability to fall in love (particularly during their competitive, striving years), whereas women may too readily resort to surrender as the primary mode of establishing their identities. However, the male propensity to hold back from surrender is as much a liability as is the female propensity to rush into it. Many men appear so constricted by the need to assert the self at any cost (as a corroboration of their masculine gender identity) that they miss out on the transformative potential of passionate love. On the other hand, by taking men as devotional objects, an act which requires a corresponding devaluation of self, women may focus so exclusively on the transformational aspects of love that the very core of the self is put at risk.

But there is no absolute difference between men and women. While

women may show a greater propensity to establish their identities by
defining themselves as nurturant givers, both sexes appear equally vulnerable to masochistic distortions of love. And, at the other extreme, both may
be too jealous of the prerogatives of the self to fall in love.

Sweet Surrender

The temptation or motivation to surrender oneself unilaterally in love
is perhaps best stated by Simone de Beauvoir when she suggests that
"blind obedience is the only chance for radical transformation known to
a human being." Surrender in love constitutes an escape from the limits
of the self or, through transformation, the creation of a new self, which
is, of course, a more extreme form of escape. In idealizing the Other,
identifying with or even vicariously living through the Other, one is
redeeming an unsatisfactory self by reconstituting it. Here, then, is the
connection between love and religion. In religion the emphasis is upon
surrender in relation to God, the symbol of worth and power before which
every mere self is imperfect, though made in his image. We try to redeem
our imperfections and transcend our mortality in union with him. The
lover's purpose, like the mystic's, is to achieve redemption through surrender, hence the striking overlap between the language of love and that of
religious mysticism. (I worship you, adore you, want to serve you, you are
my savior, and so on.) Recognizing his own weaknesses and ultimate
limitations, the lover hopes to achieve meaning, strength, and future
purpose from his identification with the beloved. Consequently, surrender
may sometimes be experienced as sweet, as happy, even when it is one-
sided.

Though the extremes of surrender—enslavement, masochism, self-
destruction in love, call it what you will—are to be found among members
of both sexes, the classic stories of sweet surrender are largely stories of
women in love. Historically, of course, women have known the limits of
self all too well, and sometimes have found escape through love to be
almost the only route open to them. (Consequently, in this section, the
lover will be designated as "she.") But men, too, eventually come to know
the limits of self, and then they may also turn to love as a mode of
transcendence.

There are many biographical and fictional accounts, particularly in the
nineteenth century, in which the lover submerges her own goals in favor
of those of the beloved and is happy in her self-surrender. The lover deems
the beloved to be worthy of the sacrifice, and, if the beloved is an eminent

man, friends and onlookers may reinforce the idea that the sacrifice is not only justified, but ennobling. Moreover, in the nineteenth century, female powerlessness in the real world certainly facilitated the ideal of surrender in love as a mode of establishing identity.

Born in 1831, Isabelle Arundell, who would eventually marry the extraordinary explorer, Orientalist, linguist, and adventurer, Sir Richard Burton, was one such woman. While still a girl, she became enamored of the exotic through some chance encounters with gypsies and her familiarity with Disraeli's Oriental tale, *Tancred*, a book she was to keep near at hand throughout her life. Writing in her diary before her "first season," she confided her longing for "Gypsies, Bedouin Arabs and everything *Eastern and Mystic: and especially a wild and lawless life.*" This was a yearning that seemed destined to be disappointed, considering her conventional upbringing and the limits of her world. But after meeting Burton at a summer resort, she committed herself to him, while he, of course, was unaware that she had chosen him as her destiny. She followed his daring exploits from afar and remained faithful to her almost obsessive fantasy of the future—that she would meet Burton again and marry him. Her dreams seemed to gain credibility from a gypsy fortune teller who foretold that through her marriage she would be of their tribe and find a husband with whom she would share "One soul in two bodies."

Indeed, it is remarkable that Burton so neatly fit the fantasy that Isabelle already entertained. Years later, she and Burton did meet again; this time he was won over by her adoration. For her, he was the living embodiment of her own self-projection; as she wrote later to her mother, *"I wish I were a man. If I were, I would be Richard Burton; but being only a woman, I would be Richard Burton's wife."* More years passed, but finally Isabelle and Burton married. However while she chose him as her destiny, his destiny remained the East. They lived together over thirty years—years often interrupted by his lengthy travels and adventures—but her devotion to him never waned. It is even said that she secured his fame through her unflagging efforts on his behalf. But, of course, surrender such as Isabelle's may also be cannibalistic. In the end, as one biographer suggested, Burton was caged by her devotion. After his death, she did what many contemporaries judged unpardonable; presumably fearing revelations that might damage his reputation (or that of the marriage) she burned his journals and *The Scented Garden*, which he considered his master work. In so doing, she disregarded his express wishes and preserved his legend as she saw fit. It was perhaps her ultimate assertion of her domination over him, claiming him utterly as her own, canonizing her idealized image of him for posterity and protecting it against the possibility of being sullied by the real man.

Another instance of a woman submerging her identity in that of an extraordinarily creative man, despite the fact that she had previously had rather a lively and autonomous identity of her own, is that of the actress Juliette Drouet who gave herself over to a lifelong devotion to Victor Hugo. Hugo, whose personality was said to have been constricted in certain regards before he met Juliette, was like a drunken man in the initial stages of his love affair with her, utterly intoxicated with the realization of love and probably an expanded sense of his sexuality. But he never ended his marriage or entered into Juliette's world. Instead he took her out of her world, installed her in an extremely modest apartment, and for a dozen years, virtually forbade her having any social intercourse. During that period of isolation, while waiting endlessly for his visits, she wrote him approximately seventeen thousand letters that chronicle both her great happiness and her great sorrow. Some claim that before she met Hugo her acting career was foundering and that she saw no real artistic future for herself, but her devotion to Hugo was apparently genuine. She was steadfast throughout the many changes in his fortunes and the fluctuations in their relationship, even managing to overlook an eight-year liaison he had with yet another mistress. Juliette eventually achieved some greater serenity and fulfillment with him and was clearly acknowledged as his primary relationship after his wife's death.

The continuing idealization of one particular object and the perpetuation of one's self-surrender, as in the case of Juliette Drouet, may be facilitated when one's own idealization of that person is reinforced by public opinion. It must be remembered that Hugo, like Byron before him, was the supreme idol of his age, and that, consequently, Drouet's appraisal of him found external validation. The public elevation of one man above others is part of what makes him a magnet for those with an impulse to surrender, hence the near fanatic worship of "stars" in every historical epoch.

Some instances of self-surrender are time-limited. The object of such surrender, feeling burdened, may of course bolt, but the surrendering lover may also have a change of heart. Such was the case, in the twentieth century, of Virginia Haggard who wrote of her "Seven Years of Plenty with the Master," Chagall. Haggard, married to an impoverished painter and the mother of a small child, was employed to take care of Chagall after his wife had died. Her role expanded quickly from that of caretaker to that of lover as well, and to Chagall it seemed that his dead wife Bella had sent Haggard to care for him. She submerged herself in him, bore his son, and sent her daughter away to boarding school so as not to disturb Chagall. (Much later her daughter affirmed that her mother's seven blissful years were quite the opposite for her; during that time, she had felt utterly displaced from her mother's affections.) But eventually Haggard, feeling constricted by the demands placed upon her as mistress of a famous man, resolved the problem by running away with a Belgian filmmaker who was doing a film about Chagall. Chagall himself, though mystified and enraged, was of course able to find a devoted replacement soon after.

Throughout the years, the stories of surrender to artists and creative people are legion. Consider Alice B. Toklas's devotion to Gertrude Stein and Gertrude Stein's assumptions (or presumptions) in penning *The Autobiography of Alice B. Toklas*. Sometimes the lover is extremely creative in her own right, her own gifts suffering because of her deference to the master. Even so spirited and gifted a woman as Alma Schindler gave up her creative aspirations in favor of her husband-to-be Gustav Mahler. At the time of her engagement she was a pupil of the composer-conductor Alexander von Zemlinsky (a fellow student was Arnold Schoenberg). According to Alma, in writing to Mahler, she happened to say that she would not write any more that day as she had some work to finish, meaning composition, which up to then had taken the first place in her life. But in her memoirs, Alma writes that "the idea that anything in the world would be of more importance than writing to him filled him with indignation, and he wrote me a long letter, ending up by forbidding me ever to compose anymore. It was a terrible blow. . . . I buried my dream and perhaps it was for the best. It has been my privilege to give my creative gifts another life in minds greater than my own. And yet the iron had entered my soul and the wound has never healed." Mahler died after they had been married nine years and Alma was yet to embark on the string of illustrious affairs and marriages that would make her famous in her own right. In a sense she forged a career out of her sexual and romantic alliances with famed men.

However, the protagonists in the great dramas of surrender are usually not famous. In fact, the urge to surrender comes from within and is often merely rationalized by invoking (or inflating) the personal gifts of the beloved. In his short story "The Darling," Chekhov gives us a classic tale of surrender in love as a woman's means of establishing self-identity. The Darling finds her identity, sole self-expression, and raison d'être in her devotion to a series of love objects; without love, she sinks into depression. As Chekhov describes her, "She was always fond of some one, and could not exist without loving." Married to Vanitchka Kukin, a theatre manager, she adopted his opinions and tastes, and became a great advocate of the artistic and social merits of the theater. She always delivered her thoughts by invoking the authority of the combined "Vanitchka and I," so much so that the actors jokingly called her "Vanitchka and I" or, more affectionately "the Darling." (For the Darling, Kukin was idealized and elevated as much as Picasso was for Françoise or Jacqueline.) Kukin died suddenly and the Darling was, of course, profoundly saddened.

She revived only a few months later, however, when she married a timber merchant. In response to her new husband, she now immersed herself in business and assumed *his* values. Even her feelings toward the theatre, which she had loved so dearly, were transformed. When a friend suggested a play for relaxation and amusement, the Darling replied that she had no time for such nonsense. She had six glorious years as the wife of the timber merchant, but then found herself widowed once again.

She recovered from this latest grief only when she took up with a veterinary surgeon. Again she found her interests and values through him and was now adamant about the need for veterinary inspection to control animal disease. But her lover became embarrassed and resented her speaking as though she herself were a veterinarian. He eventually abandoned her and she fell once again into a depression, from which she recovered only years later when the veterinarian's son was given to her care. Through immersion in the child she once more regained her radiance, composure, and her purpose in life.

Different readers respond to "The Darling" in markedly contrasting ways. I first read the story in the 1950s, when it was given to me by my militantly anticonformist uncle. He cited the tale as an example of the troubles that can befall women who give up any claim to autonomy. At first, I reacted to the Darling just as it appeared to me that Chekhov himself did, horrified at her emptiness. But from a more traditional vantage point, the Darling embodies the noble attributes of self-sacrifice and self-abrogation in the interests of someone else. Tolstoy, commenting on the story, viewed it from this latter perspective and is critical of Chekhov's attitude towards his creation: "The author evidently means to mock at the pitiful creature—as he judges her with his intellect, but not with his heart." Tolstoy admits the absurdity of the Darling's series of love objects, but concludes that despite Chekhov's manifest intent, he had nonetheless inadvertently blessed her, for "the soul of The Darling, with her faculty of devoting herself with her whole being to any one she loves, is not absurd, but marvellous and holy."

Reading "The Darling" again, I am struck by what might now be considered its proto-feminist stance—its "disapproval" of the values embraced by apparently submissive women. But Tolstoy's point, despite some strains of misogyny in his characterization, is well taken. The story is not about a power relationship that results from either the external condition (or plight) of woman. The psychological insight in the story resides in Chekhov's portrayal of the Darling's need to devote herself entirely to a beloved and cloak herself in his identity. The scenario of surrender is hers, her invention and her need. This is a tale of surrender, not one of submission. Here, surrender is a matter of character, not of situation.

Were Kukin, the Darling's first husband, to have lived, would anyone fault her devotion, or would she be praised as the ideal embodiment of nurturant altruistic love? It is her bad luck in being twice widowed which reveals that the inspiration for her devotion does not originate with the beloved but with her—that she is in fact one of those creatures for whom the surrender itself is what is most desired in love, and that she will always find someone to whom to surrender. This is, of course, offensive to anyone who imaginatively puts himself in the place of the beloved, who wants to be validated for his unique and irreplaceable qualities, not simply to serve as the blank screen onto which love is projected. And it is equally disturbing to lovers who see their love as unique, inspired by the beloved. They feel confident that they would only surrender themselves in a singular "great" love. But for the Darling it seems that almost anyone can serve as the beloved. The Darling comes too close to being promiscuous in love, and that is why she makes us uneasy.

Despite the subjective experience of the lover who idealizes the beloved and thinks that only this particular person could elicit such a response, surrender is in part impersonal; a lover prone to surrender will find an "appropriate" object to whom to surrender. The Darling is an extreme example of this predilection for surrender.

At the other extreme are those who are unable to let go at all and for whom no one (or at least no one available to them) seems quite good enough to warrant their love, the tribute of themselves; they are inhibited from falling in love altogether and completely miss out on the creative potential of love.

Most of us fall in between these two extremes: not everyone will do as an object of our love, but there is considerable latitude of choice. This is the dismayed observation of Tomas, Kundera's protagonist in *The Unbearable Lightness of Being,* as he views his beloved mistress, Tereza, dancing with another man.

They made a splendid couple on the dance floor, and Tomas found her more beautiful than ever. He looked on in amazement at the split-second precision and

deference with which Tereza anticipated her partner's will. The dance seemed
to him a declaration that her devotion, her ardent desire to satisfy his every whim,
was not necessarily bound to his person, that if she hadn't met Tomas, she would
have been ready to respond to the call of any other man she might have met
instead. He had no difficulty imagining Tereza and his young colleague as lovers.
And the ease with which he arrived at this fiction wounded him.

Tereza may have been out of touch with any such inclination in herself,
attributing her feelings solely to Tomas's worth. But Tomas had a moment of clairvoyance in which he saw through to Tereza's need to surrender almost irrespective of the object and as a consequence suffered a blow
to his pride in being loved.

Tomas brings to mind a man I once knew who tortured himself
imagining that were he to die, his wife, as a newly minted rich widow,
would rapidly assuage her grief by falling in love again. He felt the need
to believe that his wife could only feel the feelings she felt with him and
with no one else, that there was absolute specificity to her capacity to give
herself in love to him. When he fantasized that she might love another,
it seemed to make her love for him tawdry, and he grew sullen in his
unspoken resentment toward her.

The impulse to surrender that seems to have been so widely acted
upon in earlier eras is still with us. But it is no longer accorded the same
positive reinforcement from onlookers and friends. That is partly because
our current culture places such a high value—indeed an excessive one—on
autonomy. In addition, many mistake surrender for submission. These are
by no means the same thing, though they may overlap. The difference
consists of this: in surrender, the impulse is from within; its purpose is
self-purification or self-expansion through the transcending of the self and
identification with the attributes of the Other. In surrender, it is a purged
"reconstituted" self that is saved: the very act of surrender is a kind of
recovery of radical innocence. No self-will stands between the lover and
her secular god. This it shares with the religious impulse and it yields the
same gratification. Surrender is autonomous—it is unforced and it has no
covert agenda such as manipulation. Its purpose is to merge, lose, and
enlarge the self all at once. As Dante has it, "In la sua volontade e la nostra
pace." (In His will is our peace.)

In contrast, in submission, the response is to an external power differential; one is attempting to control a superior and dominating force, and
to preserve one's will and autonomy insofar as one can. Submission,
though it implies an external dominant force, real or imagined, also
implies manipulation. It has a covert agenda, to manipulate the Other in

order to maintain the self. The two—surrender and submission—are often admixed, one with the other, but they are not identical. Animals can submit to one another; only human beings can surrender. Self-surrender sometimes has the potential for happiness. Submission never does.

Surrender can certainly be understood in purely existential terms as the attempt to escape solitude and the solipsism of the self. Yet self-surrender is often experienced as conflictual, for the threat it poses to the self. Moreover, the impulse to self-surrender may be motivated, to varying degrees, by conscious or unconscious feelings of inadequacy, dependency, powerlessness, even worthlessness, and the need to counter them. Then the lover is no longer motivated primarily by the wish for self-transcendence, self-expansion, or self-purification; rather she is pursuing other aims—the bolstering of a fragile self, the restoration of a damaged self, the glorification of an impoverished self, the cohesion of a fragmented self, the empowering of a powerless self, or the obliteration of a hated self. When love is motivated by aims such as these, it is regressive rather than progressive—an attempt to secure the protection and support longed for early in life. It is in this range that surrender is problematic and symptomatic of an underlying weakness in the lover. In essence, the impulse to self-transcendence will have been perverted in ways that may be reparative or adaptive over the short term, but the long-term outcome may not be so sanguine. Some lovers will be able to form new identifications that become the basis of autonomous growth; but many others will find their potential growth stunted and their self-esteem even more grievously eroded. To the degree that the lover necessarily visualizes the beloved as superior, more capable, and powerful than herself, she may value herself *only* through identification with the exalted personage of the beloved. Then the transcendent and transformational potential of merging in surrender has been almost completely supplanted by the need to submerge.

Ambivalent Surrender

There are those for whom the threats implicit in surrender are so great as to preclude falling in love. The fear of falling in love is usually rooted in early life experiences. If one's parents were experienced as too intrusive and one's autonomy only dearly won, a love of any kind may appear threatening, and romantic love in particular because of the surrender inherent in it which is experienced as either submission or a loss of autonomy. Such fears may effectively preclude the possibility of romantic love, for the ability to achieve those moments of union that characterize passionate love requires the courage to let go, the willingness to risk one's autonomy.

Many tentative forays into love are aborted either because they pose real or symbolic threats to selfhood. Even when the integrity of the self is not at risk as it is in enslavement, pride and self-esteem may be (or appear to be) endangered. The lover may become frightened at the strength of his impulse toward surrender and the lack of autonomy he thinks it implies and he may make strenuous efforts to disengage. Or, out of self-protectiveness, he may pick an Other who does not reciprocate his feelings, and, consequently, one who sets external limits to his attempt to merge. Fearing merger, he thus sets up a situation which will prevent it. Similar motives dictate the behavior of the lover who after moments of great intimacy, particularly sexual moments, reasserts his separateness by withdrawal or by starting a quarrel. The more soulful and intimate the love-making, the greater may be the dread of loss of self, of dissolution (or emptiness) afterwards, and the sadness or distancing that surfaces in response to that dread. (Some people are only able to let go sexually as they disengage emotionally, being too afraid to surrender in both domains simultaneously. Consequently, one sometimes hears of a woman who may be orgasmic for the first time as a relationship unravels.)

In surrender, the lover wants to be incorporated into the beloved. Extreme or unilateral forms of surrender may lead the lover to submerge his tastes, interests, beliefs, and values, and either assume those of the beloved in toto (as in "The Darling") or give them complete priority over his own. Such a lover looks for the meaning of his life in his association and identification with the beloved. At first, he is happy to be encompassed by the beloved, and the sense of self expands. Paradoxically, it is only in spending the self that one can enrich the self, only in giving that one receives. (As many commentators have noted, in the West, even the mystical surrender to God is accompanied by the hope for personal salvation.)

Yet, unfortunately, such happiness can be short-lived, the radical surrender of self ultimately offending both lover and beloved. Insofar as he surrenders himself, the lover can be depleted if the beloved comes to devalue or scorn him. What began as a quest for transcendence can end in the impoverishment of servitude or even slavery. Or, as sometimes happens, the lover discovers the beloved to be less than a god and becomes disenchanted.

Surrender can also become unhappy when the lover feels that the self he had wanted to purify and expand by union with the beloved is instead impoverished, that he has, for fear of endangering the relationship, given up too much of himself, to the ultimate diminishment of a self-respecting core. He comes to fear his own regression to an infantile and dependent state from which he may never emerge. The fearful lover may pull back abruptly from his own impulse to surrender; and he may do so in extreme anger, leaving the beloved completely bewildered. As one man who was the object of such an abrupt reversal in his lover's feelings put it, "First she turned *to* me, but soon enough she turned *on* me."

To remedy fears of losing self, a lover may have recourse to still more strenuous measures. The threat to autonomy can give rise to an impulse to flee the relationship altogether, or to enter into another affair and thus preserve an identity separate from that of the beloved. In James Salter's novel *Light Years,* the husband can muse affectionately on his wife once he has a mistress:

He had a glimpse of her crossing the hall and a feeling of great warmth came over him, affection for her hips, her hair, the bracelets on her wrist. In some way he was suddenly equal to her; his love did not depend on her alone, it was more vast, a love for women, largely ungratified, an unattainable love focused for him in this one willful, mysterious creature, but not only this one. He had divided his agony; it was cleaved at last.

This is frequently the operative mechanism when an affair is utilized in order to "save" a marriage, and explains why the meaning of an extramarrital affair is not always what it appears to be. Though sometimes it is a search for an alternative, and as such a threat to a marriage which is already seriously compromised, at other times an affair serves as an "equalizer" which gives the lover a renewed sense of autonomy, and thereby allows the marriage to continue.

The lover's attempts at pursuing or preserving his autonomy may be sparse, laconic, symbolic, and indirect. One very intelligent and accomplished woman, passionately in love with a world-famous academician and theoretician, was unable to force herself to read his work. She feared she would be overcome by the sheer force of his intellectual prowess and would experience her own gifts as inferior; therefore she shielded herself from any firsthand knowledge of his genius. Even so, she knew her self-esteem was dependent on his admiration and love. She basked in his glory, but was simultaneously fearful of being overwhelmed by him. She remained poised between the impulse to surrender and the impulse to flee.

Following the end of a "love" relationship in which he felt engulfed, the lover may eschew any subsequent form of intimacy whatsoever. One man I know, on the rebound from a truly passionate love, one in which (though he didn't understand this at the time) he had felt swamped, married an altogether timid, constricted woman. Only after the end of that marriage, doomed from its beginning, was he able to reconstruct what had happened. At the time of the passionate affair he had been aware only of the passion and liberation he felt. As he put it, "I was too busy feeling the feelings, not observing them." But later, in reflecting—no longer reacting—he sensed how frightened he'd been at the prospect of losing autonomy, and understood how that fear had dictated his subsequent behavior. "Afterwards, in varying degrees, I made myself unavailable to women, most often just emotionally, sometimes emotionally and sexually. And in looking back, I could discern, after the fact, that I had felt invaded . . . that's why I married the woman I did. She was not threatening in any way."

A standard mechanism for resolving the conflict between one's simultaneous wishes for surrender and autonomy is to choose an unyielding love object. One can yield to the impulse to surrender if one has the safeguard of a partner who refuses to reciprocate, to yield in turn. Thus flinging oneself against an unresponsive love object is not as purely self-destructive as it so often seems. Such a love object sets an external boundary to the lover's self-abnegation.

This is the fundamental mechanism in one of the most commonly observed love relationships, the "see-saw" affair, in which first one and then the other of the lovers appears unilaterally head-over-heels in love with an unresponsive partner. Only when the lovesick partner begins to withdraw does the other dare yield to his own impulse to surrender. These love affairs appear peculiar to outsiders, but it is the very lack of simultaneity that allows the lovers "turns" at surrender. The participants themselves appear to suffer, but they are clearly in the grip of an intense, all-consuming passion, which takes precedence over mere happiness.

Though one can never with any degree of certainty uncover the complexities of motivation of persons long deceased, the love affair between George Sand and Alfred Musset, as described by their biographers, may well have been a flamboyant enactment of this genre of love. In 1833, longing to see Italy, the pair traveled to Venice, where they took rooms in the Hotel Daniele. But it was far from a romantic retreat for them. Musset precipitously announced to Sand that he no longer loved her, and he launched into an episode of what Sand's biographer, Maurois, calls "romantic debauchery." Though traumatized, she stayed with him.

When he became sick, she called in a young Italian doctor, Pagello, who subsequently became her lover. Only then was Musset's passionate interest in her restored. Musset returned to Paris and wrote to her, "I am going to embark upon a novel. I feel a craving to write our story. To do so would, I think, work a cure on me, and raise my spirits. I long to build an altar to you, if need be, of my bones. . . . You should feel proud, my great, courageous George, for you found me a child, and made me a man." Naturally their affair was far from over. After some months, Sand dismissed Pagello, and once she and Musset met again they resumed their relationship. But their life together "was as it had been before, furious scenes alternating with passionate notes." Sand dismissed Alfred again. But as Maurois depicts it:

Man is so made that he turns from what he can have, and pursues what he cannot. It must have been with no small a feeling of surprise that George Sand realized Musset's willingness to accept the breach, and, having done so, she at once ceased to want him to take her at her word.

Sand then cut off her hair, which she sent him. Only then was he prepared to receive her. And once more they resumed.

From breach to breach, from reconciliation to reconciliation, their dying passion twitched and gibbered in the nervous spasm of approaching dissolution. They were like two men fighting to the death, both drenched with blood and sweat, clinging together, raining blows on one another, beyond the power of the onlookers to separate.

Lack of simultaneity between lovers, so that one of the two is always less responsive, is often the safeguard that permits the headlong leap into unchecked passion, unbridled surrender. External barriers to a union can afford similar protections. It is for this reason that love often burns brightest and endures longest when there are obstacles standing in the way of the permanent consummation of the union. Such circumstances allow one to enjoy both surrender (in intense albeit limited doses) and autonomy; a rare opportunity to have one's cake and eat it too. This is the secret of the intensity in long-distance romances, parting scenes (as in "parting is such sweet sorrow"), stolen interludes, even death scenes. In one of the most tragic-ironic instances I know, a man married a woman diagnosed as suffering from an incurable form of cancer, which it was believed would kill her in three to five years. Theirs was one of the great glorious passions until she was miraculously cured. Her cancer and his ardor receded in tandem.

In divorce or separation, when the lover no longer fears engulfment, he can once again fantasize about reapprochement, reconciliation, and total reunion. Sometimes love of a spouse flowers freely only after his or her death. This is not just because one no longer subliminally fears rejection; it is also because there is no longer any threat of loss of self, of being overwhelmed by the power of the other. After the death of the beloved, the lover frequently takes on his or her ideas and mannerisms. This is a phenomenon Freud described in regard to mourning; the bereaved preserves the lost object through incorporation and identification. These psychological mechanisms provide a symbolic way of holding on to the beloved. Moreover, incorporation of attributes of the beloved, always a temptation, can now be risked: it no longer poses a threat to one's autonomy or one's boundaries. One woman was startled to see her recently widowed mother mouthing her late husband's opinions (the very ones from which she had only a short time before vigorously dissented), and even intoning them with his very inflections.

Enslavement and Masochism

In self-surrender in love, we understand the purpose, however roundabout and broadly defined, to be salvation or self-elevation. And even those for whom the experience of surrender is tinged with ambivalence may find it ultimately rewarding.

In enslavement (obsessive self-destructive love or masochistic surrender or both) the goals may be the same, but the depth and insatiability of the need doom the yearning lover to almost inevitable defeat. Sometimes, too, the impulse to surrender can be contaminated with the need for self-punishment. When this occurs and the lover comes to feel empty and worthless except for the perpetuation of his love, he has entered the realm of desperate love and he feels enslaved. The line dividing self-transformation from self-abnegation may sometimes be porous, and the deterioration of surrender into self-abnegation and self-destruction rapid. All serious critiques of romantic love point to its frequent corruption into enslavement. Without a strong core of identity and self-worth the lover's wish to merge is perverted into a wish to submerge himself into the beloved. This latter impulse may be so strong that the lover will sacrifice his autonomy, even his life in the vain attempt to achieve it. The lover may die to ensure merger in death, or being rejected, he may attempt suicide to evade separateness in life. (From this flows the paradoxically romantic contention that the lover is in love with death: Tristan,

Werther, even Antony might be considered as examples.) And in the range of masochistic distortions of love, we observe no gender difference.

Masochistic surrender in love may be akin to the ultimate pornographic dream of total objectification as exemplified by *The Story of O*. The beloved may be granted the power of God with total power over one's person; even, in extreme cases, over one's life. Then surrender appears to be motivated by guilt and outright self-loathing, not just by the sense (existential or psychological) of inadequacy, weakness, or meaninglessness. Its purpose may still be understood as salvation, but it is salvation through self-punishment and humiliation.

If one cannot be meaning to oneself, and if meaning is not supplied by a social nexus (the traditional mode of being meaningful), then one may seek to become meaningful through self-objectification: becoming an instrumentality for another. The self that feels itself to be powerless, or worthless, gives itself into the power of another: it is colonized by a foreign power. Complete surrender sustained over time rather than being experienced in brief moments is an admission of meaninglessness.

While there are those who search for a loving master and only accidentally fall in with a tyrant, still others appear to crave a tyrannical lover. Most often, in these instances of abject enslavement, the object to whom one surrenders is so visibly marred that the lover himself intuits that the impulse to surrender has been perverted. It is no longer merely the wish to merge with someone exalted, but something more complex, the self-destructive futility of which is revealed in the choice of the beloved. The following account of a three-year "love" affair was told me by an aspiring actress; her choice of a love object had none of the redeeming qualities of the man chosen by that other actress, Juliette Drouet. Retrospectively she sees the relationship as a long unhappy episode of self-abnegating love. I here repeat the story in her own words as nearly I have been able to remember them.

I'm not saying love and obsession never walk in rhyme, because that isn't so. But in this case, my case, it wasn't love. Ben was seven years older than I. I met him while I was working as a waitress in an Upper East Side restaurant. I recall the scene. It was Sunday brunch—pancakes, lox, and scones. My uniform consisted of black pleated (and stained) trousers and a pink buttoned-to-the-nose Oxford shirt. I used to pin my hair on top of my head like Gypsy Rose Lee and there was always a piece dangling, a sure-fire giveaway of the committed waitress. I wore flats and too much rouge. He used to methodically drink mimosas and order food he'd never touch. He had an obvious drinking problem which, naturally, I chose to ignore. He was very boyish looking, with straight blonde hair and a couple too many teeth, and at that time was extremely thin. He attributed this to his using cocaine every day. His little silver vial was ever-present, and he made countless trips to the men's room, always passing me at the service bar, where I would get him a refill of champagne.

I looked forward all week to brunch because I'd see this apparition, a genuine party boy. The self-destructive blueprint begins to take form. I would go to Bloomingdale's on Saturday to buy a new shade of lipstick. He told me the shape of my lips took his appetite away. (It was actually the cocaine that did that.) I spent a small fortune on gloss and lip liner. My entire week revolved around this ninety-minute meal with this disturbed, excessive, tormented person. If I met a guy like that now I'd run for my life. But he was like a defective piece of Steuben glass; if you turned the cracked part toward the wall, you couldn't really notice it. I wanted to bathe him in ammonia and watch him sparkle. I never fantasized about him making love to me; it was always me playing the aggressor, rubbing his tired nostrils, massaging his overworked liver with liniments of love and soul camphor, a false adoration. I rationalized my behavior as a tremendous need to heal. Maybe I needed someone pathetic to rescue. It was my 'Joan of Arc' period.

We slipped into a relationship. He was the son and I was the mother, cradling him to my breast like an infant. He was the laborer and I was the boss, always giving orders, astounded if he didn't carry them through. He was usually just too high to do too much of anything. He was the prisoner and I held the keys. But in truth, I was the one incarcerated. The claustrophobia I experienced at that time due to the bars I erected around myself was stifling. All I thought about was him. What was he doing? Who was he with? Did he stop anywhere on the way home from work? Did he go home alone? Did he phone anyone once he got there? Nothing else existed in my life. I barely functioned. I lived for his visits, they were the only time I was sure I knew where he was. My jealousy was unfounded. He wasn't particularly sexual. I always had to initiate everything and it was usually sheer submission on his part. He allowed me to have sex with him. He agreed to let me attempt to arouse him, but he was usually so intoxicated on either liquor, coke, or valium that he couldn't get it up. I thought I wasn't sexy enough for him. The last year we never made love at all. The sexual failure was silently accepted. I shined his shoes instead, went over to his apartment once a week and scrubbed the bathroom.

I used to look in his wallet while he was asleep to check for infidelity. Now I'm appalled. I'd wake up in the middle of the night and pour myself a juice glass full of brandy to keep myself from trying his number to see if he was home. I'm talking three or four in the morning. I paced like a crippled cougar, figuring, planning, piecing things together. The energy I wasted on love.

But where was the love that was supposed to exist, especially in the bloom of a new relationship? I am not sure it ever existed, but I thought it did. I realized afterwards that I got more affection from my cats. He was like a living piece of sculpture propped against my pillows. Finally, when the end came, I miraculously survived the loss. I was definitely sitting on the ledge but I chose the stairs rather than the window.

Looking back I see my love affair as a breakdown, as simply illness. It was a sickness, an emotional plague. It was equally as threatening as an alcohol or drug problem. I can honestly say it was the worst feeling I ever experienced. It's like being trapped in an elevator. You feel like evil has totally taken the controls of your life, and all you can do is comply with its wishes and watch your own destruction, as though you were viewing yourself and your actions on a tiny TV set: The Demon Channel. All your self-respect, esteem, dignity, and integrity are washed away like a sand castle. You are helpless. You hear people chant "What do you mean helpless? Out of control? Can't help it? That's insane. Just stop what you are doing." Like they say, "Throw that candy away. Put out that cigarette! Flush those pills! Tote that barge!" Insane is an appropriate word. That is just how you feel, like you are under some spell and you find yourself doing amazing things. Suddenly you realize you excel in being a sneak, a detective of sorts. You creep about like a cat burglar, searching for clues of betrayal, hints of disloyalty, signs of confirmation for all the crimes you suspect he's committed. At the time you assume it is love from start to finish. But when the holocaust comes and you are lucky enough to survive, in retrospect you will see there was no love, just a terrible need.

The actress was so terrified by the excesses of her experience that she subsequently withdrew from men altogether for several years after the end of the affair. She described herself as a love anorexic. The story is one of obsessive love, certainly contaminated with masochism, but the impulse to rescue her beloved is at the center of her story. She did not choose a lover she regarded as exalted, but one she saw as needy. Her story points to the complexity of motives in obsessive, enslaved, and desperate love. The manifest need to rescue the beloved appears as a component in many tales of self-destructive love.

Insofar as the impulse to surrender is perverted, it often happens that the beloved, far from being exalted, embodies the worst (often repressed) characteristics of the lover himself. The choice of the beloved is thus a reflection of the lover's negative self-image. In attempting to rescue the beloved, the lover attempts to rescue himself. To redeem the beloved is to redeem and purify the self. This is purification through martyrdom, not through surrender to someone exalted; it may also be an attempt to redeem part of the self that has been projected onto the Other.

Just as women are believed to be more preoccupied with love than men, it is also generally assumed that women suffer more in love. There is an almost cavalier assumption that men are relatively immune to the masochistic degradations of love (just as they are believed to be immune to the obsessive longing for love which is supposedly so rampant among women). But this assumption is erroneous. It might be that women are simply more open in communicating their suffering. The impression I get from my patients, where both sexes are committed to honestly articulating their feelings, is that men suffer just as much and are just as prone to enslavement.

One of the enduring fictional accounts of a man's enslavement in love is depicted in W. Somerset Maugham's novel, *Of Human Bondage*. As a young medical student, Philip Carey finds himself preoccupied with—and ultimately in love with—an extremely commonplace, but high-handed, waitress. Wounded by her initial disdain for him, trying to recover his bearings by overcoming her indifference, he falls in love with her. But what a strange love it is, for to Philip "it seemed impossible that he should be in love with Mildred Rogers. Her name was grotesque. He did not think her pretty. . . . She was common. . . . He remembered her insolence. . . . He had thought of love as a rapture which seized one so that all the world seemed spring-like, he had looked forward to an ecstatic happiness; but this was not happiness; it was a hunger of the soul, it was a painful yearning, it was a bitter anguish, he had never known before." She accepts his attentions reluctantly, and only yields to him when she finds herself pregnant by someone else. But despite his goodness to her, she betrays him time and time again. Even after she leaves him and he discovers she has become a prostitute, he takes her and her child into his home. Though by this time the passionate phase of his love has faltered and he is more repelled by her than ever, she continues to exert a deep power over him.

Finally, Philip, like the young woman of the previous tale, recovers. But what impels him? Mildred does not appear to be part of his secret self; that is, he is not fundamentally identified with her. Maugham has highlighted one of the gradients between Philip and Mildred that draws him to her: he who is psychologically crippled by his club foot, inward, diffident, and easily humiliated appears to be enthralled by her apparent self-sufficiency, her insolence, her very airs and pretensions. However Mildred is not the standard destructive woman to be found in life and literature. She is herself persistently self-destructive in her passionate choices and throws away any possibility for her own happiness by her affairs with two inconstant, insincere men, men to whom she relates much as Philip relates to her.

Maugham said his novel was an autobiographical one: "the emotions are my own, but not all the incidents are related as they happened, and some of them are transferred to my hero not from my own life but from that of persons with whom I was intimate." He claimed the book freed him from the pains and unhappy recollections that troubled him. (It may be worth noting that the two great literary accounts of men enslaved and obsessed by love—Maugham's Carey and Proust's Swann—were both penned by male homosexuals.) One may or may not recover from obsession and enslavement in love; in some instances, as with Philip, the damage to the self was reversible, but with Mildred it was irreversible.

There is a good deal of cultural and literary evidence to substantiate the male's vulnerability (and attraction) to self-destruction in love, documented by Leslie Fiedler among others. While male novelists have mythicized the Pure Maiden, they have also established the Dark Lady as a powerful temptress who sometimes lures the male protagonist to his death. From Lilith and Delilah, to Shakespeare's Dark Lady of the sonnets ("For I have sworn thee fair, and thought thee bright / Who art as black as hell, as dark as night") and through the romantic *Belle dame sans merci* to the present, literature asserts the fact (and fear) that men can destroy themselves in pursuit of romantic love. However, some male writers seem to see the danger as originating in the woman, not in any internal proclivity of the man for self-destruction. Yet this is a misunderstanding, a projection externalizing what is an internal psychological need. As pointed out by Fiedler, F. Scott Fitzgerald, perhaps more than any other novelist, uses the Pure Maiden as a disguise for the Dark Lady. Just as in *Tender Is the Night* Dick Diver is ultimately destroyed by his relationship with Nicole, so, too, is Jay Gatsby's demise brought about through his love for Daisy. As Fiedler said of Fitzgerald's work:

There is only one story that Fitzgerald knows how to tell, and no matter how he thrashes about, he must tell it over and over. The penniless knight, poor stupid Hans, caddy or bootlegger or medical student, goes out to seek his fortune and unluckily finds it. His reward is, just as in the fairy tales, the golden girl in the white palace; but quite differently from the fairy tales, that is not a happy ending at all. He finds in his bed not the White Bride but the Dark Destroyer; indeed there is no White Bride, since Dark Lady and Fair, witch and redeemer have fallen together.

Fitzgerald seems to have viewed himself as no less a victim than Jay Gatsby or Dick Diver. Of his own life he wrote, "I left my capacity for hoping on the little roads that led to Zelda's sanitariums."

Von Sternberg's movie *The Blue Angel,* based on Heinrich Mann's *Professor Unrath,* is the classic film portrayal of a man's degradation in love. The story is that of a high school professor who, discovering his students looking at picture postcards of the provocative entertainer Lola Lola, sets out to reprimand her for her bad influence on them. But after visiting her in her dressing room, he finds himself hopelessly enthralled by her seductiveness and the awakening of his own slumbering sexuality. Having spent the night with her, he precipitously proposes, abandons his teaching position, and goes on the road with her. The movie tells the story of the professor's steep decline into degradation. In the end he becomes no more than a comic member of his mistress's troupe, and Lola Lola enters film history as one of the legendary Dark Ladies of fantasy, one whose erotic power sentences a man to humiliation and ultimately to death.

The wish for humiliation or self-punishment often surfaces in male sexual life as the fantasy of the big-breasted, high-booted "phallic" woman with a whip. But the masculine wish for self-punishment and self-destruction just as often finds expression in a romantic preoccupation with the Dark Lady. She is specific to and a staple of male fantasy life. And a man drawn to the Dark Lady in fantasy often arranges to find her in the real world. Men are just as capable as women of using love relationships to gratify their unconscious longings for humiliation, self-punishment, or self-destruction.

Effects on the Beloved: Boredom, Claustrophobia, and Depletion

Excessive surrender not only damages the lover but also threatens the beloved. The beloved often experiences the lover as too dependent and may come to find his love so claustrophobic that she feels imprisoned. What the lover exalts as desire, the beloved may experience as cannibalism.

Furthermore, the lover's impulse to surrender can alienate the beloved who is its object if she becomes horrified at the lover's abjectness and is therefore no longer able to admire or even respect him. In fact, the lover may sometimes become the object of the beloved's disparagement and negative feelings precisely because he too completely *fulfills* her fantasies. Insofar as the lover attempts to gratify all the material and emotional needs of the beloved, the beloved either overidentifies the lover with a maternal figure and feels stifled, or regards him as little more than an adoring puppy. The beloved cannot idealize a lover who has abandoned any pretense of autonomy. She feels the lack of stimulation, of tension.

She feels she knows the lover too well, that the lover can say nothing which will expand her intellectually, do nothing which will stretch her emotionally. The relationship becomes threatened not by any tension between two autonomous people, but by the very lack of it.

The beloved may come to feel depleted or overwhelmed by the lover's manifest dependency. The lover's needs may even seem terrifying to the beloved. A twenty-eight-year-old divorced teacher implored her lover not to leave her, proclaiming both her love and need; she pleaded that her young son was sick and she was being considered for a promotion and she needed his support. Her lover reassured her, but bitterly complained to a friend that her declaration of love sounded more like a simple proclamation of weakness. Yet we all expect the plea "I need you so much" to be interpreted as a manifesto of love. "I need you," "I want you," "I cannot live without you," and "I love you" are statements that have an emotional coherence (at least to the one who is uttering them) if not a rational one. But the magnitude of need, insofar as it reveals the depths of the lover's dependency, may make the beloved feel trapped, and the consequent longing to escape may cause guilt. The beloved may squelch the longing to flee, yet feel enormous resentment. There is a profound debilitation experienced by the beloved—this once autonomous person—as he or she dutifully performs in the roles of savior, parent, and nursemaid.

A needy lover can be hard to escape. But perhaps no noose is tighter than that of the oversolicitous lover. We are all familiar with stories of a matriarch so overwhelming that her whole family could relax and expand only after she died. In a similar way, the beloved can come to experience her adoring lover as her jailer, feeling that she is imprisoned in a nightmarish distortion of solicitude. The wedding ring, once the token of the promise of eternal love, now becomes an emblem of bondage.

In Huxley's "The Gioconda Smile" Mr. Hutten is in Florence with his devoted and grateful second wife:

He had need to be alone. It was good sometimes to escape from Doris and the restless solicitude of her passion. He had never known the pains of loving hopelessly, but he was experiencing now the pains of being loved. These last weeks had been a period of growing discomfort. Doris was always with him, like an obsession, like a guilty conscience. Yes, it was good to be alone.

Consider also Benjamin Constant's complaint (in *Adolphe*): "She was not circumspect in her sacrifices because she was concerned with making me accept them."

When the lover is insistent on presenting self-surrender as a gift, there is a tacit (or sometimes explicit) demand that the beloved feel gratitude. In some wearing and tiresome marriages, one partner assumes the moral superiority of selflessness. The beloved is trapped by a sense of duty or by guilt. She feels an inability to move, believes that escape is impossible, but at heart she revolts.

Not only does she feel suffocated, stifled, but she is burdened by the vast expectations with which the lover attempts to saddle her; she is made to feel her own inadequacy by virtue of the exaggerated esteem in which she is held. It is wearying to try to live up to others' expectations of us. Sometimes the beloved has the urge to transgress simply as correction to the exalted image foisted upon her. She may look for stimulation elsewhere, telling herself that she is looking for larger horizons. In this way, she recapitulates the experience of previous separations from her "engulfing" family, now finding the lover as narrow, provincial, and constricting as the adolescent once found her parents.

The lover, sensing the beloved's defection, recognizes that he has changed in surrender; he knows he cannot be regarded as an object of desire. His freedom and independence have yielded to servitude, and he is no longer perceived as fascinating or desirable. Knowing this, the lover may attempt to withdraw and play "hard to get." Such is the advice mothers give their daughters, and such is the stuff of Hollywood comedies. In films, the ploy is invariably successful; in life, it may or may not be. But even if successful, the ploy leaves the lover new—and unwelcome—information; he now knows he cannot safely yield to his impulse to total self-surrender.

If the lovers give themselves over to sustained mutual surrender, there ceases to be an autonomous Other who can serve as an avenue for transcendence. These relationships, without any external sustenance, subsisting almost exclusively on mirroring, devolve into ennui. Boredom is the result of many relationships, partly because the intrinsic stuff of the self is not limitless. Some lovers counter such boredom by cultivating a small joint passion for amusements, grounding their mutuality in the external structure of games or a shared social life, whiling away the time pleasantly. By externalizing mutuality, they counter the threatening void.

Surrender is an integral part of love, at least at moments, allowing merger to be approached if not achieved. No love can be sustained without those periodic moments in which the lovers feel they have achieved merger—a sense that they are one.

For those who have the capacity for surrender it becomes problematic rather than exhilarating or enriching only when it is the sole aim of love. For then, paradoxically, the lover is concerned only with self, not with the beloved. True love is ultimately the granting of full subjectivity to the Other, which demands that each lover maintain enough of a separate identity to serve reciprocally as an object for transcendence and surrender. The lover must not only have the capacity to idealize the beloved; he must also hold himself worthy as an object for idealization. Unilateral surrender is doomed. Love cannot serve as religion; the lover cannot be redeemed solely by surrender. The lover will become disillusioned or the beloved burdened; whichever comes first, love will be shattered, or devolve into an obsessive torment. Therefore, while surrender is indispensible to passionate love, it must be measured, intermittent, and reciprocal in order for love to endure.

Fortunate lovers are able to oscillate on the continuum between merger and separateness with relative ease. They are best equipped to solve the paradox of how to achieve merger and yet maintain autonomy. As to the surrender implicit in love, the magnitude of the impulse is not the same for everyone, nor necessarily the same for any one person at different points in his life. For some, love comes close to total abdication of self; for others, such self-abdication is utterly implausible. These differences, as we shall see, depend on age, on gender, on culture, and on individual psychology. These are not inconsequential variables; they are decisive both for the ability or inability to love (in essence, to let go) and for the magnitude of danger to which one exposes oneself when one does open up in love.

CHAPTER SEVEN

The Link between Love and Power

L OVE AND power would seem to be mutually exclusive. A love relationship can be achieved only through mutual choice, which demands that both participants be sovereign subjects. Even if someone of very high status falls in love with someone of lower status, it is the very act of love which obliterates the external power differential. In contrast, a power relationship is based on the domination of one person by another, the dominant partner attempting to effect through domination or control what lovers seek by way of mutual grace. Yet, despite the apparent dysjunction between love and power, love is never completely free from the influence of power and many loves are corrupted by it.

Whenever there is a question of priority—and there always is, in every human relationship—some balance of power is established or a struggle for power ensues. Power relationships are the ground of human experience. Power may be role-related, as with teacher and student, employer and employee; age-related, the power gradient operating against both the very young and the very old; it may be affected by social, sexual, physical, or financial factors; or it may be related only to force of personality. Because all relationships involve power balances, so, too, do all love relationships. The power relationship in love may or may not be discussed by the lovers; it may not even reach conscious awareness. But whatever its terms and regardless of whether or not the lovers are consciously aware of these terms, the balance (or imbalance) of power is a fact of life—and love.

Those lovers who have achieved a measure of happiness and stability in their relationship have by definition arrived at a workable balance of power, often so subtle and so apparently automatic in its operation that neither the lovers themselves nor outside observers even notice it. Sometimes the understanding of the lovers is not the same as that of outside observers. In one female-dominated relationship with which I am well acquainted, both husband and wife believe that the husband is the controlling force. Both are most comfortable in asserting that their relationship conforms to the prevalent *cultural* expectation of male dominance and female subordination, despite their actual balance of power. However intricate, varied, and surprising the arrangements worked out by different lovers to achieve a balance of power, the only criterion that can be used to judge them is whether the lovers themselves feel satisfied that neither the one nor the other is being unduly exploited.

A power balance is always delicate and can be easily disrupted by small intrapsychic or interpersonal changes. Even when an equilibrium appears secure it can be disrupted and give way to a power struggle. (One must also remember a lesson of the woman's movement: the power equilibrium that serves to stabilize love may simultaneously hobble the individual development of one or the other of the lovers.)

The commonest way love is contaminated with power is manifest in the tug-of-war, the pervasive power struggle that so often occurs when love is on the wane. When, for example, the expectations awakened in passionate love go unfulfilled, the wish to give and sacrifice for the beloved devolves into resentment and a desire to receive. Then the lovers enter into a power struggle for fear of being cheated or short-changed. Mutuality is replaced by the struggle for priority. Here it is not so much a question of love being intertwined with power as of love failing and the struggle for power emerging as a consequence of that failure.

But power struggles need not await the death of love; power enters into love in a way that is specific to love. Just as there is an impulse to surrender in love—"I'm yours,"—so, too, is there a will to possession—"I want to own you body and soul." Dramatic and even paramount in lust, the wish for possession is also and always, in some degree, a component of love. The lover, by definition, hungers for solace from the beloved, for nurturance and for acknowledgment, and so he may be said to be dependent on her. Consequently, he wants to possess the beloved, to attach her to himself permanently, control her, and thereby insure her "love" for him. Love may unleash an insatiable hunger, a wish to devour the beloved. Domination and conquest are mobilized in the service of that hunger. This is the meaning of Socrates' profound reservation about love—already noted in the Introduction: "As wolves love lambs so lovers love their loves."

But, underneath, at the same time that the lover strives to exert tyrannical power over the beloved, he is himself enthralled, enslaved, and possessed. He is captive to the beloved and to his hunger for her. To the degree that he feels threatened by his own inner sense of powerlessness, he may escalate his attempts to dominate, thereby creating a vicious circle from which he finds it increasingly difficult to escape. Voracity and possessiveness, on the one hand, and enthrallment, on the other—the drive to power and the sense of powerlessness—are qualities that appear to be part of the essential nature of passionate love.

Power must be seen as an integral part of love, but it ought not to be confused with aggression or hate. Love may indeed conceal an element of resentment at the dependency implicit in loving and it can degenerate into hatred, but it is power with which love is more fundamentally connected. When love *is* contaminated by aggression, sado-masochistic relationships rather than simply dominant-submissive ones are the result.

Power, then, can be exercised in love in the service of a variety of different but related goals, among them: the desire for possession, the desire to preserve self-assertion and autonomy (when confronted with the internal pull to surrender), the desire for priority, or the desire (particularly when the first flush of love has faded) to get as good as one gives. Domination and submission are both power maneuvers to effect these ends—opposite sides of the same coin as it were.

The Devouring Nature of Love

Love unleashes primitive urges and fantasies. Among them is the lover's devouring hunger for the beloved which, along with the corollary urge to be enslaved, forms the dark side of love. This is because all passionate love leaves the lover dependent upon the beloved, and *only* her, for fulfillment. Insofar as love is called into being or sustained by need and dependence, it always involves a power differential. The lover, feeling himself ravished, is driven to possess the beloved. In his heart he feels that only possession will guarantee fulfillment and give surcease to the "wheel of desire." Therefore, the urge to possess appears to be part of desire.

The danger to the lover—in feeling that another person has power over him—leads him to counterattack by attempting to impose his will upon the other in order to even up the power differential. Helplessness breeds resentment, anger, all those emotions that tend to destroy the very possibility of the love that has triggered them in the first place. Morgenthau suggests a chilling, but compelling hypothesis: "An irreducible element of power is requisite to make a stable relationship of love, which without it would be nothing more than a succession of precarious exaltations. Thus without power love cannot persist; but through power it is corrupted and threatened with destruction."

While the wish for possession is an intrinsic part of the hunger in love, it is also a perversion of love. Possession is a form of denying the humanity, subjectivity, personhood (call it what you will) of the Other; as such it undermines respect for the Other and hence the value of the acknowledgment and recognition the lover requires of the Other.

The desire for possession often leads the lover to demand that the beloved love him solely. Ultimately, however, this is not possible. W. H. Auden, in "September 1, 1939," writes:

> What mad Nijinsky wrote
> About Diaghilev
> Is true of the normal heart,
> For the error bred in the bone
> Of each woman and each man
> Craves what it cannot have
> Not universal love
> But to be loved alone

Even without concrete evidence, the lover of course knows that the beloved does not exist solely for him. It is not in the nature of the human heart to love exclusively. Even if the beloved gives the lover priority over self, she is still moved by considerations for others. She treasures people other than her lover, whether they be parents, children, or the memories of past lovers. And her "infidelity" rankles the lover.

The lover's need to possess the beloved may be unknown to him—the possibility even denied—until the very moment he feels that his possession of the beloved is threatened. In *Man's Fate*, set in the early days of the Chinese revolution, Malraux gives one of the earliest fictional accounts of what has come to be known as an "open" relationship. To his surprise and dismay, however, the husband Kyo finds himself wracked by his wife May's confession of sexual infidelity, which he experiences as a wedge between them.

"I have something to tell you which is perhaps going to annoy you a little . . ."

Leaning on his elbow, he gave her a questioning look. She was intelligent and brave, but often clumsy.

"I finally yielded to Langlen and went to bed with him, this afternoon."

He shrugged his shoulder, as if to say: "that's your affair." But his gesture, the tense expression of his face, contrasted with this indifference.

The freedom which he had vested in her was given so that it should *not* be exercised; underneath their surface agreement as to their mutual freedom, he wanted her to belong to him.

The essential, what agonized him, was that he was suddenly separated from her, not by hatred—although there was hatred in him—not by jealousy (or was jealousy precisely this?) but by a feeling that had no name, as destructive as time or death: he could not find her again. . . .

She was getting away from him completely. And, because of that perhaps, the fierce craving for an intense contact with her blinded him, for a contact, no matter what kind—even one that might lead to fright, screams, blows. He got up, went over to her. He knew he was in a state of crisis, that tomorrow perhaps he would no longer understand anything of what he was feeling now, but he was before her as before a death-bed; and as towards a death-bed, instinct threw him towards her: to touch, to feel, to hold back those who are leaving you, to cling to them.

At other times, for other lovers, the need for possession is much more consciously experienced. In attempting to possess the beloved, the lover exposes his longing to be in the absolute realm of the dyad; he obstructs any force that might form a wedge between him and his beloved. He feels justified in his claims to the beloved, his need that she belong totally and exclusively to him. The lover presumes that the beloved should exist solely for his benefit. The force of this possessive passion, justified as a right, can only be compared to the omnivorous claims of the omnipotent infant, or those of the Oedipal child. It is the lover's belief that the beloved is obligated to him, in fact owes him whatever he wants, that leads to his violent sense of betrayal if his wishes are not met.

The following passage from *Portrait of a Lady* (Isabel Archer reflecting on her husband Gilbert Osmond's estrangement from her) conveys the picture of a husband disappointed in love by his inability to possess his wife:

. . . she could see he was ineffably ashamed of her . . . The real offense, as she ultimately perceived, was her having a mind of her own at all. Her mind was to be his—attached to his own like a small garden-plot to a deer-park. He would rake the soil gently and water the flowers; he would weed the beds and gather an occasional nosegay. It would be a pretty piece of property for a proprietor already far-reaching. He didn't wish her to be stupid. On the contrary, it was because she was clever that she had pleased him. But he expected her intelligence to operate altogether in his favour . . . He had expected his wife to feel with him and for him, to enter into his opinions, his ambitions, his preferences.

What are the psychological factors that intensify the need for possession? Love is always shadowed by the lover's fear that he will cease to please the beloved, that he will give offense and may even lose her, and sometimes the lover is correct to intuit a possible threat to the relationship. But some lovers have a psychological vulnerability which leads them to sense a fragility in love where none exists. To the degree that the lover fears rejection (perhaps because he feels unworthy) or has exaggerated dependency needs, his resentment will be magnified and his predisposition to invoke power will be exaggerated. For some, particularly those with any neurotic predisposition, the fear of dependency may evolve into terror. In a desperate effort to allay such a disaster, the lover attempts to achieve permanence by manipulation, either through domination or ingratiation. This, of course, parallels the stratagems that impede opening up in courtship, but it occurs much later. On the other hand, those lovers whose dependency needs were fully met in childhood may feel less threatened in later life when entering into relationships where they are once more dependent. Consequently, they are less driven to invoke power plays in self-defense.

The more insecure the lovers, the more volatile and out of control their feelings may become. Then power is sought frenetically in an effort to stabilize and to preserve love, to cling to the beloved. Fearing rejection, attempting to forestall the end of love, or vulnerable to some narcissistic injury, the lover uses whatever power he has—personal, physical, financial, social—to hold on to his beloved and control her. But the fears invoked in love may never be consciously experienced; in fact, the lover's impulse to dominate masks his fear, the act of domination permitting him to feel strong and to perceive the beloved as weak. (In a similar way, the addict who uses drugs to alleviate anxiety or depression may do so in such a way that he never has to become aware of his underlying feelings.)

Domination and Control in the Service of Possession

The lover's need for possession takes many forms; it may be manifested as either dominance or submission. In attempting to dominate or control the beloved, the lover may promise benefits (financial rewards or social access), threaten misfortune should the beloved not comply, physically coerce her (beatings), or sometimes appeal to some external authority (religious, legal, or familial). He may attempt to overpower the beloved and dominate her sexually. The lover may also utilize either the ingratiation of flattery or the seduction of his personal charm.

Out of his longing to possess the beloved exclusively, the lover may try to separate her from her other loved ones. He may resent her ministrations to her parents or children. He disapproves of her close friends and may openly or secretly subvert her relationships. He is jealous if she praises someone else. He disparages her interests, the better to be able to control her. He wants to know where she is at all times. In public, his arm around her shoulder signifies possession, not intimacy. At a cocktail party the lover sees the beloved talking to an imagined rival and hastens to her side. Later he may provoke a scene. He monitors her clothes and forbids the slinky black dress; he finds it too sexy but rationalizes his interdiction by labeling the dress vulgar.

In the last chapter I wrote of Juliette Drouet's surrender to Victor Hugo. But if she needed to be captive, he was an eager captor. Embarking on what appeared to be a light-hearted romance, he declared to her, "If ever love was complete, profound, tender, burning, inexhaustible, infinite, it is mine." Yet he was not so easy to please as he claimed and he proved to be a jealous and possessive lover, troubled over Drouet's past affairs and her extravagance with money. Hugo and Drouet tormented one another, splitting up and reconciling. But then Hugo conceived of a program for Drouet's "redemption" and she began to long for "absolution." He undertook her salvation utilizing spartan measures. According to one of his biographers, "worse than everything else, was the form of claustration that her tyrant lover now imposed upon her. As Victor Hugo became completely bound to her, and she became an inextricable part of his life, his 'Spanish' jealousy pursued her. He separated her from her former friends, female as well as male, he watched her, came in at unexpected moments; he demanded that she live alone, accounting to him for all her time. She was shut in, like the concubine of an oriental despot, receiving none but her lord and master." He even forced her to save money on fuel so the apartment in which he had installed her was often cold. And so he kept his firebird for twelve years, from 1834 to 1846. Though she was not allowed to share his public life, he tried out his speeches on her, showed her his finery before he made his public appearances, and apparently loved her. Why indeed did he ever let her out? It's been suggested that perhaps he finally felt she was redeemed, or more cynically, that her beauty had faded. She feared, probably correctly, that he no longer loved her as much. His "faithfulness" to her ended, though their strong bond lasted a lifetime.

Such extreme examples are not hard to come by; Françoise Gilot, writing of her ten years with Pablo Picasso, describes him as an absolute master of all the ploys of domination. Picasso never lived with Dora Maar, the mistress immediately preceding Gilot (and overlapping with her), but kept her on call. According to Gilot, Maar "never knew whether she would be having lunch or dinner with him—not from one meal to the next—but she had to hold herself in a state of permanent availability so that if he phoned or dropped by, he would find her there. But she could never just drop in to his place, or phone to say she would not be available for dinner that evening." One of the first ideas Picasso had about Gilot was that she should live with him secretly, dress in black, with a veil over her face, so that in that way no one else would have her. "He had the idea that if someone is precious to you, you must keep her for yourself alone, because all the accidental contacts she might have with the outside world would somehow tarnish her and, to a degree, spoil her for you." But possession never satisfied him, and he was apparently always involved with more than one woman. He also seemed incapable of completely severing the ties with his discarded women, proffering just enough interest or encouragement to keep them bound to him. Gilot may have been one of the exceptions in her ability to finally break with him.

Picasso was hardly alone in his demand for on-call availability. Many men and some women seek this, particularly in the sexual sphere. When I was growing up, in the fifties, men still felt free to voice such a desire for total possession and control quite undisguised: "Keep her pregnant in the summer and barefoot in the winter."

There is yet another quintessential fantasy of complete control over the beloved; it may be found in the various versions of the Galatea and Pygmalion legend. In the Greek story, a misogynist king who was also a sculptor, carved an ivory statue of a woman with which he fell in love. He prayed to Aphrodite to give life to the statue, and he married this creature of his own invention. Variations on this theme are found in Ovid's *Metamorphoses*, William Morris's *The Earthly Paradise*, W. S. Gilbert's *Pygmalion and Galatea*, and in George Bernard Shaw's *Pygmalion* and its musical adaptation, *My Fair Lady*. The story of Trilby and Svengali is a sinister variation of the Galatea and Pygmalion story; Svengali controls Trilby's singing through his hypnotic powers. In a certain regard, these might be considered to be perverted transformational stories in which the beloved is changed not by any internal psychic process but by the action of the lover upon her; she is created according to his specifications or transformed in accordance with his wishes.

The Pygmalion fantasy does not always remain in the realm of the imaginary; it is enacted in one or another symbolic form more often than we might imagine. But the assorted Galateas do not invariably stay in their subordinate roles; they may rebel or escape or turn the tables. Versions of the Pygmalion story are perhaps most commonly observed in the theatre or film world, when a film director or agent or manager undertakes to make over or invent an actress. Edward Judson changed Rita Hayworth's hairline, created her as a sex goddess and married her. John Derek is said to have fashioned a number of glamorous stars including wives Linda Evans and Bo Derek, and Sonny engineered Cher. But, for me, the most interesting of the Pygmalion stories to come out of the movie industry is that of the relationship between Marlene Dietrich and the director Josef von Sternberg, partly because of the intricate crossovers between their lives and their films. Their story, like those of other film pairs and some variants of the Galatea-Pygmalion legend itself, reveals the complexities and ambiguities of the motivations of both the protagonists as well as the reversals that their relationship may undergo. (And, as I shall argue later, it is perhaps the thrill of playing Pygmalion that predisposes some male therapists to fall in love with their female patients, or, short of that, to become emotionally overinvolved.)

Josef von Sternberg, having seen Dietrich perform, fought for her to have the role of Lola Lola in *The Blue Angel* in which Emil Jannings was to star. Marlene Dietrich was a small-time player whereas Emil Jannings was one of the supreme stars of his era. Von Sternberg insisted on the part for Marlene Dietrich despite opposition from everyone else connected with the film, including Jannings. Years later, Dietrich is reported to have said, "He had only one idea in his head—to take me from the theatre and make me a movie actress, to become my Pygmalion." She claims that he was originally enticed through an inner resistance or withholding he sensed in her; she did not think she had a chance for the part and therefore wasn't going out of her way to try and get it. (There is, her circumstantial explanation notwithstanding, a basic inner reserve that one senses in her, at least in her films.) Ironically enough the role von Sternberg had in mind for his Galatea was that of Lola Lola, the classical portrait of a woman as seductress and castrator. According to one of Dietrich's biographers, von Sternberg, "in love with his star already, seemed to be obsessed, drugged, all through the shooting." The romantic and professional liaison between Dietrich and von Sternberg was complex from its beginning; it is said that though von Sternberg was prone to romantic obsessions with women, these relationships were complicated by the fact that he also "looked down at women from some macho position."

The Blue Angel made Dietrich a star. Von Sternberg brought her to Hollywood, where he undertook to remodel her completely. She was instructed to lose thirty pounds; her teeth were pulled to accentuate her cheekbones, which also were shadowed; her eyebrows were plucked and painted high on her forehead, her nose was shaded to make it look narrower, and her hair was sprinkled with gold dust. While filming her in the series of pictures that made them both famous, von Sternberg forged the image that made her, along with Garbo, among the most glamorous women of her day. He was notorious for the innumerable takes he demanded before he was satisfied with any film sequences, focusing particularly on lighting Dietrich in such a way as to bring out her beauty. (This lighting was so effective that Dietrich insisted on it even into her 60s and 70s when she had fashioned the cabaret act she took around the world.) According to Sam Jaffe, von Sternberg did all the scenes with Dietrich over and over again, "not to humiliate her, but to insure she was perfectly glamorous. In my opinion, he was completely responsible for the Dietrich the world knows."

Revealingly enough, in 1924, five years before von Sternberg ever laid eyes on Dietrich, he had written and published his own version of the Pygmalion-Galatea story, a short story called "The Waxen Galatea." As reported by Donald Spoto, it is the story of a shy man who falls in love with a wax dress shop mannequin. Every day he looks at this figure longingly, but eventually comes upon a woman who is the living embodiment of the wax figure and becomes enamoured of *her.* Following her, he sees her meet another man and is humiliated. Stung to the quick, he vows never to love anything again except a lifeless mannequin. As Spoto points out "the filmmaker . . . stressed the gloomy fate of the worshipful lover, doomed to entertain an idealized and unattainable love." In a certain way the story appears to have been prophetic of von Sternberg's relationship with Dietrich. There were of course external impediments to their relationship, including the fact that both were married to other people. When von Sternberg's wife sued him for divorce, Dietrich's husband and daughter were brought over from Germany to smooth over appearances and give the impression that she had a happy marriage. But spouses aside, Dietrich and von Sternberg's relationship seems to have been tumultuous from within, particularly because of his possessiveness and ambivalence. According to one report, at a time when von Sternberg felt he was losing Dietrich, he suffered from insomnia and seemed to be on the verge of a nervous breakdown. The final break in their intimate relationship came in the mid-thirties; some say she finally dumped him ignominiously. Von Sternberg never recovered professionally, but Dietrich, having made some of her greatest films with Sternberg, went on to enjoy a distinguished career without him.

Von Sternberg's warring feelings about women, his vacillating stance

with them, and his preoccupation with domination and surrender surfaced not only in his relationship with Dietrich but with the female
characters he created for her. Subjugation and domination are nowhere
better illustrated than in those von Sternberg/Dietrich films.

I described *The Blue Angel* in Chapter 6, but variations on the theme
are found throughout von Sternberg's Dietrich films. His next film after
The Blue Angel, Morocco, is almost a rewrite of his Galatea story. In it,
the Marlene Dietrich character first appears as a Lola Lola figure, one who
has complete emotional ascendency over the very rich and elegant Adolphe Menjou. But the denouement of this film is different from that of
The Blue Angel. Dietrich does not destroy Menjou; she falls in love with
the young legionnaire Gary Cooper and, in the end, abandoning her
aspirations for worldly success, follows her legionnaire into the desert,
tagging onto a group of native women. It has been remarked that von
Sternberg wrote himself into the Menjou role, that of the man of the
world who loses his woman, and that Menjou even looked like von Sternberg. But in *Morocco,* the Dark Lady herself becomes a sacrificial victim
to love, one who totally surrenders to her man. Von Sternberg's other
films also catch those complexities of personality that can lead one to act
sequentially as seducer or victim, sometimes dominating and cruel (or at
least aloof), other times only too willing to surrender. In the very campy
movie *Shanghai Express,* the Marlene Dietrich character first appears as
a Dark Lady. Separated from her lover for years through some misunderstanding, she meets him once again and the following exchange takes
place: "Well, Doc, I've changed my name." He asks her if she means that
she has married and she responds "No, it took more than one man to
change my name to Shanghai Lily." She explains, "The white flower of
China, you've heard of me—and you have always believed what you've
heard." But hard and brittle though she may appear, she complies with
the advances of the Chinese villain to save the man she still loves (another
instance of noble sacrifice). Here von Sternberg has portrayed the whore
as Magdalen, and just so the movie-goer won't miss the point, Shanghai
Lily's real name *is* Magdalen—the Dark Lady defanged and resurrected
as the Pure Maiden. Part of what emerges in von Sternberg's work is his
intuition of the psychological vulnerability that, paradoxically, may propel
its opposite in action and appearances.

In life as in the movies, the possessive lover's enactment of dominant
scenarios fails to obscure his need. Despite his manifest belief that the
beloved has entered into an irreversible covenant with him, the possessive
lover belies his certainty by his behavior. In attempting to enforce what

should be automatic, the lover ensures that his show of strength becomes the emblem of his weakness. The magnitude of his weakness and raw need is often readily apparent, both to others and to the lover himself. When the lover tries to offset his feeling of ravishment (enslavement) by his power in domination, he travels in a futile, vicious circle. The weakness underlying the need for control and the doomed aspects of that need are perhaps nowhere clearer than in the plaintive lines of the old popular song: "I'm goin' to buy a paper doll that I can call my own; a doll that other fellows cannot steal. And then the flirty, flirty guys with their flirty, flirty eyes, will have to flirt with dollies that are real."

While domination may insure possession, it acts to destroy love in at least two different ways. First, in asserting his own superiority, the lover may undermine his beloved's worth and ultimately destroy his grounds for exalting and admiring her. For some lovers, love can only be experienced as longing because reciprocity is invariably interpreted as submission, which automatically elicits devaluation. There is the classic example of the singer who was notorious for his deluxe whirlwind courtships; the problem was that he lost interest as soon as his conquest was accomplished. He was said to soothe himself in his woebegotten affairs by listening—while he had sex—to tapes of himself singing. (Perhaps it wasn't only his narcissism at work: he may have felt need of this reminder to his woman of who he really was.) And he felt free to dispose of his devalued girlfriends by passing them along to his friends. His deepest love was for a woman who would not stand still long enough to be possessed and was more promiscuous than he.

Secondly, even if the dominating lover is able to preserve his idealization of the beloved, he can no longer believe in the reality of her love for him; having demanded it, he can never again experience it as freely given. By trying to manipulate what cannot be manipulated, to force what cannot be forced, the lover inadvertently corrupts the experience of love. Every lover wants to be loved spontaneously and for himself, not as a result of coercion or ingratiation. Sartre cuts to the core of the lover's dilemma when he suggests that the lover wishes to possess the beloved as an object and yet simultaneously wishes that she remain a free subject—free to love him.

Recourse to domination in order to insure love is doomed for yet another reason. It aims at possession, but spirit in the Other is always inaccessible; it becomes visible only through behavior. Hence the prime goal in domination must be to govern the Other's behavior. But this is never enough for the insecure lover; he fears the invisible resistance or refusal: "You may have my body, but not my soul!" The only way out of the dilemma is to metaphysicalize domination. The lover must attempt to make the spirit of the Other fully visible in the body so there can be no secret refusals, no withholdings. When domination is "metaphysicalized" the body is not simply a vehicle *for* spirit; it is identified *with* spirit. (If someone attempts to use power as the primary means to transcendence, it often takes the form of sexual domination, as can be seen, for example, in the Marquis de Sade's writings.)

For the reasons just described, possession through domination cannot ever be entirely satisfactory. Either love will fade or the attempt to dominate will be escalated, forever doomed to fall short of the mark. The escalation is a vicious circle leading inevitably to jealousy, whether or not there is cause for it in either the behavior or the secret wishes of the beloved. The desire to insure possession and to guarantee union may even result in the most extreme of acts: the lover, in a desperate attempt to extinguish all possibility of independent thought or actions by the beloved, may kill her (and himself), thus literally enacting a perversion of the Liebestod.

Sometimes domination merges into sadism. Some individuals, by virtue of their early experiences or perhaps their nature, are unable to transcend ambivalent relationships. For them, rage is an intimate and necessary part of relationships, and may emerge in the form of sadism. Whereas in domination, the lover is motivated to secure the dependency of the beloved on himself, in sadism, his additional aim is to cause the beloved humiliation and vent his own aggression. Sadism serves to inflate the self through the degradation of the Other. Excesses of behavior sometimes point to the lovers' true motives. Consider, for example, the lover who in ecstatic embrace persuades the beloved to give him a child. Upon discovery of her ensuing pregnancy, however, he insists that she have an abortion. Or there is the man, passionately enamored of his wife, who was insanely jealous of the affairs she had before they met. Yet, on occasion, he demanded that she sleep with a friend of his in his presence, and that she perform sexually with the other man with ecstatic abandon. He wanted to own his wife's sexuality entirely and yet reduce her to creature status, a slave who anxiously awaited his command. Later, enraged, he would call her shameless and undignified. Because both sexes are vulnerable to the same misfortunes of early life that can corrupt the capacity for love, both can enact either masochistic or sadistic variants of love. Nonetheless, recourse to violence, both as a mode of domination and the expression of rage, is much more common among men.

And what are the effects of domination on the beloved? Though often enough the objects of such attention see fit to flee, there are those others who are sometimes too abject to extricate themselves. Sometimes, too, they intuit the raw need beneath the lover's force and rationalize it as pure love. (At the extreme, some case workers of battered wives are dismayed to discover that a few of the wives find evidence of their husband's love in the beatings they receive.)

A word might be said about the power of the beloved enacting a role as the unattainable object of desire; it is a weak kind of power because it always depends upon the lover's continuing interest in the beloved. It can only be exerted insofar as the lover is left unsatisfied, not allowed full possession, and it is most frequently exercised through sexual withholding. But a sane lover will eventually tire of unfulfilled longing. The transience of this power, and the fantasies it awakens and dashes in both the object of desire and the doting admirer are marvelously depicted in Bertrand Blier's movie *Menage*. Bob (Gerard Depardieu) butts into a fight between a husband Antoine (Michel Blanc) and his wife Monique (Miou Miou) and forms an instant triangle. Antoine adores Monique but she is contemptuous of him. Bob seduces the couple into a life of crime and, at the same time Monique is falling in love with both the high life and him, he is falling in love with Antoine. In order to maintain her new goodies and her access to Bob, Monique encourages Antoine to submit to Bob. The centerpiece of the film is Bob's lovesick longing for Antoine, Antoine's horror (at the homosexual implications), his ultimate surrender, and the predictable outcome—Bob's need to domesticate Antoine and thereby disengage from his personal torch song. Feeling abandoned, Antoine strikes back. Both Bob and Antoine are brought low by their mutual enactment of different power modalities. One strength of the film is to detach the story of passion that is tamed when realized—and the corruption of love through power—from its usual stereotypical heterosexual frame, and to reveal the way power works in love irrespective of the gender of the protagonists.

Submission in the Service of Possession

Submission may serve the same goals of possession as domination. While submission is often believed to be nothing more than a realistic response to being in a subordinate position (in which case it might be regarded merely as the only adaptive response available to the weaker party), it is also often deployed as a power maneuver, one expressed in the "passive" voice. Then submission is a ploy, which, like domination, consists of a series of psychological maneuvers aimed either at controlling the Other or securing dependency gratification. The difference between them is that submission substitutes manipulation for coercion or force as the means of control. The lover's strategy is to please the beloved and make himself seem indispensable, or to bind the beloved to him through guilt. Submission's repertory of devices includes seduction, ingratiation, flattery, minute ministration to the needs of the beloved, and the elevation of the beloved's priorities over one's own.

Insofar as the lover can induce the beloved to depend on him, even exploit him, the lover feels indispensable and achieves a kind of security. The lover submits in order to hold on to his beloved and occasionally share in her power. He feels a sense of permanence and importance in being indispensable to someone important. But this mode of relating to the beloved necessarily carries with it a sense of self-impoverishment. The lover sacrifices himself to the security of the relationship. Unlike the impulse to surrender, where the aim is transcendence, the motivation here is not so grand. The lover does not seek to obliterate the self so as to be reborn, or enlarged, but seeks to secure the truncated self. Subordination is deeply damaging to self-esteem, so the lover may have recourse to covert "equalizers," such as affairs.

A subtle power modality, one that appears benevolent by comparison with some of the other modes, is that which is disguised as caretaking. Some lovers are extremely nurturant in order to disguise their underlying and unacceptable feelings of dependency. The lover indulges the beloved's inclination toward dependency by assuming the role of the indulgent provider of both emotional and material goods. This sometimes camouflages a conscious condescension or disparagement of the beloved. More often, however, it masks a profound identification with the beloved's dependency wishes.

In such cases, the "we" appears to be composed of a mature, centered lover who is dominant over a needy and infantile beloved. Sometimes, however, one may see a dramatic reversal in roles, which reveals the true meaning of the need to dominate, showing it for the terrible weakness that it is. One of the most gripping fictional accounts of a couple engaged in such a dynamic is Fitzgerald's portrait of Nicole and Dick Diver in *Tender Is the Night*.

Dick Diver, a psychiatrist, meets Nicole, a patient at a psychiatric sanitarium. Nicole, who is psychologically disturbed and perhaps even schizophrenic (by virtue of an incestuous relationship with her father), recovers her health through a series of letters she writes to the dashing Dr. Diver.

Following her recovery, the two are married. Nicole's life appears to be structured by Dick, but in reality both their lives are structured around her. Nicole has a relapse in response to Dick's interest in another woman. Dick becomes the head of a sanitarium in order to provide the setting in which to nurse Nicole back to health. In curing her he becomes uncentered, emptied (or was he always?) and her apparently complete domination by him and the subsequent reversal of the power balance are revealed in two deceptively small exchanges.

Dick, gradually showing signs of emotional exhaustion and deterioration, has been drinking too much. Nicole's lover-to-be, Tommy Burban tells her:

"There are those who can drink and those who can't. Obviously Dick can't. You ought to tell him not to."
"I!," she exclaimed in amazement, "*I* tell Dick what he should do or shouldn't do!"

Not long after, Tommy visits the Divers and complains of a sore throat. Nicole gives him the last jar of special camphor rub over Dick's objection. It is the first stand Nicole takes in opposition to Dick, and it is prophetic.

"There was no necessity for that gesture," Dick said.
"There are four of us here—and for years whenever there's a cough _____"
They looked at each other.
"We can always get another jar—" then she lost her nerve and presently followed him upstairs where he lay down on his own bed and said nothing.

Dick immediately understood the significance of the incident. Later, when they had agreed to separate, it was without drama. "Nicole felt outguessed, realizing that from the episode of the camphor-rub, Dick had anticipated everything."

In the end she, the fragile, sick one, was more prepared for life. "Nicole had been designed for change, for flight, with money as fins and wings. The new state of things would be no more than if a racing chassis, concealed for years under the body of a family limousine, should be stripped to its original self." He, on the other hand—the charming, engaging, and energetic Dick Diver—was fatigued, emptied out, destroyed, and destined for obscurity. During their relationship, despite surface appearances, she gained in strength while his fund of strength was eroded, and his underlying weakness revealed.

Some lovers try to control one another by eliciting guilt. This maneuver almost always fails, further estranging them. The turn to guilt as a mode of control and belief in its efficacy constitute a regression to an earlier mode of interaction: children and parents attempt to control each other through guilt. As it turns out, attempts to elicit guilt more often provoke anger. But guilt can be invoked to lock in a relationship, albeit an unhappy one.

In *Ethan Frome*, Edith Wharton has given us a chilling account of a woman who established her influence over a man through caretaking and then destroyed them both through her infirmities and reproaches. Zeena, who was Ethan's relative, came to nurse his mother through her final illness and she filled the quiet house with conversation. "Zeena seemed to understand his case at a glance. She laughed at him for not knowing the simplest sick-bed duties and told him to 'go right along out' and leave her to see to things. The mere fact of obeying her orders, of feeling free to go about his business again and talk with other men, restored his shaken balance and magnified his sense of what he owed her." When his mother died he feared to be alone again, but, afterwards thought he might have been spared had his mother died not in the winter but in the spring. For the respite from his lonely life was short enough. Within a year, Zeena had herself succumbed to sickness, largely imagined, and had become the new stone around his neck, as the two sank into stultifying silence. Seven years later, when Zeena's young cousin Mattie came to live with them, Ethan's heart grew lighter and he felt warmth and the stirring of love. But Zeena became jealous and retaliated with escalated sickness and reproaches and plotted to send Mattie away. "Ethan looked at her with loathing. She was no longer the listless creature who had lived at his side in a state of sullen self-absorption, but a mysterious alien presence, an evil energy secreted from the long years of silent brooding. It was the sense of his helplessness that sharpened his antipathy." Yet he was powerless to thwart her plans. The night before Mattie was to leave, he took her for a last sleigh ride, intending suicide, but at the last moment averted the fatal crash, avoiding death but crippling them both. Mattie, confined to a chair, lived on to be nursed by Zeena, the three locked in an unending agony.

By and large there is a gender difference in the techniques of control that each sex favors, though these are by no means invariable. Woman more often exerts her control through either a dependent or caretaking modality. As the submissive one, eager to do her lover's bidding, she manifests her moral superiority, and manipulates by eliciting guilt in the beloved. She ensnares and manipulates the beloved through her submission and her high moral standards, through her self-sacrifice and faithfulness. The time-honored question "How could you?" simultaneously conveys reproach, helplessness, and moral superiority. Traditionally, too, she can control the beloved through the granting or withholding of her sexual favors. Man, on the other hand, generally opts for dominance, coercing and manipulating more directly by physical or verbal abuse, economic, social, or other kinds of sanction. These differences reflect both gender socialization and a real difference in the power positions of men and women in our society.

Both sexes, in pursuit of possession or priority, may utilize any or all of the available techniques of power. These may appear to succeed and may stabilize the love (or, if not love, then the relationship intended to approximate love). But recourse to the instruments of power, whether domination or submission, even when it is successful at stabilizing love, ultimately leaves the lover with a sense of sadness, a feeling that love is not naturally his due, but rather that he has had to elicit it by force or secure it through guile. To be loved as a consequence of coercion or guile is to forego the experience of feeling loved for oneself.

Dominant-Submissive Adaptations among Couples

Lovers for whom mutual dependency is a primary concern often form very troubled but durable relationships in which there appears to be a strong dominant-submissive gradient between them. They sometimes attempt to perpetuate the fiction that the dominant partner is strong and free. This allows them both to participate in his apparent "strength." Nonetheless, whether dominant or submissive, the lover engaged in the drama of power is utterly dependent on his beloved. In submission, the lover needs the beloved as the source of strength; in domination, the lover needs the beloved as the objective guarantor of his own strength. In each case, he senses his abject dependency on the Other. And however he may try to suppress it, the knowledge of his vulnerability acts to intensify his need to cling to the beloved, the result being that he needs to dominate or submit even more. A vicious circle is initiated, one that is extremely hard to break.

Whether dominant or submissive in such relationships, the self is diminished, and the assertion or enactment of power in love will most often lead to mutual resentment, anger, and even aggression. Nonetheless, while the psychological maneuvers of power can dilute the purity of love,

on occasion they also stabilize love. It would be naive not to acknowledge
that some of the most intimate and intense love affairs are generated
within the context of manifest power relationships, bondings which draw
their passionate intensity from the highly charged mix of love and power.

And, interestingly enough, such lovers may struggle hard to hold on
to each other, even to the extent of living through power reversals. In
other words, the master will sometimes become the slave when his relationship is threatened by his slave's revolt, and this may, for some people,
be an effective stratagem.

I know very well a woman who was a gifted businesswoman but
inhibited in the pursuit of her own career by her slavish devotion to an
eminent lawyer. She worked on his behalf every night, entertained for
him, and spent time scheming to get him ever more glamorous clients.
Some years into their courtship, she was astonished to discover that she
was but one of two mistresses. He offered very thin excuses and made no
move to make amends. Although hurt, she went on catering to him, by
this time caught up entirely in the fantasy that she could only realize her
ambitions through him. Eventually, however, she found the courage to
have a surreptitious affair of her own, and considered marrying this second
man. But she revealed her intention to the lawyer, and what followed was
an amazing transformation in each of them and in their relationship.

The lawyer, formerly dominant, demanding, and controlling, now
became abject and pleading. Whereas before he had claimed he would
not abandon his other mistress for fear that she would commit suicide,
now he decided to give her up. He was disconsolate and despondent to
the point of threatening suicide himself if his beloved would not marry
him. She, in turn, exhibited more dignity, self-respect, and presence than
she had had in years, and put off giving him an immediate answer.
Eventually, though, she was clearly moved by his apparent transformation
and hyperbolic promises, and, although cautious, was ultimately persuaded to return to him and they were married. Of course, their relationship gradually drifted back to its original power balance. But, subsequently, whenever she became sufficiently alarmed at the intensity or
direction of his involvement elsewhere she threatened divorce or had an
affair. This was always enough to precipitate a recurrent suicidal crisis in
him which was invariably resolved through a joint reaffirmation of their
mutual love.

The moral of the tale is not that she was seduced and abandoned, for
that never happened. In fact, both seemed to thrive on the intensity of

their involvement. It was not a distant relationship but an extremely intimate one, the subacute pain and suffering notwithstanding. This love was precariously balanced in the direction of her subordination and his domination. She served him, investing all her hopes and plans in him, while he played the tempestuous, sensitive, suffering soul who longed to be true to her but was unable, by nature, to do so. However, the tension and intensity of the relationship was kept alive by their mutual knowledge that she might bolt.

A few of their intimate friends claimed to feel a little bewildered and off-center in their presence (though they were always extremely good company). There was something definitely wrong between them, and her fundamental subordination rankled some, but at the same time they always appeared to be more intensely involved than most other couples. And each openly professed a deep affinity for the other, a deep spiritual bond. He regretted her insistence on fidelity, but also cursed himself for his obsessive womanizing. She sincerely believed (or rationalized) that, despite her periodic suffering, they were bound by love and that he would eventually change. Their relationship was important to them both and they had a variety of strategies for preserving it, including their mutually reinforcing rationalizations for his behavior. And hers! For it must be added that part of their pact was to proclaim her sound mental health and superior nurturing skills. They both rationalized her submission as a kind of spirituality that placed her above the mundane concerns for fidelity and conventionality demanded by other women in other relationships.

In addition to their almost ritualized roles and rationalizations, they also contrived to have a good friend in attendance most of the time. This was sometimes his mentor, sometimes a soulful friend of one or the other, but always someone who cared for them both and perceived them as a loving couple. This third party was part confessor, part conciliator, but in whatever capacity served a strategic function: to validate the existence of their love should their own belief in it ever waiver. While this maneuver appears to triangulate the relationship, its mode was not Oedipal; that is, the third person was never a potential rival for either of them. Instead he (or she) served the roles of externalized conscience and guarantor of the relationship. A large part of the couple's psychological investment was in the "couple" itself, in the "we" they presented to the world.

This relationship illustrates a "successful" love dance of power. It is through a delicately balanced power relationship (sometimes with fluctuating power positions), that some intensive, passionate relationships are maintained for very long periods of time. It is as though the choreography of power is intuitively understood by both lovers, and the dance that emerges is nothing if not intricate.

The Existential and Developmental Links between Love and Power

The relationship between power and love is often an intimate one, the interconnection mandated by both the overlapping aims of love and power and by love's developmental history.

The aims of love and power are closely related though the means utilized by each are different. According to Hans Morgenthau, "Love and power both try to overcome loneliness, and the sense of man's insufficiency stemming from this loneliness, through duplication of his individuality." In both love and power, the Other is mobilized as an affirmation of the lover's subjectivity and will. It goes without saying that both are attempts to overcome his sense of weakness as well, and that both answer his dependency needs. Given the fact that the aims of love and power are so close yet can never be entirely achieved, it is inevitable that the one may be called upon to bolster the other. (Though it is not our primary concern here, it is also true, as Morgenthau suggests, that power seeks a modicum of love: "The political philosophies which emphasize the stability of power relationships, such as those of monarchies and autocracies, make a point of appealing to the love of the subject for the ruler.")

The intermingling of love and power is also facilitated by the developmental history of love. Affectionate bonding has its earliest roots in infancy and is closely tied to the child's state of dependency. In part, socialization of the child proceeds because the child fears the loss of love should he not comply with parental demands. Similarly, the adult lover often harbors the underlying belief that the beloved must be placated in order to insure her constancy. Because of the early link between affection and dependency, subsequent attachments often reflect the deep-rooted idea of an inherent power differential in love. Rieff takes this argument even further. According to him, because love is related to the "parental fact of domination," it follows that "Power is the father of love, and in love one follows the paternal example of power, in a relation that must include a superior and a subordinate." Moreover, he argues that while Christianity proclaimed the ultimate authority to be the source of love, "Freud discovered the love of authority." (Here, one sees part of the impetus to the birth of love in therapeutic situations, where the close relationship between love and the love of authority predisposes the patient to believe that she is in love with the therapist.) The lover may identify with either the all-powerful parent or the helpless child. Affection often originates along this power gradient—where is almost beside the point. One may overcome this proclivity, but only if he has the good fortune to become his own authority.

Thus far, I have primarily discussed the ways in which power acts adversely in love. However, as has been suggested, there is always, between all lovers, whether it is acknowledged or not, a period of jockeying for their respective positions in a balance of power. The balance of power establishes the relative priority of claims between the lovers. The subtle adjustment that results concerns not just matters of priority, but who cares about coming first and in which areas. (Nonetheless, the ultimate balance of power most often resides in the partner who is least fearful of losing the relationship.) It is when such a balance is disrupted (typically when one lover unilaterally desires to change the "rules") that a power struggle ensues. This may never happen and then the balance of power need never be articulated. It is only when an unspoken understanding about the balance of power is disrupted that the struggle for priority serves to destabilize love.

As for the more fundamental impulses to domination inherent in love, the need for conquest and possession can be restrained but not obliterated. The desire for possession appears to be an essential component of passionate love. What sometimes restrains the lover from the attempt at absolute possession is his intuition that it must fail. Then, too, the lover feels more than just the need for possession alone. He also cherishes the beloved and wants to surrender himself to her. He tries to relinquish his possessiveness and he tries to free himself from his own impulse to surrender. Passionate love oscillates around a point midway between these diametrically opposed but intimately connected impulses.

However, love is most likely to evolve and be sustained when both lovers are sovereign. That is one of the underlying themes of Chaucer's extremely complex tale of *The Wife of Bath*. In that story, a young knight in Arthur's court is sentenced to die because he has raped a girl. Arthur's queen commutes the death sentence on one condition: that within twelve months the knight tell the queen what it is that women most desire. The knight travels the country and receives diverse replies: women want riches, clothes, love, and many other things. But no two people agree on a single answer. Near the end of the year, fearing for his life, he happens upon an old hag. She promises to answer the question on condition that he do her bidding when his life is again his own. He agrees and gives the hag's answer to the Queen: women want sovereignty. The women gathered in the Court—wives, widows, and maids—all agree, and the knight's life is spared.

The hag then asserts her claim to the knight and orders him to marry her. Although loathing the old woman, he feels obliged to comply. She, however, notices his distaste for her and gives him two alternatives: she will be a faithful and loving wife as an old hag, or, if he prefers, she will be young and beautiful, but he will then have to take his chances regarding her fidelity. And how does the knight choose? Very wisely, in light of what he has just learned about what women really want: he leaves the choice to her. Granted her sovereignty, the hag responds generously; she transforms herself into a woman both beautiful and faithful. Thus he learns by his own experience the meaning of that "sovereinetee" that women desire above all things. And she, transformed by the trust he puts in her and the unconditional freedom of choice he allows her, becomes that which he had wanted her to be—but does so of her own free will.

The knight could be gratified in love only when he had been "educated" as to the true nature of women. He who had exercised an extreme form of sovereignty over a woman—rape—now grants total sovereignty himself, and is rewarded with a wife who then "obeyed him in everything that might give him pleasure or joy/And thus they lived to the end of their lives/In perfect joy."

CHAPTER EIGHT

Disillusionment

HAT MANY lovers long for is the perpetuation of the excitement of love's passionate phase. However, wishing does not always make it so. Love's critics often cite loss of intensity as its major hazard. Even friendly critics of love point to what they consider the inevitably transient nature of love's passionate phase, the excitement of courtship giving way—in the happiest of circumstances—to the serenity of commitment. Passion, then, is generally viewed as the introductory phase of love, a mere prelude to a more muted relationship, which can be described as affectionate bonding. There are some, myself among them, who believe that a passionate core can be maintained beyond the "falling in love" period, but, of course, that is far from the most common outcome. Alternately, and less happily, love may simply die when passion fades, swamped either by the boredom and restlessness that often ensue in the absence of intensity or by the sense of betrayal or fear of abandonment or anger that may follow the more fundamental loss of idealization or mutuality.

Initially passion draws on the excitement and anxiety generated by the uncertainty of the amorous quest. And here is the sorrow: for many lovers the pleasures of realization cannot match the thrills of the quest. But it is only human to want both; the lover craves the calm and peace of mutuality, intimacy, and commitment—love in pastel colors in a pastoral setting—at the same time that he hungers for the danger of life on the edge—electric love in a torrential landscape. He simultaneously longs for the safe haven and the bright lights, Jane Austen's drawing room and Emily Brontë's wild heath, quiet conversation and peak experience, serenity and the exhilaration of the chase, peace and strife, familiarity and mystery. The achievement of the one must, of necessity, compromise the other to some (though not always to a fatal) degree, and this contradiction of aims lends a restlessness to love, a sense that its complex and contradictory longings can never be completely satisfied. In attempting to mediate this contradiction, some lovers are able to find a source of excitement other than that of the perpetual quest for new objects. For them, the creative synthesis in love fosters a richness and complexity of internal experience that is at least as exciting as the thrills of novelty and uncertainty. These lovers, however, seem to be in the minority.

For many others, excitement appears to be necessarily grounded within either the riskiness and adventure of courtship, the mystery of the Other, or the intensity of sexual passion. But all these sources of excitement are unreliable. Courtship is by definition impermanent and fleeting, intimacy encroaches upon mystery, and lust is one of love's most vulnerable and often transient components.

Thus it is that many lovers who are able to avoid the extremes of surrender and domination still succumb to a different kind of longing for absolutes, leading to another set of disappointments and problems. And if idealization and harmonious mutuality—components of passion which are just as important as intensity—give way too, then love in all its manifestations may fade, to be replaced by either apathy or loathing. The apparently safe harbor may turn into a trap, a place in which one feels becalmed in a desultory, stifling atmosphere.

All these failures of feelings—the loss of idealization, mutuality, and excitement—are the result of the internal dynamics of love, its inherently contradictory aims and needs. But each of them can be neurotically elaborated as well, thus compounding the problems. Or, they may be minimized, thus enabling lovers to enjoy one of life's great pleasures: enduring love.

The Loss of Idealization

When love unravels, the lover's idealization of the beloved may give way to a radical de-idealization. Aristotle Onassis's disenchantment with his wife Jacqueline Bouvier Kennedy (as reported by Maria Callas's biographer) appears to have followed this pattern: " 'Coldhearted and shallow' is how he was now describing Jackie, who had only two years earlier been 'like a diamond, cool and sharp at the edges, fiery and hot beneath the surface.' "

Because romantic love is based on idealization which is by definition an act of imaginative exaggeration, it is believed by all love's skeptics that love will inevitably fade when confronted by the exigencies of daily life. It seems almost preordained that the lover, having idealized at the beginning, will come to de-idealize the beloved, and that the new realistic perception will spell the death of love. According to these analyses, the original idealization of the beloved is a distortion, a projection of the lover's fantasies of perfection onto the beloved. But, in truth, the fate of idealization is variable: it may be preserved, modulated, diminished, or utterly shattered.

Furthermore, the degree of idealization is itself quite variable. Sometimes the lover's idealization of his beloved clearly does represent an extreme overvaluation, sometimes a total misperception, and it is for this reason that love is often called "blind." But while such perceptual distortions are common, they are not ubiquitous. Insofar as the valuation of the beloved is not vastly exaggerated, idealization—hence love—can endure.

During the course of any relationship, there are invariably changes in the content and nature of idealization. Fitzgerald in *The Great Gatsby* gives us a wondrous account of the way not just people but things may be vested differently when lovers finally come together. At one point in the book, Gatsby has just gone to great lengths to arrange a meeting with Daisy, the great love of his life, who had married someone else while he was away in the army. She is now visiting him at the vast estate he had bought solely because its closeness to her home would allow him to gaze across the bay to a space he knew she occupied.

"If it wasn't for the mist we could see your home across the bay," said Gatsby. "You always have a green light that burns all night at the end of your dock."
Daisy put her arm through his abruptly, but he seemed absorbed in what he had just said. Possibly it had occurred to him that the colossal significance of that light had now vanished forever. Compared to the great distance that had separated him from Daisy it had seemed very near to her, almost touching her. It had seemed as close as a star to the moon. Now it was again a green light on a dock. His count of enchanted objects had diminished by one.

This de-investment is in the service of love. But others may diminish love.

Even in the most successful of love relationships, idealization is not static. The lover feels waves of hostility towards the beloved, sometimes entirely irrational, sometimes in response to the most insignificant of transgressions. These usually take the form of fleeting de-idealizations, flashes of negative, possibly even degrading feelings and thoughts about the beloved. In happy love, these thoughts, though momentarily unsettling, are usually quickly dismissed. But what causes such fluctuations in perception and feeling? In part, de-idealization seems implicit in idealization, awaiting only the first outbreak of anger at the beloved or the introduction of some new piece of knowledge about her. In part it has to do with the latent anger existing in all love, which can perhaps be explained as the lover's defense against the threat to autonomy which is invariably posed by love's thralldom. Or resentment may be the expression of the lover's latent envy of the beloved's good qualities, those very virtues which drew him to her.

In *A Sport and a Pastime*, Salter catches that sudden feeling of disillusionment and then the equally sudden restitution of admiration. The lover, Dean, is musing about his beloved French girl:

Dean is a little bored. It's an effort to speak French. He's weary of it, and English is no better, hers is so uneven. Her mistakes begin to be irritating, and besides, she seems disposed to talk only of banal things: shoes, her work at the office. When she is silent, he glances at her and smiles. She doesn't respond. She senses it, he thinks. Suddenly, he feels transparent. The eyes that return his somewhat mechanical glance are the eyes of a knowing child, and all the evasions, poses, devices become foolish. The windshield has faint streaks of blue like air. As he looks through, at the road ahead, he is conscious of her calm appraisal. She understands effortlessly. Life is all quite clear to her. She is one with it. She moves in it like a fish, never wondering if it has a bottom, shores, worlds above it . . .

Such waxings and wanings of idealization are common to all lovers. Within the space of a single evening, how often we may feel a mixture of pride in the beloved, embarrassment, annoyance, boredom, and affection.

Quite different are the radical de-idealizations that signify the end of love. The potential for de-idealization, always present, can be catalyzed by any fundamental shift in the lover's feelings, whether motivated by hurt, disappointment, anger, or an attraction to someone else. Anna Karenina, after meeting the dashing Vronsky, returns to St. Petersburg where she notices that her husband's ears seem much more prominent and his habit of cracking his knuckles more exaggerated. And so it is that our perceptions tend to follow our feelings. (This is no less true of our self-perceptions: Some mornings we look in the mirror and find ourselves ugly and other mornings quite attractive.)

Sometimes de-idealization may be precipitated by the discovery of previously unknown shortcomings in the beloved. One shrewd but scrupulous businessman's love was destroyed when his beloved revealed to him that she gave kickbacks to buyers. He was unable to marry her; she, in turn, was startled by his rejection since she assumed that her behavior was consonant with his code of ethics. A homosexual man was shocked to discover that his beloved hated women; this became the fatal flaw around which de-idealization—and then rejection—crystallized. In the case of

Onassis, it has been suggested that his fundamental disenchantment with Jacqueline had two immediate causes: ". . . as Jackie spent an estimated $1.5 million in the first year of her marriage, removed his favorite allegorical friezes from the *Christina* and completely, extravagantly and by no means always to his taste, redecorated the Skorpios house, Onassis began to feel invaded and used." But "the turning point came . . . when all the letters Jackie had written to her former escort, Roswell Gilpatric, fell into the hands of an autograph dealer and were published around the world before they were returned to Gilpatric under the terms of a court order." Though the letters revealed nothing about Onassis, they suggested a degree of intimacy between Jackie and Gilpatric that Onassis apparently found extremely distasteful.

Sometimes de-idealization may be set in motion when changed circumstances show the beloved in a different light. (Lovers prone to over-idealization are particularly vulnerable to such disappointments.) For example, one woman, who had always admired her father for his well-acknowledged contributions to the local community, fell in love for the first time in the 1970s with a successful musician. He seemed to her to have the same kind of vitality and imaginative engagement with the people around him as her adored and idealized father; and thus she pursued her beloved, yearned for him and forgave him his infidelities and indiscretions, experiencing it as a great victory when she finally persuaded him to marry her. But fifteen years later, her opinion of her husband was remarkably changed, admiration and idealization having worn disastrously thin. Was the decline in her feelings, as she experienced it, merely because her husband turned out to be an essentially cold man? Or was it also because musical tastes had apparently changed so much that the current market was not the best showcase for her husband's particular talents and musical idiom? He dined out more on his past successes than on any current ones. In any case, her inner need to idealize someone did not diminish; it simply got redirected to a series of different people. To her friends, the increasing estrangement between husband and wife seemed as much a product of her exaggerated need to attach herself to someone of considerable prominence as it was of her disappointment at her discovery of her husband's emotional limitations.

The common fate of idealization in love—its diminution over time— tells us something in general about the failure of imagination that ultimately affects most lovers. But de-idealization may also tell us something specific about the failings of a particular lover. One divorced man fell in love with a series of remarkable women, each of whom he idealized for her uniqueness and achievements, but each of whom was past the child-bearing age or unwilling to have more children. At the threshold of the altar, he invariably discovered he could not give up the prospect of being a father once again. The first time it happened it seemed entirely plausible that he was genuinely overtaken by a sudden realization of his wish for more children, and that this insight dampened his enthusiasm for his beloved. If this were the whole story, one might have expected that he would, in the future, have looked to younger women. When his pattern continued virtually unchanged, his friends came to suspect either that he harbored some underlying fantasy of revenge against women, or that he feared sustained intimacy—but whatever the cause it was one that invariably spoiled his fabled romances.

Sometimes rapid de-idealization is clearly neurotic. We all know of individuals who are prone to repeated intense infatuations accompanied by exaggerated idealizations. These are subject to radical de-idealization and subsequent withdrawal of love, so sudden that the love has ended long before the lover can have come by any real knowledge of his beloved.

If the idealization is markedly exaggerated, the overvaluation has neurotic determinants, and the subsequent disillusionment is likely to be as exaggerated as the initial idealization. Psychoanalysts are familiar with the kind of extreme underlying ambivalence that gives rise to such oscillations, rendering the idealization of the beloved vulnerable to the massive incursion of rage in response to even slight provocations. The textbook example of overidealization and the problems that follow in its wake found in Thomas Hardy's *The Well Beloved* has been explored by the psychoanalysts Werman and Jacobs. The protagonist of this novel, as a child, first falls in love with a little blue-eyed girl of about eight or so. Even in the first enraptured stage of his crush he could not help noticing that the girl's flaxen hair, coming down to her shoulders, attempted to curl "but ignominiously failed!" This became the fatal flaw through which he came to de-idealize her. His oscillation of feelings in this early episode was prophetic of the pattern that would characterize his subsequent loves; the girl with the flaxen hair was followed by many other well-beloved ones, all of whom were at first extravagantly admired despite some evident "flaw," and then radically de-idealized.

There are several problems, most often interrelated, that make some lovers vulnerable to sharp devaluations of their love objects. The lover may be impelled by the reactivation of anger connected to former love objects (a chronic ambivalence) or by a lack of self-esteem which is projected onto the beloved with whom he identifies.

Projection of the lover's own self-devaluation onto the beloved is one of the most common of all factors in the disequilibration of a love relationship. Perhaps the easiest of all mechanisms to understand, it is best summed up in Groucho Marx's famous dictum: "I wouldn't join any club that would have me as a member." Translated to the realm of love, this simply means that if the lover has sufficiently low self-esteem, he regards anyone who truly loves him as by definition deficient, wanting in taste. I know a woman who describes the surface manifestation of this kind of dilemma in her own life, though without fully understanding its implications. She makes a joke of her disregard of her current lover: "I don't know why I don't love him. He's completely devoted and he'll spend three hours on oral sex. I need somebody to make trouble, give me a hard time. He's too easy." To prove his worth, he would have to be reticent, hard to get, hard to please, and less eager to please her. This same mechanism, of course, accounts for the romantic allure of those who appear somewhat unapproachable or reserved, who possess what one might call the attractiveness of narcissistic distancing.

One man, kind to a fault, found himself excessively critical only of his wife and, before her, of his first wife. He came to understand that he aimed his harsh judgment only at himself and those few intimates whom he regarded as part of himself. (It's always hard to live with someone who has a harsh superego; such people seldom can restrain their punitive impulses towards themselves *or* their loved ones.) The self-hate and judgmentalism that characterize those ruled by a primitive, harsh superego have led many theorists of love, most notably Erich Fromm, to the conclusion that healthy self-love is a prerequisite for on-going mutual love. Serious fluctuations in self-esteem and self-evaluation have the potential to destabilize the healthy idealization of the beloved that is a prerequisite of ongoing love.

There are other root causes of de-idealization. Sometimes when idealization comes to grief, it is in response to real changes, but change within the lover's psyche rather than any change in the beloved. For example, with the advent of the women's movement, some women who had previously admired their take-charge husbands came to resent their husbands' inability to share the decision making. A problem may also emerge if the lover manifestly values one accurately perceived quality but, in fact, unbeknownst to himself, needs another, as is the case, for example, with the lover who idealizes the beloved for her independence but is fundamentally threatened by it.

De-idealization may affect not only the beloved, but also the "we," the joint identity that the couple has created. This joint identity is sometimes so concordant with the aspirations of each lover's ego ideal that it provides the matrix for a lasting mutual love, but the pride and pleasure invested in the "we" may also give way to sharp devaluation and de-idealization. When married lovers encounter the emergence of psychological problems in one of their children this may prove the destabilizing event that precipitates a break. Very often parents attribute their children's difficulties to a negative dynamic between them, one they believe is implicit in the "we," or they may reject the internalized concept of the "we" altogether and project all blame onto the partner. Either scenario can result in the complete erosion of the pride previously invested in the union.

Illness can be the disruptive factor between previously stable, happy lovers. It can lead to an altered perception not just of the afflicted lover, but of the relationship itself. This is a frequent occurrence, for example, when a militantly self-sufficient man has a heart attack. While many couples readily adjust, some pairs are pulled asunder by the necessary restructuring of the "we" during that period of time when the husband is incapacitated and the wife must care for him (or vice versa).

Sometimes, too, lovers have specific aspirations for themselves as a couple. These aspirations often find their proving ground on the social plane, where the couple's joint popularity and social mobility confirm their value as a unit. Thus the social world is the field in which the couple, the "we," can sustain positive reinforcement, or, alternatively, insults, slights, and disparagement. A negative evaluation by their peer couples can create a profoundly negative effect on the lovers' evaluation of themselves as a couple. The blame for the deficiencies (real or imagined) may be projected solely onto the partner, at the expense of the lover's idealization of both the beloved and the relationship, the "we."

Sometimes idealization is at risk because it was so weak to start with; in those instances, "love" is more related to the wish to be tended to, looked after, adored, than to any adoration of the beloved. Then one might say that *romantic* love never took firm hold in the first place. H. G. Wells describes a kind of love unrelated to idealization of the Other: "With me the Lover-Shadow never became, as it becomes in many cases, a sought-after saint or divinity. My innate self conceit and the rapid envelopment and penetration of my egotism by socialistic and politically creative ideas was too powerful ever to admit the thought of subordinating my *persona* to the Lover-Shadow. This fair and lovely person, who was to be my protagonist, was to be friendly and understanding. . . . I do not recall that . . . I had any dream or thoughts of my finding something perplexing in her and studying to understand her." Moreover he claimed to recognize the same impulse in Rebecca West when she urged him to leave his wife and marry her. " 'Jane is a wife,' I argued, 'but you could never be a wife, you want a wife yourself—you want sanity and care and courage and patience behind you just as much as I do.' " (Despite his intransigent insistence on his due as a man and genius, it is remarkable that, in attributing a desire for a "wife" to Rebecca West, he anticipates one of the slogans of the woman's movement—"I want a wife"—by forty years.)

Insofar as relationships resemble those Wells describes, they are based predominantly on a one-sided longing for admiration and tender nurturance. They often prove extremely vulnerable because the idealization of the beloved is so fragile, the estimation of her worth so trifling, that the value of her admiration is itself severely compromised. Insofar as a man believes his beloved to be inferior, her esteem cannot warm him.

To the degree that the lover's fantasies are of being loved and catered to, not of mutual love, he might be considered narcissistic. Sometimes such narcissism appears to be the product not of personal pathology, but of gender socialization. Men have been socialized to expect their lover to be nurse, mother, wife, mistress, and muse; everything, that is, except a subject, a transcendent person in her own right. But this is clearly not mutual or passionate love as it is generally understood. Although relationships involving marked degrees of domination or subservience may sometimes be extremely intense, the inequality of the lovers makes the idealization one-sided (if it exists at all) and diminishes the possibility of the kind of mutuality that is an integral part of ongoing passionate love. There may be another kind of mutuality, in which one lover "services" the Other and both, presumably, obtain some kind of satisfaction from the transaction. But by and large, relationships based on a power differential of any magnitude are conventional and tepid, at least on the part of the dominant partner. Here the problem is not lack of mutuality, but lack of exhilaration, a failure to be absorbed in the other, hence the impossibility of feeling liberated from the self into another, superior, identity (either that of the Other or the couple).

Men are not the only ones who sometimes overlook certain "limitations" in the beloved in favor of other priorities and thus fail to achieve full idealization of their beloved, at the expense of passion. The following excerpts from actress Evelyn Keyes's autobiography detail some of her ambivalence about Mike Todd at the inception of their romance.

This Mike Todd was most entertaining during my Hollywood stay, but nothing more than that. Who could take him for a steady diet?

He talked of marriage immediately. "I got love," he would say, "what else can I do." Though I admired his whirling dervish ways and jumping *joie de vivre*, he wasn't really the "artist" type I was inclined toward, the creator of things rather than the hirer. And that eternal cigar. The atrocious grammar. "Anyways," he would say. The repetition of certain phrases. "Walk around money." "He's around 49th Street" (somebody's age). . . .

But none of that was the real reason why I got caught in his web. For a daddy-prone person like me, Mike the planner, the organizer, the doer, was made to order. It was too easy to let this dynamo make all the arrangements; he was doing it anyway: where to go, when, how, tickets, reservations, cars. In no time at all he had taken the place of the studio I had relied on, and was missing terribly. Big Daddy had returned.

So she got herself a daddy, and seemed to think him a good bargain. When Todd later rejected her in favor of Elizabeth Taylor, she claimed to take it hard. "When I wasn't looking, I had been delivered a knockout punch. I felt jilted." Nonetheless, she did seem able to look at the positive side: she announced that she felt relieved never to have to hear his colorful but crude language again.

It is the nature of all valuations, including idealization, to change over the course of time. But this does not necessarily mean that idealization must diminish. In many relationships it does; but in many others the idealization evolves, changes, and ripens. One may be disappointed, but one may also become more deeply appreciative of the beloved as gratifications and shared pleasures accrue. Even the course of a downward spiraling relationship can be reversed when, in crisis, one partner puts aside his accumulated resentments and rises to the occasion, thus evoking the other's admiration.

The course of the relationship, and the degree to which each partner is able to idealize the other, depends on many factors that may change over the years. The outcome depends not only on the individual health or neurosis of the lover, but on the external events that impinge upon the lovers separately and together, and, most important, on the "fit" between them, the question of whether over the long haul their wishes, needs, and values (both conscious and unconscious) continue to prove more compatible and mutually reinforcing than conflictual. As an example, we might take the following hypothetical case and write three different denouements. We start with a sublimely happy struggling couple. The wife is quite fulfilled as a kind of earth mother, scrimping and saving, making do, never complaining, and sponsoring her husband's creative potential. The husband, of course, is extremely grateful, holding her up as a paragon to all their friends. They truly idealize and idolize one another.

In the first case, their great happiness is finally ruined by the husband's success, preeminence, and affluence. On the conscious level, the wife comes to deplore his growing materialism and defection from the pure life; but subconsciously, she is succumbing to envy of her husband's realization of his creative potential and dismay over the obsolescence of her accustomed role as sole support of and believer in her husband. Moreover, with the new freedom from the duties of her previous role, she may now be forced into an entirely unwelcome questioning of her own purpose in life. The marriage ends. In her next marriage she is careful (unconsciously) to pick someone whose creative struggle is ultimately limited by his potential; she and her new husband live contentedly on the fringes of the artistic, literary world where she is once again doted on as the good wife and she dotes (in turn) upon her new husband as an unrecognized, uncorrupted creative genius.

In the second denouement, the couple's happiness is also ruined but for a different reason. The wife is extremely happy at her husband's success and rejoices both for him and for the new opportunities that his success affords them both. But the husband, now less needy, reevaluates his wife negatively. Retroactively he feels humbled, infantilized by her nurturance, and therefore angry at her. He wants no one around to remind him of leaner, needier days. Now he finds her limited and second best and longs for someone more worthy of his newfound stature.

But in the third denouement, both wife and husband rejoice at their great good fortune. He is authentically grateful for her help and she genuinely fulfilled. Now that it is no longer necessary for her to spend so much time stretching so little so far, her creative energies find a new outlet in some worthwhile community project, and he admires her even more for her authentic selflessness. For them, their mutual appreciation grows, and their initial idealization of one another evolves into an even richer more accurate perception of each other's real strengths and virtues.

There is, of course, an enormous range in the nature and fate of idealizations in love. At one extreme are the unrealistic and primitive idealizations, at the other the more differentiated and realistic kind. To the degree that idealizations are unrealistic or neurotic, they are more likely to break down over time, and to generate a good deal of rage as they do so. But, as in the example of the good wife and her creatively limited second husband, a neurotic fit may have viability over the long haul and insure the continuation of mutual idealization.

While "mature" idealizations tend to endure, they, too, can waver, if two "healthy" lovers happen into a crisis that tests their values and disturbs their arrangements. For my grandfather, who passionately loved his second wife (though not his first), whom he married when he was sixty-five (lying about his age and claiming to be only sixty), there was no decline in his feeling for her until some thirty-four years later. When he was ninety-nine and still running his second-hand bookstore, his by then ailing eighty-year-old wife wanted to stop cooking and keeping kosher and move to an old-age home. His unflagging admiration for her womanly virtues was almost shattered. (No more apple strudel!) Thirty-four years of idyllic love gave way to recriminations and accusations of bad faith. The crisis was only resolved by a marriage counselor. My grandparents moved to the home, where they continued to keep kosher with massive assistance from my grandmother's daughters, and my grandfather got a driver to take him to work every day. Most important, their love was restored. My grandfather died a year later, and his truly beloved quickly declined into senility.

The Loss of Harmony and Mutuality

In the beginning, lovers create an illusion of *perfect* harmony. Part of what they give each other is a surfeit of tenderness and nurturance, expressed either physically (through petting, stroking, or the administering of tea and chicken soup) or emotionally (through supportiveness, spontaneous sympathy, understanding, and approval) or in both ways. They convey to one another that each values the Other's subjective needs and desires, and in fact, considers them central to their shared world—not inconvenient, irrelevant, or irritating. In harmonious interaction, the lover feels he has transcended any unilateral craving for passive gratification, that he and the beloved are naturally attuned to each other's feelings and wishes and need only respond to them spontaneously. And so lovers dwell on the rightness of their "fit," sometimes finding their physical relationship emblematic of their emotional unity, as when, for example, she says to him: "I fit perfectly into the crook of your arm," and so on.

Paradoxically, these aspirations to unity are sometimes most threatening when they come closest to being fulfilled. Exquisite mutuality may prove too much of a good thing, for it carries with it the danger of appearing stifling and intrusive to the beloved (or feeling invaded oneself), and of reinvoking parental imagoes and the incestuous inhibitions that accompany them. Such dangers can be deadly to love; however, it is relatively rare when mutuality becomes so perfect as to be threatening.

More often, the lovers' expectation of continuing mutuality and harmony are doomed to disappointment. The sense of perfect harmony between lovers often proves as illusory and fragile as that to which it harkens back—the oceanic oneness of mother and infant, the natural interplay between the good mother (or father) and the young child. Such aspirations are generally frustrated because of the inevitable limitations of the beloved, or the contradictory nature of the lover's implicit wishes and demands, or simply the existential limitations to any human being's power to completely fulfill another's wishes. Consequently, over time the lover loses hope that his desires will be gratified by the beloved (while holding on to the belief that they can be, perhaps, by someone else) and he becomes disenchanted with the beloved. Finally, the lovers' hopes are clouded by their knowledge of the finiteness of all things—love and life itself. Writing of Tolstoy's Levin, the happy lover in *Anna Karenina,* Troyat says, "In the early days of his marriage he thinks he has gone beyond the reach of sorrow and fear. But love is a frail bulwark against the spectre of death." And Levin, a stand-in for Tolstoy, ultimately looks to a religious resolution of his existential angst.

Sometimes, even in the idyllic phase, the fantasy of perfect mutuality goes unrealized. In such cases, the initial passion can never blossom into true love. H. G. Wells, in his autobiography, provides a marvelous example. (Given his insistent need to engage in passionate encounters, and his inability to sustain one, his memoirs are a treasure trove for illuminating the fatal flaws in love.) Speaking of his interlude with Dorothy Richardson, he reminisces:

She wanted me to explore her soul with wonder and delight. But a vein of evasive ego-centered mysticism in her has always made her mentally irritating to me; she had an adorable dimple in her smile; she was most interestingly hairy on her body, with fine golden hairs, and then—she would begin intoning the dull clever things that filled that shapely, rather large, flaxen head of hers.

Not only was he unwilling to explore her soul, but he was also somewhat contemptuous of what he viewed as her pretentiousness. There was a double failure, both of idealization and mutuality. Such a relationship, with such different expectations and priorities on the part of the two participants, could never soar. No mutual aims could be realized, no real harmony achieved. And, as we already know from his reflections on his relationship with Rebecca West, however much he might be carried away on the currents of passion, his abiding wish was for someone to take care of him and minister to him, not the other way around.

Even when mutuality and harmony appear well established in the early intensity of a love affair, they cannot be sustained in their perfect state. And I believe it is this failure which is the most serious enemy of love, not, as is commonly believed to be the case, the taming and domestication of the passions that follow upon their institutionalization. That is, routinization is less of a danger to ongoing love than the failure of the lovers' sense of reciprocity and mutuality.

Over time, even among the happiest of lovers, there are two almost universal threats to complete and harmonious mutuality: the act of sex and the birth of a child. While both sexual union and the birth of a child can be profound symbols and enactments of mutuality (even merger), paradoxically, they also present a powerful potential for disharmony.

Sex gives lovers the enormous gift of collapsing the tension between body and soul that each feels. When love claims sexuality as a means to merger, the body is made to serve the soul instead of tugging at it to remind it of the bestial. If sex becomes the instrument by which one soul touches another, the body is vindicated. Through it, the lover validates not only his own body, but that of the beloved, which is but the material expression of her soul. But potential discord continues to lurk within the lover's sexuality.

One of the problems that many lovers face is the fact that their sexualities are not well matched. Consequently sexual encounters, which psychologically ought to be the expression par excellence of perfect harmony—the physical union symbolizing the longed-for spiritual union— turn out instead to be the occasion for the discovery of irreconcilable differences, or at least differences that require rational mediation and "work." Among male homosexuals, one occasionally hears that a successful union is undone by the fact of sexual preferences that don't mesh, for example, both partners preferring to be recipients in anal intercourse. Among heterosexual couples, such differences may be less dramatic, but are probably more widespread.

As more has been learned about female sexuality, it has become better known that men and women may also have quite different sexual preferences. Some women like oral sex, though their partners do not, and vice versa. Men and women often have different sexual rhythms. Men may not have enough staying power, or women may require too much time, depending on how you look at it. Even when lovers are sincerely dedicated to each other's pleasure, and willing to stay their own satisfaction in order to please their partner, these differences and sacrifices are affronts to the fantasy of complete affinity and perfect harmony. They contradict the sense of spontaneous mutual accord and are the concrete evidence of divisions in taste and temperament. This is why the very notion of having to "work" at sex is so unsettling to many lovers.

But the problem of sexuality is larger than any simple difference in preference would suggest. There is a potential for pre-emptoriness and possessiveness in sexuality that may result in love-making which has none of the feeling of gentle communion that mutuality requires. And some individuals' sexualities are infused with a commitment to aggression, or to perverse strains, that conflicts with the fantasied twinship of soulful union.

Moreover, despite its transcendent function in love, sex is so clearly of the body and the body is always problematic when we aspire to true transcendence. In part, this is because of its connection to excrement. For some of us the body is ludicrous if not downright disgusting, and sex is contaminated by our negative feelings about the body. Sex, though it yields so much pleasure, is not immune to the negativity the body invokes. Freud, paraphrasing Napoleon's dictum that geography is destiny, postulated that anatomy is destiny. Although this phrase is generally misunderstood (it is widely and erroneously believed to refer to female "castration"), Freud was explicit in his meaning. The shame of sexuality is that the sexual organs are intertwined with the organs of excretion. The transcendence toward which sex strives is compromised by reminders of excretion. Swift has poignantly and humorously captured this dilemma:

> And yet, I dare confide in you;
> So, take my Secret, and adieu.
> No wonder how I lost my wits;
> Oh! Caelia, Caelia, Caelia shits.

The problem of the body is larger still. Our animal, mortal nature is an affront to our human spiritual nature, for in the end we all perish. Ernest Becker, who sees fear of death as the central motivating force in man's life, writes in *The Denial of Death:* "Man is literally split in two: he has an awareness of his own splendid uniqueness in that he sticks out of nature with a towering majesty, and yet he goes back into the ground a few feet in order blindly and dumbly to rot and disappear forever." Sex, even when it seems to liberate the self, may also remind us of our irreparably animal nature.

The birth of a child can spell the end of harmony as decisively (and paradoxically) as sex sometimes does. That a child should prove a threat to the passion of a union is of course ironic, since a child is desired as the very embodiment of the merger fantasy. Sometimes, particularly in a first pregnancy, both partners do indeed revel in their common venture. But even then, the pregnancy generally belongs more to her than to him. Moreover, shortly after the child's birth, one of the parents (more often the mother) usually falls in love with the child. The beloved no longer comes first, his needs no longer take priority. He may adore the woman in her maternity, but she is now separate from him. Even when the new father is able to transcend his feelings of exile and exclusion, the new mother may inadvertently place another burden on him. She expects him to love the child with the same intensity and singleness of purpose that she does. To the degree that he is unable to do so, she begins to regard him as selfish. To the degree that she insists his feelings ought to mirror hers, he begins to find her narcissistically preoccupied and controlling. The residues of an old Oedipal wound are reawakened in this new triangular configuration. Jealousy and envy complicate his feelings. The previous mutuality of desires and priorities recedes. And once mutuality is disrupted in one or more areas, the dissonance may spread to still others—often to the conjugal bed. It is very common for the birth of a child to precipitate a period of disharmonious love-making or even a more fundamental estrangement, as we know from the frequent references to that fact in both life and literature.

In Grace Paley's short story, "A Woman, Young and Old," a mother imputes the cause of her husband's defection to the birth of their children. Her daughter remembers her mother's insistence on blaming *her:*

My father, I have been told several hundred times, was a really stunning Latin. Full of *savoir-faire, joie de vivre,* and so forth. They were deeply and irrevocably in love till Joanna and I revoked everything for them. Mother doesn't want me to feel rejected, but she doesn't want to feel rejected herself, so she says *I* was too noisy and cried every single night. And then Joanna was the final blight and wanted titty all day *and* all night.

In another of Paley's stories, an abandoned wife recalls the exact moment when all her happiness was shattered:

It was like trying to move back into the dry mouth of a nightmare to remember that the last day I was happy was the middle of a week in March, when I told my husband I was going to have Linda. Barbara was five months old to the hour. The boys were three and four. I had to tell him. It was the last day with anything happy about it.

She anticipated, correctly as it turned out, that the news would push her husband out of her life.

Even when it presents no affront to mutuality, birth, like sex, may still cast a shadow onto love. It, too, is of the body and therefore a reminder of death. Because birth is of the flesh, sorrow intermingles with joy. Many parents are shocked to discover, in the midst of the joy they feel in being new parents, that the baby in their arms gives them intimations of their own mortality, the baby reminding them that they are but links in the great chain of being, the unending cycle of birth and death. In our child's beginning, we sometimes intuit our own end. The reminder of death dilutes the pure joy we might otherwise experience.

In any ongoing relationship, there are more than ample opportunities for failures of empathy. Inevitably, one or the other lover comes to feel misunderstood (on however minimal a provocation). Something happens which leads the lover to feel profoundly insulted; he takes umbrage and sulks. The lover waits for the beloved to acknowledge his wound, indignant that she does not intuit both his suffering and its cause, too proud and hurt to complain. He tumbles even further into despair; even at night lying on the bed beside his beloved there is no surcease to his anguish. Frustrations, wounding slights, stinging off-hand observations, broken hopes—all these prey on his sense of harmony. This deep hurt is compounded by the realization that his soul is opaque to the Other; in the end, he fears, she will never know him.

Perhaps even worse is the hurt when the lover has been understood, but not cherished, as in the case where the beloved intuits his feelings quite accurately yet chooses to ignore them, whether because she is momentarily tired and drained or has come to experience the lover as perpetually needy. Sometimes one lover fails the other out of his own neurotic inhibitions, as, for example, when one man, terrified of illness and death, "forgot" to meet his wife when she was scheduled for a breast biopsy. His wife never truly forgave him and began to find more and more evidence of his self-protectiveness and selfishness.

Betrayal may be purposeful, but most often it is inadvertent. Raising children, for example, presents ample opportunities for such betrayals. In Judith Rossner's novel *August,* Lulu and Nathan's marriage was intertwined with his adopting her daughter Sascha. After Lulu and Nathan were married, Lulu used to say "that Nathan had adopted Sascha before marrying Sascha's mother, and while this was a jest, it had been clear Sascha was an important part of the package." They were a threesome. But much later when Lulu became pregnant and Sascha, in a rage, asked to spend the summer with her *real* father, Nathan was devastated. "He was staring at his adopted daughter in an agony of disbelief. There were tears in his eyes. His lower lip was trembling." He was to find himself even more wounded because Lulu promptly replied to Sascha "that this isn't the time or place for our first conversation about your father." As soon as the words were out of her mouth, Lulu knew what had transpired. "She didn't have to look at Nathan to see the betrayal and reproach that would be in his eyes. After twelve years of having been folded away neatly in a box, the truth had sprung up out of the box and punched them all in the nose." And so, one of the consoling illusions of the marriage was inadvertently shattered.

Some degree of mutual betrayal is almost inevitable in every love relationship, inherent in the conflict between each lover's simultaneous need for mutuality and self-realization (self-assertion). In the early stages of love, the conflict temporarily disappears because the process of falling in love and establishing a new identity as a couple is compelling enough to absorb the lovers entirely. The joint project, that of establishing the "we," takes priority over all other projects, and, by definition it serves both to establish mutuality and to facilitate each lover's self-realization as part of a couple. But once the "we" is established, a need for new joint projects is born.

Mutuality is an exhausting and time-consuming labor of love. Insofar as the lovers' separate commitments are demanding, the time each lavishes on the other is at risk. It is hard to discover that point at which separation, instead of making the heart grow fonder, backfires. But once that point is reached, the lovers sense withdrawal and a vicious circle of self-preoccupation and mistrust may be set in motion.

Then, too, as so often happens, the lovers' outside interests may be intrinsically at cross purposes. Very real contradictions between the aims of mutuality and autonomy may surface. For example, a woman may feel that her lover's apparently single-minded professional ambitions prevent his paying enough attention to her, while he may feel that his ambitions are for both of them. He, in turn, may feel deprived if she is absorbed by her work and does not give him the support he feels he needs to accomplish his goals. (And, of course, the superficial conflicts are often fueled by unconscious competition, jealousy, and envy. Thus, neurotic predispositions serve to intensify the inevitable conflicts of coupling, and sometimes convert mild problems into intractable ones.) Success may divide lovers, and failure as well.

Insofar as the lovers' separate aims or wishes must inevitably conflict, each couple needs to develop some automatic mechanisms to work out differences. Otherwise, the mutuality of happy love will give way to the irritations and hurts that arise from conflicting sentiments and priorities.

Consider for example, the deterioration in Ruth Benedict's marriage as she describes it in her diaries. The beginning of her marriage appears to have been particularly ecstatic, coming as it did after a fractured childhood and before she found her life's work in anthropology. Benedict writes in her diary in 1914, after she had been married about a year:

I have so much, so much—life seems so incomparably rich these days. I have been happy, happy this summer, as I did not think it was given to be unless one were very young or very blind. We have had love and companionship.

But her marriage, begun in high hopes, ended in disillusionment. Scarcely six years later, she writes:

There is good in me, and Oh! there is great good in Stanley. And we've both of us a decent measure of self-control. Why must we go on hurting each other so cruelly? . . . he's taken me one for all—the intimacy is proved, established; all he asks is to keep an even tenor. And, knowing this, for years I can keep away from subjects which disrupt the quiet—my own ambitions. . . . But I'm made on the exactly antithetical scheme—it is my necessary breath of life to understand and expression is the only justification of life that I can feel without prodding. The greatest relief I know is to have put something in words, no matter if it's as stabbing as this is to me; and even to have him say cruel things to me is better than an utter silence about his viewpoint year in and year out. —And so it's insoluble—a wanton cruelty to him no less than to me. So we grow more and more strangers to the other—united only by gusts of feeling that grow to seem more and more emptiness in our lives, not part and parcel of them; and by an intolerable pity for each other as human beings cruelly tormented.

Love can be seriously damaged by mutual accusations of selfishness. Each lover feels that he has sacrificed and that the sacrifice has gone unappreciated. An accusation to that effect often elicits the retort that the original gift or sacrifice was not made in love at all, but only for concrete gain, as a means of manipulation, or with the explicit expectation of a quid pro quo. In the midst of these quickly escalating charges, one lover may sense that the divergence between them may be nearing the point of no return, when a final rupture is inevitable. The interim period, when the point of no return is approached but not yet reached, may be quite extended. But once one lover recognizes the danger, the impulse is to escalate, to put the beloved to a final test of his love. Some of the most dramatic conflagrations between lovers take place at this juncture, and these have about them the high stakes and deadly determination of Russian roulette. Instead of sacrifices, impetuous and imperious demands are now made: "If you really loved me, you would disinherit your daughter" or "cancel your trip" or "tell so and so to go to hell." The lover anxiously waits to see if he has indeed pushed the beloved past the point of no return or whether his will has prevailed and the relationship has been preserved.

The rage triggered by the frustrations of disappointment may be freely vented upon the beloved. It may coalesce with rage from an earlier developmental period, particularly the rage experienced toward a frustrating parent—hence the lovers' often accurate mutual accusations: "You're treating me as though I'm your father (or mother)."

In an attempt to redress a perceived injustice, the lover may not be content merely to vent his anger, but may avenge himself by beginning a sexual affair, which simultaneously reconfirms autonomy and validates his discontent with his partner. ("Now I realize she never really understood me.") This diverts attention from the real issues and trivializes the love relationship. Or a lover may withhold sex as another expression of power vis-à-vis the Other.

There is another kind of triangulation to which lovers may resort, one informed not by erotics but by recourse to an external authority. One or the other lover takes his complaints to a sympathetic friend or listener, very often an older and trusted member of the extended family, sometimes a marriage counselor. The purpose is to take the outside judge's pronouncement back into the dyad, sometimes merely to bolster the lover's own position, though sometimes, of course, the resort to an external authority represents a genuine attempt to assess where the responsibility for the "mess" actually lies. In the process of seeking help, the unhappy lover relinquishes some of the couple's sacred secrets and the union is invariably compromised to some degree. Nonetheless, such triangulation may prove beneficial, even necessary, from time to time. But it surely changes the fundamental nature of the dyad's boundary with the external world; the "we" is no longer a closed entity, its boundary is permeable. In the unhappiest situations, the nature of the lovers' relationship changes so radically that they cease to be an adult "we"; they are no longer authentically seeking help, but have regressed to the level of squabbling, competitive siblings in search of adult mediation and intervention or validation.

If one lover is disaffected, disappointed but out of touch with his feelings, he may simply withdraw, become apathetic, depressed or bored. Some lovers are so frightened by the prospect of falling out of love that they deny any negative feelings or thoughts. Under such circumstances they may manifest signs of physical revulsion towards the beloved, and though apparently unconnected with any underlying feelings of unhappiness, these should be taken seriously as possible warnings that something is amiss. Or the discomfort may be displaced onto someone safe. I have come to believe that the constant complaining and mutual commiserating about household help among middle-class and upper-middle-class women is often a coded communication (usually unconscious) about a much more serious failure of support from their husbands. These women feel neglected and resent the burden of carrying the lion's share of responsibility for sustaining their marriages. Fearing to confront their unhappiness, however, they have transferred their complaints to a safe target, the "help," in a way that is socially acceptable and even sanctioned. Still other lovers keep their own counsel, suffer silently, but begin to look for other options, new lovers, new opportunities. They become self-interested and proffer just enough to the relationship to "float" it until the moment comes when they can leave.

However, one of the most common responses to love's disappointments is neither anger nor apathy, but an overwhelming anxiety which takes the form of a fear of abandonment or rejection in the favor of an imagined rival. Even without any change in the manifest relations between two lovers, one may intuit a diminution of emotional involvement and be plunged into agonizing ruminations over what seems an inevitable debacle, the *certainty* that he will be abandoned. Such obsessive ruminations and their accompanying affects may mushroom to such a degree that they begin to resemble an agitated depression of clinical proportions. But despite his suffering, the lover most often makes a conscious—and generally unsuccessful—effort to keep his feelings to himself, fearing that should they be revealed, they would only serve to distance the beloved even more. When a tormented lover gives way to his impulses to reproach the beloved, his worse fears appear confirmed as she becomes defensive, and then his anger turns to self-reproach and guilt—and yet another abortive attempt to shrug off despair and placate the beloved.

Tolstoy writes movingly of the unraveling of the love between Anna Karenina and Vronsky in which Anna feels a loss in intensity of Vronsky's passion and Vronsky resents Anna's inability to accept the limitations of their situation. Anna is increasingly overwhelmed with despair which she tries to control with morphine, meaningless flirtations, or orchestrated activities. But despite her best efforts, her self-confidence is increasingly eaten away.

In her eyes the whole of him, with all his habits, ideas, desires, with all his spiritual and physical temperament, was one thing—love for women, and that love, she felt, ought to be entirely concentrated on her alone. Yet that love was diminishing; consequently, as she reasoned, he must have transferred part of his love to other women or to another woman—and she was jealous. . . .

And being jealous of him, Anna was indignant against him and found grounds for indignation in everything. For everything that was difficult in her position she blamed him.

Naturally there are both psychological and situational factors that predispose one or another lover to respond to love's disappointments with renewed hope, stoicism, apathy, anger, or the fear of abandonment. The fear of rejection and abandonment anxiety appear more commonly among women, both by virtue of social strictures and the specifics of female developmental life (see Chapter 11). But they often find extreme expression in those who have suffered from actual loss or emotional distancing early in life, or in others who harbor so much conscious hostility that they fear retaliation in the form of abandonment.

Unhappily, many of the reactions to waning love merely serve to accelerate the process acting to separate the lovers, each lover having lost that sympathetic understanding which enabled him to enter into the subjectivity of the Other.

Mutuality, like idealization, is often fragile but sometimes proves surprisingly hardy. The harmonious accord between lovers can deepen over time as lovers come to know one another. And sometimes, even when disrupted, it can be reestablished. This, of course, is what couples attempt to do on "second honeymoons" and stolen getaways; there they hope to reconstitute the sacred boundary between the two-personed dyad and the external world. Sometimes lovers are able to maintain their closeness, intimacy, and mutuality throughout all the stages of a committed relationship, but for many it can only be reconstituted after their children have grown and left home, and the triangle can revert once again to the dyad. As with idealization, much depends on the degree to which there is a concordance of conscious and unconscious fantasies, needs, and values.

The Loss of Sexual Passion

Carnal love is an important feature of passionate love, but is only one part, not to be mistaken for the whole. Nonetheless, its loss can present a major impediment to the continuing intensity of passionate love. Though it is extremely difficult to maintain the high pitch of purely lustful passion in mutual love, the absence, or even the diminution, of sexual passion is alarming and on occasion devastating to lovers. It is in fact so hard to confront that sometimes they will ignore what might seem obvious and become aware of it only when an inadvertent comparison with others is forced upon them. In Sue Miller's novel, *The Good Mother*, Anna and her husband Brian are visiting friends.

> In bed that night, he and I lay far apart, our bodies curved away from each other, two crescent moons, each in a separate universe. We could hear Louise and Mark making love, her greedy cries of "Yes! Yes!" thickened and muted through the walls. I lay still, breathing evenly so Brian would think I was asleep, and wondered when this had happened to us, when we'd stopped noticing or valuing the separateness of the Other.

They were divorced within the year.

Passionate sex is vulnerable in love because previously defeated Oedipal demons do not always remain vanquished. In realized love the lover vests the affectionate and sexual in the same object, and achieves sexual passion. Initially, of course, insofar as the object has some incestual resonance, the sense of transgression (and refinding) contributes to the intensity of love, in both its emotional and sexual aspects. The lover's pursuit of the secret and the forbidden heighten the intense excitement of sexual passion. However, in long-standing love, incestual fixations are often revivified to a greater degree and the prohibitions against them come to inhibit sexual passion.

Refinding may be necessary in order for the chemistry to be right, but too much similarity can create problems. Most of Freud's writings on love point to the rupture between sex and affection due to incestual constraints. Why should these resurface in a long-standing relationship, when they appear to have been overcome? This may happen when one lover too forcefully reinvokes and comes to embody an old parental imago for the other. The transformation of lover into parental imago sometimes occurs after the couple has had a child. (Couples with children often call each other "Mother, Father.") But it happens at many other junctures as well—when, for example, the beloved becomes so maternal, so caretaking that she evokes too strong a connection to mother and the reverberations of infantile life, or when there are physical changes in the beloved as a consequence of aging.

Aside from the incestual taboos that may inhibit sexuality and love in cases where there is too much likeness between the new love object and the old, there are other ways in which the past can hurt the present, making the selection of the beloved problematic. Freud demonstrated not only the continuity in the series of love objects, but also the fact that specific unconscious memories and experiences pertaining to the earliest love objects have a decisive role in the adult lover's experience of love, shaping and sometimes limiting it. The course of love is influenced by our personal histories and our childhood loves. As an example, consider the child who was smothered by maternal solicitude; to the degree that he experienced his mother's caretaking as intrusive, he may, even as an adult, experience closeness as invasive or persecutory.

As regards sexual inhibitions, they are evoked not only because of incestual constraints; they can also arise as protection against the aggression mobilized in sex. Anger may be reinvoked, directed against the beloved who is a stand-in for the earlier object. But aggression also may be part and parcel of ongoing sexual excitement. In either case it may be experienced as potentially threatening to the integrity of the relationship.

The lover, fearful of both his own (or his beloved's) secret sources of aggression, holds back and becomes unable to forget himself in the act of love-making. Once the superego is mobilized by love and conscience to protect either the self or the beloved, inhibitions pre-empt passions. Therefore, while tenderness plays a necessary role in love, it may also destroy some of the roots of sexual passion. It is in this sense that love (which aims at tenderness) may be fundamentally at odds with passion (which aims at possession).

Most mental health professionals assume that sexual passion is characteristic of the early stages of relations and gradually disappears, generally for the reasons just suggested. Yet others have taken the position that it can endure. For example, Kernberg states that "Sexual passion is a basic ingredient of what keeps couples together, as expression of (as well as guarantee of) the active, creative functions of love." For him, the Oedipus complex is not ever resolved, but continues to contribute to the excitement or passion of sex. However, as he goes on to say, "sexual passion, a precondition for the couple's stability is also a potential source of threat to it, so that a most viable, creative love relation is by implication also more threatened than one characterized by a relatively quiet harmony and feeling of security."

The Rhythm of Love

Some lovers are willing to sacrifice intensity for the quieter joys of affectionate bonding; others manage to preserve intensity within a relationship. But still others appear to require a constant level of excitation and exhilaration, lived out through some external tumult. Among this latter group, one sees people who "choose" adaptations particularly suited to maintaining a high pitch of excitement. These include love addicts (those who are continually falling in love but unable to stay in love), Don Juans and Juanitas (lovers who separate sexual excitement from intimacy and have a series of passionate sexual encounters) and those who choose unattainable lovers (thus prolonging the uncertainty of courtship indefinitely).

In the normal course of any love, passion will wax and wane. In successful love, there are always resurgences of intense feeling, sometimes even exceeding the intensity originally experienced. Many lovers are familiar with this phenomenon and may tell one another they are having a "love attack"—similar to storms of lust. Such resurgences account for the capacity of even faded love affairs to rebound.

While mutuality, idealization, and passionate intensity are closely related and are usually lost more or less in tandem, with the result being emotional disengagement, they are by no means identical. One thing that distinguishes them is the degree to which they are recoverable. It is my impression that the sense of mutuality can often be restored after periods when it has disappeared. Similarly, the flagging of intensity is often a reversible phenomenon. Think how often failing passion can be piqued by the threat of a potential rival or a looming separation. Loss of idealization, however, poses a more serious, though still not necessarily irreversible, blow to love. Insofar as the lover still feels some respect or admiration for the beloved, even if he thinks he hates her, his love may be revived. However, though love may survive betrayal and disappointment, it cannot be retrieved if the perception of the beloved is so altered that she is now viewed as prosaic, inferior, or bad. In that sense, sustained idealization may be more of a prerequisite to love than either the sense of mutuality or passionate intensity.

As suggested earlier, idealization and affinity are not wholly imaginary or "projected." Because they are based on what are often authentic appraisals and perceptions, above all on some sort of emotional "fit," they have more potential durability than love's critics suppose. It is for this very reason that lovers rightly dread the chance appearance of a sweetheart from the beloved's past: they know how little it may take to kindle the dying embers of an old love into renewed flames of passion. Even after a traumatic rupture or long separation, lovers may feel a "spark" when they meet again.

I have known more than a few women in their mid-sixties who, despite the statistical odds and the conventional (and accurate) wisdom about the "double-standard of aging," found true passion with lovers who had first felt a spark for them some decades before under circumstances where the love could not be fully realized. (Interestingly enough, attraction and idealization based on the memory of a younger incarnation seem to have enough imaginative power to override the typical desexualized response to the older woman.)

When a relationship is in abeyance, the problems that plague it may be forgotten, while the memory of the lost exaltation becomes the focus for romantic reverie. Nostalgia stokes the fantasy—one more instance of the ongoing pull of lost objects. For example, it is not unusual for divorced people, alone and feeling bereft even though they may have initiated the separation, to find their thoughts and fantasies returning obsessively to their discarded spouses. Some lovers may then discover that reconciliation is possible. No one is surprised to hear of couples who divorce, experiment elsewhere, and come together again. (Elizabeth Taylor and Richard Burton impressed this pattern upon almost everyone's consciousness.) Sometimes this works out and sometimes it does not. A new self-knowledge on the part of one or both—and a new acceptance of each other—may not only enable the old spark to flame again but may keep it going for the duration. If the grievance between the lovers was fundamental, the reconciliation is of course doomed, and the lover will sooner or later arrive at the sorry conclusion that it was the reunion, not the separation, which was all a mistake. One man expressed relief that his estranged wife had called and driven him crazy in conversation. He had been fantasizing about her, but when she called, "I remembered how infuriating she is, how she doesn't make any sense when she talks." And so he was able to reconfirm the wisdom of his decision to separate.

The classic account of rediscovery, rekindled hope, and rapid disillusionment can be found in Katherine Mansfield's short story "A Dill Pickle." Two former lovers accidentally meet, after a six-year hiatus, in a tea shop. At his invitation she sits down with him and their conversation turns to his adventures during the intervening years; she is somewhat evasive about her recent past. As they reminisce their memories take them back to their joint past and they gaze at each other soulfully. "In the past when they had looked at each other like that they had felt such a boundless understanding between them that their souls had, as it were, put their arms around each other and dropped into the same sea, content to be drowned, like mournful lovers." Despite her memories of his cheapness and insensitivity, both of which had bothered her greatly, she enters into his upbeat romanticized recall of their days together, is won over by his apparent sensitivity and begins to think she had thrown her happiness away in throwing him over. Suddenly his mood shifts, and he rather crudely interjects some deflating observation, unintentionally breaking the magic spell. She, forcibly reminded of all her previous well-founded reservations about him, excuses herself and leaves. He, completely puzzled, asks for the check. Thunderstruck though he may be, he is not so distracted as to forget to ask the waitress not to charge for the cream; after all, he reasons, it had not been touched.

Despite the parting of the ways that occurs at the end of the Mansfield story, one of its implicit themes is that attraction is not as random as we tend to think. The idealization of the Other upon which attraction is based, so apparently fragile and unreal, is sturdy enough that it can often be at least momentarily revived, even between lovers who have long since parted for reasons they have neither forgotten nor dismissed. This is so because idealization is often based on accurate perceptions of characteristics we truly value. Moreover, idealization can modulate, deepen, and mature. Consequently, idealization has more durability and capacity for revival than is generally supposed. This is one of the qualities that, under advantageous conditions, allows love to wane and wax, rather than simply disappear.

With the revival of admiration and of idealization, hopes for reciprocity and mutuality may also revive, and sometimes lovers are enabled to retrieve the old intensity. But there are also a very fortunate few for whom the predominance of harmonious wishes over conflictual ones has resulted in the preservation of idealization and mutuality, and they won't ever have lost that intensity in the first place. Their numbers may be small, but they do testify to the potential viability of the impulses that inform love.

CHAPTER NINE

Triangles

TORIES OF triangles exert almost as much imaginative power over us as do tales of two lovers. Some of us have pondered over Rose Kennedy's reaction (or apparent lack of one) in the face of the long-standing affair between her husband, Joseph Kennedy, and Gloria Swanson; have either felt or been appalled by the furor when Ingrid Bergman left her husband for Roberto Rossellini; have been deeply affected by the disclosure of Franklin Roosevelt's unfaithfulness to Eleanor; or have tended to obsess over one or another triangle of which we chance to hear. The intensity of the response to the story of Gary Hart's alleged infidelity to his wife is not unusual; it's simply more vivid because the incident is more recent. We may be fascinated, horrified, even threatened, as we relate such episodes—regarded from the viewpoint of any one of the participants—to our personal situation and imaginatively play out the possible future scenarios in our own lives.

We have an immense curiosity about triangles. And why not? Given our developmental history, this should not be at all surprising. Triangles are intimately connected with the dyads of our early lives, and are imbued with profound desires and fears. Our first triangular (Oedipal) involvement marks our separation from too much infantile dependency on mother, our entry into the world as independent contenders. The love dialogues of development take us from the blissful mother-child dyad of infancy through the triangular Oedipal complex, which is reactivated in adolescence and resolved only when the individual achieves the glory of first love and the restoration of the psychological centrality of the original dyad. In fact, the play between dyads and triangles, whether enriching or depleting, realized or fantasized, is life-long.

Although romantic love is generally described as a "religion of two," love pairs can be infected by triangles, and may even be wholly contaminated by them. Or, more positively, triangles may sometimes facilitate love: some dyads first crystallize in the context of a triangle. Others, especially older, more established dyad may be re-energized by a triangle. And, as we know, many of the most celebrated lovers were adulterous: Tristan and Iseult, Lancelot and Guinevere, Paolo and Francesca. Moreover, some triangles are not mere way stations into or out of love, nor are they invoked as a means of protecting against intimacy or reviving intensity, but they are themselves the main event; the lover is fixated on triangles and can only achieve some of the gratification of love within a triangular configuration.

Envy and Desire

Walking alone, seeing the world go by in pairs, one can abruptly feel bereft, lonely, and disconsolate; one feels envy and more, as though one suffered from some unnamed deficiency. "Why not me? Am I the only one alone?" One senses that one's full potential and pleasure can be realized only in love. If one is a partner in a perfunctory couple whose union never blossomed into love or whose love has long since faded, one may feel more than envy; one may feel hopelessness or a bitter rage at having life's possibilities perhaps permanently thwarted.

Envy runs deep in the psyche, but it is the twin of desire. Perceiving or imagining that two other people are together sexually or romantically incites us to find a love of our own. Reading or watching a love story we are imaginatively engaged: we want that story, or one like it, to happen to us. So it was with Francesca and Paolo, the brother of her husband. Descending into the second circle of hell, Dante inquires of Francesca how she came to fall in love with Paolo, and she replies,

> On a day for dalliance we read the rhyme
> of Lancelot, how love had mastered him.
> We were alone with innocence and dim time.

> Pause after pause that high old story drew
> our eyes together while we blushed and paled;
> but it was one soft passage overthrew

> our caution and our hearts. For when we read
> how her fond smile was kissed by such a lover,
> he who is one with me alive and dead

> breathed on my lips the tremor of his kiss.
> That book, and he who wrote it, was a pander.
> That day we read no further.

The story of Lancelot evoked the imaginative possibility of love for one another in Francesca and Paulo's hearts.

For the fortunate, desire is awakened in response to the characteristics of the Other, and a dyad comes into existence without any direct reference to a third person. But for many, as for Paolo and Francesca, desire is mediated through the perception of oneself in relationship to a couple. In other words, we desire what another like us has, or what a couple appears to share. But envy and emulation may take another form— literally to want what another has rather than to simply crave something similar. Then our desire erupts as the impulse to cut through an envied couple, and to replace one of the protagonists. At such times it almost appears as though desire were created (or intensified) by the very fact that someone is already spoken for, desired by someone else. The aim may be to capture the beloved, but there also appears to be a competitive element at work. In such cases, we may say love's purpose is dual: erotic longing for possession of the beloved is coupled with the wish for competitive defeat of the rival.

Many professional women have noticed that when they marry they seem to become sexually and romantically more appealing to their male colleagues than they had been when they were single. Part of the reason for this may be that some men feel protected by built-in limitations to the full flowering of a potential relationship. But just as important, the husband-rival is always in the background, and through him the desirability of the beloved becomes established. Though women may appear more alluring in this light, sometimes they may be little more than prizes to establish the challenger male's priority in a "phallic, narcissistic" competition.

Moreover, in such a situation any rebuff directed toward the would-be lover can be rationalized away. In *Anna Karenina,* there is a passage depicting Vronsky, at the stage when he is still lovesick over Anna and not yet successful in his pursuit of her, apologizing rather disingenuously to a friend for how ridiculous he must seem in his passion for Anna: "He was very well aware that he ran no risk of being ridiculous in the eyes of Betsy or of any other fashionable people. He was very well aware that in their eyes the position of an unsuccessful love of a girl, or of any woman free to marry, might be ridiculous. But the position of a man pursuing a married woman, and, regardless of everything, staking his life on drawing her into adultery, has something fine and grand about it, and can never be ridiculous."

The strength of the impulse to desire what is someone else's and its competitive implications are revealed in a common adolescent male taboo. Although young males may share sexual exploits they usually respect one another's territorial rights and do not have sex with each other's girlfriends. Those who defy the taboo are known in some circles as "buddyfuckers." There are always boys (and men) who specialize in "buddyfucking." In fact, some men appear to be fixated at this level; for them, such competitive behavior continues as a major mode throughout adulthood. As the phrase itself reveals, the real object of "buddyfucking" may be the buddy, not the woman, the goal in such cases being competitive destruction of a rival male. Those men who respect the taboo have replaced competition with a shared identification; they have accepted the laws of rightful possession. For many of this latter group, however, the sense of loyalty to their male friends transcends their loyalty to their own wives. Although horrified at the thought of sleeping with a good friend's wife, they may feel quite comfortable with the idea of sleeping with their own wife's best friend. Their moral code is fundamentally tied to male solidarity (a code I believe to be a machismo resolution of fears engendered in the childhood Oedipal rivalry with father).

Alma Mahler, who was married to or had romantic liaisons with any number of famous men, including Gustav Mahler, Walter Gropius, Franz Werfel, Oskar Kokoschka and Max Burckhardt, may have been the beneficiary of male sexual rivalry. Either she was a great femme fatale, or the passion she inspired in each of her lovers was mediated by the images of her previous lovers, which were reflected in her and thereby defined her worth as an object of desire (or perhaps both propositions are true). One is reminded of the husband of a woman who had been Byron's mistress, who hung a portrait of Byron in his drawing room. The husband thus elevated himself through his indirect, triangular association with Byron.

Some lovers can fall in love *only* with someone already involved with another. For them, envy seems to be a prerequisite for desire; the triangular configuration is required for the inception of romantic longings. Among some groups of single women, the taste for married men seems to have reached almost epidemic proportions—that is, if all the magazine articles dealing with this "problem" are any clue to its actual occurrence. This proclivity is sometimes misunderstood as simply the self-defeating wish for someone unattainable or inappropriate, and is lumped together with such misguided desires as a penchant for alcoholics, failures, or men who fundamentally dislike or fear women. But this over-neat formulation overlooks the specific and very real preoccupation with triangles as such.

Of course, the lover may be drawn to the beloved by virtue of her own qualities, without any reference to triangles, but the longing for her may be intensified by knowledge of a rival. The rival may not even exist in the present; he may simply be fearfully anticipated in the future, or vividly imagined from details gleaned about the beloved's past. In Fitzgerald's *Tender Is the Night,* Dick Diver, burdened by his marriage, is romantically drawn to the young actress Rosemary. By chance, one of her suitors confides in Dick that she is not so innocent or physically cold as he might think. In fact, she and a young man once locked themselves in a train compartment and drew the blinds in order to engage in some furtive love-making, but they were interrupted by the conductor. Hearing of this incident causes a profound reaction in Dick Diver:

With every detail imagined, with even envy for the pair's community of misfortune in the vestibule, Dick felt a change taking place within him. Only the image of a third person, even a vanished one, entering into his relation with Rosemary was needed to throw him off his balance and send through him waves of pain, misery, desire, desperation. The vividly pictured hand on Rosemary's cheek, the quicker breath, the white excitement of the event viewed from outside, the inviolable secret warmth within.

From the moment he learns of Rosemary's aborted tryst, Dick's subsequent romantic reveries about her begin with the conversation he imagines in that distant train compartment:

"Do you mind if I pull down the curtain?"
"Please do. It's too light in here."

Even in realized love, lovers may have attacks of jealousy, minutely scrutinizing the past for evidence that an earlier love was grander, fresher, or deeper. Questions multiply: "Do you love me more than you've ever loved anyone else?," "Do you still think of her?" and so on. What is puzzling, if we fail to take account of the stimulating effect of triangles, is that the *wrong* answer, the answer that fails to reassure us, may intensify our love, longing, and particularly our sexual arousal. The threat of triangulation is a jog to passion, whether it is past, present, or merely in the conjectural future. One must also accept that behind one's doubts of the beloved's reliability lurks one's own penchant for wandering. Frequently enough, the impetus to jealousy is not any observable threat on the part of the beloved, but a subliminal self-knowledge. Put simply, jealousy is sometimes merely the response to the projection of our own prurient feelings onto the beloved.

The link between desire and envy becomes especially clear in the long-standing Western preoccupation with adultery. According to Tony Tanner, Western literature begins with a tale of adultery, and "it is the unstable triangularity of adultery, rather than the static symmetry of marriage, that is the generative form of Western literature as we know it." In the *Iliad*, Homer's epic narration of the Trojan War, the conflict is precipitated by Paris' abduction of Helen, wife of Menelaus. The preoccupation with adultery clearly continues throughout the period of chivalry; but though adulterous, the prototypical romantic love songs of the medieval troubadours were chaste. As Leslie Fiedler pointed out, the convention that marriage heralded the death of love obscured the fact that the beloved in tales of courtly love was *always* married, indeed must be married, though to someone other than the lover. These highly stylized romances almost literally reduplicated the Oedipal constellation of the knight's childhood: mother-father-son. The beloved was surely idealized, but she was surrounded by the equivalent of an incest taboo. Although the knight might long for the lady, he also respected his commitment to his Lord, generally the husband of his beloved; and consequently the knight kept his love in the realm of the ideal, thus preserving the allegiance due his symbolic "father."

Only later did the *breaking* of the adulterous taboo become one of the major themes of Western literature. According to Denis de Rougement: "To judge by literature, adultery would seem to be one of the most remarkable of occupations in both Europe and America." Alberoni goes even further when he states that, "For hundreds and hundreds of years, falling in love was presented as a rupture of the conjugal couple: adultery."

Adultery has remained a prominent theme in Western literature to the present day. De Rougement takes the adulterous relationship between Tristan and Iseult as the paradigmatic love story. Tanner traces adultery as a major theme in Shakespeare's last plays and in Restoration drama. And many of the great nineteenth-century novels touch on it. Among these, one thinks immediately of *Madame Bovary* and *Anna Karenina*. In these novels the theme of adultery dramatizes issues of authority and transgression not only in individual psychology, but in the social order as well. When the adulterous impulse is enacted it violates the rules of possession both in the private and public spheres, most often with unfortunate results.

Nonetheless, in life as in literature, some of the most passionate love affairs occur when one of the lovers is married. The intense feeling in adulterous love appears to draw some of its energy from the dual transgression of both social and psychological taboos. Adultery, then, is not always an incidental byproduct of love; for some it is the precondition.

Triangles and the Oedipus Complex

The profound pulls of the triangle exert constant pressure throughout the cycle of love. Lovers who come together originally through a desire unmediated by the presence of a third party, and who wish only to establish a glorious dyad, may still be vulnerable to the process of triangulation.

Triangles are often invoked defensively to protect against the hazards of dyads. Either lover may be tempted to introduce a third person to escape the intensity of love, to fend off the threat of self-obliteration implicit in a desire to surrender to the beloved. Other individuals, too frightened to risk full-out one-on-one dyadic love, restrict their romantic liaisons to a regular series of cameo appearances in triangles.

Triangulation may be used to punish a disappointing or errant lover, or to even out the score. A husband may believe he has forgiven his wife after she confesses a prior affair, only to feel himself drawn into a love affair of his own shortly thereafter. Triangulation may also be used to re-establish a sense of gender adequacy when one's femininity or masculinity has been damaged by a competitive defeat, either erotic or non-erotic. For example, a man who has received a shattering blow at work may be more than usually vulnerable to the ministrations of his adoring secretary. Alternately, triangulation may be used to alter not one's own self-image, but one's image in a lover's eyes, with one lover hoping to pique the other's interest and coax fading love back to full intensity through the agency of jealousy. Triangulation may even be used as a self-punishment. A lover who is radiantly happy in love may experience guilt at his great good fortune, and he too may embark on a triangular liaison—as a means of destroying this happiness he does not think he deserves. (Embarking on a triangle is often felt to be a crime, and because of the anguish it brings, a punishment as well.)

Our culture is so saturated with Freud that when anyone alludes to triangles, our thoughts immediately go to the most basic of all triangles, the Oedipus complex. Because erotic and sexual longing first come together in the early Oedipal period, we can appreciate why desire may be readily elicited by triangles, and why the secondary triangle of wife-husband-lover is easily viewed as a derivative of the primary triangle of mother-father-child. But, love in the face of any taboo, whether of class, religion, race, or incest, is, at least in part, a reworking of the original Oedipal taboo. Indeed, all love bears some relationship to the Oedipal.

However, it will not do simply to declare that triangles are basically Oedipal in nature and leave it at that. We must distinguish two primary kinds of triangles: "rivalrous" triangles and "split-object" triangles. The distinction is important because each type is wrapped around a fundamentally different psychological core. In the rivalrous triangle, the protagonist is competing for the love of the beloved. In the split-object triangle, the protagonist has split his attention between two objects. Any individual may find himself or herself in one or the other triangle at different points in life, and may even be in both kinds of triangles simultaneously, as I will elaborate later.

These two types depict the different perspectives inherent in any triangle, and their different psychological substance. Each of the protagonists in a triangle will obviously have different hopes, anxieties, and preoccupations. Though they inhabit the same objective triangle, their subjective triangles (the meaning of the triangle in their psychological lives) will be different. While all these meanings can be related to the Oedipal complex, they represent different variants of it.

Consider, for example, one of the simplest triangles, a married couple and the lover of one of the spouses. Let's say that an unmarried woman is in love with the husband. From the perspective of the other woman (and of the wife, if she knows of the triangle), the tension in the triangle revolves around a rivalry. This is a straightforward "rivalrous triangle," a reincarnation of the Oedipal triangle of early life, and the major emotions accompanying it are jealousy, and, sometimes, anger. (It should be noted that this configuration may sometimes bring not just pain but also increased intensity.) Participation in a rivalrous triangle is sometimes a transient phenomenon in the lover's life, but some lovers may be fixated on such participation.

From the husband's point of view, however, the triangle has an altogether different make-up. For him, the triangle is a split-object triangle and it is *not* a duplicate of the Oedipal triangle of early life. The main tension he experiences is the division in his emotional life between two women; the principal emotion most often guilt. The split-object triangle may have multiple purposes, perhaps one of the most frequent being to serve as an escape from intimacy. Sometimes triangulation is a late derivative of the child's propensity to play his parents off against each other; from this perspective, the split-object triangle is a power maneuver. And sometimes it is nothing more than the product of the lover's dissatisfaction with the reality of his lot and his insatiable quest for ever-elusive perfection.

But the husband's triangle may turn out to be what is best described as a "reverse triangle," a specific subcategory of the split-object triangle. The reverse triangle is a split-object triangle that has a particular motive behind it. It is invoked as an attempt to undo the humiliation of once having engaged in (and lost) a rivalrous struggle (whether Oedipal or more recent). In other words, though the form of the split-object triangle and the reverse triangle are the same, the reverse triangle always has a very specific unconscious meaning. Whereas the split-object triangle is invoked as the solution or pseudo-solution to all kinds of current problems and conflicts, the reverse triangle bespeaks a lingering resentment at having been an Oedipal "loser" in the past, and is an attempt to redress that injustice. The reverse triangle actually *reverses* the configuration of the Oedipal triangle: One is no longer in competition with a rival but is the object of a rivalry. The underlying dynamic motivation of the protagonist would determine which term—"split-object" or "reverse"—might best apply. In the case of a lover whose erotic career reveals a preponderance of split-object triangles, one must suspect that he had some underlying resentment at "losing" the Oedipal struggle and was prone to enacting scenarios of reversal and revenge.

The vagaries of love play on the constant movement from dyad to triangle and back. Some individuals by virtue of their individual psychology or psychopathology have more propensity to seek out forbidden triangles or to feel any established dyad as incestual. Still others are prone to experience the constraints of dyadic love and seek escape in triangles. Some are only comfortable in the illusory power position of the reverse triangle. Then, too, some people transfer (or project) their Oedipal fixations onto others, creating triangles with two members of another family. This is a special form of a reverse triangle and might well be regarded as a "displaced incestuous" triangle. Each of the major kinds of triangles generally has certain specific features attached to it. But, as we shall see, a lover may move out of a rivalrous triangle and into a split-object triangle and vice versa.

Rivalrous Triangles

In the early stages of romantic liaisons, when the loved one is either married to or significantly involved with someone else, the lover's obsessive preoccupation is nonetheless the same as that of other lovers, consisting primarily of thoughts about the beloved. But in such rivalrous triangles (as these are by definition), an obsessive preoccupation with the rival may gradually come to compete with the erotic longing for the loved one. Both erotic longing and competition play a pivotal role in this erotic configuration, and the lover's relationship with his rival has its own significance.

In the beginning of adulterous relations, the claims made on the beloved may be modest: "You may make love with him. I understand you have to. But please, do anything except this very special thing (whatever it may be) that we do together. That is ours." Even so, reveries of love may come to be replaced by jealous fantasies in which the beloved is pictured with the rival. As time passes the lover becomes consumed with jealousy, visualizing the beloved in the rival's embrace, and he comes to resent the rival. The lover's obsession gradually shifts from the beloved to a preoccupation with his rival: what the rival has, over and against what the lover can claim for himself, becomes the focus. That the beloved loves him (or claims to) is not enough, for the rival can claim endless time, holidays, material possessions and social priority.

The lover's obsessiveness may also take the form of invidious comparisons between himself (herself) and the rival. The female lover fears she is not as pretty as the wife. The male lover doubts his ability to look after the beloved as well as her husband does. The lover has a dread of being compared with the rival. The lover may become consumed with self-depreciation and envy of the rival. The lover's unremitting suffering and self-doubt, his jealousy and envy, are sometimes so exaggerated as to suggest that he is masochistic. Indeed, simply to reach for what is someone else's may elicit the fear of retaliation, with ensuing guilt and self-punishing rumination.

If the betrayed spouse knows of the existence of the triangle, he or she, too, experiences jealousy and envy. It is common to wish the disloyal spouse dead rather than contemplate losing her (him) to the hated rival. Generally, however, the rival becomes the repository for all hatred, so that the feelings toward the beloved can be preserved. The mutual jealousy and hatred of both lover and spouse can survive even the death of the beloved. For example, a betrayed wife may forbid the appearance of her husband's mistress at his funeral. Such, for example, was one of the unhappy events in her past life that Maggie confides to Quentin in Arthur Miller's *After the Fall*. Her liaison with a judge was terminated by his death, and the family closed her out of the mourning process.

And such vengeful feelings can be carried to extreme lengths. One beautiful young woman's rivalry with the other woman outlived her erotic

longing for the lover. One week she groomed herself with unusual attention in order to look particularly stunning in anticipation of going to a
professional convention, where she was anticipating seeing her former
lover. A year before, while passionately in love with him, she had discovered an infidelity, and after a heated confrontation, they had split—he to
embark on a live-in relationship with the other woman. Ever since, she
had harbored a fantasy of revenge. She no longer wanted him back, but
she wanted him to do to the other woman what had been done to her.
The other woman, not her former lover and betrayer, had become the
object of her hatred. She went to the convention and engineered her
triumph. She slept with her former lover in his hotel room and managed
to pick up the phone when his girlfriend called. The new girlfriend acted
on cue; she broke off her relationship with her lover. The result the young
woman had fantasized about for so long—the end of the detested bond
between her old lover and her rival—was achieved. But she claimed to
have no further ambitions in the affair, not wishing to resume a love affair
or even a sexual relationship with her former lover, and having no conscious wish to hurt him. Her passionate commitment to competitive
revenge had outlived her love. However, it must be acknowledged that she
did, in fact, damage her former lover. Though this was not her conscious
intent, such a desire may well have played a role in her unconscious
motivation.

What generally happens in rivalrous triangles when the lover emerges
victorious? If the lover has successfully plucked the beloved from another
dyad, he may feel all the expansiveness and exhilaration of an Oedipal
victory, and often enough he lives happily ever after. Such victory may
be easier to enjoy when the love has not been evoked by the triangle per
se, that is, when the triangular complication is merely incidental to the
lover's motivation. But on occasion, "Oedipal victory" may precipitate
self-defeating or even self-destructive behavior. This is most often the case
when the lover has a penchant for triangles, thus indicating some fixation
on an Oedipal conflict. In some individuals, such an unconscious fixation
coupled with a tendency toward masochism leads them to construe love
as triangular even when it cannot objectively be designated as such. The
following quite typical vignette illustrates the link between love invariably
construed as triangular, and masochistic suffering and self-degradation.

A woman, drunk and almost incoherent, called her beloved with
whom she had quarreled, falsely accusing him of being with another
woman. Fearing she had taken an overdose, he hurried to her apartment.
When he arrived, she was still drunk, but her speech was less slurred than

it had been on the phone. Now, instead of being confused and incoherent, she became aggressively erotic, pleading with him to make love, begging him to do anything he wanted to her. She was ingratiating to the point of self-humiliation, resorting to crude language and gestures, wheedling and abject, but she was also coercive, toeing a thin line between utter self-degradation and emotional black-mail ("I cannot live without you!").

Similar episodes punctuated their lives together. Always in the background was her sense of being threatened by other women—his former wives or his previous girlfriends. She was obsessed with comparisons. Was his previous girlfriend prettier, better in bed? She invented triangles where none existed, demeaned herself as she compared herself to past or imaginary rivals, demanded all and promised all, yet pushed her lover away by the nakedness of her hatred toward her "rivals" and the depths of her need and her underlying rage at him. In the end, having succeeded in destroying the relationship, she felt abandoned, rejected in favor of his old ties, and was completely unaware that it was she who had undermined the relationship.

In relatively "stable" triangular relationships, the lover appears to love the beloved without ambivalence, and his resentment and hatred are restricted to the rival. Nevertheless, such a balance is tenuous. What follows is a classic story of adultery triumphant, but embedded within it is a cautionary tale of sorts. This story is not apocryphal; it has been enacted with variations by any number of different players, and you may find it very familiar in its basic components.

An aspiring female business executive had a long-term relationship with her married boss. They travelled the world together, while his wife was apparently oblivious to their affair. He was loathe to get a divorce before his second son went off to college, and the mistress grudgingly accepted her lover's decision to continue a split life. He was sincere, however, and when his youngest child went off to college (some five years after the inception of the affair), he left his wife and immediately married the executive. She seemed extremely happy, at least for the moment, especially when they had a child. But she was a proud woman, and a troubled one, and she never truly forgave him for the humiliation she had suffered as the Other Woman. Her underlying resentment and rage surfaced abruptly and took the form of berating him and finding fault. Her anger, which had previously been focused on her rival, was now directed at him. Her ultimate revenge took the form of starting a new affair with a man for whom she eventually left her former boss. (Her revenge for feeling humiliated in a rivalrous triangle was ultimately to punish her husband by putting him in the same situation. In other words, she moved from a rivalrous triangle to a split-object triangle.) And despite herself she almost relished the idea of separating her husband from his new child, remembering how he had put his consideration for his other children ahead of any sympathy he might have felt for her plight as the other woman.

The boss—and abandoned husband—found himself somewhat dispirited; it is unclear what path his amatory career would have taken eventually, for he died within a few years. His former wife, whose hatred had been aimed not at her ex-husband, whom she saw as having been ensnared by an unscrupulous woman, but at the executive, appeared almost radiant at the funeral. She was reborn as the widow, and thereafter regarded herself as such, no doubt convinced that her ex-husband (with whom she had established a cordial relationship) would have returned to her had he lived.

Derivatives of Oedipal rivalry can be observed even without any overt *erotic* rivalry. In the case of stepfamily rivalries, the intensity of the resentment between stepmother and stepdaughter (or stepfather and stepson) may be so intense and corrosive as to alienate the affections of the husband (or the wife) or to destroy the lover's own feelings. I believe this form of Oedipal rivalry is so common and disruptive that it is a major source of conflict in second marriages (a conflict often played out in terms of the allocation of financial resources). In stepfamilies, we can see the overt expression of tendencies more often kept covert in "natural" families. In general, individuals who experienced intense Oedipal struggles with their parents are apt to duplicate these struggles with their stepchildren (or their own children). Not just Oedipal rivalry, but pre-Oedipal envy is commonly expressed in Oedipal terms. One woman I know ultimately divorced her husband because of her conviction that he favored his son (her stepson) over her. The quarrel was centered on the allocation of money and time, not eroticism.

Now as I have already suggested, many individuals will find themselves in rivalrous triangles at some time in their lives, either by virtue of their longing for someone committed elsewhere, or by virtue of being the hapless spouse or lover whose partner, while still manifestly committed to them, embarks on alternative love affairs. But for most people these rivalrous entanglements, painful as they are, are no more than nodal points—though sometimes crucial ones—in their erotic histories. Even where triangular involvements are the enactment of unresolved Oedipal conflicts, they may be worked through in their very enactment, or, alternatively, experienced as so cruelly painful that they are henceforth assiduously avoided.

In contrast, there are those whose entire erotic careers, or at least long parts of them, are lived out in the context of triangles. Such was the case with Ivan Turgenev. Paramount in his personal life, triangles also found their way into his fiction, where they appear as a major theme—a parallel eloquently demonstrated by the scholar Leonard Schapiro. In 1843, when he was twenty-five and not yet an acclaimed writer, Turgenev met Pauline Viardot, twenty-two, already famous, married, and making her operatic debut in Russia. Despite all that was to happen between them subsequently, he "loved her deeply and all absorbingly for forty years, literally until his death." In the beginning, all was well. He fell in love with her at first sight, and she responded; they loved one another for some seven years. But then she broke away, and effected a reconciliation with her husband. Apparently Turgenev and Viardot never resumed their relationship at the same level of intensity, but except for two years (1857 to 1859), he was always in touch with her. In 1863, he took up residence in Baden-Baden to be near her, her husband, and their children, and from then on the Viardot household was his main emotional preoccupation. Viardot is thought to have been the dominant force in their relationship; she seemed to possess the will to command that he so admired (apparently first in the person of his father), but that he failed to embody in his own personality. Turgenev remarked that he had never been able to "weave himself a nest," but had always perched on the edge of strange nests.

In *Spring Torrents*, Sanin (the Turgenev figure) betrays his betrothed Gemma for the femme fatale Maria Nikolaevna. Here is how Turgenev describes Maria: she was "cast in the image of a young female creature who simply radiated that destructive, tormenting, quietly inflammatory temptation with which Slav natures alone . . . know how to drive us poor men, us sinful, weak men, out of our minds." But Sanin's downfall is not merely the outcome of his submissive nature; Maria is married. Ultimately, she humiliates and eventually banishes him, but his triangular preoccupation is not exhausted. Years later, alone, depressed, and depleted, he finds Gemma's garnet cross and begins to reminisce about the pure love they had once shared. He sets out to find her, finds that she has married and gone to America, and at story's end sets sail, no doubt to install himself as friend and family intimate, like Turgenev himself, to perch on the edge of someone else's nest.

Rivalrous triangles may provide some secondary gains. They may afford the lover a safeguard against forbidden impulses. If based on some derivative of an incestuous desire, for example, they may also serve to ward off that same impulse by directing it to an object who is largely unavailable. Then, too, triangles may protect the lover from his fears of falling in love, particularly from a fear of engulfment. They allow the lover to yield enough to fall in love but they simultaneously guard against the loss of the self, because complete union with (or commitment to) the beloved is averted by circumstances.

One middle-aged man, judged by his professional peers as a force to be reckoned with, nonetheless felt quite differently about himself. He experienced his public persona merely as a protection against long-standing, deep feelings of an altogether different nature. As a child, though doted on by his mother, he had been intimidated by a rigidly authoritarian and dominating father—typically Teutonic, as the son described him. Next to him, the boy had felt helpless, inferior, and unmanned, feelings that were intensified by growing up Jewish in a virulently anti-Semitic community. He remembers with amusement, how, as a boy, he felt elevated when by chance he had a casual conversation at the box office with one of the local aristocrats. He married, quite conventionally and lovelessly. As his success in the world increased he ventured more and more away from home, though his sexual affairs were essentially casual. His position, and the fact that he was often traveling, assured him some ease of access to women.

Almost by accident, he stumbled into an affair that evolved into the great love of his life. Quite apart from the fact that she was a woman who thought about and judged the world much as he, he found her both exotic and imperious. On first meeting her, he told her he found her fascinating; instead of thanking him, she accepted this homage as her due. His interest was piqued, all the more when she said that she could not see him: he was already married, and she was looking for a younger man to marry and with whom to have children. Nonetheless, she deigned to be courted, and he promised a good many things he may or may not have meant, the promises interspersed with flowers and gifts and trips. Their affair provided him with what he needed, and he probably would have remained satisfied in a split-object triangle, gradually losing interest in his new found love, except that she asserted the priority of power. What tipped the balance was her precipitous marriage to someone else, which came as a shock to him. Only then did his love reach the boiling level, and he suddenly felt life would not be worth living without her. After much Sturm und Drang, she essentially took her lover into the marriage with her (for reasons I will return to, in the discussion of the split-object triangle). Over time, he separated from his wife, but could never move out of the sphere of influence of his beloved, where he remains to this day, having renounced his lifelong propensity for split-object triangles in favor of participation in a rivalrous one, paradoxically achieving the first intense and enduring love affair of his life.

Perhaps such metamorphoses as his cannot be fully understood, for they draw on too many complexities of character. In part, though, I believe the shift in his manifest adaptation to the world was facilitated by his very success; only then, fortified by a strong sense of self, could he acknowledge his deepest longing toward passivity and his fatal attraction for someone of strong will. Yet at the same time, the triangular configuration he finally adopted, afforded him some protection against total submission and gratified and checked the fundamental passivity that was so much a part of his hidden nature.

"Split-Object" Triangles

A married woman or man who takes a lover may only be indulging in a dalliance, in which case he or she may view it as irrelevant to the marriage. But when an adulterous affair becomes a passion rather than a diversion, a split-object triangle develops with a split in valuation between the spouse and the lover, the marriage and the affair. The spouse, if not actually loathed, comes to be seen as (at the very least) limited. The marriage, if not bad, is experienced as stultifying. The lover comes to equate the unsatisfactory spouse with an impoverished marriage, and the new beloved with a rich affair. This split in the lover's evaluation is commonly simplified to a "good" situation, on the one hand, and a "bad" one, on the other. Even so, the lover is often consumed by guilt for what he experiences as a betrayal of his obligations.

One should not, however, be too quick to assume one has understood the underlying motivation in any given split-object triangle. The impulse for a spouse to fall in love with someone other than the marriage partner may be eminently sensible. Some marriages are dead and others are dreadful. But sometimes the impulse to run away from home, so to speak, reflects an inability on the part of the spouse to stay in love or to sustain ambivalence within the context of a loving relationship (in psychoanalytic parlance to coalesce good and bad object representations). Some lovers are simply incapable of risking a one-on-one commitment. In formally committed relationships such as marriage, they experience a threat to their autonomy, or they feel consumed with anger.

When love flowers in the adulterous situation, there are typically exaggerations of what normally occurs in falling in love. The lover's obsession with the beloved must now extend also to an obsession with the logistics of the affair. The lover is simultaneously rearranging time *and* concocting new explanations of his absence from his spouse—delays, longer working hours, unavailability. The attempt to conceal an affair from one's spouse takes on gargantuan—and sometimes ludicrous—proportions. The wife worries lest her husband notice her diaphragm is not in its usual place; the husband takes so many showers in order to obliterate any telltale odors that he appears overfastidious; the wife wonders if her husband notices that she wears her best lingerie on Wednesdays. But the lover must also plot to stay in touch with the beloved. Secret telephone calls must be carefully planned. Can the lover allow the beloved to call at home, when, and with what pretext?

To some extent, the lover's obsession with arrangements becomes the substitutive expression of his love; it serves as a release from the monotony of life away from the beloved because it appears to serve the purpose of love, the realization of being together. (To some extent, it may also become the source of discontent. So much arranging, when not sufficiently appreciated by the beloved, can itself become just another duty or obligation.) Vacations spent apart from the beloved are perhaps the most trying time. Not only are they not relaxing, they are anguished. The separation is hard to bear, and communication may be almost impossible to maintain. Whatever the difficulties, however, many lovers will spend a considerable amount of the vacation time trying to place a furtive call to the beloved. The lover broods about the repercussions of leaving the beloved alone and fears he will lose her.

The lover often feels the anguish of needing to make a choice. He may be torn between the guilt he feels toward his wife and children, and the guilt he feels for failing to cement his tie to his beloved. He is consumed with longing for her. Fluctuations in feeling (the uncertainty of whether he is really in love) and doubts about whether the beloved really loves him are intense, especially when they are separated. The lover reproaches himself, worrying for his children and his wife. Sometimes he will still desire his wife, and sometimes he will resent his children. They stand between him and his new love. Perhaps, if he is introspective, he may also intuit that earlier they might have come between him and their mother, causing the first breach in his marriage. He wants to spare the children and yet he wishes them out of the way. He also worries about the beloved, fearing that he may be harming her by using up her best years.

Thus far, the lover appears to be in a triangle where the problematic dynamic is a split love-object. However, his concerns can shift abruptly, and he can find himself obsessing about whether or not his beloved is abandoning hope and considering an affair with someone else. The guilty, despairing lover may now be transformed into the jealous lover, the triangle converted into a rivalrous one.

Just as the protagonist in a rivalrous triangle may invoke anger to counteract unbearable jealousy and anxiety, so too, in a split-object triangle he or she may try to evoke anger from the betrayed spouse in order to feel legitimately angry in return, and thereby surmount his sometimes overwhelming sense of guilt. One betrayed husband declared that had he, rather than his wife, been having an affair, he would have been unusually nice to her, contrary to the mean way in which she was treating him. But he failed to understand the dynamics of guilt. (His wife always held that it was his psychological naivete that was at the heart of their marital failure.)

One man, embarked on a passionate affair, stopped sleeping with his wife. Curiously enough, she never suspected any infidelity but thought he was depressed. He began to find fault with her and she retaliated in kind. Their marriage deteriorated into little more than a continual barrage of bickering. Feeling misused, she demanded more and more material things. By this time, the husband felt quite justified in his affair—he was, after all, married to a shrew. He divorced his wife, married his mistress, and sincerely blamed his wife for the demise of the marriage. According to his interpretation of past events, had she been goodhearted and patient, he feels quite certain that he would never have made a final break. As is often said, short memories preserve good consciences.

In general it is hard to predict what any particular adulterous lover will do, stay in his marriage or leave. Even if he loves his mistress, the strength of his attachment to his wife may preclude his leaving her. Then, too, in some triangles the real love affair exists between the married couple. Their love may be submerged in routine, disguised for the time being as mere attachment, but when threatened it can be reawakened. In the movie *The Women*, based on the play by Clare Boothe Luce, the mother of the betrayed wife, Mary (Norma Shearer), explains to her daughter that her husband still loves her and is not in fact tired of *her*, but tired of *himself* and therefore in need of seeing himself reflected in another woman's eyes. Women, as she explains, when they feel tired of themselves, buy new clothes or change their hair and thus renew themselves, but men don't have enough imagination to do that, so they look for another mirror in which to view themselves, rather than changing the image *in* the mirror.

Frequently enough, the mistress hopes against hope that her lover will eventually free himself, while the wife consoles herself with the belief that her husband will eventually tire of his mistress. It would appear that one or the other must ultimately be proved correct. But the split-object triangle may not come to any resolution whatsoever, lasting a very long time, sometimes even until the death of one of the participants (as was the case, for example, with Victor Hugo, Adèle Hugo, and Juliette Drouet). In such longterm situations, it is likely that the split triangle is important to the lover in and of itself, and in fact, serves the psychological function of a reverse triangle and protects him against the vulnerability of any potential abandonment or humiliation.

And sometimes, to the absolute horror of mistress and wife, the lover breaks with both only to take up with still another woman, whom he eventually marries. One man, apparently exasperated by his wife's utter lack of interest in his work, began a long romantic liaison with his assistant. He experienced the resulting split in his life as increasingly debilitating and managed to bring it to resolution by arranging (unconsciously) for his wife to come upon an incontrovertible piece of evidence pointing to his long-standing infidelity. Unable to deny the situation any longer, she asked him to leave and he did. But strangely enough, he did not move in with his assistant, perhaps, he now thinks looking back, because he did not want to merge his personal and professional life with one person. Or perhaps he was already too angry at his lover-assistant for the relentless pressure she had brought to bear on him to leave his wife, or perhaps her increasing eminence posed a competitive threat. Perhaps, in part, he felt used by her to further her own career. Whatever the fundamental reason, within the year he was utterly enraptured with still another woman whom he met on a business trip and whom he subsequently married.

It is not only men who engage in split-object triangles. Asked, prior to its publication, to read a paper on the subject of "The Professional Woman" by a colleague, I noted her comment that all her professional women patients had had at least one significant extramarital affair. I advised her against publishing the paper, because it could cause considerable trouble in her patients' lives should they or their husbands ever read it (not to mention the legal ramifications that might ensue). And so it happened that a very interesting paper was never published. Nonetheless, despite her figures and my own clinical experience, I believe there is more propensity to form *reverse* triangles among men, not because women are either more timid or moral, but for developmental reasons that I will discuss in Chapter 11.

Some people engage in what I would consider to be imaginative split-triangles. They lead conventional monogamous lives, but hold to the belief (sometimes articulated, sometimes not) that they are still deeply in love with someone with whom they once shared a great love. One elderly gentleman, in a marriage most of his friends regard as exemplary, will occasionally confide that he loved someone else early in his marriage, but that, because he was an honorable man, he stayed the course and gave up his one true love. Of course, he regards his wife as a most remarkable woman, but as for his true feelings—those, he assures his listener, are on a different plane. One sometimes senses a twofold purpose in such confidences. Often, the feelings articulated are deeply authentic ones and serve the same goals (at a safer level) as enacted split-triangles. But sometimes they are the most tentative feelers to explore new imaginative possibilities depending, of course, on the response of the confidante.

There is one important variant of the split-object triangle that brings many individuals (more often men than women) into therapy. In these triangles, the spouse is gradually but invariably transformed from the beloved into an ogre. The wife is not manifestly regarded with guilt; she is hated and feared. She is viewed as hostile and potentially threatening, yet also as the embodiment of stability (ambivalently perceived as providing safety through constraints). She serves the role of the jailer, the woman assigned to protect the husband from himself. In contrast, the beloved is perceived as the paragon of freedom and spontaneity, though perhaps not sturdy or mature enough to be relied upon. Freud spoke of the "Madonna-whore" complex, in which a man might love his wife and yet, in order to spare her his sordid sexual urges, transfer his sexual longings to the "whore." The triangles I am describing here are quite different. The spouse is not metamorphosized into an asexual Madonna; on the contrary, she is viewed as an overcontrolling, intense, all-powerful mother figure. She comes to be experienced as menacing, and is resented because of her right to place demands and strictures on her husband. To the degree that he is dependent on her, he will resent her all the more.

However, the protagonist in these triangles may gradually become aware that history repeats itself and he will find this alarming. He discovers that as soon as he achieves freedom from his tyrannical wife and commits himself to his mistress, she too becomes transformed into a locus of duty and hostility, and he will have duplicated his marriage. Then he is once more drawn to another younger, simpler, and apparently less demanding woman. To his dismay—if he has any self-awareness—it may gradually dawn on him that the succession of women he has loved have not undergone malevolent transformation of their personalities as a conse-

quence of marriage, but rather that they were transformed by his withdrawal and hostility or, even worse, that they were not transformed at all
except in his imagination. (However, excessive self-awareness is seldom a
problem that afflicts us.) Alternatively (on the theme of history repeating
itself) the mistress may fear that her adulterous lover, having betrayed his
wife, will betray her in turn. Françoise Gilot, contemplating two of her
predecessors, observed that neither the demandingness of the one nor the
compliance of the other spared them Picasso's disenchantment, and so
she was more prepared for the inevitable transformation of his perception
of her too.

Sometimes there appears to be an underlying psychological need for
a lover to de-idealize and ultimately betray his beloved. But most of us
are loath to come to such a conclusion. We prefer to rationalize the causes
of those rejections we initiate as well as those we stand witness to and (in
the role of newly beloved) benefit from, in superficial terms: "I had to
leave him before his dullness destroyed me," or "He couldn't stand her
because she had become a prattling bourgeois housewife," and so forth.
Yet, whether we acknowledge it or not, some people are psychologically
geared to betray those who love them. Usually, such a person has felt
betrayed himself (whether actually or in mere fantasy, recently or in early
in life), identifies with the aggressor, and is prepared to disrupt the lives
of successive lovers in order to seek reparation for past wrongs. (The
original betrayal that later converts the person into a betrayer is most often
a legacy of childhood.)

Such was the case with the young woman, previously alluded to, who
took her distinguished older lover into her marriage. As a child, she had
been morbidly ashamed of her ungainly mother and inordinately proud
of her charming virtuouso father. But her relationship with him was
marred by her perception that he preferred her older and less gifted sister.
Nonetheless she looked for validation and for succor from a series of
nurturant men. Her first serious love affair proved disappointing, and she
sought something more intense in an affair with the married man for
whom she worked. That adulterous affair awakened her to the profound
joys of truly passionate love, though it failed to become a permanent
relationship. Her latent anger against her father (he had dared prefer her
sister!) now found expression in the disappointed and angry feelings
aroused by her lover's failure to marry her and caused her to be on guard
with all men. How she solved this problem—her need for male nurturance
conflicting with her basic distrust of men—was to enter into a series of
split-object (reverse) triangles. Consequently, it seemed natural to her to

continue her affair with the older caretaking lover even after she married—and she did indeed seem to thrive on the emotional largesse of two devoted men. Though it might appear that she, as the dominant force in the split-object triangle, was in the power position, it is clear that she (like others in similar situations) suffered from a fundamental weakness, the inability to risk all and to love full out.

While the suffering lover in a rivalrous triangle may envy the apparent invulnerability of the lover in a split-object triangle, the latter has plenty of woes of his own, some of them profoundly debilitating. The guilt generated in the split-object triangle is itself corrosive and antagonistic to the goodness the lover feels (and aspires to) in happy love. Complications abound and the fragmented lover may come to feel depleted, no longer longing for love but for solitude—and at such a point the lover may abandon both relationships and enact one or another of the standard fantasies of escape to splendid isolation (retreat to a romantic cabin or some contemporary equivalent of the French Foreign Legion.) Such was the fate of Isaac Bashevis Singer's protagonist in his novel, *Enemies, A Love Story*. This man, a survivor of the holocaust, marries the Christian woman who at great risk to herself had saved him, then acquires a mistress, and is suddenly brought up short by the appearance of his first wife whom he had believed dead. His life, split up into too many pieces, left him little option but to disappear. For some of us, life is an endless journey as we shuttle back and forth between the solitary state and dyads, dyads and triangles, triangles and the solitary state, never finding our preferred place of rest.

"Displaced-Incestuous" Triangles

Displaced-incestuous triangles do not involve love (or sex) between members of the same family; rather, two family members share the same lover (either simultaneously or sequentially). Woody Allen's movie *Hannah and Her Sisters* is a virtual celebration of interlocking triangles and emotions. In the film, the two key triangles involve Hannah (Mia Farrow), who is portrayed as happy, mature, and envied by her two sisters. Hannah's husband (Michael Caine) lusts after her beautiful and sexy sister Lee (Barbara Hershey), who succumbs to his advances. (In the end, it turns out that he really loved Hannah all along and he stays with her). Meanwhile, Hannah fixes up her previous husband (Woody Allen) with her coked-up discombobulated sister Holly (Dianne Weist), with disastrous results. This misadventure is later redeemed when Holly and the ex-husband accidentally meet again, fall in love, and decide to marry. Essentially, then, each of Hannah's sisters sleeps with one of her husbands. (And there are still other triangles in this film. One involves the request by Hannah and her apparently infertile first husband that their good friend donate sperm so that she might get pregnant.)

The strength of the film lies in its portrayal of the rich emotional mix that informs real life: the sisters are competitive and erotic rivals but they are also affectionate, helpful, and compassionate toward one another. By passing on a discarded husband to her sister, Hannah is denying sibling rivalry (and Oedipal competition, from which sibling rivalry in part derives). Sometimes, such an act may conceal—and covertly reveal—a homosexual urge, which can be symbolically mediated through a shared man.

But what of the triangles from the point of view of Hannah's husbands? What is the impulse that leads some individuals to involve themselves emotionally and erotically with more than one member of the same family? In a general way, the desire reflects a taste or tendency for complexity and density. Such complexities may be necessary to pique the emotional life. More particularly, the urge is a variant of split-object triangles, in which the lover displaces unresolved incestuous fixations onto the objects of his affection. When displaced-incestuous triangles form a large part of an individual's erotic preoccupation, they derive from Oedipal fixations and longings which may present themselves in other ways as well. Clinically one often observes a predilection for the exotic and forbidden (as an alternating form of displacement of Oedipal desire) along with the displaced-incestuous preoccupation. This was the case with a woman I know, a proper Anglo-Saxon Protestant, who was never attracted to men of her own background, but drawn only to Asian men. (Her father had been stationed in the Far East during World War II when she was a child and apparently Asian men represented both a protection against her fantasies about him and a symbolic stand-in for him.) The single exception to her predilection for Asian men was one instance in which she was simultaneously attracted to two Caucasian brothers.

Part of the appeal of the movie *The Graduate* may have to do with the fact that it was one of the first films to deal with the fairly common male fantasy of being involved with a mother and her daughter almost simultaneously (an intense reverse triangle of the first order—the man is not competing with his father for his mother; rather a mother and daughter are competing for him.) The incestual preoccupation has been externalized and the protagonist "plays" with it at some remove. Sometimes mothers and daughters have love affairs with the same man, just as father and son may love the same woman. I have known two men who married the daughters of former mistresses—or put the other way around, two daughters who married their mothers' former lovers. In Judith Krantz's novel, *Mistral's Daughter*, Maggy, who is the model-mistress and inspiration for some of the painter Julian Mistral's best work, loses him to another woman. But later, her own daughter, Teddy, has a love affair with Mistral (for Teddy a thinly disguised case of re-finding and a rivalrous Oedipal triangle) and has a child by him.

The Erotic Appeal of the Rival and the Attraction to Couples

There is occasionally a shocking piece of self-discovery for participants in triangular love relationships: a deep sexual attraction to their rivals. This may be manifested only in apparently inexplicable dream fragments or flash fantasies. The negative Oedipal complex and a homosexual longing for the rival often come into play in the context of love triangles.

A masterful account of the complexities of triangular love can be found in Milan Kundera's *The Unbearable Lightness of Being*. In that novel, Tereza reads her lover Tomas's mail and discovers his ongoing infidelities with Sabina. She then has a nightmare in which the three of them are in a room together. In it, Tomas orders her to watch him make love to Sabina on a raised platform bed. She awakens and tells Tomas of her nightmare. The next day, Tomas goes to his desk and finds a passage in one of Sabina's letters to him which states, "I want to make love to you in my studio. It will be like a stage surrounded by people," and he realizes that Tereza has read his mail. He forgives Tereza for this, but she is unable and unwilling to forgive him for his ongoing transgressions, though she is equally unable to give him up. She remains tormented by his infidelities. Later, she incorporates the image of the raised bed and Sabina into her love-making with Tomas. "As time passed, the image lost some of its original cruelty and began to excite Tereza. She would whisper the details to him while they made love." Still later, Tereza and Sabina have an encounter with distinctly sexual overtones in Sabina's studio. It excites them both, though both ultimately draw back from it. More interesting still, Tereza ultimately models her professional identity on what she has learned from Sabina.

While the knowledge of betrayal by one's lover causes pain, it may also generate considerable sexual excitement. This fact, as well as the occasional manifestation of a deeply buried sexual longing for one's rival, point to the contamination of a love affair by unresolved Oedipal material. In particular, homosexual longing for one's rival suggests the ongoing influence of a highly developed negative Oedipus complex along with the positive one. (This is a manifestation of bisexuality, a universal propensity.) In this case, the lover is simultaneously attracted to and jealous of both partners in the couple, just as he once was toward his parents.

Some lovers do manage affectionate relationships with their rivals, and treasure ongoing relationships with them. While some wives use the occasion of the spouse's death to exact revenge on a rival, others initiate closer ties with the mistress. Together, they share their memories of their lost love.

There are also those who attach themselves amorously or half-amorously—sometimes even asexually—to both partners in a couple. This appears to have been the case with David Diamond's intense friendships both with Carson McCullers and her husband, Reeves McCullers. Diamond, a composer, was drawn to both of them from their first meeting, and his diary entries are explicit about his dual inclinations: "Now I have met *this* love—this lovable child-woman—whose loneliness hit me the moment I entered Muriel Rukeyser's apartment. . . . I met her husband, whom I know I love. . . ." "What has happened to me since meeting Carson and now Reeves, her husband. Carson, whose magnetism and strange sickly beauty stifles me, gnaws at me, and I know it is that I love these two human beings. It is a great love I feel. It will nourish me or destroy me." At first the McCullers drew him into their coupledom. But their marriage was disintegrating; and Diamond, drawn into the maelstrom, yearned for a passionate attachment first with one, then with the other, and did live for a time with Reeves. Carson, who previously had championed the legitimacy of homosexual relationships, was nonetheless devastated by this turn of events and her felt exclusion. Her biographer Carr believes that Carson's triangular relationship with Reeves and Diamond figured heavily in her fascination with the "we of me" which was to become the central motif in her novel *The Member of the Wedding*. The triangle that haunted her fictional character Frankie haunted the author in reality. According to Carr, Carson found an exclusive permanent relationship between these two men distasteful; she goes on to say: "A we of me relationship was good only as long as it suited Carson—and included her—but it was devastating if it left her out." Ten years later, after Carson and Reeves were back together, Diamond saw them again, but with trepidation and hesitation: ". . . I feel they may still be able to *force* me to accept *their* helplessness and loneliness as a part of my own." Diamond did not, however, become hopelessly stuck in his role as an adjunct to a couple. He eventually found "a meaningful and lasting liaison" one-on-one.

Sometimes it is altogether unclear whom the lover regards as the object of desire and whom the rival. One encounters men (and some women) whose preferential masturbation fantasy is the image of a couple making love. In this fantasy the protagonist is present merely as a voyeur. Now, clearly, the same manifest fantasy does not always have the same meaning for everyone, but in some cases this fantasy represents a fixation on the parental couple, in which it is the very exclusion from the parental bedroom and the fantasized primal scene that has itself been eroticized.

No love dyad is immune from triadic components. Most often, these can be incorporated into the dyadic relationship and need not be corrosive. Particularly when they take form only as fleeting fantasies, such triangles may sometimes even be enriching to love.

To the degree that triangular preoccupations are actualized in extramarital love affairs (or merely sexual ones for that matter), they are often destructive, containing, as they do, inherent fault lines and dangers. The intrinsic problems of such triangles derive from their instability, their hidden agendas, their connection to power considerations, and the inevitable frustrations and insecurities they engender in each of the three principals. This is not to say that a couple that cleaves to form a triangle may not ultimately reestablish a dyad and survive as a couple, but their love may be fractured. The lovers' sense of mutual priority and trust will have been violated in such a fundamental way that it may not be entirely retrievable.

Yet there are instances when triangles prove adaptive, or when adulterous love may be life-sustaining. Then, too, the original dyad may be dissolved and replaced by a new one.

But while for some people, triangles are merely temporary arrangements in response to circumstances or dissatisfactions, yet in others they are the primary focus. To the extent that an individual is fixated on triangular relationships (for example, when a woman only falls in love with married men), that individual has entered the realm of self-defeating behavior and the pleasures of love will be eroded.

4

THE GENDER
DIFFERENCE IN
LOVE

CHAPTER TEN

Transference Love and Romantic Love

TUDIES OF love are just now beginning to appear in greater number in the psychoanalytic literature, stimulated in part by the growing theoretical interest in transference.* Although Freud originally described the erotic transference—the patient's falling in love with the therapist—as an impediment to therapy, something to be assiduously avoided and something that might even disrupt a therapy, he came to recognize it as a paradigm for transference in general and, ultimately, as closely akin to falling in love in "real" life.

Gradually, in the years since then, the psychoanalytic view of transference has enlarged. Far from being viewed as an impediment, the development of a transference and its analysis are now viewed as the very heart of the psychoanalytic process. Transference analysis has to some degree replaced dream analysis as the "royal road to the unconscious." In fact, the patient's capacity to form a transference relationship to the analyst seems to be a key factor in facilitating change.

Interest in the erotic transference may seem a very circuitous route by which to come to inquire about love. But because the subjective experience of transference love has so many similarities with romantic love, analysts have come to make the assumption that, psychologically, the two phenomena are close kin if not identical. Transference love and romantic love do possess many features in common: not only the subjective feelings they evoke but their obvious deep connection with the subject's (patient's or lover's) innermost desires, feelings, and imaginative powers and their capacity to act as powerful agents of change. Like transference, love can create both the desire and the vehicle for fundamental change. In analyzing the strange phenomenon of the erotic transference, one that the

*I have published a more technical paper on the subject of transference love elsewhere. See "The Erotic Transference in Women and in Men: Differences and Consequences," *Journal of the American Academy of Psychoanalysis* 13:2 (1985): 159–80.

earliest analysts stumbled upon, we are given a privileged viewpoint from which to explore something of the psychological make-up of love. Transference love becomes a window into the phenomenon of love from an apparently neutral perspective. It may be that many analysts, myself included, have felt more secure in talking about the erotic transference than about love, the transference being, as it were, an observable phenomenon, something we can examine firsthand, though remaining relatively uninvolved.

Transference love reveals a gender difference and consequently it sheds some light on the gender variations in romantic love: differences both in the circumstances that serve to promote love in men and women and in the kinds of predominant existential problems to which men and women are vulnerable. Just as important, the comparison between falling in love in therapy and in "real life" identifies some of those factors that facilitate the experience of falling in love.

Transference is the general term that designates certain feelings a patient develops for his analyst in the course of therapy, the erotic transference being but one form of transference (albeit a crucial one). Now what distinguishes transference feelings from those other emotions engendered in direct response to the person (and character) of the analyst, is, as Freud pointed out, that they are re-editions of feelings the patient once had toward the most important persons in his early life. Many clinicians use the term transference in the strict sense, only as it applies to the treatment situation. And indeed, the discovery of transference had immense implications for the technique of analysis. But analysts and social scientists have been well aware that the concept of transference is also useful in understanding a number of disparate phenomena that take place outside the treatment situation, among them the propensity of so many people to attach themselves to leaders and causes, as well as to loved ones. Social scientists interested in finding the psychological roots of the predisposition to slavishness have discovered a veritable Rosetta Stone in the concept of transference.

Freud utilized the concept of transference in order to understand among other things the roots of religion. According to Freud, the emotional content of transference—toward a parent figure or toward God—is the child's longing for a powerful parent or surrogate who can serve "as a protection against strange superior powers"; first for the child, and then for the man, transference is invoked by his "need for protection against the consequences of his human weakness." Transference, then, is a natural outgrowth of the terrors of the human condition—a means of "taming terror." In essence, Freud suggests that each of us seeks union with some representation of parental potency, not only out of erotic (libidinal) desire but also out of weakness and fear.

As the child empowers the parental figure, so in later life will the adult empower the transference object. But once empowered, the transference object (like the parental figure it reincarnates) becomes a controlling agent. The child, and then the adult, deals with the transference object by conciliation, accommodation or manipulation. Thus, while the transference object is longed for as a means of saving an individual from a dreaded fate, it instead becomes his fate (in the same way that the beloved to whom we look for freedom from the prison of our old lives often enough becomes our new jailor.) No sooner do we attach ourselves to a transference object in order for that object to take care of us and protect us than we may discover a whole new set of fears; our safety and well-being are still not within our own control and we displace our fears onto the transference object. We dread losing or antagonizing the transference object, of not being able to survive alone: in short, we remain haunted by our own helplessness and dependency needs. Positive transference always contains within itself the potential for negative feelings because of our resentment for our inordinate need for the object, and we may project onto it our childish angers and our grievances against our parents. We may even come to experience the transference object as the primary source of our unhappiness.

The less actual power one has or feels, the stronger the transference must be. In this schema it is transference and its derivatives that make the world go round.

Transference Love: Falling in Love in Therapy

Even for those unacquainted with any of the tenets of psychoanalysis, it is common enough knowledge that people sometimes fall in love with the doctors or nurses who tend to their physical ills, thereby demonstrating the same proclivity as those patients who fall in love with their psychotherapists. In the movies, one thinks of (among others) Bette Davis in *Dark Victory*. She plays the role of a very spoiled rich young woman, stricken with mysterious fainting spells. During the course of her medical treatment, she falls in love with the neurologist and, ultimately, he with her. In falling in love and struggling with what turns out to be an incurable brain tumor, Davis is transformed from a bratty immature woman into a mature, happy, and feeling one. Similarly in real life, many aging or ailing men fall in love with their nurses. The latest well-known figure to have done so is the novelist Joseph Heller, who fell in love with his nurse while recuperating from a neurological disease. Thomas Merton, while a cloistered monk, did the same with a nurse he met when he was ill. Some men have been known to disinherit their families in favor of their nurses, even when close to death and not likely to achieve a fully realized, mutual love. (Closely related are those love affairs between aging men and their housekeepers: among them one thinks of the recent example of Mr. J. Seward Johnson and the Polish-born housekeeper whom he married, much to the consternation of his disinherited children.) Reciprocally, many women are known to fantasize about nursing a man back to health or falling in love with an injured or mutilated man. The story of Jane Eyre is perhaps the ultimate nursing fantasy. And doctors, too, like the neurologist in *Dark Victory*, fall in love with their patients. In this context, one is also reminded of the pilot of a fatal airplane crash who afterwards fell in love with and married one of his passengers, the singer Jane Froman, who lost her legs in the crash. Indeed, rescuing or being rescued surely ranks as one of the great romantic themes.

Falling in love with one's doctor in psychoanalytic therapy is a common enough phenomenon that, as already noted, it has a special name—the *erotic transference* or *transference love*. This refers to some mixture of tender, erotic, and sexual feelings that the patient has towards the analyst, and, as such, it forms part of a positive transference (though like all positive transferences it necessarily contains some latent negative feelings). Sexual longing or sexual transference alone—without the elements of tender longing—represents a truncated erotic transference, one that has not been fully developed or experienced. In large part, the erotic transference is a component of the wish to be loved by the analyst. The analyst may occasionally experience reciprocal feelings for the patient—what would then be called an erotic countertransference—stoked by his response to both her admiration and need. (Generally speaking, the patient longs to be rescued, the therapist to rescue.)

Today with psychoanalysis so well established and knowledge (as well as folklore) about it so widespread, many people take it for granted that patients are "supposed to" fall in love with their analysts. But the fact that patients do fall in love with their doctors with some regularity is, when you think about it, astonishing. Of course, analysts call these feelings "transference," but the patient often experiences them as genuine feelings of love.

Freud was the first to describe the phenomenon of the erotic transference, to theorize its meaning in our developmental lives and in the process of psychoanalytic therapy, and to make a connection between transference love and romantic love. But an understanding of the erotic transference did not spring full-blown, even to Freud. His introduction to the phenomenon began with a strange series of events which he learned about through his mentor and collaborator, Josef Breuer.

The "talking cure," an early precursor of psychoanalysis, developed more or less by accident in the course of Breuer's therapy with Anna O, a woman with many hysterical symptoms. She had initiated the process of a kind of free association, in which her speaking of the origins of each symptom magically caused it to disappear. But this therapy was finally disrupted by events in the world outside the consulting room, and it was the disruption itself that led circuitously to the conceptualization of transference, specifically the erotic transference and its hazards to both patient and doctor.

Breuer, who had become increasingly fascinated with Anna O's treatment, is thought to have ignored his wife and thereby provoked her jealousy. Belatedly recognizing the nature of his wife's reaction, Breuer terminated Anna O's treatment. Shortly afterward, he was called back to find his patient in the throes of an hysterical childbirth. He calmed her down but, the next day, took his wife on a second honeymoon. Freud recounted the story in a letter to his own wife. According to Freud's biographer Ernest Jones, Martha "identified herself with Breuer's wife," and hoped the same thing would not ever happen to her, whereupon Freud reproved her vanity in supposing that other women would fall in love with her husband; "for that to happen one has to be a Breuer." Freud, then, denied even the possibility that such a phenomenon might occur in any of his patients, while Martha, rejecting the idea that the infatuation could be attributed solely to Breuer's personal prestige and charisma, seemed intuitively to understand the universal nature of the dynamic. (The mere possibility of triangulation can apparently sharpen one's intuitive abilities!) Only later did Freud come to see Anna O's reaction as the rule rather than the exception, thus enabling him to turn his attention to its central theoretical significance. (It may be of some interest that Anna O was in fact none other than Bertha Pappenheim, who went on to become an eminent social worker and a pioneer of the European women's movement.)

It's been suggested that it was perhaps inevitable that the theoretical observations of the phenomenon were originally made by someone other than the therapist involved. In other words, because Anna O was Breuer's patient, not Freud's, it was easier for Freud to assume an observing role toward her sexual and erotic communications than if they had been directed at him. But even then it wasn't so easy. Simply being a fellow analyst seems to have brought Freud too close to the phenomenon for comfort, and he only appreciated gradually what his wife intuited immediately. Freud's reluctance to acknowledge the phenomena may be some measure of the power—and threat—residing in it.

Nonetheless, by 1905, Freud had formulated fairly explicit concepts about transference, linking the patient's reactions to the therapist to previous reactions the patient had experienced to one or more significant figures from his childhood. Freud described transference reaction as:

new editions or facsimilies of the impulses and phantasies which are aroused and made conscious during the progress of the analysis; but they have this peculiarity, which is characteristic for their species, that they replace some earlier person by the person of the physician.

In this formulation, emphasis is placed on the repetition inherent in transference and not on its subjective reality for the patient. According to one present-day analyst, "Freud's stress on repetition was in part a response to real and threatened public disapproval of the erotic transferences that female analysands developed in relation to their male analysts." (And here we have an implicit acknowledgment of the fact that this supposedly universal phenomenon is in practice much more common between women patients and men doctors.) But whatever Freud's reason for stressing that transference feelings are "merely" a re-edition of earlier feelings, the truth is that the patient experiences "transference" as a very powerful reality in the present tense. In fact, even a patient who has fallen in love with two therapists in a row finds it hard to accept the idea that her feelings are nothing more than transference. Only the doctor can view the patient's feelings from such an Olympian distance—and, as already discussed, doctors aren't always successful either, hence the phenomenon of the countertransference. Usually, however, the therapist keeps such feelings at bay, in part by invoking the theory of the transference, which thus becomes not only an aid to understanding the patient, but also a defense against a situation which threatens the analyst.

Freud himself was not unaware of the fact that transference looked different to the patient and the doctor. By 1915 he had begun to formulate a theory about the relationship between the erotic transference and the state of being in love. At that time, though, he still maintained his belief that the erotic transference was solely an impediment to therapy and advised that the therapist demonstrate to the patient that she fell in love with him only in the service of resistance to the analysis, as a means of avoiding the painful discoveries about to be made. Even so, Freud acknowledged that transference love and love had certain shared qualities in common.

> I think we have told the patient the truth, but not the whole truth regardless of the consequences. . . . The part played by resistance in transference-love is unquestionable and very considerable. Nevertheless the resistance did not, after all, *create* this love; it finds it ready to hand, makes use of it and aggravates its manifestations. Nor is the genuineness of the phenomenon disproved by the resistance. . . . It is true that the love consists of new editions of old traits and that it repeats infantile reactions. But this is the essential character of every state of being in love. There is no such state which does not reproduce infantile prototypes. It is precisely from this infantile determination that it receives its compulsive character, verging as it does on the pathological. Transference-love has perhaps a degree less of freedom than the love which appears in ordinary life and is called normal; it displays its dependence on the infantile pattern more clearly and is less adaptable and capable of modification; but that is all, and not what is essential.

According to Freud, then, all love is a re-finding, and repeats infantile reactions; but transference love, for reasons he did not specify, was said to be even more dominated by the strait jacket of repetition than was romantic love. (One present-day analyst, Martin Bergmann, has suggested the reverse—that in real life the lover simply displaces or suppresses his negative feelings about the beloved, making it likely that they will eventually wend their way back into the relationship and corrode it, whereas in psychoanalysis the negative feelings can be both experienced *and* worked through so that what began as a compulsive repetition can end by becoming a freeing experience.)

Knowledge of the erotic transference was crucial to Freud's formulation of the phenomenon of re-finding in love. His observations in the consulting room enabled him to see that the object of both transference and romantic love is a re-edition of the original love object of childhood. But insight into the erotic transference is important to our understanding of love in several other interrelated ways as well. Transference can be demonstrated to be an imaginative act, an idealizing one, and, perhaps most importantly, an *act*—a process that the patient causes to happen and participates in, not something that happens *to* him, and in all these ways it confirms certain of our assumptions about romantic love.

Transference also sheds light on love as an agent of change, because transference, too, can be a major catalyst for personal change and growth. In fact, as already mentioned, analysts no longer fear transference as an impediment to analytic process, but rather look to it as the very vehicle of that process. Nonetheless the erotic transference, like love itself, can sometimes prove disruptive rather than constructive.

Perhaps even more important than the similarities between transference love and romantic love is one enormous *difference*. Transference love is far more predictable than love, such a regular feature of so many analyses that it almost appears to be promiscuous, whereas love in "real" life is much more selective. For insight into the whys and wherefores of falling in love, we must try to understand the frequency of transference love (at least for women patients in treatment with men) compared to the less predictable, more erratic inception of romantic love in everyday life.

The Transformational Potential of Transference Love

It's well known that positive transference alone sometimes catalyzes radical change in patients, hence the term "transference cure." Patients come into treatment and sometimes as a result of transference (and their dependency on, or identification with, their therapists) their symptoms disappear or the patients rapidly mobilize into life. However, analysts are at great pains to argue that such change is superficial, and that the symptoms may well reappear if treatment is interrupted. But this does not always appear to be the case. Many patients use their short-term gains to consolidate a different (and better) self-perception and self-appraisal over the long term.

How one regards transference and transference love has implications for both technique and theory. Schafer neatly captures the double and perhaps contradictory sense in Freud's conceptualizations of transference love, and the ramifications that bifurcation has for current therapeutic ideas.

On the one hand, transference love is sheerly repetitive, merely a new edition of the old, artificial and regressive (in its ego aspects particularly) and to be dealt with chiefly by translating it back into its infantile terms. (From this side flows the continuing emphasis in the psychoanalytic literature on reliving, re-experiencing, and re-creating the past.) On the other hand, transference is a piece of real life that is adapted to the analytic purpose, a transitional state of a provisional character that is a means to a rational end and as genuine as normal love. (From this side flows the emphasis in our literature on the healing powers inherent in the therapeutic relationship itself, especially with respect to early privations and deprivations). We are not in a position to disagree entirely with either conception of transference, transference neurosis, and transference-laden therapeutic effects. The problem is, how to integrate the two.

Bergmann, however, believes that transference love "is not by itself adaptive. It is only the sublimation of this love with the aid of the analyst that makes it adaptive for the purposes of cure, when inquiry is substituted for gratification." He argues that it offers a new opportunity for the reworking of Oedipal material and the making of new and better choices.

But sublimated or not, the positive transference seems to be an absolute prerequisite to analytic change, part of the fuel that propels the therapeutic process. As subspecies of the positive transference, the erotic transference must also be acknowledged as a potentially useful, if dangerous, tool in therapy.

The psychoanalyst Bergmann, despite all his caveats to the contrary, catches the transforming power of love and the role it plays in psychoanalysis:

In a historical perspective, Freud's twin discoveries that the transference feelings of his patients contained psychic energy that could be harnessed in the service of a treatment procedure that aimed at insight, and that the emotion of love could be subjected to analysis, because it was based on the refinding of infantile love objects, is an astonishing example of a secular utilization of Plato's ladder of love. That love can be diverted from its natural course where it seeks gratification and mutuality and be pressed into the service of bringing about intrapsychic change confirms Plato's original insight into the plasticity of Eros.

But, of course, love is not *pressed* into the service of bringing about intrapsychic change; that is part of its very nature, that *is* "its natural course."

There are clearly dangers in emphasizing that some form of love that the patient feels for the doctor can be transforming in and of itself. The most obvious danger is that such an emphasis can be used as a justification for the erotic and sexual exploitation of patients. But there are less flamboyant pitfalls, too. When the erotic transference is experienced but not fully analyzed, it often becomes the major resistance to the analysis. The limitation of these therapies is a tendency for the strength of the erotic

transference to obscure other important dynamics and conflicts. Therefore, much caution *must* be observed. But, at the same time, truthfulness
demands acknowledgment of those instances when transference rather
than analysis seems to be the change agent, or at least one of the most
significant factors.

This surely appeared to have been the case with one of Jung's early
patients. A love affair between Jung and Sabina Spielrein has recently
come to light. Its history has been reconstructed by an Italian analyst,
Aldo Carotenuto, who accidentally came into possession of Spielrein's
diaries and letters. As a young woman Spielrein is reported to have suffered from either a schizophrenic disturbance or a severe hysteria with
schizoid features and she was hospitalized in Zurich. What follows are the
bare bones of what is known of Spielrein, her treatment with Jung, and
their romance.

Spielrein was born into a well-to-do Russian Jewish business family in
Rostov-on-Don in 1885. Though extremely bright, imaginative, and
gifted, from an early age she suffered psychological symptoms of some
severity. By age three or four she retained feces; later she began to
ruminate about defecation and "anyone she saw was imagined as engaging
in that act." She herself dates the onset of her illness to the sixth grade
when she was almost eleven, at which time her younger sister died. By
the time she was eighteen she could no longer look at anyone and experienced alternating fits of weeping and laughing, screaming and crying.
Her parents conceived of sending her to Zurich where she might simultaneously study medicine and undergo treatment, and they probably took
her there in 1904. Bettelheim believes she was among the first of Jung's
patients—if not the first—whom he treated by the psychoanalytic
method. (Jung also engaged her to assist in his word-study tests.) At some
point, she was well enough to leave the hospital as an inpatient but
continued her therapy with Jung. By 1905 she had enrolled in the University of Zurich to study medicine. By 1911 she received a doctor's degree
on the basis of a study of schizophrenia.

At the time they met, Spielrein was eighteen or nineteen; Jung was
no more than thirty, having worked at the sanitarium for four or five years,
and only just embarked on the studies for which he would subsequently
be acclaimed. He was judged to be charismatic to women patients and,
according to Carotenuto, Jung's wife wrote to Freud that, "Naturally the
women are all in love with him."

It's unclear at what point in time the love affair between Jung and
Spielrein blossomed. Carotenuto surmises from the correspondence be-

tween Jung and Spielrein that Jung probably realized he was in love with
Spielrein by the beginning of 1908. It's also unknown whether or not the
love affair was ever consummated sexually. Carotenuto thinks not, but
Bettelheim, as he states in his introduction to Carotenuto's book, thinks
so. The lack of certainty may have to do with the fact that Jung's heirs
did not give permission to publish the letters that Jung had written to
Spielrein (though Carotenuto read them and quotes from them), and the
letters themselves may not be conclusive.

By 1909 their love affair had come to light. Someone—thought to be
Jung's wife—had written an anonymous letter to Spielrein's mother warn-
ing her that her daughter was involved in a possibly damaging relationship
with Jung, and asking her to put an end to it. At that point, Jung wrote
to Freud that "a woman patient, whom years ago I pulled out of a very
sticky neurosis with unstinting effort, has violated my confidence and my
friendship in the most mortifying way imaginable. She has kicked up a
vile scandal solely because I denied myself the pleasure of giving her a
child."

In a bizarre correspondence between Jung and Spielrein's mother (if
Spielrein's account of it in a letter to Freud is accurate), Jung indicates
that were he to be paid—his fee being 10 francs per consultation—the
mother would not have to worry about any further irregularity in the
doctor-patient relationship. There was a stormy falling out between Jung
and Spielrein, including one scene in which she pulled a knife on him
though she apparently succeeded only in cutting her own hand. She was
then removed from Zurich by her parents.

In 1910, on the occasion of submitting her thesis for a doctorate, she
reinstituted contact with Jung. She writes in her diary at that time that
he reassured her he knew no one to replace her—it was as though he had
a necklace in which all his other admirers were pearls but she the medal-
lion. Because she felt their love grew out of a "deep spiritual affinity and
common intellectual interests," she continued with him as her mentor,
re-establishing their love and their "poetry" (which Bettelheim assumes
was sexual) though with the clear understanding that he would never leave
his wife. And so the relationship continued for another year or two. She
toyed with giving him a child, the fantasied boy-child Siegfried (to unite
Jews and Christians—a theme of ongoing importance to her).

The relationship drifted over the next few years but Spielrein always
maintained an intellectual correspondence with Jung even after she had
moved into Freud's camp and Freud had broken with Jung. The love affair
was extraordinary in many ways, for both participants. Whatever the

precise nature of his relationship with Spielrein, Jung derived his theory of the unconscious from the experience—if not directly from her. In a letter from Jung to Spielrein, one of the last letters, dated September 1919 (long after their love affair had ended), Jung states: "The love of S. for J. made the latter aware of something he previously only vaguely suspected, that is, of the power in the unconscious that shapes one's destiny, a power which later led him to things of the greatest importance." Bettelheim concludes: ". . . whatever the specific contributions of Spielrein or Jung to the Jungian system, Jung asserts . . . that it was in their love affair that the system itself originated."

But, for our purposes, what is more important than what Jung got from Spielrein, is what she, as a result of a therapeutic relationship seriously "compromised" by an erotic transference and countertransference, got from him. In the course of their relationship she recovered from a very serious illness and went on to lead a productive life. Despite Jung's intense involvement with his patient, his inconstancy, and his abandonment of her when he may have feared that his career was threatened by exposure, this formerly psychologically crippled woman did not shatter; instead she healed, and was even able to preserve her feelings for Jung. Furthermore, it was in the treatment—and no doubt in her identification with her beloved Jung—that she found her own life's work. Spielrein seems to have transferred her love for Jung into her commitment to work, as symbolized by her using the name Siegfried, which she had once applied to the child she longed to have by Jung, to designate a paper she offered to him in fulfillment of her "duty" to him. The transposition of the child, Siegfried, from a real hoped-for child to the work is explicit. In a letter to Jung in 1912 (probably before her marriage) she writes, "Dear One, Receive now the product of our love, the project which is your little son Siegfried. It caused me tremendous difficulty, but nothing was too hard if it was done for Siegfried. If you decide to print this, I shall feel I have fulfilled my duty toward you."

Bettelheim is very disapproving of Jung's behavior, as well he might be, particularly given what we now know of the dangerous potential for acting out for both patient and analyst when there is an erotic transference-countertransference. However, he is careful to note that one's judgment of Jung must ultimately be tempered by the fact that the treatment cured Spielrein, and he raises a question which is peculiar indeed, but nonetheless valid: "In retrospect we ought to ask ourselves: what convincing evidence do we have that the same result would have been achieved if Jung had behaved toward her in the way we must expect a conscientious therapist to behave toward his patient? However questionable Jung's behavior was from a moral point of view—however unorthodox, even disreputable, it may have been—somehow it met the prime obligation of the therapist toward his patient: to cure her. True, Spielrein paid a very high price . . ."

I tell this story in part because, now that therapists are more knowledgeable than they were in the early days of psychoanalysis about the perils of transference-countertransference, there are many fewer present-day examples to draw from. Back then such interactions between analyst and patient occurred with some regularity. But I also tell it because of the profound changes that took place in both doctor and patient and must be largely attributed to the transformational power of love.

There is another dramatic story—also just recently come to light—in which transference love appears to be the prime catalyzing agent in a young woman's psychic transformation. In the holocaust memoir, *An Interrupted Life: The Diaries of Etty Hillesum*, a young woman who would later perish in a death camp describes her relationship with Julius Spier, a disciple of Jung. Spier was a practitioner of "psychochirology" or palm reading, and Etty became his student, patient, lover, and disciple. Despite the fact that he emerges for the reader, even through Etty's adoring eyes, as second-rate, and probably disreputable and dishonest as well, Etty was able to use her relationship with him to effect within herself a profound realignment of values and priorities. Ultimately her journal bears witness to a liberation of the self into a sphere of ever widening possibilities—even under the shadow of the holocaust.

But it is important to note that, however many such anomalous stories there are, unanalyzed transference love is much more likely to result in harm than good. Furthermore, those benefits that are possible in transference love accrue much more reliably from the analyzed transference, and this is of course the point Bergmann was making, and the reason transference interpretation has become so crucial to analytic therapy. Through an analysis of the transference, and an understanding of how the dynamics of the transference correspond to real life situations from the past, the patient can gain insight and free himself from the strait jacket of unanalyzed emotional material. (Analyzing the absence of an erotic transference can also yield insight, if the analyst can relate that absence to those inner resistances that militate against falling in love, as is the case with many male patients). Insofar as transference love is repetition—a reprint—it brings to the fore many of the excessive and unrealistic demands and conflicts that have insinuated themselves into the process of loving in real life, and thereby demonstrates to the patient how these tendencies have been destructive of real-life relationships. Only when self-knowledge frees the patient from the endless cycles of repetitive compulsion that contaminate his adult experiences of love can he enjoy the creative or restorative aspects of love. The working through of the erotic transference has this self-knowledge and liberation as its goal. Transference love can in this sense be a preview of and a route to the creative, restorative powers of romantic love.

But as I have already suggested, transference love is not an invariably positive or therapeutically useful experience. Like love itself, the erotic transference has within it the potential for pleasure and pain, good and evil. Not a simple emotion, it is fused—again like love itself—with pre-Oedipal components; it can mask dependency yearnings, competitive strivings, and hostile feelings as well as self-loathing. But within the therapeutic situation, it can become the basis for a transforming analytic experience—or alternately it can disrupt the therapy. Transference love may offer the energy for change, but only when it is rigorously analyzed can one be certain of the direction of that change. Despite its therapeutic potential, the erotic transference continues to this day to confound psychoanalytic therapies; it remains both gold mine and mine field.

Erotic Transference and Countertransference: Gender Variations

Insofar as we view transference as a response to our deepest human needs (and anxieties), we might expect there to be no gender difference in transference manifestations. Nonetheless, although many analysts contend that transference love is gender-blind, I believe it to be more common among women, particularly women in treatment with men. At the same time, the erotic countertransference—the feelings of love the therapist has for a patient—appears to be more commonly a problem for male therapists. What this suggests about differences between the sexes is that they are socialized to different forms of mastery over both themselves and the world and are the products of different developmental experiences, but for all that are both vulnerable to falling in love, albeit in different circumstances. By examining the erotic transference, we may shed light not only on the underlying impulses and facilitating factors resulting in love, but on gender differences and how they affect love.

A woman analyst, Eva Lester, was the first to make explicit note of this most interesting gender discrepancy in erotic transference and countertransference. She pointed out that there are almost no references in the psychoanalytic literature to the phenomenon of male patients experiencing strong erotic transferences to their female analysts. Lester reported she had encountered strong erotic transferences in her female patients, but only mild, transient, muted, and unstable ones in her male patients. Karme, in a case report, discusses a male patient's erotic transference to her, but it consists mostly of allusions to triangular situations in associations and dreams, with only a few explicitly erotic dreams and fantasies about her.

When there is an erotic transference in a male patient–female therapist pair, it seems to differ in significant and signifying ways from the comparable experience in female patient–male therapist pairs. In the latter case, the erotic transference tends to be overt, consciously experienced, intense, long-lived, directed toward the analyst, and focused more on love than sex; in the former, it is less overt and less sustained, more often relatively short-lived, experienced indirectly in dreams and triangular preoccupations, frequently transposed to a woman outside the analytic situation, and it is generally sexual rather than loving in its manifestation.

While male patients' sexual fantasies may be quite graphic, they tend to be devoid of erotic longing. A sexual thought, such as "sucking her cunt," may appear as an ego-alien thought and be accompanied by embarrassment. Frequently, what one witnesses are the defenses against the erotic transference rather than the transference itself. Even so, male patients can be extremely sensitive to imagined slights, demanding attention, or special accommodations, even while denying any personal involvement or desire. Like women, they may idealize the analyst, but they tend not to merge idealization with erotic longing (just as it so often happens that men are unable to direct both romantic, erotic feelings and affectionate, dependency feelings towards one object).

Generalizing from the transference experience in therapy, one might simply conclude that women are more susceptible than men to falling in love were it not for the observation that male analysts appear to have a greater proclivity to falling in love with their female patients than women analysts do with their male patients. From the early days of the psychoanalytic movement, before the dangers of the erotic transference and its reciprocation had been explored and codified, we have accounts of numerous instances in which male analysts fell in love with their female patients. In fact, the temptation to fall in love in the therapeutic situation when the analyst is at low ebb and the patient is young and attractive (and has either hysterical charm or the mystery of madness about her), turns out to be a very strong one on both sides.

Jung's affair with Sabina Spielrein is one such example, but he had another relationship of even greater moment, both romantically and intellectually: a forty-year-long romantic liaison with Antonia Wolff, first his patient and later his colleague. Toni was the daughter of Arnold Wolff, a rich businessman, and member of one of the oldest, most distinguished Zurich families. In 1910, she went to Jung as a patient, partly because she had failed to adjust to the death of her father and partly because of difficulties with her mother. Sometime during 1911–12 their relationship changed its character, escaping professional constraints, and their ensuing love affair was serious enough to produce complicated repercussions on Jung's family life. According to one biographer, "Jung's affair with Toni might have been less troublesome if he had not insisted on dragging his mistress into his family life and on having her as a regular guest for Sunday dinner." But Jung was proud of the triangle he had created and preserved, whatever the sacrifices and conflicts it caused his wife Emma and Toni. Toni Wolff, like Spielrein, became a practicing psychoanalyst and seemed to serve as Jung's inspiration, contributing to and elaborating upon many of his central ideas. She wrote a description of the four typologies of women: Mother and Wife; Hetaera or companion and friend to Man; Amazon; and Medium, the mediator between the conscious and unconscious. And apparently for Jung, she was both Hetaera and Medium.

Otto Rank is another analyst who seems to have participated in a passionate relationship with one of his patients, Anaïs Nin, whether or not they technically became lovers. One of Rank's biographers, James Lieberman, believes that they were. Nin spoke of herself in her famous diary as Rank's patient. Though she does not say they were lovers, Lieberman states that it is generally assumed they were, both by readers of the diary and his informants. Nin, who was married to the engraver and filmmaker Ian Hugo, never divorced, but lived apart from him much of the time, pursuing her interests and relationships. In 1931 she began an intimate and lasting friendship with Henry Miller in Paris. In 1933 Miller, impressed with Rank's work, wrote to him, met with him as a patient, and soon enough pronounced himself cured. Through Miller, Nin, too, went to see Rank as a patient. Shortly after her therapy ended, Nin decided she would become a therapist, and apparently "trained" with Rank. The following year, after Rank had moved his practice to New York, he asked Nin to join him there. According to Lieberman, she was willing to help Rank start a new life just as he'd done for her. But she delayed and Rank wrote her desperate letters reminding her of things he had done for her in her hour of need and asking her to reciprocate: "Well, I am dying now. Come to my rescue." She did join him in the States, where Rank set her up as a psychotherapist and his collaborator (and where she took him dancing in Harlem). Rank wanted Nin to condense some of his books, a task that struck Nin as overwhelming. Eventually, the excitement of playing help-mate to Rank and psychotherapist to patients lost its allure for Nin. Rank and Nin became less compatible as she felt asked to subordinate her autonomous creative life to his. She complained that his pleasures were too much of the mind, and it was apparently she who left him. She went back to Paris, having concluded that her attachment to Rank was a continuation of a father fixation. Lieberman quotes her on her liberation from psychoanalysis (or at least from Rank):

> I entered with impunity the world of psychoanalysis, the great destroyer of illusion, the great realist.
> I entered that world, saw Rank's files, read his books, but found in the world of psychoanalysis the only metaphysical man in it: Rank. I lived out the poem and came out unscathed. Free. A poet still.

There are many other instances, continuing even to this day, that show the proclivity of male therapists to fall in love with their female patients whether they act on these feelings or not. Some of the enacted affairs are well-known, even infamous, within the psychoanalytic community. Others remain relatively obscure for the perpetrators can come from all parts of the theoretical spectrum and all levels of training. Anyone who has worked in the wards of a mental hospital knows the frequency with which feelings of erotic transference and countertransference are engendered and sometimes acted out between patients and the various tiers of their support staff. Still other affairs are the stuff of popular fiction and films. The movie *Lilith,* for example, based on Salamanca's novel of the same name, portrays the destruction of an occupational therapist in training (Warren Beatty) who is seduced by a schizophrenic patient (Jean Seberg).

Lucia Tower points out, "Virtually every writer on the subject of countertransference . . . states unequivocally that no form of erotic reaction to a patient is to be tolerated. This would indicate that temptations in this area are great, and perhaps ubiquitous." Speaking of such relationships between women and their male analysts Phyllis Greenacre remarks: "That this is not so infrequent as one would wish to think becomes apparent to anyone who does many reanalyses. That its occurrence is often denied and the situation rather quickly explained by involved analysts as due to a hysterical fantasy on the part of the patient . . . is an indication of how great is the temptation." Many women analysts can confirm from the evidence of their own practices the frequency of such encounters, since they often have to deal with the results. This is so because women patients who have had sexual relations with therapists are frequently sent to women analysts in order to assure the patient that such an experience will not be repeated. The magnitude of the male therapist's proclivity for sexual acting out is further suggested by looking at the figures on sexual encounters between women patients and physicians (not just therapists). In the results of a survey of 460 physicians published in 1973, Kardener and his coworkers found that between 5 and 13 percent had engaged in erotic behavior with patients, although the psychiatrist was in fact the least likely to do so. In a more recent study of psychiatrists, Gartrell and her coworkers reported that 7.1 percent of male respondents and 3.1 percent of female respondents reported sexual contact with their own patients, but 88 percent of all such contacts took place between male psychiatrists and female patients. (It might be added that this article reports the highest percentage of female therapists ever implicated in this kind of sexual misconduct.)

The relative restraint of female therapists is not because of any special virtue on their part. Differences between the sexes in their experience of the erotic countertransference—and their enactment of it—reflect differences between them outside the consulting room: the reaction of a younger dependent female to an older, authoritarian male is traditionally conducive to an erotic relationship. By contrast, it is traditionally taboo for an older, experienced woman and a younger, inexperienced man to have erotic feelings for each other—though this prohibition appears to be weakening. (This dichotomy parallels the family experience in which father-daughter incest, while not sanctioned, is less abhorred than mother-son incest.) In short, women have a tendency to eroticize relationships with men in authority, men to split sex and dependency. This happens in the therapy situation and outside it as well. While both sexes may be drawn to love across a power differential, men tend to need the safety of the power advantage, women to fall in love within the apparent shelter of male power. Thus the relative subordination of patient to analyst makes the emergence of an erotic transference-countertransference reaction more likely in a male therapist–female patient configuration, because it is congruent with our society's prevailing romantic fantasies (fantasies which seem relatively untouched by the changing roles of women in the workplace). And so it is that the consideration of why a phenomenon like transference—a response to humankind's most basic needs—has a gender component ends up telling us much about men and women, and about love.

Promiscuity and Selectivity: Transference Love versus Romantic Love

There is a further mystery about transference love (and countertransference love, too)—one that if "worried" enough may yield even greater insight into love. The mystery is this: Falling in love is a phenomenon so erratic (or seemingly so) and inexplicable, so dependent on the incalculable, so much a product of what for want of a better word we call chemistry, the love object a re-edition sometimes so removed from the original as to seem more like a translation than a re-edition (and a very murky one at that), obscuring rather than revealing the original—in short, falling in love is such an idiosyncratic, unpredictable phenomenon—that it is hard to understand why its analogue, transference love, occurs so frequently and with such predictable regularity.

In trying to solve the mystery, the gender difference described above may give us a clue. Given the fact that transference love occurs with relative frequency among women patients and men analysts, and with less frequency when the positions are reversed, and the further fact that eroticism comes into play much more frequently in the analytic encounter (with the gender difference noted) than in nontherapeutic encounters, we have to try to identify what facilitates erotic longing in the therapeutic situation. Conversely, this may give us some insight into what inhibits it in "real" life. I will look first at the facilitating factors for the patient.

What is it that impels love—and why does it take place so frequently within the therapeutic context? Why should the erotic transference be called into being at all? Are we simply drawn to anyone who is caretaking and powerful—a potential rescuer—and if so, why? And how does this kind of leaning-love relate to romantic love?

In part, we can answer these questions by returning once again to Plato's great insight that love is a restoration—not just a longing to be reunited with the missing half, but the longing for restoration of a grander self. This is how Freud put it several millennia after Plato: "He [man] is not willing to forego the narcisstic perfection of his childhood," and when "he can no longer retain that perfection. . . . he seeks to recover it in the new form of an ego ideal." It has long been postulated that the infant's original sense of omnipotence—of being the center and mover of the world—is whittled away by the sequential frustrations and humiliations of childhood: hunger, weaning, repeated discomforts, toilet training. Consequently, the child projects onto the parents his lost omnipotence and for a while sees them as perfect. But they too fail to live up to his characterization of them as omnipotent and perfect, and finally the child must incorporate his image of perfection into his own psyche as a kind of guiding light. The "lost" ideal parents of one's childhood are thus internalized so that they become the basis of the superego (the restraining aspects of the parental function—the conscience) and the ego ideal (the inspiring aspects of the parental function).

Our hope of restoring our "lost" omnipotence rests then on our ability to live up to the dictates of the ego ideal; or, alternatively, on the opportunity to unite with someone else onto whom we have projected that ideal. To the degree that we live up to our internalized ego ideal, or come close to it, all is well. We are satisfied and comfortable. To the degree that we fail to do so, we are depressed and our sense of self is diminished. Thus love can be seen as a roundabout quest for perfection, for restored narcissism. Through idealization of the Other, and identification with that Other, we hope to regain our own perfection. This is the sense in which Alberoni (See Chapter 1) suggested love was always motivated by weakness. I would say, not just (or always) by weakness, but by some discontent or wish for something more.

Here, then, we come to one of the fundamental reasons the patient in analysis is so prone to fall in love. The patient comes to analysis only when he or she experiences some psychological disturbance or discontent, hence some wish for change. Whatever its cause, the fact of the patient's own psychological insufficiency or discomfort is of course a blow to her narcissism, to her sense of perfection and wholeness. She is on the lookout for an external remedy. Thus there is, in analysis, a clear prior tendency that would facilitate "falling in love" with the therapist. And, in fact, it is not uncommon for a prospective patient to have fantasies and dreams about the analyst even *before* analysis has begun. There is, as it were, a preformed transference, needing only the blank screen of the actual analyst on which to project itself. The analyst is the perfect foil for such fantasies because he (she) is, by and large, esteemed, respected, believed to be wise and mature, and, in the context of the therapy, the leader, therefore a candidate for automatic and instantaneous idealization. The preformed transference reminds us forcibly of one of the aspects of love—its imaginative component. Need, imagination, and a blank screen on which the imagination can go to work—these sometimes seem sufficient to galvanize transference love into being.

But there are still other features of therapy that facilitate erotic longings and feelings, features specific to therapy and common in it, but much harder to come by in everyday life. As such, these features may further account for the propensity to fall in love, and to long for reciprocal love in therapy rather than the much less predictable appearance of love outside the consulting room. First, it is the nature of analysis to promote regressive wishes, and part of the substratum of love is comprised of such wishes. Second, there is a sense of intimacy; one-sided though such intimacy may be, the patient feels the analyst knows her better than anyone else in the world. Thirdly, knowing the patient this profoundly, the analyst remains nonjudgmental and accepting. Fourth, because all the attention during the session is focused on the patient, there is some narcissistic gratification attached to therapy. And, finally, due to the privacy of the consulting room, the patient and doctor are secluded. By definition, they form a dyad, one which has a distinct boundary separating it from the external world; their interchanges are marked by privacy, intensity, communion, a sense of mission, and shared secrets. And, just as there is a unique dynamic characterizing the transactions between each pair of lovers, every therapeutic dyad, too, has its unique rhythmn and tone. The analyst is not exactly the same with any two patients, and of course it sometimes happens that the communication between the partners of a particular dyad is indeed extraordinary. (This is something seasoned analysts know and sometimes discuss among themselves, which somehow gets diluted in the analytic literature into generalities about analysts that tend to make them sound disembodied, utterly impersonal, literally blank screens.) Transference love may also be facilitated by the fact that very few demands are placed on the patient, not for sex or any kind of emotional reciprocity. Transference love can flourish as "a special hothouse variety of love." One can see that it in this way resembles other forms of truncated romance, for example of the pen-pals variety.

If therapy facilitated only the patient's eroticism, we might attribute that finding primarily to the regression that analysis fosters. But the frequency of erotic feelings in the therapist as well (countertransferential feelings) suggests that there are other factors of equal importance. For the therapist, one of the facilitating factors is the immense security of being admired and idealized. Moreover, the intimacy of the treatment situation, the seclusion of the treatment dyad, and the sense of a joint mission of some importance are predisposing factors for the analyst as well as for the patient.

The frequent occurrence of transference love, and to a lesser degree that of countertransference love, suggest that the impulse to fall in love is much more omnipresent, though in latent form, than one might otherwise imagine. It can then be seen to be *released* in the therapy structure, where the facilitating factors are so prodigious and the protection accorded to the integrity of self so considerable—enough that patients quite regularly take the risk of letting go enough to fall in love. The impulse to fall in love is obviously a tender, tentative one, one that needs a great deal of nourishment to grow. The analytic process provides much of that nourishment. Moreover, the caretaking implicit and explicit in therapy (whether one is patient or doctor, passive or active) stimulates some of the component fantasies of love.

However, as we might imagine from the dynamics of transference love, psychoanalytic therapy is not the only special situation that facilitates the experience of falling in love. Whenever a series of ongoing encounters between two people is structured in such a way as to foster intimacy within the context of a holding environment (one in which limits are set), love may be promoted.

This sometimes appears to be the case among clients of prostitutes for whom the fantasy of the whore with the heart of gold gets elaborated into love. The reasons why this development—so seemingly odd at first thought—should take place with some frequency are not difficult to fathom. Among high-priced call girls, those with steady customers, the following conditions obtain: the encounter is secret, exotic, and intimate. Like therapy, the meetings are concerned with the needs of the client. And like therapy, the encounter has certain limits: in particular, no demands are made on the client, the experience is designed for *him*. Regressive wishes are fostered and honored; the call girl is accepting and nonjudgmental. Moreover, the best of the call girls—like the best of therapists—often have uncanny insights into the needs and wishes of their clients (one intuitively gifted call girl conceived the brilliant idea of tying up her paraplegic client, thereby "normalizing" his disability). Unlike the therapy situation, where the therapist may be older and is seen as a power figure, thus suppressing the male client's tendency to fall in love, the call girl is young and is seen as less powerful, possibly herself in need of being rescued. And although she appears accessible, she is inaccessible too; she sets limits on her time and availability, and these very limits make her more desirable. Like analysts, the best of the call girls know about transference and how to handle it. And, in fact, some of their guidelines resemble those of analysts: they tend to discourage the personalization of the experience, they are loathe to take advantage of their clients, and are fundamentally more interested in other men (often their pimps) who appear to *them* as more powerful than their relatively needy clients.

It's also my impression, though this is harder to verify, that love blooms with some regularity among alcoholics attending AA. Elmore Leonard tells of one such love story in his novel, *Unknown Man, No. 89.* In it, a process server, Ryan, finds himself ruminating over an alcoholic girl, Denise, whom he has met while trying to track down a tough guy, Robert Leary, Jr. He must relocate Denise, whom he has discovered is Leary's wife. But his thoughts turn to Denise as a person.

He realized he wasn't just thinking about her in relation to the money, the fifteen thousand he'd get. He was thinking about her as a person. She had called for help and he had let her down.

At that point in the novel, it appeared somewhat perplexing—at least to this reader—as to why he should be so drawn to someone he had last seen in an alcoholic stupor. Later when Ryan locates Denise at an AA meeting, where she has gone for help, it becomes clear that he, too, had been an alcoholic, and the deep roots of his attraction towards Denise become more intuitively available to the reader. Speaking at the AA meeting Denise says, "I have the feeling everything I say you've heard before . . . but I guess that's part of it too. We can empathize, put ourselves in each other's place." Ryan falls in love with Denise and, together, they are able to outwit the bad guys and give up alcohol. In love affairs that ignite in comparable circumstances, one of the facilitating factors appears to be the ease with which two people, already sharing similar experiences and vulnerabilities, come to establish a sense of intimacy. Fear and shame may be confessed within a setting that guarantees both understanding, acceptance, and support. And, of course, analogous to the formal arrangements in the two other kinds of structured encounters already discussed—the therapeutic situation and the prostitute-client relationship—the periodicity and regularity of AA meetings promotes the simultaneous closeness and distance that may allow for both longing and crystallization to take place.

By contrasting real-life love affairs with several kinds of structured encounters that promote the experience of falling in love, we are made aware of the many impulses to erotic sentiment which float through mental life, destined for oblivion for lack of a controlled atmosphere in which they can flourish. Love appears to be a perpetual possibility waiting to be born, and flash fantasies of romantic encounters may sometimes figure as prominently as flash fantasies of sexual ones. Such impulses to love are formed in those situations in which a desirable object simultaneously appears to be accessible and forbidden. But they are ultimately nipped in the bud, except in circumstances that provide both some guarantee of safety from rejection and some hope (or illusion) of reciprocation, while allowing enough structured separation that the imaginative work of falling in love can take place.

CHAPTER ELEVEN

Modes of Self-Realization: Women and Romance, Men and Power

OTH SEXES have the same capacity to experience the pleasures and pains of romantic love. Women and men describe being in love in similar terms. This is surely as we would expect since the deep impulses that give rise to love and the capacity to synthesize those impulses derive from our human nature; the potential for exaltation, transcendence, and transformation is fundamentally unaltered by the accident of gender. In love we are more alike than different.

Still, there are some important differences between women's and men's experiences of romantic love, particularly in the incidence of the different distortions to which love is prone. As explained in the preceding chapter, women in treatment tend to experience the erotic transference more readily than do men, while men seem more susceptible to the temptations of the erotic countertransference. This observation parallels a popular assumption about women and men: that women are more at ease with the mutuality implicit in love, as well as the surrender, while men tend to interpret mutuality as dependency and defend against it by separating sex from love, or alternatively, by attempting to dominate the beloved. Women may well be more vulnerable to distortions in the direction of surrender, men to distortions in the direction of dominance.

These differences sometimes appear so great that some observers believe the very nature of love is different for the two sexes. Nietzsche expresses the latter view succinctly:

The single word love in fact signifies two different things for man and woman. What woman understands by love is clear enough:—it is not only devotion, it is a total gift of body and soul, without reservation, without regard for anything whatever. This unconditional nature of her love is what makes it a *faith*, the only one she has. As for man, if he loves a woman, what he *wants* is that love from her; he is in consequence far from postulating the same sentiment for himself as for women; if there should be men who also felt that desire for complete abandonment, upon my word, they would not be men.

Simone de Beauvoir agrees with Nietzsche. According to her, "The word *love* has by no means the same sense for both sexes, and this is one cause of the serious misunderstanding that divides them." Of course, the focus for both de Beauvoir and Nietzsche is twofold: the female capacity (and taste) for surrender and the male fear that surrender would undercut the essence of masculinity—in Nietzsche's words *"they would not be men."* De Beauvoir believes that total surrender is more in keeping with female psychology, but locates that proclivity in woman's situation, rather than in her nature. In de Beauvoir's view, as in mine, the experience of love is potentially the same for both sexes, but in actuality is shaped by each gender's differing experiences in the family and in society. It is clear from her exegesis that she believes surrender to be harmful for women. To some degree she is no doubt correct, but the corollary is also true: the male's inhibited capacity for surrender is damaging to him, for it tends to preclude the possibility of the kind of liberation from the confines of self that comes with surrender.

Not just distortions in loving, but the basic experience may be shaped to some degree by gender. Many observers, both casual and professional, agree that men and women generally value romantic love differently (at least consciously), tend to act it out in what might be called typically "masculine" and "feminine" ways, and are often variously susceptible to its siren call. Although men and women face the same existential problems in life—death, aloneness, insufficiency, imperfection—they attempt to solve these problems in different ways and utilize love differently. Why? First, because there is a strong cultural component to love, and there are different cultural imperatives for the sexes, different prescriptions urged upon them. Second, the psychological development of each sex preordains different central problems and different strategies for resolving them. And finally the ongoing cultural context locks in the preexisting tendencies toward difference.

Because of their different socializations, men and women are predisposed to different passionate quests—the passionate quest being, for us in the West, that which constitutes the central theme of our lives. This passionate quest supplies the context for our pursuit of self-realization, adventure, excitement, and ultimately transformation and even transcendence. The passionate quest is always a romance in the larger meaning of romance, but it is not always the quest for romantic love per se. For women, however, the passionate quest is almost always predominantly interpersonal in nature, and generally involves romantic love, while for men it is more often heroic, the pursuit of achievement or power. One might say that men favor power over love and women achieve power through love. (In years gone by, though it is not now an obsolete phenomenon by any means, the woman indulging in megalomaniac visions of power imagined obtaining it vicariously, through bewitching some great ruler and ruling through her command over him—so the legend of Delilah, the actuality of Eva Peron.) Most commonly, women incline toward defining themselves in terms of romance, men in terms of work.

Sometimes these different imperatives for the sexes are covert, sometimes they are all too explicit, as in this conversation between two characters in *Man's Fate*. (The conversation also embodies a profound racial prejudice.)

"Far fewer women would indulge in copulation," answered Ferral, "if they could obtain in the vertical position the words of admiration which they need and which demand a bed."

"And how many men?"

"But man can and must deny woman: action, action alone justifies life and satisfies the white man. What would we think if we were told of a painter who makes no paintings? A man is the sum of his actions, of what he has *done*, of what he can do. Nothing else. I am not what such and such an encounter with a man or woman may have done to shape my life; I am my roads."

Socialization seems to be one of the predominant factors in creating the different dreams by which each sex shapes its narrative life. There is a second equally powerful source for these different modes of achieving self-realization—one that resides in earliest psychological development. Each sex has the fundamental task of organizing a gender identity, by which I mean each of us constructs a way of being in the world which is either feminine or masculine. The consolidation of an inner psychological identity is based by and large on a fundamental identification with the same-sex parent. (One can argue endlessly about whether or not this female/male dichotomy is an inescapable fact of human life. It appears to be universal, having been demonstrated in every known culture. But the specific content of femininity and masculinity is culturally variable—sometimes to a startling degree.)

For the girl, whose earliest identifications are with her mother—generally the primary caretaker—the task of identity consolidation is in some ways more straightforward than for the boy. Most women feel the pull to reduplicate the maternal identity by falling in love, pair-bonding, and becoming mothers themselves. Love is experienced as part of the girl's destiny, the cornerstone for consolidating her female identity; and, growing up as she does by the side of her mother, she learns firsthand how to achieve this destiny. The skills she seeks are psychological, the goal is mutuality, the model is the nurturing mother. The "calling" most likely to compete with the primacy of romantic love is motherhood, not work.

Just as the girl must establish a feminine identity, so, too, must the boy establish a masculine identity. Part of what it means for a man to love *successfully* is that he finally accepts both his father's right to his mother, and the fact that his mother has loved his father as she has not loved him, the son. But he can only grant this "independence" to his parents full-heartedly when he has integrated their story into his own, when he has become his own father precisely in the act of loving the woman who stands to him at the deepest level as a substitute for his mother. However, the resolution of the boy's problem of achieving a masculine identity is not so direct as the girl's consolidation of a feminine identity.

While the girl establishes her femininity *through* love, the boy must establish his masculine credentials by another route. In primitive societies, there are initiation tests and ceremonies that prepare and signal the boy's accession to manhood; but in more developed societies the boy enters the adult male world chiefly through his becoming economically independent. Historically, this has often meant following in his father's footsteps—that is, taking the same kind of job, apprenticing to the same trade. Thus, in a sense, the boy's arrival in adolescence at a "penile equivalence" with his father is marked by his entering into the father's economic role, a line of continuity which operates to reassure him of his masculine identity at the same time that it equips him financially to repeat the parental pattern. But this is increasingly difficult to achieve in complex societies.

Some of the inner conflicts experienced by men today may be the result of the prolongation of dependence upon the father's economic authority well beyond the period when it is optimally acceptable to the boy's psyche, and the attendant delay in the consolidation of masculine identity—and autonomy—that this implies. To remain "dependent" well into their twenties, through college, and more and more frequently graduate school, imposes upon men an emotional and psychological burden from which it may be difficult to recover—that is, out of which it may be difficult to emerge into true autonomy and from there into the psychological freedom to fall in love.

The path by which the boy consolidates his masculine identity is achievement-oriented. For the male, his quest, like that symbolized in initiation rites, involves a test he must pass before being allowed to assume his place in the world. It's doubtful there is ever the same element of risk in women's *rites de passage*.

For the male, then, love is not usually the first prerequisite in consolidating his identity (though of course there are exceptions). Generally, he must first seek affirmation of his masculinity through his autonomous exploits. And this remains for him an activity of highest priority, taking precedence over romantic love. (For the male, in contrast to the female, it is work rather than parenthood that most often conflicts with romantic love.)

The difference between the sexes depends then not just on socialization, but the way in which socialization acts through early psychological development. The fundamental psychological difference between the sexes appears to be perpetuated by the fact that the girl is raised by a caretaker of the same sex, the boy by a caretaker of the opposite sex. This difference predisposes to greater ease for women in achieving a feminine identity than for men in achieving a masculine one. Both the mother-infant dyad and the Oedipal triangle are different for the two sexes. This difference not only shapes the basic nature of the passionate quest for the sexes, but it determines the discrepant psychological skills necessary for the journey and calls into being the conscious and unconscious fantasies about the demons and enablers who will be encountered along the way.

In response to the universal human state of existential aloneness and the corresponding wish for wholeness, each sex looks to different modes of establishing self-identity and transcendence. For the woman, both needs—for self-identity and self-transcendence—can be fulfilled in the trajectory of love that leads to marriage and motherhood. For the male, self-identity and self-transcendence are established in different trajectories, self-identity in autonomous achievement, self-transcendence in love or sometimes (abortively) in power. (Consequently for many males, love may become contaminated by self-assertion and domination.) Though both sexes may ultimately achieve love as a transcendental experience, a mode of simultaneously enlarging and escaping the self, the degree to which one or the other—escape or enlargement—is stressed may again depend upon gender. The tapestry of an individual's love chronicles, his need for love, capacity for it, and specific vulnerabilities, are always woven of a complex mix of social and psychological imperatives, penchants, and possibilities. Many of these are contingent on gender, and gender issues in turn have both social and psychological components.

Women and Romance

Life's central romance, at least for many women, is the quest for an ideal love relationship. It is the only quest readily available to most women except for motherhood, and this generally (though of course not always) awaits pair bonding. The rewards of this feminine quest are elegantly stated by Rachel Brownstein in her book *Becoming a Heroine:* "The marriage plot most novels depend on is about finding validation of one's uniqueness and importance by being singled out among all other women by a man. The man's love is proof of the girl's value, and payment for it. Her search for perfect love through an incoherent, hostile wilderness of days is the plot that endows the aimless [life] with aim." Brownstein, like many others, emphasizes the crucial distinction between the female search for feminine identity through intimacy and the male search for masculine identity through achievement. (The woman finds her identity through the self-in-relationship.)

It is in the problems a woman encounters in her amorous quest that the history of her psychological development is most clearly reflected. These problems can be seen in their purest form in romance novels—that enormously popular genre whose enduring appeal reveals the female appetite for romantic love. As shown in Janice A. Radway's study of the romance novel, the central plot generally revolves around the ability of a beautiful young woman to melt the cold and indifferent stance of the slightly menacing, withdrawn hero. The plots of these books, like those of fairy tales, recapitulate both the cultural directive that women are to seek romance *and* the major psychological barriers they must face before bringing that quest to a successful conclusion.

Radway describes the typical heroine as feisty, independent, and spirited—this, paradoxically, despite her ultimate goal of surrendering her autonomy to the powerful hero, of losing herself in a romantic union. The man who is sought is distinguished by his extreme masculine characteristics (a stallion of a man, like Rhett Butler in *Gone with the Wind*); this preference is striking because it seems almost to preclude fulfillment of those desires for tender nurturance that are part of the central longings in love. In fact, the nature of both these archetypes—fiery, independent heroine and powerful, aloof, even frightening hero—points to the same need: to separate the conscious experience of romantic love from its infantile origins. Apparently, for any of us, female or male, to identify with a romantic story, we must be reassured that the nurturance sought is of a different order from that offered by maternal love.

Just as in real life the tomboy stage seems to separate a girl from her identification with (and dependence on) her mother, the literary characterization of the heroine as willful and high-spirited assures us that she is already emancipated, a free woman. (These personality characteristics make it easy to see why Bette Davis and Katharine Hepburn made such marvelous heroines in the films of the forties.) Alternatively, the heroine may be orphaned, alone in the world—another route that establishes her separateness. Similarly the stereotypic fantasy of the sought-after romantic hero is so different from the imago of the nurturant mother that we are prevented from seeing any continuity between the longing for maternal solicitude and the longing for romantic solicitude. Thus the archetypical romantic fantasy provides for tender nurturance, simultaneously proclaiming that the heroine's internal separation from her pre-Oedipal mother has taken place and confirming her femininity and heterosexuality. Moreover, the drastic Otherness of the male lover wards off the dreaded consequences of fusion—loss of self—at the same time that it provides a vehicle for transcendence. Union, even merger, with somebody distinguished by such dramatic qualities of Otherness may help to preserve the sense of intactness of the boundaries of the self. (In real life this romantic solution to developmental needs may not work out so neatly. Men distinguished by so many characteristics of extreme "masculinity" may prove insufficiently nurturing. Consequently, many women must eventually get their nurturance at one remove—not by refinding their mother, but by becoming one. But this is another subject altogether.)

The heroine must not only grapple with those issues of separation just described, but, in order to come into her own as a woman, must also deal with internal prohibitions against sexuality (generally emanating from fear of the internalized Oedipal mother). The plot of the novel *Rebecca,* by Daphne Du Maurier, dramatically illustrates the conflicts present in the feminine quest for romantic love. *Rebecca* brings to life the unconscious female longing for paternal rescue from a malevolent female Oedipal figure. The impoverished heroine (interestingly enough never designated by a Christian name throughout the novel), an orphan employed as a companion for the shallow, snobbish, and demanding Mrs. Van Hooper (the first of many withholding, disapproving "bad" mothers in the novel), meets Max de Winter, the older, recently widowed owner of Manderley, a beautiful and famous English estate, at a resort hotel where they are all staying. Because Mrs. Van Hooper falls ill, the heroine's time is her own and she is startled when Max chooses to spend time with her, taking her for long morning drives. To her utter amazement, Max falls in love with her, proposes, and takes her home to Manderley and, thereby, it might be noted, rescues her from her enslavement to the altogether unsympathetic and selfish Mrs. Van Hooper. She has already noticed Max's moodiness and periodic withdrawal, and mistakenly, almost tragically, attributes it to his ongoing grief for his dead wife, Rebecca. At Manderley, the shadow of Rebecca hovers over her happiness even more, intensified by the machinations of the housekeeper, the evil Mrs. Danvers, who had been Rebecca's loyal and loving servant. Curiously enough—or perhaps typically enough—the heroine cannot confide her misgivings and unease in her husband, feeling herself to be a poor replacement for the brilliant, beautiful Rebecca; consequently, it is only in the context of a hair-raising and threatening series of events that she discovers the true fate of Rebecca.

Naturally, as in all happy fantasies of Oedipal victory, it turns out that Max was never in love with Rebecca at all. In fact, because Rebecca had taunted Max with the fact that she was pregnant by another man (even this turns out to be one of Rebecca's vicious lies), far from mourning Rebecca's untimely death, Max had actually been the cause of it. In this female fantasy, no real rapproachement is ever made between the heroine and the rivalrous and menacing female Oedipal figures who haunt or torment her; instead the heroine is rescued by recourse to a union with a protective paternal figure, and triumphs over her rivals. These fantasies apparently subsume the child's longing for the mother, which has been renounced but lingers on, into the tender nurturance she seeks from the father-husband. Yet, in *Rebecca*, the ultimate limitation to this resolution is clear. The Oedipal victory is incomplete; Mrs. Danvers burns Manderley to the ground and the lovers live out their lives cast out of the Garden of Eden. (This sequence parallels the dangers of the erotic transferences women form toward their male analysts if they remain unanalyzed. If they fail to achieve a positive identification with a beloved or respected maternal figure, their unconscious guilt at being Oedipal winners spoils their happiness in one way or another.)

Rebecca, first published in 1938, proved enduringly popular with the public. In fact, it was the phenomenal success of this novel that is said to have inspired the launching of two series of romance novels, at Ace and Doubleday, in the early 60s at a time when mystery novels were declining in sales and the publishers were looking for a best-selling genre to replace them. I make the assumption that no novel can win such a huge female audience without touching some fundamental chords in female fantasy. This is, of course, the premise the publishers were working on, and it surely proved out commercially. The chords struck by *Rebecca* and other more simplistic imitations from the same genre sound out the themes of separation and Oedipal conflict. They reverberate throughout all female erotic fantasy, and generally reach resolution (or sometimes merely suppression) only with the arrival of Prince Charming.

Fairy tales as well as romance novels are very revealing on the subject of the intersection of the pre-Oedipal and Oedipal struggle in female life. Bruno Bettelheim in his classic study *The Uses of Enchantment* points out the difference between girls' and boys' Oedipal problems as revealed in fairy tales. "What blocks the oedipal girl's uninterrupted blissful existence with Father is an older, ill-intentioned female (i.e, Mother). But since the little girl also wants very much to continue enjoying Mother's loving care, there is also a benevolent female in the past or background of the fairy tale, whose happy memory is kept intact, although she has become inoperative." (In contrast, Bettelheim notes how seldom the wicked stepmother figures in fairy-tales with a male protagonist.) In other words, the girl splits her image of the mother into the good pre-Oedipal mother and the wicked stepmother. The girl's internal maternal demons find symbolic expression in many of those fairy tales that focus on courtship and marriage. The fairy tales depict the heroine as bound to the past, sometimes by virtue of an evil perpetrated on her by one or the other of her parents (or parent surrogates—witches, enchantresses, step-parents). Until set free by love. Rapunzel was locked away in a tower by a wicked enchantress, awaiting rescue by the prince; Cinderella, too, was in the clutches of her past, in her case bound to do wretched service for her wicked stepmother. One thinks again of Mrs. Van Hooper and Mrs. Danvers in *Rebecca*. In all these stories, the girl's actual father, like her mother, is ineffectual (his ineffectuality has the added advantage of providing a defense against any residual incestual longings) and so her rescue must await the prince.

Daphne Du Maurier, whose imaginative powers seem to have tapped directly into the female psyche, played an interesting variation on the Oedipal theme in still another best-selling novel, *Jamaica Inn*. There, the heroine Mary Yellan goes to live with her mother's sister Patience and Patience's husband, Joss Merlyn. The once beautiful Patience is now aged, fearful, and broken, living in dread of her boozing bullying husband at Jamaica Inn, which is an isolated, desolate place on the moors, deserted save for intermittent dark-of-night visitations from her husband's nefarious acquaintances. Mary is horrified by her new surroundings; only through her quiet dignity and inner resources does she escape some of the worse hazards of her situation.

And here, of course, Du Maurier has given us the theme of the menacing, threatening Oedipal father, potential rapist and brute, coupled with an Oedipal mother who is good but too weak to protect either Mary or herself. But just as there is an internalized good mother and bad mother image for most of us, so, too, is there a good father as well as bad father image. In *Jamaica Inn*, the bad father is personified in the figures of the drunken uncle and Frances Davay, the evil vicar of Altarnum. But Mary is ultimately rescued by her uncle's brother, Jem. While Jem is initially viewed as threatening—and he is, in fact, a horse thief—nonetheless he is a good man and literally rides to the rescue in the happy ending. (While I might write about Du Maurier's plots tongue-in-cheek, she is, nonetheless, a magnificent storyteller and I find myself just as spellbound by her tales as any other reader. These primal fantasies take us past our surface sophistication because they speak to something so deep within us.)

In real life, too, and not just in fairy tales and novels, we are bound to and by our past, generally through the internalized images of our parents, who continue to exert an influence on our lives. Only when an internal psychological separation is finally effected can the Oedipal constraints be symbolically overcome and love prevail. But whereas romance novels and fairy tales generally have happy endings—though not always, the denouement in *Rebecca* and some others of the genre being ambiguous—in real life even relatively healthy women often continue to suffer from unresolved aspects of Oedipal (and pre-Oedipal) conflicts. Some women, as many observers have remarked, prefer nonsexual caresses and verbal reassurances of love and commitment to sexual ones. While this may perhaps reflect some fundamental differences in female and male priorities regarding sex, it certainly also suggests that such women have not fully escaped the threat posed by their personal equivalents of Rebecca and Mrs. Danvers, of nay-saying internalized Oedipal mothers. Sexual inhibition may be the price some women pay for the shortcuts they take to self-identity. These women may opt to find selfhood through a headlong rush into romance rather than through the kind of autonomy possible only to those who have integrated identifications with good and strong women into their sense of who they are. Autonomy through vicarious identification with one's lover is ultimately no substitute for one's own accomplishments, particularly in today's world, and it sometimes tends to preclude the full development of parts of the self.

Moreover, in their refusal to confront the spectre of female competition, some women may be left with the nagging fear that another woman will intervene and steal away the beloved. Even women who are firmly ensconced in a love relationship often fear or anticipate its end without any external cause for doing so, just as the second Mrs. de Winter feared the hold of Rebecca on Max. Fear of loss of love can take the form of fear of abandonment or rejection by the beloved, even when this is an extremely remote possibility. If threatened by abandonment, real or imagined, women may feel not only unloved but bad and unlovable.

Women's preoccupation with pair-bonding and the fear of its disruption can perhaps best be understood in the context of specific features of the female Oedipal constellation. The fact that the girl relinquishes her first object—her mother—in favor of her father has several important ramifications. First of all, in giving up her mother for her father, she is giving up a love object whose feeling for her was unconditional and automatic in favor of one whose love she must act to win. Moreover, she realizes that her mother, now her erotic rival, remains her major source of dependent gratification, a situation that intensifies her fears of retaliation. The fear of losing the dependency object (the mother) leads to a dread of loss of love and consequently of sustenance, a fear that is displaced from mother onto all subsequent love objects. This formulation of the problem emphasizes the uncertainty of the girl's relationship with her father, and also the girl's special vulnerability to the threats of the Oedipal period, when her rival is also still her much-needed caretaker, which would account for the preponderance of wicked stepmothers in fairy tales with female protagonists. But this formulation is in direct opposition to the classical one in which the girl, already "castrated" and therefore having nothing to lose, is said to bypass Oedipal competition comparable to what the boy experiences. My reading is completely different from the classical one; insofar as competition is differentially experienced, I believe girls are *more* vulnerable, because what is at risk is their very sustenance. (In my opinion, it may be this dilemma that makes females so susceptible to anorexia.)

To recapitulate: The girl's difficulty (fear of competition) at the threshold of the Oedipal period is reinforced by the consequences of her renunciation of her mother and simultaneous turn to her father. She feels she has abandoned her mother for an uncertain substitute and she fears retaliation. Further, the renunciation of her mother is felt as a loss. One could therefore say that all heterosexual women have experienced the loss of their first love object, whereas the same cannot be said for men. It is this early loss (and fear of retribution) along with the threat of the loss of the new dependency object that appears to be at the core of the female's pervasive dread of losing love. In some women, the fear is activated not by any slight on the part of husband or lover, but by an adulterous impulse on her own part. In contrast to men, this dynamic (adulterous impulse leading to fear of losing love) occurs so regularly that it seems to recapitulate some earlier confusion: Did the girl renounce her mother or was she rejected by her? For women, the lifelong problematic seems to be the uncertainty about achieving and conserving a love relationship.

Men and Power

Cinderella and the Prince, Penelope and Odysseus: She must be good and patient, sometimes no more than meltingly beautiful, but He must quest. His road to love is through actively establishing his masculine worth, thereupon being enabled to claim his prize. Sex roles may have changed to some degree, but the quintessential love plots appear to have considerable durability.

Just as women's popular fiction appears to be preoccupied with romantic love, so men's appears to concentrate on the adventurous (though the adventures are interspersed with encounters with women who supply spice and sex). Much of popular male fiction stresses the heroic, the adventurous, the virile, and sometimes the cruel. (I would include here writers such as Harold Robbins, Norman Mailer, and Eric van Lustbader.) I have suggested elsewhere that the appropriate name for this genre might be "Herotica." Just as the female romance novel has been called the female "pornography," I think a case could be made for "Herotica" as the male "romance." (The one recent, and in my judgment excellent, novel which appears to be a hybrid and incorporates elements of both Harlequin and Herotica is John Le Carré's *The Little Drummer Girl*. It is a gothic embedded within a thriller format.) This difference in fantasy fodder reflects the differences both in the "romances" to which each sex is socialized and in their psychological development as well.

For men, the typical adventurous journey recounted in fairy tale and epic is prelude to and embodiment of the amorous quest; the male must establish his masculine identity *before* he is internally free to love. In the archetypal adventure, the hero, alone, sets out somewhat innocently, unaware of the immense tests he will inevitably face. The hero, like the lover, is often looking for something lost—magic sword or holy grail (his full phallic strength perhaps); he is bent on defeating a threatening dragon or confronting other grave dangers (to self or country, king or maiden). The danger he faces is externalized. It is not Father who presents the problem, but the evil dragon.

In the course of the young man's journey he encounters many obstacles and through confronting them, learns the full measure of his personal resources, which often depend on magic he has received—either because of his goodness or kindness—from someone older and wiser. (In the amorous quest, the figure of the enabler might be thought of as a benevolent Oedipal figure who gives sanction to the quest.) The hero's excitement derives in part from the dangers he faces, in part from the challenge to his own strength, and the need to draw on undiscovered regions of himself. His journey is based on mystery, transgression, illusion and elusiveness, struggle, and the promise of a magic resolution at the end. The joys of claiming the prize are of course enhanced by the hardships along the way. And, as Bettelheim has pointed out, that prize is often a female who has been held in captivity—what better stand-in for Mother, who is surely not with Father of her own accord?

In love, too, the lover encounters much that is strange, mysterious, even threatening and therefore exciting, on his journey. He, too, must test his mettle. In order to possess the Other, he must confront certain prohibitions and demons. But unlike the hero, whose demons are found in the external world, the lover's demons are frequently found to reside in his own unconscious. Just as the hero, confronted by external demons, draws on the magic of the sorcerer, so, too, the lover, whose demons are within, must fight using those internal resources that have been given him—positive identifications and the benevolent imagoes of good parents—as a legacy of growing up. (Both the demons *and* enablers are, of course, different sides of the internalized parental imagoes. In the Wife of Bath's Tale the old hag who gives the protagonist the magic secret is finally transformed into the beloved—a most dramatic instance of refinding!) In the end, the lover, like the hero, discovers new capacities in himself and, therefore, the basis for an expanded sense of self-worth. In successful quests, the lover's personality is reorganized at a more complex level; as an adult who has come into his own and achieved a new maturity, he then takes his place as ruler of the kingdom.

Just as the heroine confronts and resolves certain basic psychological conflicts, so, too, does our hero. But the boy's inner psychological journey of separation, individuation, Oedipal thrust, and ultimate re-union is somewhat different from the girl's. In marked contrast to women, the problem of obtaining nurturance does not appear to loom as large for men. And why should it? Women are socialized and psychologically groomed to give nurturance, men to receive it. The hero's problems have more to do with establishing his masculinity, with the potential threat of castration from another male, a father "competitor," with devising strategies for defeating the father competitor and taking his place, and with the question of whether or not he is powerful enough to fulfill—fill up—a woman. This is as true for Tristan as for that foiled lover, the tireless seducer Don Juan.

By and large, most psychoanalytic accounts of male development focus on the boy's struggle with his father, as do the heroic accounts of male adventure. The fundamental problem is viewed as the struggle to achieve phallic strength and power vis-à-vis other men.

To understand male development in more depth, one must also take into account the primary impact of the mother-son relationship at different points in the boy's development. Too often, the female has been portrayed more as a prize than a protagonist in the boy's development.

Yet there are essentially two very different images of woman that run through male fantasy life: woman as temptress, seductress, femme fatale; and woman as nurturer, comforter, earth mother, eternal mother. In the first category are images of the sirens, the Bride of Darkness, the Whore of Babylon, Medusa, Delilah, Carmen, Cleopatra—all the images of the Dark Lady to be found in literature. In the second category are the Muses, Lady Luck, Beatrice, the pure Virgin, Goethe's Lotte whom Werther first sees distributing bread to children. (These same images are also part of the woman's repertoire of potential imaginative roles; in *Gone with the Wind* we have Scarlett and Melanie. Curiously enough, I've encountered only a few women who have identified with Melanie rather than Scarlett.) In Frank R. Stockton's short story "The Lady or the Tiger" the whole plot turns on the hero's ability to guess who the lady really is: Is she the loving self-sacrificing woman who will try to save him by relinquishing him to another woman, or is she the serpent woman who will let him go to his death rather than let another woman have him? Perhaps Ibsen in *Peer Gynt* comes closest to portraying men's fantasy life when he divides his protagonist's life between Anitra, the sensual woman, and Solveig, the maternal one. And, as noted in the previous chapter, we have Jung's theoretical distinction between different types of women, which provided the rationale for his forty-year triangular involvement with the maternal woman (his wife Emma) and the eros-muse (his mistress Toni).

How is it that the bountiful nurturant mother of childhood is so often imaginatively transformed into the snake woman, the emblematic kiss of death? Or, alternatively, how is it that so few men seem able to find satisfaction with one woman only? Just as the girl may register problems with the Oedipal father and not just the Oedipal mother, so, too, does the boy's erotic development show the traces of tensions with *both* Oedipal parents. The history of the boy's development as regards his mother is fairly complex. Freud, Horney, and, more recently, some of the French theorists have suggested that the first blow to the boy's narcissism is his *inability* to secure his mother's exclusive love. In other words, the boy's fear of his father and the threat of castration (at the hands of the father) are not the only factors in the boy's renunciation of his mother. He also withdraws his emotional investment in her because he does not have the genital equipment to compete with his father. His sense is that his mother rejects him because his penis is too small, that he is altogether an inadequate replacement for his father. In essence, the boy, like the girl, must renounce his libidinal tie to his mother, though for different reasons and at a different time—the boy both out of fear of Oedipal retaliation and out of his mortified realization that he is inadequate to replace his father. This is a narcissistic wound that persists; it may be revealed later in life through fears about the size and adequacy of his penis, and metaphorically, though perpetual questing for the sword, the grail, and so on. For many men, the sense of masculine inadequacy never abates despite years of adequate sexual performance and stable relationships.

In addition, the boy's sense of masculine inadequacy may become linked to aggression directed towards women. The blow to the boy's sense of genital adequacy (and to his masculine self-regard) may serve to remind him of earlier frustration (oral, anal) sustained at the hands of that same mother. Consequently, in accordance with the talion principle of an eye for an eye, a tooth for a tooth, as Horney puts it, "The result is that his phallic impulses to penetrate merge with his anger at frustration, and the impulses take on a sadistic tinge." This might be regarded as nearly universal, but essentially transient. However, if the anger and sadism are great, the female genitals and the female herself (again by virtue of the talion principle) will become a secondary source of castration anxiety and the mother, along with the father, will be seen as a potential castrator. And so it is that the Dark Lady is born in the imagination.

While sexual sadism is hardly universal among adult men, nor the fantasy of the Dark Lady either, the anxiety connected to masculine self-regard seems to be. According to Horney, "the dread of being rejected and derided is a typical ingredient in the analysis of every man, no matter what his mentality or the structure of his neurosis." The dread of rejection is, for men, connected with anxiety about inadequate endowment and performance—whether sexual, emotional, or economic. And, as I have already suggested, the typical male fantasy—as depicted in myth and Herotica—entails the protagonist's journey either to recover or validate his masculine prowess.

Confirming masculinity rather than achieving love appears to be the male's central dilemma, a preoccupation that permeates many aspects of his life. In order to compensate for anxieties about his masculine adequacy, men resort to power remedies. I use the term "power" in the sense of a set of impulses intended not just to defeat male competitors, but also to control women, so as to insure the availability of the source of gratification without jeopardizing his own independence. The man's control of the woman becomes a device compensating him for his childhood sense of inadequacy and inferiority vis-à-vis both parents. Out of revenge, the man reverses his infantile experience: he stands ready to demand sexual and amorous fidelity while disavowing it himself. His defensive structure is essentially counterphobic.

For all these developmental reasons, men seem to be more susceptible to initiating reverse triangles for safety's sake and more vulnerable to the corruption of love through power than are women. In his compensatory fantasy (or desire), the male may split his erotic and sexual desire among a number of different women, usually those whom he sees as occupying a position inferior to his own. This allows him to control the source of his gratification by insuring that there are backup objects in the event that one vanishes. To this end, he fantasizes about omni-available women and dreams of sex with two women at a time. Often he seeks simultaneous love relationships with two women or, alternately, he tries to thoroughly dominate and possess one woman.

The male's fear of the female (and his anger at her) stems from different developmental levels: fear of the pre-Oedipal mother of infancy who abandons/engulfs; of the phallic-narcissistic mother who confirms/denigrates masculinity; of the Oedipal mother who cannot be fulfilled, who rejects and falsely seduces, and who prefers the father. Out of these fears arises the male propensity to divorce romantic longing from sexual longing. Alternatively, some men protect themselves either through overt domination over the beloved or through recourse to reverse triangles.

By and large, women escape into love, whereas men fear being made vulnerable by love. Women establish their feminine identity through loving, whereas men must secure their masculine identification in order to be able to fall in love.

Cultural Conditioning

As already suggested, to the degree that differences exist in the female and male experience of love, they are not due simply to differences in psychological development but to differences in cultural conditioning. What then, of the current gender revolution and its impact on the experience of love? We are indeed witnessing a change in the prescribed gender roles for women and men, but primarily as these involve women. For women, the gender revolution prescribes a shift in the concept of the ideal feminine role. Traditionally, woman is said to have thought of herself as the "Other," seeking vicarious fulfillment through her nurturance of both husband and children. In the feminist view fulfillment must be sought through autonomous achievement as well, and work and career have consequently assumed greater significance in women's lives. Nonetheless, when it comes to love, the impact of the gender revolution has not had so large an influence. Although some women and men feel they have blasted through social and psychological stereotypes, more often love stories appear to be the same. Moreover, it is not altogether clear precisely what the aims of change are (or might be) as regards love. There appear to be two different schools of thought, with some theorists arguing that women should be freed from the harmful injunction to seek romantic love, while others (perhaps fewer in number) urge men to give up some measure of worldly success in return for the pleasures of intimate bonding (fatherhood and perhaps romantic love as well).

Many feminists, while willing to confirm the potential benefits of affectionate bonding and love, object to *romantic* love because they feel that it demeans and enslaves women. Too often, they feel, the woman finds meaning in life only as the romantic object of a sovereign male. Because love is central to her identity, woman subjects herself to a man's whims in order to placate him and preserve "their" love. Preserving the relationship then takes priority over authentic feeling. Insofar as women lack avenues for the consolidation of autonomy, they cannot be free to love because they are forced to forego spontaneity and authenticity in favor of manipulation through submission and ingratiation. Some feminists, like Shulamith Firestone, claim that romance rationalizes woman's suppression. She is among those who point to the glamorization of love and courtship as a disguise for women's subordination in marriage. "Who can resist this conclusion?" asks Phyllis Rose, and—perhaps sardonically—answers her own question: "Only millions of romantics can resist it—and other millions who might see it as the bone thrown to men to distract them from the bondage of *their* lives."

Approaching the problem of the difference between the female and male commitment to love from the opposite vantage point, that of its deleterious effects on men, some feminists (interestingly enough including Firestone) also point out that the inequality between the sexes interferes with the oppressor male's ability to love. I am in sympathy with both these positions, which are not so contradictory as they appear to be at first glance. Essentially, each is a plea that one sex move away from its gender's major distortion and vulnerability in loving. While women are urged to move away from any tendency towards submission or enslavement, men are urged to open themselves to the riches of intimacy and love. Surrender in love (as distinguished from submission) can then be seen as a valuable goal for both sexes—the ultimate act of courage and generosity, and of liberation, too.

Thus far, however, despite the injunctions that women become more like men, or men more like women, our patterns of loving have proved relatively resistant to change. Perhaps the chief complaint against women is that they continue to value love too highly and think about it (whatever their personal situation) too obsessively. For women, the "desired" change has not yet been forthcoming for a number of different reasons. Among them is the fact that equality has not yet been achieved in the work place or in economic life (for reasons that I need not go into here) and the fact that, even if it had, professional achievement is not an adequate substitute for intimacy in women's lives.

Those who have pinned their hopes on professional achievement as a means of freeing women from their enslavement to love cannot be fully satisfied with the results. The contention that successful professional women, by virtue of their strong career identities, would be less vulnerable to the tortures of uncertain love than other women has not been demonstrated. However, since professional distinction and fame have been no inoculation against tormented love affairs for men, it is hard to see why they should be for women.

Then, too, many women are still fearful of succeeding professionally because of the negative impact they believe—correctly, as it turns out—this might have on their intimate relationships. Gertrude Ticho, a psycho-analyst, reported the following history of a shy, unassuming physician:

When she was accepted by a prestigious medical school, she was so afraid of failure that she worked very hard. To her amazement, she became the second best student in her class. Some of the male students made sarcastic remarks about competitive women, and from then on, afraid that she would be rejected by her peers and be all alone, she deliberately kept her grades down.

The threat of social ostracism particularly by men, is especially potent because women are still socialized to believe that feminine success is defined primarily by the degree of their desirability to males and, ulti-mately, by the marriage they make. So it is that the status quo is per-petuated by the still dominant cultural imperatives of the society in which we live.

Not just early socialization but on-going social realities continue to play an important role in reinforcing the female preoccupation with pair-bonding. Single women are still considered freaky—"losers," rather than "choosers" of their solitary state. And there are concrete liabilities in being a woman alone—among them the social devaluation that still makes the single woman less sought after by the average hostess or host, the threat of random male violence that renders a woman's physical safety precarious when she is alone in certain situations, and the economic privations she suffers since she is still far from being a man's equal in earning power.

Women are not only concerned with establishing relationships, but also are more involved in attempting to preserve them. Psychologically, of course, both sexes are equally at risk after unhappy love. But tradition-ally, and even to some degree today, women often have more to lose—at least in the coin of the external world—when love ends badly. The phrase "seduced and abandoned" conjures up many of those old dreads haunting women—dreads we sometimes think of as anachronistic—but they were real enough only yesterday and some are still with us today. Though anatomy is surely not destiny, biology sometimes is. Women have always risked pregnancy as the outcome of a sexual love affair. And that particular sorrowful scenario—seduced, abandoned, and with child—is still the un-happy sequela of many love affairs. The educated classes and the upper-middle classes have a tendency to forget recent history; but to remember the dilemmas their mothers and grandmothers faced, they have only to look at the plight of their own contemporaries who are less materially advantaged, less well informed, or more desperate.

And finally we come to one of the major problems that confronts women today, and contributes to the transformation of a perfectly healthy longing for love into a kind of deadly preoccupation. The frequent female obsession with love is in part the result of a demographic imbalance with profound psychological ramifications: unlike men, women live in a scarcity economy; there simply aren't enough men to go around. This problem is compounded by the fact that men often consider women less desirable as they grow older. Here is Edmund Wilson, aged sixty, on the subject of women and age, sounding a trifle self-congratulatory for being different from his peers:

> Unlike some elderly men, I have no appetite for young girls; the women who occasionally attract me are invariably middle-aged married women. The women of my own age, however—or the age that corresponds with mine—are now too old to attract me: their breasts have collapsed, their hair is turning gray, they have gone through a change of life and are likely to have had hysterectomies that have left them unresponsive and juiceless.

After a certain age women know their chances of finding love (and sex) are radically reduced. The term "double standard of aging"—coined by Susan Sontag—describes the reality of older men being attractive to younger women, without the converse—older women being attractive to younger men—being true. This double standard puts women at an enormous disadvantage. To put it bluntly, in our society it is much easier for a man to replace a woman than the other way around. Both sexes subconsciously know this, and that knowledge forces women to become the "keepers" of the relationship, not out of greater love but out of a greater fear of the consequences of disrupting that relationship. While men may have the same (perhaps even greater) dependency needs and affiliative yearnings as women, they are less fearful that these will go unfulfilled. In order to achieve equality between the sexes it is not only economic power and job opportunities that must be equalized, but access to the possibility of finding love and sex throughout the life cycle.

Unfortunately, redressing this imbalance may prove more difficult than it first appears, my suspicion being that the male aversion to female aging is deeply rooted. In part, the aging woman probably comes to represent an incestual maternal figure. Perhaps more importantly, past the child-bearing age, the woman no longer offers the imaginative possibility for a child, which seems important to men whether or not a real child is desired. As already suggested, the fantasy of having a child together can concretize the possibility of the longed-for merger between lovers. For the male, his impregnation of the female also signifies his potency (masculinity) as well as his possession of her. (The escalating aversion to aging female flesh is so critically important to our understanding of the possibilities of love between the sexes that I long to see an in-depth study of the aversion, something citing data from different epochs, different cultures, and perhaps some studies of the special characteristics—if any—of those men who have been able to love a woman across a significant age gap. And there are well-known examples: Benjamin Disraeli and Mrs. Wyndham Lewis, Claude Lanzmann and Simone de Beauvoir, among others.)

Yet, despite the cultural factors that tend to lock women into pair-bonding, many women intuitively know the difference between love that leads to self-realization and love that leads to self-impoverishment—or they come to know the difference through experience. For women, the problem in romantic love has not been the possession of too limitless a capacity for surrender, but rather the dire economic and psychological straits in which they may find themselves should love fail. A true romantic union, one that allows the growth of both participants, has more chance of success when each is capable of being functional in his or her own right. Marriage or some form of pair-bonding is not then the end point (though some therapists may ill-advisedly pronounce their female patients "cured" when they achieve it), but it is rather the institution or arrangement in which two people are sometimes fortunate enough to find the conditions for their individual and mutual growth and fulfillment.

As regards men, opening up and indulging in the kind of intimacy that so many women crave entails acknowledgment of self-doubt, insecurity, and weakness that is sometimes not compatible with their self-definition of masculinity. Moreover, as some men probably correctly intuit, many women, despite what they say and consciously believe, are attracted more to macho men than to "feminized," soft, intuitive, and liberal ones (perhaps as earlier suggested because such men may too closely resemble the "nurturant mother"). And, in fact, while some men who appear to be liberated from gender stereotypes actually are, still others are simply masking gender conflicts and dependency problems with a rhetorical overlay.

There are some fundamental issues about love and the gender difference that are only now beginning to be explored in the psychological and feminist literature. In an intriguing article entitled "The Feminization of Love," Francesca Cancian argues that those scholars (and feminists) who espouse verbal intimacy as the sine qua non of love, by emphasizing that women's identity is based on attachment, men's on separation, may inadvertently "reinforce the distinction between feminine expressiveness and masculine instrumentality, revive the ideology of separate spheres, and legitimate the popular idea that only women know the right way to love." In fact, it is almost a cliché of popular women's magazines that women have a gift for verbal intimacy which is erroneously taken to be synonymous with intimacy (while, actually, intimacy is often wordless) and Cancian does well to point to this distortion. She herself proposes a more androgynous concept of love. I'm sympathetic to her analysis and share her alarms at some of the more reductive analyses of love in which woman emerges as purer and abler, but am less sanguine about her proposed solution because of the importance of *otherness* to the process of falling in love.

The longing in love is almost always across a perceived difference, otherwise the lover has essentially chosen a narcissistic love object and the enormous transcendent power of love is lost. (Perhaps the need for difference as the inspiration for love is nowhere better illustrated than among some male homosexuals. No longer having easy recourse to a difference grounded in biological sex, it is quite extraordinary how many homosexual lovers choose the love object across striking differences in age, culture, background, and general abilities and interests.) And here, perhaps, we come to another of those irreducible conundrums of love, one so intuitively apparent as to be almost a commonplace: opposites may attract, but that difference which sparks love may turn out to be the very difference which ultimately unravels it. The disorganized woman who loves the structure her obsessive husband brings to their lives nonetheless increasingly resents his nagging her to be neat; in essence she admires some, but not all, of the manifestations of his basic personality, yet they are all of one cloth. So, too, with the timid fearful man who enjoys his wife's adventuresomeness so long as she does not insist on dragging him into "dangerous" situations or leave him alone too long while she indulges her proclivities. Sometimes we appear more drawn to the idea of otherness than to its concrete expressions.

The Expression of Female / Male Differences across the Life Cycle

The cultural prescription that women achieve identity through coupling, men through achievement and autonomy, is reinforced by consequences of the asymmetry in female and male pre-Oedipal and Oedipal constellations. These differences are clearly expressed in the strikingly different problems men and women face in the pursuit of love, and in the different prototypic stories of the passionate quest; they may also contribute to a different timetable for love.

In contemporary culture one of the most prominent differences between men and women as regards passionate love is that their capacity for it—and vulnerability to it—may well peak at different periods in the life cycle, a different timetable that is the result of both socialization and of discrepant object relations. Although both sexes experience first love at about the same time, in adolescence or young adulthood, the subsequent pattern is often different. Men may be more vulnerable to the sorrows of first love, an experience which can be such a blow to masculine self-regard that it causes some men to withdraw from any subsequent emotional exposure to avoid being hurt. In young adulthood, women feel a great readiness and urgency to fall in love. Many young men, too, continue to be prone to love attacks, but other men may be willing to run the risks of romantic love again only in middle age or later. Inhibited in the search for love by fear of either loss of autonomy or power (or both), such men return to it only after repetitive conquests are finally perceived as empty, or the limits of achievement have been explored and have either confirmed masculine identity or been found wanting. For other men, love comes when waning power facilitates the re-emergence of merger fantasies, particularly as accompanied by a fantasy of vicariously sharing in the youth of a young woman. While the appetite for romantic love does not always abate in women, some opt in later adult life for the rewards of different pursuits, in particular motherhood or work. For many, these years offer the first opportunity to pursue power, to seek a different kind of identity consolidation and transcendence in the work of the mind or the imagination.

Overlapping cultural, contextual, developmental, and perhaps biological factors, too dense and intertwined to weigh separately with any degree of authority, affect the male and female experiences of love. Cultural imperatives regarding masculinity and femininity play a role, as do early object relations and the asymmetric structures of the Oedipus complex. The main problematic in (heterosexual) love is the female's longing for it, the male's fear of it. Consequently, women often distort love in the direction of submission, men in the direction of dominance—though these distortions are not invariably gender-linked, individual psychology taking priority over cultural directives. As far as I can make out, homosexual lovers incline as much to enactments of dominance and submission as do heterosexuals (surely male homosexuals do).

I am not personally sanguine that a power differential in love can ever be totally eradicated. The image of the slave of love (the submissive partner)—and by imaginative extension, the master (the dominant lover)—is too entrenched for me to think of it as merely a cultural distortion accounted for by socialization. While not inevitable, its frequent appearance seems almost mandated by the existential nature of love which simultaneously demands self-transcendence (the loss of the strictures of self-boundaries) and self-affirmation. Many pairs of lovers attempt to maintain some balance through a strict division of labor, one lover being committed to the transcendence of the self through surrender, the other to the affirmation of the self through domination, and both of them (presumably) integrating both properties through forging a mutual identification. Here, the feminist critique seems incontrovertible: such a balance of power leaves the surrendering lover—usually the woman—more at risk, the other lover better able to disengage and embark on a new relationship, and generally not so dependent financially. (But the dominant lover may lose the transcendant and transformational potential of love.)

Liberation from gender stereotypes may help unlink the roles of slave and master from gender, though it is unlikely that it will obliterate the roles altogether. Even so, such a corrective would be an immense forward stride. But the greater liberation—for both men and women—requires more than the transcendence of gender; it requires the ability to transcend the self.

5

THE FATE OF LOVE

CHAPTER TWELVE

Unhappy Love: Experience and Consequences

EVERY LOVE story is different, its beginning unique, its outcome unforeseeable. For some love is the saving grace: it endures and prospers. For many more, passionate love modulates into affectionate bonding. For others, however, love is thoroughly unhappy. It may end in great pain for the lover who is rejected, in guilt for the lover who is doing the rejecting, or, even worse, it may not end at all for the lover who persists in an unrequited, obsessive love or a mutually destructive, tormenting one. Perhaps the saddest and dreariest of fates is when feeling subsides but the erstwhile lovers stay together imprisoned in an empty, conventional relationship. The unrequited lover, the rejected lover, the disenchanted lover, and those lovers who feel trapped all suffer, though in different ways.

The kinds of suffering that result, and the depth of that suffering, tell us something about how profound an experience love can be. Love reawakens wishes and fantasies from one's earliest life. If it does not culminate in their fulfillment, the resulting devastation to the lover's ego reveals how much of the lover's feeling of self-worth is at stake, how inextricably the lover's self-identity has become intertwined with that of the beloved. To witness the unravelling of love is to learn something about its genesis: the role of the imagination in sparking love becomes clear when we see the equally forceful role it plays in trying to forestall (or deny) love's end or, paradoxically enough, in bringing it to an end; and the power of the old submerged dreams is attested to by the grief the unsuccessful lover experiences in relinquishing them.

However, the worst horrors of unhappy love should not blind us to the enrichment that may occur even in painful love. When the outcome of love is unhappy, the lover may nonetheless have experienced the liberating effects of love and be able to preserve the fruits of that liberation, whether in expanded creativity, enlarged insight, or a subtle internal reordering of personality. There are even instances in which an unrealized love has served as the organizing force in a creative life: Dante is the classic example. For some, the memory of a lost love may provide the sweetness of an entire life. It is no wonder then that lost love is one of the great resonant themes of our lives, hence of literature and film.

One of lost love's great powers is that it may allow us to savor indefinitely the fantasy of what might have been. We have only to conjure up the memory of lost love as it is evoked in *Casablanca* or *Gone with the Wind* to see how compelling a fantasy this is. The dream of "what might have been" is a significant one, playing an adaptive or reparative role in our mental lives. Its power and persistence are testimony to its ongoing importance within the lover's psyche. Paradoxically, nostalgic fantasies about what might have been confirm our belief in what could still be, affirming our belief in the possibility of perfect love in the future. They keep alive the hope of realizing old dreams.

Imagination in Love versus Imaginary Love

Perhaps one of the most original and penetrating insights into the relationship between imagination and love comes from Troyat writing about Tolstoy's creation of the character of Anna Karenina, and how he loathed her before he came to love her.

[Tolstoy's] attitude toward Anna Karenina . . . changed in the course of the book, almost as though the creator had gradually been seduced by his creature. Behind the love story of Anna and Vronsky lay the love story of Tolstoy and Anna. At first, Tolstoy did not like his heroine: he condemned her in the name of morality. He saw her as an incarnation of lechery and, oddly enough, did not even make her beautiful. . . . Her personality is that of a man-killer. . . . She is the agent of evil in the world. Both husband and lover are her victims. . . . In a word, two choice characters, in contrast to whom the diabolical Anna stands out blacker than ever.

However, Tolstoy unconsciously begins to be intrigued by his sinner. She moves him, disturbs him, disarms him. He is on the verge of declaring his love. Suddenly he can no longer deprive her of her beauty. Plastic surgery is called for: the operation is a resounding success. The troll with the turned-up nose emerges a *sylphide.* . . .

Now the tables were turned. Neither of the two men was worthy of her. With cold rage Tolstoy divested them, one by one, of the qualities he had freely bestowed upon them. He debased them in order to elevate and justify Anna.

Troyat's depiction of Tolstoy's changing attitude towards Anna somehow resonates with Tolstoy's accusation against Chekov that the latter failed to understand his own creation, the Darling. Both Troyat and Tolstoy imply that fictional characters acquire their own reality—as much for their creators as for their readers.

When a creative genius falls in love with a figment of his imagination, we sometimes get great literature. With ordinary mortals, the issue is more often love at first sight (and sometimes unrequited love). But imagination is crucial to all loves—realized, idealized, or wholly imaginary. Frequently, our yearnings for impossible—or perfect—love find expression in vicarious imaginative modes (our identifications with lovers in movies and novels, for example), or in private fantasies, which we may sit back and enjoy as the imaginative excursions that they are.

However, for some lovers, there seems to be little or no internal pressure ever to bring their yearnings to any realization in the external world; they are content with their imaginative excursions. And here the imaginative component comes to border on the imaginary. For frightened or timid lovers who are too insecure to test love in reality, such insubstantial fantasied gratification may prove sufficient for short periods of time or during certain developmental phases. Many different motives can serve to entice a lover into preserving ideality at the expense of reality, thus tipping love in the direction of the imaginary. There are lovers who loathe carnality, who cannot tolerate the fact that "Celia shits"; lovers who dread the exposure of their sexual inadequacies; lovers who experience their self-boundaries as so fragile that they prefer distance to intimacy; lovers who are too guilt-ridden to claim the forbidden prize.

The imaginative component in love is also much in evidence in those extremely long-lasting but attenuated affairs in which the contact between the lovers takes place mostly by mail or telephone. While these affairs may offer many kinds of gratification, there is little real impetus to convert them into primary love relationships that become part of one's daily life. Sometimes the lover is almost deliberately protecting the ideality of his experience. But sometimes these intermediate forms are simply the tail end of once meaningful love affairs which one lover (the rejected one), or both, find it difficult to relinquish. Even long after it has ceased to have much of a role in everyday life, the lovers may perpetuate love's existence in their own and each other's imagination. In this latter instance, even though the love is cut off from daily life, it is not wholly imaginary insofar as the lovers validate each other's wishful preoccupations.

Sometimes, the "imaginative-imaginary" type of love has as much to do with situation as with psyche. Consider, for example, the plight of the orphaned or impoverished nineteenth-century governess given a precarious perch in an affluent family. Such women, with few outlets for living or loving, often contrived a passion for the master of the house, a passion very rarely reciprocated. It is in this version of unrequited love (which is not the most extreme kind) that we are perhaps best able to see love's imaginative component gone awry—crossing the boundary into the realm of the purely imaginary. Unrequited love of this kind is a maladaptive expression of the imaginative component in love, the lover persisting in his love despite the lack of any reciprocal response.

Such was the situation of Charlotte Brontë, who yearned for a Mr. Heger while working as an instructor in his school in Brussels. Her "fixation" was in part a function of situation, but also a product of psyche. Charlotte Brontë had not been without opportunity for marriage; she had already turned down two proposals. Of the second refusal, she wrote a friend, "I am certainly doomed to be an old maid. Never mind, I made up my mind to that fate since I was twelve years old." Her separation from home aside, it may have been Heger's unavailability as well as his position as charismatic teacher that accounted for Brontë's passion. According to one account, at that point in her life, "Like Mina Laury, the creation of her youth, she had to be able to call a man 'Master'." Dispatched home by Madame Heger, who possibly intuited the situation, Brontë obsessively mourned her "loss," though Heger had never given her any hope of reciprocation.

Charlotte Brontë's last letter to Mr. Heger, written after Madame Heger had sent her home, dwells revealingly on feelings common to all unrequited—as well as rejected—lovers, including shame over the very obsessiveness of those feelings:

I tell you frankly that I have tried meanwhile to forget you, for the remembrance of a person whom one thinks never to see again and whom, nevertheless, one greatly esteems, frets too much the mind; and when one has suffered that kind of anxiety for a year or two, one is ready to do anything to find peace once more. I have done everything; I have sought occupations. . . . That, indeed, is humiliating—to be unable to control one's own thoughts, to be the slave of a regret, of a memory, the slave of a fixed and dominant idea, which lords it over the mind. Why cannot I have just as much friendship as you, as you for me—neither more nor less? Then should I be tranquil, so free—I would keep silence then for ten years without an effort.

Her letter was never answered. But Brontë recovered, probably aided by her literary endeavors. Her great novel *Jane Eyre* portrays a woman hired on in the home of a man with whom she falls in love and whom she marries in the end. In a rather interesting reversal of roles (and reversal of Brontë's own past history), the dependent, unworldly governess in love with a worldly man of wealth and power has, by book's end, become a strong, resourceful woman who must care for her now blinded, dependent but still beloved Mr. Rochester. Perhaps this tale may have been a kind of fantasied enactment and exorcism of Charlotte Brontë's own yearnings as the rejected lover.

We often see unrequited love in its more sublimated forms; for example, in the bonds of devotion some unmarried women contrive for their bosses. These relationships—real in a narrow sense, but elaborated imaginatively—come to form the essential emotional sustenance for those women cut off by external circumstances or psychological inhibitions from fuller participation in reciprocal relationships. One thinks again of Turgenev and his lament that he was doomed to perch on others' nests.

Even if utterly inappropriate or hopeless, unrequited love becomes totally imaginary and destructive only when it is fervently insisted upon and the dream cannot be relinquished. When the imaginative wish and need take priority over reality and the lover presses for the dream's actualization despite its hopelessness, he has entered into the realm of obsessive unrequited love. In extreme cases, such love seems to be related to madness—when wishes and dreams undermine the lover's perceptions of reality, and, further, when it acts to preclude any other lived relationships. Such was the case with Adèle Hugo, the daughter of Victor Hugo. Her story, dramatized in Truffaut's film The Story of Adèle H., is haunting.

Whatever the underlying causes of Adèle's bizarre attachment and intense suffering, the little we know of her biography is surely evocative. Adèle was the fifth child born to her mother in seven years. After her birth, according to family tradition, her mother, tired out, refused herself to her husband and initiated a sexual withdrawal. This was followed by a mutual emotional withdrawal and Victor Hugo's subsequent involvement with Juliette Drouet, a triangular involvement that lasted the remainder of his life. In 1843, when Adèle was only thirteen, her older married sister, the favorite child of Victor, was drowned in a tragic boating accident in the Seine. Hugo could not be reached because he was traveling incognito with his mistress, Juliette, and he remained unaware of the tragedy for five days.

When Adèle was about thirty, Hugo's family and his mistress Drouet followed him into political exile in England. Adèle languished there. There were no appropriate choices for marriage, and her father forbade her to see an English officer in whom she had expressed interest. She grew sad and listless, and withdrew in solitude to the second floor of the family house, where she endlessly played the same piece of music. Apparently she met her English officer in secret and, discovering that he was due for transfer to Canada, decided to follow him.

En route to Canada, Adèle wrote to her family that she had married the officer. Her mother interceded on her behalf with her father, and they agreed to accept her action and put a notice of the marriage in the paper. Soon after, to their horror, the marriage was denied by the young officer's family; according to them, the two were not married and had never even been engaged. Truffaut's film depicts Adèle's endless shadowing of the officer, her utter obsession with him and his refusal of her. In one of the film's most startling scenes, Adèle is so involved in her interior vision of her beloved officer that she literally fails to register him when she chances to pass him on the street.

Finally, she wrote her parents explaining that her officer had abandoned her and she needed money, although she persisted in claiming to have been married. Her brother was sent to fetch her home. By that time, however, Adèle was demented beyond recovery. She survived for fifty years in an asylum. Her story is surely one of the most extreme cases of imaginary love.

This kind of imaginary love is destructive of both reality and creative imagination. And yet, within it are potent reminders to all of us of what our loves have in common with Adèle H.'s, which may explain the feeling of horror experienced by some of the viewers of Truffaut's movie. In fact, most lovers resemble the unrequited lover to some degree: in their fascination with the elusive object, their stubborn and exaggerated idealization of the beloved, their obsessive preoccupation with love, and their belief that happiness depends solely upon the realization of that one love and no other.

There are in the psychoanalytic literature two brief reports by the psychoanalyst Robert Bak that shed some light on the psychology of extreme unrequited love. Bak saw "a young married woman doctor who fell in love with the head of her department about a year after her father's death." Up until that time, she had been functional and intelligent, and Bak believed that only retrospectively could one see in her a general readiness to assume that men were in love with her—a kind of erotomania. At the outbreak of her illness, she conceived the idea that she was in love with the head of her department and that he reciprocated her love. But she spoke very formally of her new love and her divorce, in such a detached way that it aroused Bak's suspicions that something very peculiar indeed was at work, not mere romance. He asked for a consultation and was told by a senior physician that the reaction was indeed imaginary and represented "delayed and displaced mourning." While Bak agrees that the trigger to her deterioration was related to mourning her father's death, her insistence that her love was reciprocated turned out to be a prelude to a schizophrenic deterioration reminiscent of Adèle Hugo's. In both cases one senses an extreme, through displaced, incestual fixation.

The second case Bak reported was that of the Hungarian poet Josef Attila in whom schizophrenia first came to the surface in an intractable transference love. Subsequently, Attila was sent to Bak and in this new treatment the schizophrenic process seemed to be arrested, up until the point when Attila fell in love again. As was the case with his thwarted transference love, this new love, too, was unrequited and his schizophrenia became unmistakable. For him the only escape seemed to be death, and ultimately he did kill himself.

Such individuals appear unusually sensitive to object loss. For them, love relationships do not simply assuage past losses and separations; they seem absolutely essential to maintain the integrity of the self. If this kind of lover feels rejected (as is almost inevitable), despite the fact that he may come to see the beloved person as totally bad, he persists in an unconscious identification with her in the hope of maintaining the integrity of his own ego. But the aggression toward the lost object persists and is ultimately turned against the self, against the part of the self-identification which is the merged or fused image of lover and beloved. As Bak puts it, "The oblivion sought for in the arms of the loved one finds a grim substitute in suicide."

The Rejected Lover

Since realized love is experienced as an expansion of the self, it is not surprising that its loss is felt as a contraction and diminution. When the lover is rejected, the power implicit in union must give way to the vulnerability of the solitary self. Then the "we" that encompassed a world is reduced to the "I" that is but an atom. The uniqueness that the lover felt as a consequence of being in love vanishes and leaves him feeling depleted, worthless, his life voided of meaning. When one is rejected in love, the sense of loss can afflict the very core of the self, fracturing that self, rendering one an emotional amputee.

Rejection presents itself in many and varied forms. The lover may be rejected during the early stages of a love affair, or long after, when passion has been institutionalized in marriage. The rejection may be abrupt (as, for example, when the beloved suddenly announces she has fallen in love with someone else and is leaving) or, more often, gradual. The first clues may be no more than small changes in love-making or conversation.

Lovers who are attuned to each other develop ways of communicating nuances of meaning. They can convey secret or subtle messages to each other even in crowded rooms via a code known only to them. As one of them withdraws, this subtle process is undermined. The impending rejection is heralded by a new tone of voice, or the use of a given name instead of the customary term of endearment. In the beginning, the slights are often small, perhaps acts of omission rather than commission.

But such subtle alterations in communication may be very pronounced indeed to the lover who is being rejected. Consider, for example, Aleksey Aleksandrovich, betrayed husband of Anna Karenina, who has just begun to realize that he may have lost her to another man. He waits for her to return home one night, and when he tells her he must speak to her, she replies:

"Why, what is it? . . . Well, let's talk if it's so necessary. But it would be better to get to sleep."

And now her very imperturbability begins to give her away to Aleksey:

She looked at him so simply, so brightly, that anyone who did not know her as her husband knew her could not have noticed anything unnatural, either in the sound or the sense of her words. But to him, knowing her, knowing that whenever he went to bed five minutes later than usual she noticed it and asked him the reason; knowing that every joy, every pleasure and pain she felt she communicated to him at once; to him, now to see that she did not care to notice his state of mind, that she did not care to say a word about herself, meant a great deal. He saw that the inmost recesses of her soul, which had always hitherto lain open before him, were closed against him. More than that, he saw from her tone, that she was not even perturbed at that, but seemed to say openly to him: "Yes, it's shut up, and so it must be, and will be in the future."

The lover who is being rejected may be aware of these clues without knowing what to make of them. If confronted, the rejecting partner may deny any change of feeling. She is not necessarily duplicitous; she may be disengaging gradually, so gradually that she is not even fully aware of doing so. The fact of rejection often becomes a palpable reality very slowly for both the disenchanted lover and the rejected one. The rejected lover gradually senses the loss of harmony and becomes unsure of his acceptance by the beloved. He senses that he has to force or fill in gaps in the conversation. An unbearable self-consciousness sets in and he cannot seem to get his voice or his behavior under control, cannot resume the easy ways he was accustomed to in his relations with his beloved.

So it is with Aleksey Aleksandrovich after he begins to suspect that his wife is in love with Vronsky. His agony manifests itself in his behavior, which becomes extremely artificial and arch as he tries to distance himself from acknowledging the impending reality. When Aleskey and Anna are at the racetrack (he to keep up appearances, she to watch her lover compete) and he engages in the worldly banter he knows so well how to sustain, Anna hears "that loathsome, never-ceasing voice of her husband" and mentally accuses him, whom she is betraying, of falsehood:

". . . it's the breath of his life—falsehood. He knows all about it, he sees it all; what does he care if he can talk so calmly? If he were to kill me, if he were to kill Vronsky, I might respect him. No, all he wants is falsehood and propriety," Anna said to herself, not considering exactly what she wanted of her husband, and how she would have liked him to behave. She did not understand either that his peculiar loquacity that day, so exasperating to her, was merely the expression of his inward distress and uneasiness. As a child that has been hurt skips about, putting all his muscles into movement to drown the pain, in the same way Aleksey Aleksandrovich needed mental exercise to drown the thoughts of his wife . . . And it was as natural for him to talk well and cleverly as it is natural for a child to skip about.

And so it is with any lover who becomes unsure of his acceptance by the beloved. His uncertainty is reminiscent of his fluctuating mood when he was first falling in love, except that while he was uncertain and hopeful then, he feels uncertain and progressively less hopeful now. Eventually the beloved announces her intent, or the lover confronts her and insists on facing reality and having it out.

But the period of uncertainty leading up to the moment of truth may be a very protracted one. Given the gradual nature of the beloved's withdrawal, and sometimes the beloved's failure to be honest with herself as well as with her lover, false hope may be kept alive all too long. And the lover's wishfulness—the felt necessity of preserving the status quo—makes him vulnerable to imaginative distortions. Letting go is never easy.

Sometimes the rejected lover refuses to recognize even the clearest communication. When we look closely at the way the rejected lover holds on to hopes for reconciliation against all reason, we are forcibly reminded once more of the importance of the imaginative component in love, of the distorted perceptions that may accompany it, and, most of all, of the dreadful need behind such distortions. We see this particularly when the lover tells outright lies to himself, refusing to read signals of rejection even when they are crystal clear. Simone de Beauvoir tells us about a friend of hers whose capacity for self-deceit was prodigious. She simply refused to face the fact that she had been rejected and said of her erstwhile lover's long silence: " 'When one wants to break off, one writes to announce the break'; then, having finally received a quite unambiguous letter: 'When one really wants to break off, one doesn't write.' "

The lover distorts reality in order to preserve his dreams. He infers nuances and finds ambiguities, small omissions, or quirks in communication that allow him to hold on to the fantasy that mutual love will be restored. He prolongs his agony by tormenting himself with false hopes. Even after rejection is made explicit, he mishears and misconstrues, inferring promises where none were intended.

But the distortion is not always a product of the lover's wishful imagination. Sometimes the beloved intentionally or inadvertently misleads the lover. One thinks, for example, of *Gone with the Wind,* in which Ashley continues to dangle hope before Scarlett O'Hara, fanning the flames of her fantasies, even after he marries Melanie. Perversely, he renounces his seductive posture with Scarlett only after Melanie dies! What motivates the beloved to perpetuate these deceptions? His vanity may be flattered by the lover's attention, or he may regard his admirer as someone to be held in reserve should other options fail to materialize. On the other hand, he may innocently wish to soften the blow of rejection through deliberate ambiguity, saying, "I really care for you, but now is not the right time." Or he may fear the prospect of being thought of as "bad" or "cruel," and hide his real feelings in order to preserve his lover's (and his own) good opinion of him. More fundamentally, the beloved's identity, like that of the lover, is often still intertwined with the "we" from which he is attempting to extricate himself.

The following story is typical of the lover who persists in self-deception against all odds. A gentle, kind, but shy man, led on both by his own need to distort what he heard and (initially) by his loved one's deliberate manipulations, prolonged a courtship long after it was clear that his beloved was not altogether sincere. For months, he was unable to acknowledge the fact that she was seeing less and less of him at the same time that she was seeing more of other men. Finally, she told him that, while she was fond of him, she was not really in love with him and was therefore unable to commit herself to him.

Still he continued to hope, even to the extent of rejecting the attentions of another woman who had in the meantime fallen in love with him. And he became increasingly obsessive, brooding about the beloved's intentions and whereabouts. Sometimes by reasoning with himself he could snap back to normal for a few hours. Once an image from the movie *Of Human Bondage* made him see an aspect of his own "love" relationship, and the realization momentarily freed him of his morbid preoccupations. But his relief was short-lived. Now, in addition to the anguish of loss, he suffered the humiliation of knowing himself enslaved to a morbid passion and being unable to control his thoughts.

His hope for ultimate reconciliation focused on progressively smaller ambiguities. When at last he was told by his beloved that she no longer wanted to see him, he asked her to return some money he had lent her. Four days went by without her complying, during which he nearly convinced himself that she was working out her "problem" and wanted to reconcile, otherwise she would have done as he asked immediately. It never occurred to him that her priorities were such that she simply had not yet gotten around to it—or that she resented his request.

When she finally did return the money, he was devastated and described his feelings in the language typical of the rejected lover: "I'm all alone. There is no future." But he was so unwilling to surrender his last hope for reconciliation that he managed to read encouragement even into the perfunctory note that accompanied the returned money, for it was signed, as he pointed out, "Yours."

It is not just *naïfs* who are capable of self-deceptions of this magnitude. The very worldly Swiss novelist Max Frisch, writing of himself in the third person, reminisces about the end of one of his marriages:

He was said often to have spoken as if he knew what was going on. He did not ask: Where have you been? She squeezed his orange juice before leaving the house. He knew she was fond of him, and he resisted the temptation to make inquiries: He loved her. Now and again he made a joke, to prevent himself from taking his suspicions seriously; he was making things comfortable for himself. This made the daily deceptions easier: There was little need for lies when silence would do. In fact, he knew the other man and admired him greatly. If this was love, he thought, he would be told of it sooner or later. . . . But it was difficult for her, the way he kept coming up with plans for a journey together, pleading, in ignorance of the true situation. Why did he not ask straight out? She told herself that he did not want to know. . . . Gradually he stopped suspecting entirely. That was his mistake; a man who does not notice that a woman has come to him from another bed is no truly amorous man. He simply noticed that she showed little interest in his work. . . . He noticed how infrequently he was able to persuade his wife whatever the topic of conversation was. All the time she knew that he was living in ignorance of his true position, so how could she not believe he was not equally wrong about everything else?

A year later, his wife finally told him the truth—that she was in love with another man and wanted to live with him. Frisch claimed he understood why they had not told him: ". . . he had given them no assurance that he, a man of sixty, would not on their account have shot, poisoned, or hanged himself." In the end, having denied his anger at his betrayers, he displaced part of it onto a very close friend who had known of his wife's infidelity and not told him.

That "the husband [or wife] is always the last to know" is often true because, in the words of Thomas Gray: "Where ignorance is bliss, 'tis folly to be wise." Even when the lover has clearly been betrayed, he may willfully distort his perceptions in order to preserve the illusion that his love is ongoing and unthreatened, for it is the locus of his hopes and ambitions, it is his raison d'être. If he acknowledges that their love is transient or his lover less than worthy, then he fears his feelings were without foundation. Moreover, insofar as the lover has experienced a sense of self-fulfillment or self-enhancement in the realization of love, what is now at stake is his good opinion of himself. If he acknowledges the present reality, he fears relegating the past good to the realm of fantasy. There is only a Hobson's choice: The lover must face reality, accept the current loss, and give up his sense of self-worth and enlarged identity, or deny the current reality and overlook, forgive, ingratiate himself—and hope. It is this kind of self-deception that gives love a bad name and leads outsiders to question the sense of reality and even the sanity of lovers. But lest we judge love too harshly, we should remember that self-deception is not peculiar to love; human beings are prone to it in every area of life.

When the rejected lover finally acknowledges reality, he usually tries one of two strategies: he presses his suit, often desperately, or abandons his love. In the first instance, he may woo, buy gifts, make promises, attempt to change. He tries anything he thinks may be effective, including a pretense at aloofness in an effort to make his beloved jealous. Rejected lovers, particularly rejected spouses, may sometimes pretend (to themselves and others) that they are themselves responsible for the demise of their love, the implication (and hope) being that they can resurrect what they destroyed: They lament, "If only I had understood, been more sympathetic, given more." Or they may assign the beloved's rejection to a kind of momentary lapse, madness, or loss of senses. "He's acting out a mid-life crisis," or "She's being self-destructive." The grieving lover pleads with friends and family to intervene and help salvage the relationship. These intermediaries are required to carry messages. According to the lover's version of the reasons for the breakup, these messages are either promises of reform or dire warnings of the harm the lover will ultimately do himself if the rift is not mended. All these tactics postpone the acknowledgment of the finality of loss.

If the rejected lover adopts the second strategy, that of abandoning the love, he tries to convince himself of the beloved's unworthiness. He may contemplate suicide, but since the surest cure for an unhappy love is a new love, he is more likely to try to fall in love again (hence the familiar phenomenon of love on the rebound). If men appear to be less hurt by rejection than women, I think this is partly because the second option, finding a new love, is more commonly available to them. For a whole constellation of social, psychological, and statistical reasons, men clearly have easier access to new partners than women do, especially as both get older.

The usual pattern in the last days of love is that the injured party continues to suffer, eventually ceases to hope, alternates between apathy and depression, and gradually recovers. During the protracted and painful process of letting go, the rejected lover may indulge in long periods of peculiar behavior about which he is morbidly ashamed. Just as the woman fearing rejection may get pregnant, the rejected woman may feign pregnancy. The rejected lover telephones the beloved and hangs up without speaking. Calls to determine the beloved's whereabouts are common responses to betrayal. The lover shadows the beloved, waiting to see whom she is with. The lover arrives at the beloved's house unexpectedly, invents pretexts for "legitimate" calls, and endlessly imagines "natural" ways to meet in apparently chance encounters. These behaviors usually cause him to feel ashamed, but they are almost impossible to control. In fact, they are standard means of acting out a major obsession—regressive aspects of the personality that are inevitably released when the self is fractured by rejection.

Objectively, this behavior is hard for friends and family to fathom. Worse yet, it is inexplicable to the lover himself. The lover puts himself in a demeaning position and simultaneously risks the pain of encountering the beloved with someone else. But the lover holds to the unrealistic expectation that any one of these acts may remind the beloved of him, speak to her unconscious, tap some underlying remnant of love and elicit reciprocation. At the same time, there is a masochistic component. The self-torture and self-humiliation are an expiation and repetition compulsion belonging to an ancient fantasy and its inevitable punishment: the excluded child, in a frenzy of Oedipal longing, interrupts its parents and is punished, excluded anew, and humiliated.

Morbid preoccupation in rejected love is like a reverse image of the happy obsession in the time of idyllic love, with the emotional valence of the obsession now negative rather than positive. Instead of feeling liberated, as one does when falling in love, the lover now feels enslaved to his obsession.

The rejected lover who has finally acknowledged his loss may sometimes experience an impotent rage as a result of his feelings of helplessness. When it is conscious, the rage may be directly expressed. Even when not consciously experienced, it may surface in conversations or letters aimed at making the betrayer feel guilty. Letters of rejected lovers may be filled not only with regrets but also with reproaches and accusations of bad faith.

I had occasion to observe one dramatic instance of hostility in the guise of devotion. A charming au pair, employed by a friend, had unwittingly encouraged the advances of an insecure young man who lavished all sorts of gifts on her, including regular deliveries of flowers. She let him know as tactfully as possible that she disliked roses. As she felt increasingly suffocated by him (and wary of his obsessive preoccupation with her), she broke with him. On the occasion of her twenty-first birthday, a few weeks later, he surprised her with an astonishing gift—twenty-one dozen roses. Only when they were all delivered did the unconscious intent become clear. Her room resembled a funeral parlor. He later put her name and telephone number in a public toilet, so that she was hounded by obscene phone calls until the number was finally obliterated.

If the lover has been rejected in favor of another, he may be consumed by a jealous frenzy, tortured by the image of his lover and the rival together, causing him to focus his rage primarily on the rival. Like fugitives from Dostoyevsky's novels, some spurned lovers display a roaring emotionality, the capacity for not only a grand passion but a great obsession, and a matching grandiosity of rage directed at the other woman or the other man. By venting all rage at the rival, the lover exonerates the beloved. Part of the mechanism involved here is Oedipal: the rival parent is deemed the villain. This allows rage to be discharged while preserving the goodness of the beloved. The alternative, to accept the culpability of the beloved, would mean that the lover would have to rewrite history and belittle the importance of the beloved and hence of the love affair. Furthermore, it is necessary to preserve a good opinion of the beloved in order to maintain hope for a reconciliation, which is the only happy ending imaginable.

Just as self-esteem is enhanced in love, it may plummet as a result of rejected love, because self-worth has become so bound up with the love relationship. Not only is the love object lost, and the "I" (previously valued so highly by the beloved) cheapened, but also the "we." To the extent that the lover defines his identity through being part of a couple, he will be denuded of an identity when he is forced back upon a single state. Then he grieves for the loss of the good opinion of those who had admired his relationship, and fears their disapproval. The sense of estrangement from a social circle is one more in the series of losses that rejected lovers may suffer.

Another of the losses experienced when love dies is the feeling of being coddled and protected. In mutual love, fantasies of being cared for and nursed can be reawakened, often after a very long slumber (many adults experience such wishes as being so childish that they effectively suppress them until relatively late in life). To the degree that such longings are reawakened, acknowledged, and accepted in the full tide of adult love, a profound frustration ensues when their realization is denied. Then the suffering and humiliation in rejection are experienced with particular intensity. The lover will hurl accusations of craziness or infantilism at himself, feeling demeaned and diminished by his needs. Those with lifelong dependency problems who have been rejected may feel more desperate still, faced not only with the pain of rejection but also the horror and terror of having to function alone, and uncertainty about their ability to do so. Their sense of helpless abandonment may make death seem the only possible reprieve.

Perhaps the most basic and universal suffering endured by the rejected lover is the feeling that his deepest self, which is exposed in love as it seldom otherwise is, has been viewed and found wanting. To the extent that the lover is uncertain about his self-worth, rejection will confirm his underlying sense of badness or inadequacy: someone else has looked into the deepest recesses of his soul and found him shallow, or ugly, or discovered his anger.

The suffering experienced in rejected love exists on a continuum between unhappiness and morbid despair. When it is self-identity and not just self-esteem that love has confirmed, the suffering over its loss will be all the greater.

Most people suffer for a while and finally recover. While passing fantasies of suicide or murder are fairly common in rejected love, they are not generally acted upon. They usually become preoccupations or are actually carried out only by those few personalities in whom there is a primitive core. Experiencing uncontainable anger at the rupture of a symbiotic dyad, the primitive lover regresses to the rage of the distraught and furious infant confronting object loss. Infants and others with weak or as yet unformed egos react to loss by splitting, in which an all-good object is converted into an all-bad one. The rejected lover may then view the beloved, once seen as all-giving and nurturant, as entirely malevolent and cruel. Insofar as the lover's pathological omnipotence and narcissism are deflated, he can be thrust into a morbid depression. Unfortunately for the lover, it is precisely this kind of primitive love—because of the excessive demands for nurturance and attention that it generates even in the early stages of love—that so often leads to rejection by the beloved.

Even after "recovering" from the end of a love, the lover can store away the fantasy or memory of the entire love affair in a form I have called the lover's reel. There it may languish in obscurity, until some concatenation of circumstances causes it to be replayed. In *The Love Object*, Edna O'Brien depicts a woman who had recovered from the end of a love affair with a married man. Eventually they resume seeing each other from time to time, but the man she meets later is not the man in the lover's reel within her mind:

We do meet from time to time. You could say things are back to normal again. By normal I mean a state whereby I notice the moon, trees, fresh spit upon the pavement; I am part of everyday life, I suppose. There is a lamp in my bedroom that gives out a dry crackle each time an electric train goes by, and at night I count those crackles because it is the time he comes back. I mean the real he, not the man who confronts me from time to time across a cafe table, but the man that dwells somewhere within me. He rises before my eyes—his praying hands, his tongue that liked to suck, his sly eyes, his smile, the veins on his cheeks, the calm voice speaking sense to me. I suppose you wonder why I torment myself like this with details of his presence, but I need it, I cannot let go of him now, because if I did, all our happiness and my subsequent pain—I cannot vouch for his—will all have been nothing, and nothing is a dreadful thing to hold on to.

The memory complex may lie dormant for years, awaiting only the right stimulus—perhaps something so simple as the crackle of a lamp—to return to life. It is this feature of love that explains the ease with which old love can sometimes be recalled or, if circumstances further conspire (if for example the real he comes to correspond once more to the "reel" he), can even be renewed.

But whether or not the "reel" lover ever reappears to play a real-life role, the memory of him always "dwells somewhere within" as O'Brien's character realizes. She experiences something object relations theorists have emphasized: images of people with whom we have had significant interpersonal relations enter into our ongoing mental representations and continue to play a role in our emotional lives and self concepts.

The Disenchanted Lover: Falling out of Love

The lover, passionate though he may have been in the opening phase of a love affair, may fall out of love. Sometimes love simply seems to disappear. It fades and is replaced by apathy, boredom, or restlessness, if not resentment and rage. It can happen gradually or suddenly, as a result of recurring disappointments, with or without overt anger. Sometimes love fades for both lovers. People who think that such disenchantment is natural and inevitable, far from acknowledging the emptiness that can be experienced when it happens, tend to urge a conservative position upon the lovers, particularly married ones: "Don't do anything rash," "Try to work it out," and so forth.

We may mistakenly believe that there is no great suffering attached to falling out of love, no price to be paid. But while falling out of love may not be as acutely painful as being rejected, it exacts its own sorrows. (These can be muted by falling in love with someone else, or pretending that one was never really in love at all.) The bewildered lover, who has fallen out of love as mysteriously as he once fell into it, now feels disappointed, let down, and depleted. What he once held to be the most important thing in his life has now lost its meaning. And he experiences overwhelming sorrow not only for the loss of love, but for the loss of the faith, hope, and innocence that go with it. It is not just this love that has ended but also the belief that any love can last a lifetime.

For the disenchanted lover, there can be an erosion of the imaginative life, a subtle fraying at the edges of personality, and, for some, a definitive failure of the imagination. Perhaps no novelist has depicted this so clearly as Proust. Proust portrays with utmost sympathy and in the most nuanced detail the grand obsessive passion of his creation, Charles Swann, for a woman we all—reader, Swann (in flashes of objectivity), and Proust—know to be "unworthy" of it. Proust loses patience with Swann only when Swann's objective mind triumphs once and for all over the act of the imagination that had allowed him to love Odette. At the end of their affair, Swann revisits his passion for Odette in a dream and awakens, cold-eyed and cold-hearted, deploring the lamentable dereliction of taste that had allowed him to love Odette rather than one of the plump pink beauties to whom he was more naturally drawn. "To think that I have wasted years of my life, that I have longed for death, that the greatest love that I have ever known has been for a woman who did not please me, was not in my style!"

It is not Swann's initial lapse of taste in loving Odette which is lamentable so far as Proust is concerned, but his subsequent failure of the imagination. That is why he characterizes Swann's cry from the heart as a moral failure, a lowering of "The average level of his morality," a sign of "that old intermittent fatuity which reappeared in him now that he was no longer unhappy." Swann has committed a crime against love, against himself, and against imagination by being unable, now that he is no longer in love, to enter into the consciousness of the man he once was when he loved Odette.

Sometimes the disenchanted lover is able to rationalize his loss of feelings. He may point to his own neurosis or immaturity at the time he made such an inappropriate choice as a way of accounting for the end of love. She says she outgrew him; he says he now finds her boring. In some instances, these appraisals are accurate. In the warmth of the security provided by a steadfast lover, a person may indeed reach new levels of self-awareness and creativity which propel him into new positions in the world and open new possibilities for internal and external change. The loyal partner who sponsored such growth may not be equipped to adapt to these changes. At this point, the "enlarged" lover may "sacrifice" and stay in the relationship, or he may disengage from it. For example, of the eight founding partners (all men) of a well-known professional firm, all dynamic achievers from constricted immigrant backgrounds, only two remain married to their first wives. Such occurrences are nowadays actually the rule rather than the exception. We imagine that we understand the implications of this immediately—"she was good enough for him when he was nobody"—but we really understand on only one level. It is true that some people do act out of narrow self-interest, placing great value on how the world perceives their partner, or deciding that wealth and power can buy them something better than the old model spouse. (Husbands and wives, like cars, can be traded up.)

But such simple motives cannot account for the depth of the distaste some people come to feel for their ex-lovers. While external pressures and temptations may be enough to end a marriage based primarily on convention or convenience, they are no threat to relationships in which authentic mutual love has been achieved. That's why it's commonly said that an outsider can't break up a healthy marriage, only one that is already in trouble. Love more often dies because of internal ambiguities and paradoxes than because of external temptations or shifts.

Once feelings of exploitation, loss of autonomy, failed mutuality or any of the multitude of other problems already discussed come to outweigh the gratifications experienced in love, then hurt, resentment, disillusionment, and finally anger and depression ramify and overwhelm our emotional investment in loving. But typically there will be a period during which, in the interest of preserving both love and the status quo, the lover tries to ignore his negative feelings, tends to discount them, or blames himself for any failures in the relationship. Gradually, however, the accumulation of unacknowledged differences and difficulties takes a toll in depression or apathy. Usually these feelings are allowed to break through with full force only when the lover senses some other prospect for his future life—often, but not always, the possibility of a new love relationship. When the feelings break through even in the absence of any apparent alternative to the existing relationship, the sense of despair can be staggering, the feeling of being trapped suffocating indeed. For many women in the seventies the alternative that presented itself was the hope for personal growth and autonomy through an independent work life—hence that decade's proliferation of movies and novels about the excitement of being a career woman.

The new life plans may succeed or fail, but at the very least they empower the disenchanted lover to acknowledge his negative feelings. In the happiest of circumstances, once the resentment is acknowledged, the lovers may be able to devise an effective mechanism for confronting and resolving their differences.

When love fails irretrievably, however, it is transformed into a series of negative emotions, a sort of reverse image of the positive emotions characteristic of falling in love. The specificity of the distaste and even revulsion that the lover feels for his former beloved can be remarkably powerful. He complains of her odors; she hates the way he chews with his mouth open. These complaints assume an importance completely out of proportion to the stimulus (after all, he always chewed with his mouth open, and her smell is unchanged). They are as intense and idiosyncratic as the feelings of enchantment evoked by such concrete signs of grace as her beauty mark or his crooked grin during happier times, when the lovers were in the process of falling in love. During the reverse process, when love is failing, disengagement is often expressed through an almost concrete revulsion to the physicality, flesh, and intimate habits of the former beloved. What has been lost—among other things—is the sense of cherishing the *inwardness* of the other: hence the flesh no longer encloses a treasured spirit but assumes a stubborn solidity that one may come to regard as the whole person. One's revulsion at the physical is often commensurate with one's loss of regard for the Other's subjectivity.

The disenchanted lover is bored. Silence, which once signified communion, now echoes his sense of emptiness. Hours together, once experienced as timeless, have become endless. Dining out, the lover notices married couples eating together in stony silence and wonders how he and his beloved came to such a state of emotional bankruptcy. He feels isolated from her but has no desire to attempt a restoration of their relationship. The lover feels as though he were with a "stranger," but one without mystery or appeal. He is no longer interested.

Whereas the lover worried about whether he was good enough for the beloved (or at least as good as his rivals) when he was falling in love, now, having abandoned love, he compares his beloved with others and finds her wanting. He feels he could "do better" if only he could regain his freedom. He finds her flawed, and dwells on all her inadequacies. The disenchanted lover may even entertain cruel or sadistic flash fantasies about his "beloved" in which he sees himself inflicting harm on her either physically or psychologically. Gratuitous insults, bad-mouthing, public humiliation, and punishing silences are the instruments of angry disengagement.

Thoughts of escape now preoccupy the lover as much as adoring reveries once did. The lover who feels bound to someone he no longer loves comes to resent his responsibilities. He feels he is being depleted, perhaps even cheated, by the money, time, and energy he must continue to expend on her behalf. Matrimonial lawyers testify to this almost inevitable outcome of lost love, advising their female clients to settle early, while their delinquent husbands may still feel guilty, because "no one likes to pay for a dead horse."

Falling out of love has a trajectory which is the reverse of falling in love; like the latter, it is a discontinuous process, issuing forth in bursts of negativity (instead of adoration) sometimes interspersed with renewed wishes for reconciliation. This vacillation continues until one of the lovers decides to end the relationship and separate. But the disenchanted lover may experience a desire to reconcile even after separation and, as already suggested, may sometimes even fall back in love. The process of falling out of love, like that of falling into love, ranks as a grand obsession, but the emotional valence is exactly reversed. Generally, the lover who falls out of love will mourn the end of love, even though the "choice" was his.

Contrary to the usual assumptions, it seems that falling out of love is an event of some moment for the disenchanted lover, and a painful one.

Empty or Hurtful Relationships that Endure

Some marriages that are judged from the outside to be successful are indeed highly functional on a superficial level but are dead at their emotional core. Mutuality, idealization, and real intimacy are no longer a fundamental part of such relationships. Social dictates have utterly replaced the dictates of the heart. Couples like these are generally attached to the public persona of the "we" and find great security and small pleasures in the routine of married life. They may luxuriate in the warm protection of the institution of marriage, even while loathing the conjugal embrace. Such couples maintain their relationships with their children, do not squander their money on two households (as they would in a divorce), enjoy a joint social life and even manage a civil relationship with one another. They may function smoothly, may know how to do things well together—travel, entertain, divide chores. In fact, they may have everything necessary to a successful relationship except for passion and intimacy. For each participant in such a relationship, it is the social self rather than the inward self that is validated.

Such a couple shares a joint project, however, and that is the tacit agreement to present an imposturous relationship to the world. In essence, they have constructed a joint narrative, but what is missing is the resonance of a meaningful subtext. These marriages may be more stultifying than overtly troubled marriages because in the latter some passion still exists, and the participants are freer to talk frankly to their friends and each other; they do not operate under the constraints of having to present a fictionalized appearance of happiness.

Some of the participants in empty marriages are themselves unaware of the emotional bankruptcy of their lives. They are reassured by those skeptics of love who have always proclaimed that passion is brief; since they believe that de-idealization invariably follows idealization, and that stifling boredom is the inevitable end of love, they do not necessarily feel cheated. They rationalize their situation as being the norm and compliment themselves on their ability to adjust to adult reality. They are comforted by denunciations of the superficiality of passionate love and the immaturity of those who seek it. They would have it that their triumph lies in a realistic assessment and acceptance of their partners: "I know he's not Cary Grant, but I'm not Katharine Hepburn either." If at all affluent, they tend to substitute correct consumerism (buying the right brand, taking the right trip, seeing the latest play) for passion. Their social life comes to consume more and more of their emotional lives, and concern over whether or not they are invited to a particular party becomes the substitute for any intimacy. If both partners are reliably passionless, the "we" lasts but the individuals who made the pact have generally long since compromised their individual aspirations for love, either companionate or passionate. A threat to the stability of these relationships exists when one partner still has the potential for passion and consequently may still seek and find an alternative relationship.

The toll on the participants in loveless marriages may far exceed the mere impoverishment of their relationship. To preserve such a bond often requires the deadening of one's general emotional availability and the suppression of one's imaginative life. Many people die psychologically decades before their biological deaths.

But how are we to understand the transition from the ebullience and hopefulness of newly committed lovers to the resignation, emptiness, and hopelessness (conscious or not) of disenchanted lovers, the descent from idealization and mutuality to enmity and boredom, if not outright torment? Love need not lose its affectionate component even when intensity is gone, so something more than loss of passion must be involved to account for such emptiness or even enmity. As I have tried to show in the preceding chapters, the early promise of committed love can run afoul of a number of kinds of problems, generally exaggerations of love's ordinary existential problems and conundrums. Love can be disrupted by shifts in the lovers' power equilibrium, often more tenuous than either partner knows. Or it can break down when repeated disaffections and disappointments lead to de-idealization and loss of harmonious mutuality. The lover comes to feel criticized and reviled, or he is overcome with anger, jealousy, or envy. Sometimes the couple simply appears to have used up its emotional capital, having failed to replenish it with either an enriching sexual life or an ongoing emotional intimacy.

The saddest, perhaps, of the many different kinds of sad love stories are those that start out with high hopes, appear to soar, and then are brought down not by external circumstances but by the lineaments of character of one lover or both. As each of us comes to know, sometimes to our astonishment, character (including our own) reveals itself only after a long time, sometimes in interaction or struggle with the Other, and sometimes only in circumstances that take us to the limit.

For years I thought I knew something of the story of Leo Tolstoy and his wife, Sophie. My understanding of that ill-fated liaison was similar to the account to be found in de Beauvoir's *Second Sex,* in which she berates Tolstoy for perpetrating the lie of the ideal couple (Pierre and Natasha as depicted in the epilogue of *War and Peace*):

> The most damning judgment against the Pierre-Natasha myth is to be found in the Tolstoy couple, Leo and Sophie, which gave origin to it. Sophie feels a deep repulsion for her husband, she finds him "frightfully dull"; he deceives her with every peasant woman in the neighborhood, she is jealous and bored to death; she goes neurotically through her many pregnancies, and her children neither fill the void in her heart nor occupy the emptiness of her days; home is for her an arid desert; for her husband it is a hell on earth. And it all ends with Sophie, a hysterical old woman, sleeping half-naked in the damp night of the forest, and with Leo, a harried old man, running away and disowning finally their "union" of a lifetime."

Yet if one reads a fuller biographical account of the Tolstoys, the story that emerges is infinitely more complex. There was, of course, a long and precipitous decline in their relationship, but in some profound way, they provided the only real bedrock in one another's lives, alternating between love and loathing. More than the sexual problems, infidelities, multiple pregnancies, and the jealousy that tormented and divided them, the real decline in their joint life seemed to follow upon Tolstoy's monumental death anxiety, which broke out almost uncontrollably in mid-life, after the publication of *Anna Karenina,* and led him to turn away from literary endeavors and fashionable life, toward religion and pacifism. Sophie, happy to accommodate to the demands of Tolstoy the novelist, was unable to share the new priorities of Tolstoy the pacifist and was resentful of having to try. He, in turn, reviled her for what he deemed to be her narrowness and materialism. Nonetheless they were profoundly bound, one to the other, and each was periodically suffused with moments of love and adoration for the other, almost until the end.

Committed love relationships, even successful ones, are always delicately balanced and require continued re-equilibration as different strains and conflicts inevitably emerge over the years, not just as a result of the passage of time, but also because of fundamental changes in the lovers' lives and situations: changes in income and jobs, the birth of children, the demands of dealing with elderly parents, and perhaps, most of all, the encroachment of aging. It is a commonplace that while the mid-life crisis may, in fact, have more to do with aging and the first faint intimations of death than with the strictures of marriage, its resolution or pseudo-resolution may well take the form of an extramarital affair or even a divorce.

Paradoxically, the easy availability of divorce, while surely a great boon to many individuals who would otherwise be locked into terrible relationships, also causes certain inhibitions in relationships. Some lovers, fearing the ever-present threat of divorce, pull their punches out of fear of provoking their partners into leaving. This forecloses any possibility of genuinely working out differences and enhances the likelihood that the marriage will devolve into a manifestly empty, covertly hostile, yet enduring relationship. Many women, especially as they get older, are fearful of confronting and provoking their husbands, because they judge, often correctly, that their husbands maintain social options in the real world that they no longer share.

It is for this latter reason—"the double standard of aging"—that many of the feminist reservations about inequality in marriage remain pertinent today, this despite some real strides toward equality that women have been able to make. But as I have previously suggested, it is somewhat naive to think that economic equality alone would equalize the power balance of a marriage. Economic emancipation is surely to be applauded—is indispensible really—but as long as older women are viewed as sexually less desirable than older men, a power imbalance will continue to exist, one that will continue to influence women to hold their tongues, keep the peace, and take the responsibility for preserving the marriage. Until these realities alter, many women will continue to behave in a way that we may deplore but must also understand and feel sympathy for: "a whole tradition enjoins upon wives the art of 'managing' a man; one must discover and humor his weaknesses and must clearly apply in due measure flattery and scorn, docility and resistance, vigilance and leniency." Real equality between the sexes, as far as relationships go, will finally depend on abolition of the double standard of aging—and that will be no mean feat.

The Aftermath of Unhappy Love

Many loves end; some sorrowfully, some painfully, and others bitterly. Nonetheless, for many unhappy lovers, the memory of the joy that was theirs, and the legacy of change that took place within themselves as a consequence of love, imbue the experience with value that endures long after the relationship has ended. Consequently, while love may end unhappily, this does not mean that the overall effects were necessarily negative. Some ultimately unsuccessful loves are growth-enhancing and self-expanding while they last. And the benefits to the lover may outlive the love. Often the real impact of the experience can be evaluated only months or years after its end.

And sometimes out of the profound shattering that can take place, there is an inner regrouping, a creative surge, even from the depths of despair. One of my dearest friends, a great scholar, wrote his finest and most personally cherished essay as he emerged from a deeply wounding love affair in which he had been rendered impotent. As a consequence of what he had suffered, he felt he had achieved a new intellectual clarity and a much deeper insight into life—and into himself. This phenomenon may be equivalent to what has been described as creative illness—a journey to the depths where it is given to one to stalk one's internal demon and to emerge strengthened. This may have been the case with Jung, who credited some of his major theoretical insights to his deep but thwarted love relationship with Spielrein (as discussed earlier). As W. H. Auden would have it, "Weeping Eros is the builder of cities." (This is quite different from Freud's view of creativity as the product of repressed, rather than thwarted or lost, Eros.)

Even during the course of unhappy or problematic love, there may be a creative surge. Emma Goldman's most creative period is said to have coincided with her tempestuous love affair with Ben Reitman. Goldman—Red Emma as she was known—was an anarchist and an advocate of free love, a fiercely political person. While the outlines of her life have been well known to political people and feminists for many years, her name, and biography, are better known today because of the discovery in 1975 of the love letters exchanged between Goldman and the love of her life, Ben Reitman, and the two biographical studies that grew out of that discovery.

In these letters Goldman speaks of a love that opened up "the prison gates" of her womanhood. For the ten years between her meeting with Reitman in 1908 and his marriage in 1917—perhaps the most productive of Goldman's life—she lived with Reitman, playing out love and anarchy. She was ten years older, he a dubious convert to her cause. For him she was "Blue Eyed Mommy"; for her, he was "Hobo." Despite Reitman's impulsiveness, "he seems to have been looking for some alternative to his chaotic, disorderly, drifting life. Emma Goldman's strength gave direction and discipline to his own grandiose fantasies of saving the world. . . . He was filled with admiration, flattered by her attention, excited by her notoriety, aroused by her passion. He needed someone to inspire and organize his life; she needed someone to help her and cheer her, to work for her by day and make love to her at night. Both in a way had found the realization of their dreams—but also of their nightmares."

The unhappy underside of their relationship was her uncertainty about his commitment and her utter preoccupation with his fidelity, or, as I should say, lack thereof. Unfortunately for her peace of mind as well as her ideals, she found herself consumed with possessiveness and jealousy. In the end Hobo left his "Mommy" ostensibly because he wanted children and a conventional family life. Though Goldman had always deplored women's fear of public opinion and urged frankness, when the time came for her to write her autobiography, she was torn about whether or not to record the tormented aspects of her love life, and, finally, chose not to. One surely understands. Sex might be revealed, but not those possessive feelings she deemed so shameful. And yet, the conjunction between her consuming passion and the intensification of her creativity tell their own important story—one perhaps somewhat at odds with her political theories about the priority of free sex in the cause of liberation. (One must surely liberate one's sexuality but perhaps love more reliably liberates the self.)

Some people maintain deep emotional attachments to those they once loved romantically earlier in their lives, knowing that no one else shares their memories and their coming of age together. This may account for the number of stories one hears about loves rekindled at high school reunions decades after their first flaming. (The reasons range from "She was everything I remembered"—the lover's reel replayed—to "He even remembered my darling aunt who died when I was in high school.") A sizable number of divorced pairs view one another as extended family. One man confessed to his ex-wife that he saw her as his ace-in-the-hole, knowing that in any serious crisis he could count on her. They had no real ongoing relationship, but when his crisis—a major illness—came and he called on her, she did indeed rise to the occasion. In the deepest sense, we come to know very few people, and so may always treasure those few with whom we enacted those basic dramas that shaped our identities and destinies. This may be especially true for our earliest loves and may account for the privileged place in memory that first love often holds.

Perhaps one of the strangest, most intense stories of a deep connection to someone no longer loved (at least not romantically) is to be found in Marguerite Duras's memoir, *The War*. Married and living in Paris, she had fallen in love with D., a good friend of both her husband and herself. Her husband, Robert L., a political prisoner of war, is reported to have survived the liberation and Duras is awaiting his release from Belsen, unsure of whether he is alive or dead. During the period of waiting she is half-crazed—anxious, depressed, and essentially nonfunctional. She cannot sleep, she cannot eat, she cannot be comforted by her lover. Walking the streets she thinks, "He's been dead for three weeks. Yes, that's what's happened. I'm certain of it. I walk faster. His mouth is half open. It's evening. He thought of me before he died. The pain is so great it can't breathe, it gasps for air. Pain needs room. There are far too many people on the streets; I wish I were on a great plain all alone. Just before he died he must have spoken my name."

François Mitterand (a fellow member of the underground) calls Duras to say that Robert L. is still alive, too weak to leave the camp, and so frail that he might not live. Duras dispatches D. and another friend to rescue Robert L. Though officially liberated, he is thought to have typhus, and, therefore quarantined, is about to be given injections that might kill him. D. and a friend Beauchamp rescue Robert L., and bring him back to Paris, where Duras, D., and the doctor are all caught up in the heroic effort to save him. Feeble, emaciated, starved as he is, food will kill him. They must nurse him back, feeding him meat extract drop by drop. As Robert L.'s strength comes back so does Duras's. She begins to eat again and to sleep, to put on weight. "We're going to live. Like him I haven't been able to eat for seventeen days. Like him I haven't slept for seventeen days, or at least that's what I think. In fact, I've slept for two or three hours a day. I fall asleep anywhere. And wake in terror. It's awful, everytime I think he's died while I was asleep." Later during his convalescence she told Robert L. that "we had to get a divorce, that I wanted a child by D., that it was because of the name the child would bear. He asked if one day we might get together again. I said no, that I hadn't changed my mind since two years ago, since I'd met D. I said that even if D. hadn't existed I wouldn't have lived with him again. He didn't ask me my reasons for leaving. I didn't tell him what they were." Nor does she tell the reader. But we are left with a vivid impression of the profound connection, devotion, and loyalty that propelled Duras to pluck him back from the dead, feelings that lasted longer than the love that first inspired them. While there may be readers who see guilt as the underlying motive that impelled Duras's heroic rescue of Robert L., for me, the tone and feeling of the memoir points more to a sense of a profound identification which she had with him; to the kind of feelings most often evoked vis-á-vis one's own children when they are threatened.

Sometimes what lovers feel after the end of love seems nothing more than an intermittent nostalgia for a lost love. Yet the strength of the poignancy and regret they experience suggests that nostalgia has unconscious reverberations of some complexity. Nostalgia for lost love is often so dear to us as to suggest it may serve an important psychic function. Perhaps that is why we respond to it so powerfully in movies as well as in life. Nostalgia is the feeling to which audiences seem to react in *The Way We Were*, an earlier generation's *Big Chill*. The movie portrays the very touching story of the courtship and marriage of a radical Jewish girl (Barbra Streisand) and a golden boy (Robert Redford) who meet in college and later marry, but who eventually encounter an irreconcilable difference—his willingness to "sell-out" and her intractable rectitude. But the climax of the film is the chance meeting between them years after they have separated—she as political as ever, he with a golden girl. What passes between them is some combination of remembered love, sorrow, and regret, but they go their separate ways. Yet, they (and the audience) know that they came of age together, that through their relationship they came to know themselves as well as each other, to accept that self-knowledge and encompass the Other's reality, and this knowledge suffuses with sadness the inevitability of their parting once again.

What hidden strings does nostalgia play upon, that it should resonate so powerfully within us? I've already suggested that the power of such films as *Casablanca* and *Gone with the Wind* can in part be explained by their evocation not just of what was, but what could still be. Their enduring appeal, like that of certain personal memories suggests that there may be a second story hidden behind the surface story, one which works its magic on the viewer even if he is not aware of its existence. In *Casablanca*, where the manifest story is one of thwarted love, the story resonating beneath the surface is that of the perfect love that might have existed—endless and eternal—had circumstances been different. If the Ingrid Bergman character were not already married, or if her husband were not a noble leader of the French resistance, and if she, her husband, and the Bogart character had not all been so pure of heart—so the movie reassures us—their love could have and would have triumphed and endured. Eric Segal's *Love Story* also derives its power from an evocation of perfect enduring love that would have prevailed if only the heroine had not been struck down—not, as some critics claim, because it echoes the death theme of the Liebestod. I've already quoted David's insight in *Endless Love*: "If endless love was a dream, then it was a dream we all shared, even more than we all shared the dream of never dying or of traveling through time." Beneath the manifest story of lost love lies the hidden more powerful story of perfect love, which confirms in us our own sweet hopes and dreams.

In *Gone with the Wind* love was doomed not by external circumstances, but by the destiny implicit in character. Scarlett and Rhett did love each other; but their timing was bad. Had Scarlett come to self-knowledge sooner, if Rhett had been more patient and forgiving, the outcome could have been different. And so, what makes the movie the enormous success it is (other than its filmic qualities) is not so much what happens, but what the screen conveys about what could have happened: two joyous, spirited creatures, full-blooded and passionate, triumphing together over the devastations of war and sickness, poverty and destruction, walking off into a blood-red sunset in each other's arms. The image of the rejected Scarlet (with which in fact the film ends) fades before the glorious image of potentiality that fills the mind's eye. The very specificity of the reasons for love's failure lends credibility to the illusion that perfect love might otherwise have been attained. And so the promise of love between Rhett and Scarlett is somehow allowed to retain its integrity. "What might have been" triumphs over "what was."

So, too, do we sometimes play with memories of our own lost loves. These in turn, reverberate with feelings carried over from our earliest love losses—the loss of our state of oneness with mother and of all that we longed for in our Oedipal years. If only we can persist in our belief that the romances of our earlier life were worthwhile, lost only because of destiny or fate or circumstances beyond our control, we are able to maintain our idealized belief in perfect love, and to preserve our hope for a future love that will finally fulfill all our most cherished dreams.

Even without any creative outcome, be it an artistic masterwork, a psychological shift, an enduring friendship, or even a sweet memory, the most unhappy or difficult love relationships are not always ultimately destructive; nor do they rule out subsequent *happy* loves. Take, for example, Colette who spent the last twenty years of her life in a comfortable love relationship, having survived two previous depleting and stormy marriages. We all know people who have been hurt, even savaged, in love, but go on to find comfortable, happy relationships and sometimes passionate ones. In fact, many people who had failed abysmally in their first marriages are able to achieve happiness in second marriages. They have learned something of themselves and of the requirements for relationships.

However, there's no denying that unhappy love can have long-term unhappy consequences for its sufferers. Given certain pre-existing psychological vulnerabilities, the sorrows of tainted or unhappy love can be

perpetuated in low self-esteem or a damaged perception of future alternatives and possibilities. Sometimes the rejected lover, or the disenchanted
lover, or the unrequited one never recovers, or appears to recover only to
embark shortly thereafter on yet another horrific experience. The rejected
lover may continue to overidealize the rejecting lover, and assume that all
the benefits of love were tied to *him*, and could never be duplicated with
anyone else. (Maria Callas seem to have felt that way after she lost
Onassis.) Consequently the rejected lover may foreclose any possibility of
future relationships and be left with negative feelings not just about
herself (having taken to heart all the complaints the beloved raised against
her), but about other people in general and the possibilities of love in
particular. Or, more extravagantly, the rejected lover may feel driven to
suicide or murder. For his part, the disenchanted lover may not learn
anything from his experience, either what qualities truly matter to him
or what qualities in himself he might hope to change, and he too may
remain bitter about love or may enter blindly into repetitive relationships
which result in the same unhappy outcome each time. The unrequited
lover may recover, as Charlotte Brontë did, going on to marry her father's
curator, with whom by all accounts she was very happy for the nine
months of married life she was able to enjoy before she died, or alternately
may never let go of the fantasied relationship—as appears to have been
the case with Adèle Hugo. The love has become obsessive and may evolve
into a kind of imaginary love.

Who will be destroyed by unhappy love, who will recover from or even
benefit from it? How can we tell when love is, as we might say, counter-
indicated? Since the sufferers of unhappy love are so many and various,
it is not very instructive to say of those lovers who are particularly devastated by love that they are neurotic. In fact, many people with a significant degree of neurosis are still able to achieve enduring and happy love.
Think, for example, of the clinging vine, who has found a degree of
happiness by finding an oak to which to cleave, oak and vine having
worked out a satisfactory, symbiotic arrangement. Consequently, it would
seem that only particular kinds of psychological problems lead to inevitable devastations in one's love life.

What are the manifestations that are predictive of the least tenable
outcomes? It is sometimes difficult to say, because there's frequently a
great deal of overlap between the normal tumult in the pursuit of love and
those neurotic variations that bode ill. However, there are certain cues
that signal the contamination of love affairs by either primitive psychic
mechanisms or psychopathological components that will destroy the possibilities of love or ravage the lover, and these cues are well-known to

clinicians. They include, among others, excessive self-doubting and self-torment when the relationship goes badly; unconscious sabotage of the relationship (particularly through unconscious manifestations of hostility) accompanied by feelings and fears of rejection; the periodic unleashing of rageful attacks followed by abject repentence; suicidal feelings whenever the relationship threatens to break up; intense outbreaks of uncontrollable jealousy, often unprovoked; repetitive choice of inappropriate or unavailable partners; the compulsive choice of lovers who are caricatured reincarnations of one's parental imagoes; the abandonment of all other pleasures, pursuits, and obligations; the complete inability to perceive realistically any easily identifiable problems in the beloved; sudden abrupt changes in feeling from love to loathing and vice versa; feelings of unworthiness; overriding wishes to rescue or be rescued; holding on whatever the emotional price or humiliation, and so on.

These are typical kinds of distortions and excesses that habitually beset the aspiring but perpetually defeated or disenchanted lover. Some of the simpler ones tend to ameliorate with time, life experience, insight, or a rare stroke of fortune. Others prove stubborn without benefit of some form of psychotherapeutic intervention, and some seem to defeat even the most thoroughgoing therapeutic attempts at insight and change.

That said, we must acknowledge that while there are indeed neurotic problems that may act to the detriment of love, there appears to be a more fundamental (and universal) psychological flaw that plagues the course of love. Though we all seem to expect it as our god-given right, happiness (in love or in any other endeavor) is hard to come by, and confronted with any unhappiness each of us tends to find the cause in the nearest scapegoat. When we are young, that scapegoat is generally a parent or a rival sibling; when we are married that person is most often our spouse. As a consequence, love bears not only its own burdens, but the weight of all our unfulfilled desires and frustrations.

In the end, the fate of love may be said to depend upon many variables, among these the lovers' temperament, capacity for tolerance, and gift for healthy denial (or oversight) and forgiveness. But it is not only what we bring to love that affects its capacity to endure. We must learn both to acknowledge the centrality of romantic love to our lives, and to maintain other relationships, other avenues to meaning. For, perhaps most important of all for the survival of love, we must not ask it to bear the weight of all meaning.

CHAPTER THIRTEEN

Love That Enriches, Love That Endures

"G OOD" LOVE is love that ultimately promotes the lover's sense of self-worth and liberates him from the strictures of self. Whether that love lasts the millennium is not the overriding consideration. In making this very point, Theodor Reik borrowed a politician's witticism: "Speeches to be immortal need not be eternal." Auden beautifully celebrates the transcendence of love, even while acknowledging its transience, in a poem that opens with the lines: "Lay your sleeping head, my love, / Human on my faithless arm;" and goes on to depict precious instants of love:

> Soul and body have no bounds:
> To lovers as they lie upon
> Her tolerant enchanted Slope
> In the ordinary swoon,
> Grave the vision Venus sends
> Of supernatural sympathy,
> Universal love and hope; . . .

Nonetheless, lovers always aspire to eternal, rather than merely immortal, love. (This aspiration is a natural consequence of the fact that the wish for all forms of gratification, including love, originates in the unconscious, where everything exists outside a temporal dimension.) Some lovers actually achieve the near impossible: the preservation of passion in love. And it is natural for lovers and love's theorists both to have a profound interest in attempting to understand those factors that allow love to be sustained in its passionate form over the course of many years.

But, just as I do not claim that passionate love is valuable only when sustained, I do not claim that passionate love is the only form worth sustaining. There are many cases of passionate love which, when formalized and institutionalized (as in marriage), evolve into a "mature" and deeply gratifying form of love characterized by bonds of duty and affection rather than passion. At a time when so many passionate loves terminate in complete rupture, even rubble, such evolution to a quieter, stable form appears highly desirable. And so it is. Another stable variant is a cross between the affectionate and the passionate: one lover is passionately in love, while the other feels fondness rather than ecstasy. And, if one wants to search out first-person accounts of "perfect" unions, one need only talk to a lover whose love was interrupted by the death of the beloved. If we count all these variants along with relationships that maintain their passionate intensity as successes, then love may often have happier outcomes than is generally supposed.

Why, then, is the skepticism about love so rampant? First of all, because some people consider successful only those loves which retain their intensity, and as must be readily admitted, they appear to be the minority although, in my opinion, a significant one.

Secondly, the literary depiction of love, from which we draw so many of our judgments about it, has had difficulty depicting happy love. Auden has said: "Of the many (far too many) love poems written in the first person which I have read, the most convincing were, either the fa-la-las of a good-natured sensuality which made no pretense at serious love, or howls of grief because the beloved had died and was no longer capable of love, or roars of disapproval because she loved another or nobody but herself; the least convincing were those in which the poet claimed to be in earnest, yet had no complaint to make." Fiction has had as much trouble as poetry in depicting realized, sustained, passionate love, and thus we have few literary models for this experience. Perhaps this is because, as Tolstoy suggested—and many others following his lead have concurred—all happy families are alike.

Thirdly, skepticism about love may be stoked by envy. Love stirs envy in observers, and the envious observer may then try to discredit love so as to quiet that envy. Such envy may well have its point of origin in the feelings of exclusion experienced by the child vis-à-vis his parents, particularly and paradigmatically when the parents seek the communion of love behind closed doors. It is of course true that lovers, so obsessed with one another, tend to exclude those around them, even those near and dear, and thus inadvertently evoke anger and envy.

The magnitude of the fascination *and* abhorrence the observers of love may feel as a result of envy is exquisitely caught in a passage in Salter's novel, *A Sport and A Pastime*. In fact, one subject of that book is an observer's perspective on a sexually passionate love affair. As such, it is truly a tour de force. Here is the narrator-observer speaking:

What had happened? They had gone off and made love. That isn't so rare. One must expect to encounter it. It's nothing but a sweet accident, perhaps just the end of illusion. In a sense one can say it's harmless, but why, then, beneath everything does one feel so apart? Isolated. Murderous, even.

In a way I could calmly expect that from this point they would begin, having discovered all there was so soon, to lose interest in each other, to grow cold, but these acts are sometimes merely an introduction—in the great, carnal duets I think they must often be—and I search for the exact ciphers which serve to open it all as if for a safe combination. I rearrange events and make up phrases to reveal how the first innocence changed into long Sunday mornings, the bells filling the air, pillows jammed under her belly, her marvelous behind high in the daylight. Dean slowly inserts himself, deep as a sword wound.

I prefer not to think about it, I turn away, but it's impossible to control these dreams. . . . I cannot stop them even if I want to. . . . My own life suddenly seems nothing, an old costume, a collection of rags, and I walk, I breath to the rhythm of his which is stronger than mine."

This narrator-observer knows he is not fully objective, that his perceptions are partly derivatives of his own imagination. Most observers of love, however, believe that they, in contrast to the lovers, are objective. In truth, the observers are often as subjective as the participants. Both see different truths and construct different falsities depending on their own unconscious needs.

Even when we are not envious, our perceptions of lovers and of couples in general are colored by unconscious expectations and fantasies. Just as each of us has an image of the "Lover-Shadow"—an unconscious dream of our own idealized beloved—so, too, do we have an image of a perfectly loving couple. Sometimes we project that image onto couples whom we know where it may or may not approximate reality. One young-ish man adored such a couple and found a good deal of warmth within their orbit. They appeared to him to be soul mates and ideal parents, creating in the country an idyllic existence antipolar to the materialistic values of his city friends. They lived modestly, but reached out to their friends with ritual and holiday feasts, touching those around them with the authenticity of their warmth and mutuality. The youngish man was so enamored of the couple that when he belatedly married, he tried to model his own marriage on that of his friends. Imagine his sense of horror and personal betrayal when the admired husband, complaining of feeling stifled, ran off with another woman.

Most of us, however, are more likely to err in the direction of harshness toward those loves that come within our purview. We see only the flaws in a relationship and come to the conclusion that one or the other of the lovers (if not both) is deluding himself so as to preserve the illusion of love, or perpetuate dependency gratifications, or whatever.

In the case of either kind of distortion, positive or negative, there is no doubt that we do see part of the truth, but we miss part of it too, and perhaps the most important part. What counts in the end for the individual is, of course, his subjective experience, provided that his distortions are not so great that "reality" will shortly come tumbling down on his head. Too often our lack of tolerance for adaptive solutions and values different from our own lead us to make inappropriate and irrelevant judgments of other people's loves.

Affectionate Bonding

"Love and marriage" may go together like a "horse and carriage" in the lyrics of an old song, but in the modern world the belief that love and marriage go together is about as obsolete as the aforementioned conveyance. In fact, conventional contemporary wisdom has it that passionate love and marriage are at odds with one another, passion diminishing as a function of commitment. (The suspicion that love cannot thrive in marriage is not merely a modern prejudice, however; it has roots at least as far back as the Middle Ages, in the troubador idealization of adulterous love.) Passion is seen as a mere prelude, in healthful or optimal situations, to a mature form of love which is usually designated as "affectionate bonding" or "companionate love." In this view, while many different kinds of people may have the experience (and excitement) of falling in love, the state of being in love will fade quickly enough and only those who have achieved a certain measure of emotional maturity (mature object relations) will be able to convert the introductory phase into a steady-state love relationship, albeit a muted one.

The traditional philosophic view echoes the psychoanalytic view in its insistence that passionate love diminishes in intensity as it approaches fulfillment. For Plato, passion is the intermediate state between yearning and possessing; it corresponds to the trajectory between not having and having, disappearing in the very moment of its satisfaction. And, surely, many love relationships—perhaps the majority—do follow that pattern, though some retain their passionate intensity.

Affectionate bonding may be what is left of a love affair after the passionate component fades, but it may also have a life of its own in a relationship that was never passionate, never had any moments of transcendence, but always provided the kind of warmth and affection, tenderness, and nurturance that bind people together. Moreover, such relationships are not the private preserve of the "healthy"; many couples with neurotic interactions nonetheless form stable loving connections.

Affectionate bonding appears in both unconventional and conventional forms. One of the more unconventional, at least to the American mind, is perhaps that of novelist and poet Vita Sackville-West and writer and diplomat Harold Nicolson. Though each of them was homosexual, their marriage was successful. Their story was chronicled by one of their two children, Nigel Nicolson. Of his book, which draws on—among other sources—his mother's diaries, he says:

It is the story of two people who married for love and whose love deepened with every passing year, although each was constantly and by mutual consent unfaithful to the other. Both loved people of their own sex, but not exclusively. . . . If their marriage is seen as a harbour, their love affairs were mere ports of call. It was to the harbour that both returned; it was there that both were based.

Later on he recounts the nature of their relationship more precisely.

What cannot be preserved except in memory is the gentleness of their reunions. They did not "leap together like two flames," . . . but berthed like sister ships. There was always a certain bustle, the business of unpacking and tea, the tour of the garden and the changing of clothes, but soon they settled down to their easy companionship, allowing words to trickle into the crevasses of the other's mind, feeding each other with impressions of what they had read or heard, stimulating, reassuring, teasing by turns—a process that was half solicitous, half provocative, always tender.

Many people may take exception to the proposition that this is a wonderful example of affectionate bonding. Even so, given the sorrows and pains that accompany so many of our human pursuits—surely including love—I think we ought not be so quick to deny the goodness of that which may be strange to us, but deeply fulfilling to the principals involved.

The difference in the judgments we make may have to do with whether or not we believe it is "justifiable" or "healthy" for the individual to separate his sexual life from his affectionate life. Theoretically, probably it is not. But historically and experientially, the arrangement surely occurs with enough regularity and frequency that we ought not to expect people to forego affection just because they can't integrate it with sex. When we compare love without sex to a more prevalent and commonly sanctioned alternative—the preservation of perfunctory sex within an emotionally depleted union—the former compromise may look very good indeed, especially when painted in the glowing colors of the Sack-ville-West/Nicolson marriage portrait.

However, affectionate bonding often is combined with sexuality, and this constitutes a very happy outcome for many lovers. In Woody Allen's movie, *Radio Days,* set in the days of World War II, there is an early scene in which the tiny old grandfather is standing behind his more-than-buxom wife, trying to stuff her into one of the full-torso corsets women wore in the 1940s. The scene is comic, but it transcends the merely humorous, evoking as it does the casual yet tender earthiness of a couple who have shared half a century of physical intimacy. The two are at ease, deeply unashamed with one another despite the ravages of time and gravity, and their intimacy is extremely moving to the viewer.

Affectionate bonding is based on mutuality and warmth and, above all, on trust and loyalty. This kind of bond provides what Lasch called a "haven in a heartless world." Our picture of such relationships conjures up hearth and home, family pleasures, a leisurely pace, and homely com-forts. In the best of such relationships, the lovers have constructed for themselves a context rich with meaning: they maintain a joint memory bank, share long-standing jokes, constantly re-edit the family mythology, update the picture albums, and exchange tokens and tidbits. Their bond is that of shared ongoing values, habits, and pleasures. In short, the lovers validate each other's lives and provide enough warmth not only for them-selves but for those around them, children and friends. If our parents had such a relationship we considered ourselves fortunate; if they didn't we envied our friends whose parents did. (Perhaps the reason is that these relationships leave room for the children, while the more passionate vari-ety sometimes does not.) However, when we think of what we want for ourselves, we usually daydream about a love that is more passionate than companionate.

Some affectionate lovers may yearn for passion but fear making any new experiments knowing only too well the negative alternatives to com-panionate bonding; they think of those who live alone and those who live in mutual combat. Some passionate lovers, reeling out of tempestuous love affairs that have left them depleted and wary of too much intensity, are eager to seek refuge in the bonds of affection. For many couples, the metamorphosis from passion to a quieter love is eagerly greeted and strongly affirmed. There is an ongoing happiness and ease and the security that the partners have come to a good realistic appreciation of one another and need not fear any sudden reverses or radical deidealization.

In addition, there is always between lovers a degree of ongoing gratitude—gratitude at being understood and affirmed and for having someone to stand by one in those inevitable moments of sorrow, hurt, depression, and reversals of fortune. The joys of tender solicitude may be ample enough, particularly if the lovers have at some point had the joys of a more ecstatic union. I say this because, having had the experience they know what it is and need not feel they've been cheated, and so are freer to appreciate the great value of what remains.

What are the prerequisites that allow for the perpetuation of warm affectionate bonding? The lovers must establish what for them will be the optimal distance between them, allowing for union without subverting autonomy through domination or submission. For most lovers, attaining the optimal distance means two things: the lover has the ability to periodically be alone without feeling empty *and* he has the ability to open up in intimacy. There must be some workable mutual accommodation to both intimacy and separation. Otherwise the most loving bonds are experienced as intrusive, or the shortest of separations is experienced (by one lover, anyway) as intolerable. The lover must be able to periodically renounce his urge to nurture the Other and allow the beloved to move away. Individuals best able to maintain the paradoxical stance required in love—the ability to achieve union without compromising autonomy, and to tolerate aloneness without collapse of the self—are often those with a strong sense of self; they do not have to succumb to the temptation of either triangles or solitude to preserve autonomy. However, there are other kinds of workable balances; for example, if both lovers have significant dependency problems, they may require and tolerate more absolute togetherness than is generally the case.

The lovers must be able to counter those disillusionments so rampant in committed relationships. These problems are easiest to counter when each lover's idealization of the other has not been too extreme, meaning that it has been based on attributes which were accurately perceived and truly valued. Most important, the lover must be able to tolerate some frustration and to be satisfied with what is good, not demanding impossible perfection of either the beloved's character or ministrations. In this sense, happy love depends in part on temperament, on the ability to look at life on balance. The lover must be able to discount some of the negatives, to blink and look away, to deny and to forgive.

Moreover, as we know, the existential problems lovers encounter can be intensified both by character and certain kinds of neurotic problems. Perfectionists suffer in life as well as in love. Any proclivity to generating and harboring anger, jealousy, or envy acts against one's ability to perpetuate love. Neither lover can be so riddled with ongoing hostility (deriving from the past, though experienced in the present) that it becomes impossible to maintain the requsite good will toward the beloved.

Enduring Passion: The Fortunate Few

In contrast to the dominant theoretical position that passion must fade, there is another theoretical proposition that suggests that passionate love can indeed abide. Georg Simmel takes this latter position:

. . . love may arise anew in the very moment of its passing. From the perspective of its meaning, love remains fixed within a process of rhythmic oscillation. The moments of fulfillment lie in its pauses. However, where love is anchored in the ultimate depths of the soul, the cycle of having and not-having describes only the shape of its expression and its outward aspect. The being of love, the pure phenomenon of which is desire, cannot be terminated by the appeasement of this desire.

I would agree with Simmel that for the fortunate few passionate intensity lasts and is not fated to be subsumed in the quieter companionate love that mental health practitioners advocate. For as long as lovers share a mutual fascination with one another, then they can manage to sustain a passionate love in which desire and fulfillment alternate without ever spelling love's end.

To ask if it is ever possible to maintain the intensity of the courtship period throughout an ongoing committed relationship is perhaps to put the wrong question the wrong way. A long-term passionate relationship is closer to what Simmel describes; it is a relationship in which the capacity for passionate engagement remains alive and emerges intermittently. While the lovers might not be as obsessed with their love moment to moment as they are during the courtship stage—such obsession is not completely consonant with functional life—nonetheless they sense that any separation or threatened rupture would quickly enough bring passion to the boiling point. Even without such a threat, the lovers experience periodic intervals of intensity—"love attacks" as it were. They maintain their interest in, and commitment to, the subjectivity of the Other. And they continue to achieve moments in which they experience soulful "merging."

However, the possibility of an ongoing passionate involvement requires certain preconditions. First of all, the lovers must be willing to make some sort of passionate commitment to one another. This need not

be legal, but it surely must be spiritual. George Sand—not herself notable
for a lifetime of faithfulness to one man—wrote her son Maurice the
following letter:

To marry without love is to serve a life-sentence in the galleys. I heard you say
not so long ago that you thought yourself to be incapable of loving anybody
always, and could give no guarantee that you would be faithful to your marriage
vows. If you really mean that, then do not get married at all, because, if you do
you will, in the long run, become a cuckold, and deservedly so. If you married
in that state of mind you would merely be sharing your life with a brutalized
victim, a jealous fury, or a dupe for whom you could feel nothing but contempt.
When one truly loves one is quite certain that one will be faithful. One may be
wrong, but one *believes* it; the vows one makes are made in good faith, and one
is happy for as long as one remains true to them. If an exclusive love cannot last
a lifetime (and I have never found any satisfactory proof that it can), it does at
least give many happy years so long as the belief that such a thing is possible persists. . . . On the day when I see you sure of yourself, I shall cease to
worry.

What George Sand is discussing here we may think of as a kind of
"existential good faith"—a willingness and ability to believe wholly in
one's commitment (or cause or work), an acceptance that is analagous to
Coleridge's "willing suspension of disbelief." Skepticism, like that which
George Sand's son apparently expressed, is often only a defense or a mask
for one's inability or unwillingness to undergo the risks of loving without
guarantees that love will succeed.

But there is no denying that preserving intensity does pose special
problems. While excitement depends on novelty, on otherness, intimacy
and security more often depend on knowledge. Therefore it would seem
almost a contradiction in terms to expect that intimate loving couples
could preserve excitement over a long period of time. The dilemma is how
to perpetuate mystery, uncertainty, and novelty while integrating them
into a stable relationship. Successful lovers intuitively (or accidentally)
solve the problem in creative ways. There are a variety of strategies that
different pairs of lovers use to cut this curious Gordian knot. Excitement
can be fostered by uncertainty, by periodic separations, by sharing external
projects, by unconventionality, and, most importantly, perhaps, by ready
access to the unconscious and the primitive reaches of one's own and one's
lover's soul. It can be renewed by threats of triangulation (though this
sometimes becomes destabilizing rather than simply exciting). And inten-

sity can sometimes be maintained courtesy of particular neurotic fits.

Those lovers who use separation (psychic or geographic) to keep love exciting, find that their periods apart offer them opportunities for inner change or insight. Creative people are more apt to avail themselves of this mode, because they more often require intervals of separation and isolation for inner development, and they can more readily turn such periods into times of growth. Those inner changes and creative insights generated in separation are then brought back into the relationship, which becomes imbued with a new mystery. When this works, it is, of course, a rare achievement, one that is arrived at intuitively, not programmed or plotted in advance. Its rarity probably relates to the fact that *both* lovers must thrive on periodic separation, and this is usually only true of one. The danger is, of course, that the separation becomes more heavily invested than the reunion.

Some lovers find their excitement in a shared external project. This may take the form of a cause that fires the imagination of both, offering them a joint source of excitement issuing from the external world. They would agree with Antoine de Saint-Exupéry's statement that "Love does not consist in gazing at each other, but in looking outward in the same direction." For many, the common cause is political, though it could be artistic, religious, altruistic, or even (thinking of Harry Helmsley and his Queen) mercantile in nature. Mutually engaged, passionate couples are often found in the wake of causes, jointly committed to doing good, righting injustice, reforming, preserving, or revolutionizing. One thinks of the proverbial left-wing couple who would never marry because they were intellectually committed to the proposition that marriage was bourgeois, but who stayed together shamefacedly faithful and passionate. Another fantasy version was embodied in the Nick and Nora Charles movies; Myrna Loy and William Powell played the ultrasophisticated, ever-loving, and romantic detectives. (This tradition has been continued in television with the McMillans and the Harts, and Scarecrow and Mrs. King, too.)

The dream of many people is to find a love relationship which is also the locus of collaborative creative work. This is relatively common in the pop music business, film, and the theatre, though the couple's attachment may or may not endure. (One thinks of the Lunts, John Lennon and Yoko Ono, and so on.) Currently, Mia Farrow and Woody Allen appear to have achieved this kind of relationship and consequently are one of today's premiere fantasy couples. By the term "fantasy couple," I mean one in which the manifest interaction between the pair becomes the stuff of other people's dreams. This ideal is clearly projected in an article based on an interview with the two of them on the occasion of the release of the movie *Broadway Danny Rose*.

The collaborative relationship that Miss Farrow has established with Mr. Allen . . . is, she says, "the most ideal thing that could happen to an actress"; and clearly it has nurtured facets of her talent that otherwise might have gone unnoticed. Mr. Allen, on his part, has also found the process inspiring. "I think it's a good thing to work for someone," he explains. "In trying to create things for a particular actress, it stretches them and it also stretches me."

Miss Farrow goes on to say:

"The biggest help was that Woody trusted me . . . and so I was a little more able to trust myself and sort of go with it. He knew what I can and can't do maybe better than I do myself."

And Mr. Allen goes on to say:

"I'm trying to create a serious thing for her to do now."

These comments embody the dream: He brings out her hidden creative potential and by doing so stretches his own imaginative processes, all within the context of a loving relationship. Nothing could be better.

Occasionally, one lover will be able to find purpose and excitement in service to the other's cause. One woman I know—not apparently psychologically subservient to any degree whatsoever—orchestrates an imaginative creative life around the centerpiece of her husband's work, which both perceive as committed, engaged, and in the service of a better and more just world. Paradoxically (to the observer), the true creativity is hers; she is one of those rare persons whose art expresses itself in the creation of those luminous shifting tableaux of daily life. She gets involved in the administration and practical aspects of his career so that he can focus his skills where most needed. But she is the emotional center, he somewhat deadened without her. Her intuitive, interpersonal, and social gifts make up for his deficiencies in those areas and enable her to hold her own in what could have been a very unbalanced relationship.

Historically, given the pre-eminence accorded to men and their work, creative collaboration usually consisted of a wife serving as helpmate to her husband's gifts and pursuits. (And such relationships are still with us today to a remarkable degree.) However, these one-sided collaborations often prove extremely vulnerable. Jane Carlyle who made a career of protecting Thomas Carlyle's prodigious productivity—and wrote wittily of her jousts with servants and noise—was almost emotionally destroyed by her husband's attentions to another woman. And Sophie Tolstoy ended up resenting her own daughter's secretarial ministrations to Leo Tolstoy. But some lopsided partnerships were (and are) gratifying to both.

Some couples, of course, share pursuits in a genuinely egalitarian manner. Frank Sheed and Maisie Ward engaged in a "lifelong affair" within their long marriage. In *Frank and Maisie: A Memoir with Parents,* their son, Wilfred Sheed, has penned a wonderful account of their extraordinary relationship. Its success seemed to grow out of many different roots. For openers, Maisie Ward and Frank Sheed rescued one another from unsatisfactory (or limiting) beginnings, shared a joint passion, and started Sheed and Ward Publishing, an enterprise that figured hugely in the evolution of contemporary Catholicism. She was the daughter of English Catholic gentry, finding herself in young adulthood at loose ends, with energy and vision but no career. He was an Aussie, in flight from a certain sterility of purpose, who found his destiny in Maisie and her family's Catholic culture.

It was commonly understood in the Sheed household that Frank rescued Maisie. Certainly *she* so understood it and conveyed a life-long sense of gratitude to him, which sweetened their marriage, however cloying and childlike this might seem to modern feminists. In fact, there was gratitude on both sides, as Frank treasured his gift in endless amazement, and it gave a vibrant endurance to their love such as I have never seen, regardless of method. . . .

. . . It was no routine case of a man saving a woman—the Wards were too proud to think they needed saving by anyone, and a lower-middle-class Aussie was a matchmaker's disaster; it was more like a stranger turning up with the other half of the code, just when one had despaired.

The code was to be the strange world of Sheed and Ward, a Siamese twin of a vocation which neither could have pursued solo.

Frank and Maisie lived a life of "joint independence," one in which Frank was constantly on the go, whether visiting branches of the publishing firm, or, after the family moved to the United States, making dangerous wartime visits to England. Though the couple shared passionate pursuits, they kept separate bank accounts and, within the context of their overall shared interests and ideals, followed slightly different activities, enthused as they were over different aspects of religious life. "It was just a matter of emphasis, each shared the other's enthusiasm more than anyone else did, but Frank the lawyer thrilled to the settlement of ancient misunderstandings, while activist Maisie loved to see the Church in motion, 'getting down to it,' or on with it." As regards their coupling, they did everything right intuitively, without benefit of any input from marriage manuals. Among the factors contributing to their good fortune as a couple, the son points out his father's total lack of envy of his wife and his full enjoyment of his wife's success, even during one period when he was in a "minor eclipse" himself.

A number of "literary couples" appear to have been quite successful in their combined love and work lives: the Brownings, Beatrice and Sidney Webb, and I would even include Virginia and Leonard Woolf. The egalitarianism and hence the stability of the Webbs and the Woolfs may have gotten a boost (in addition, that is, to the quite authentic genius of both Beatrice and Virginia) from the fact that both women married "down," thus offsetting the traditional tendency to accord priority to the male.

Then there is the relationship between George Eliot and George Henry Lewes, which doesn't just negate the standard expectations, but reverses them. Their love, generally regarded as highly successful, enabled Lewes to serve as helpmate to Eliot's literary career. Following is an excerpt from her journal, written some four years after the beginning of her liaison (which lasted till Lewes's death):

My life has deepened unspeakably during the last year: I feel a greater capacity for moral and intellectual enjoyment, a more acute sense of my deficiencies in the past, a more solemn desire to be fruitful to combining duties, than I remember at any former period of my life. And my happiness has deepened too: the blessedness of a perfect love and union grows daily. . . . Few women, I fear, have had such reasons as I have to think the long sad years of youth were worth living for the sake of middle age.

Most women love this love story; it is one of the few in which the man nurtures the woman's creativity. Lewes was extremely involved in Eliot's work and instrumental in getting her to write her first novel, handling many of the business aspects for her and sharing with her what appears to be a true marriage of minds. Thus there was a very strong element of a joint project linking them.

There was also a strong element of nonconventionality. Eliot and Lewes lived together twenty-five years without benefit of clergy—indeed in active defiance of the mores of their time. The truth was that Lewes could not divorce and remarry. Though his wife, Agnes Lewes, after eight years of marriage and four sons, had begun an affair with another man, and had children with him, Lewes had accepted, even condoned, the arrangement, and was therefore not able to justify a divorce later. (Shortly after Lewes' death, Eliot married a long-standing friend and apparently some people could not forgive her lapse into conventionality.)

Other less exalted lovers display unconventionality to similarly good effect. One loving couple was the first I knew—and the first in their crowd—to embrace an open marriage. (Though both heterosexual they might be considered a latter-day Americanized version of the Nicolsons.) By and large this never seems to me to work out very well over the long haul, jealousy being not just a conventional, "conservative" response, but one deeply rooted in early life experience. But this couple managed to incorporate sexual freedom into their joint identity as a couple because it made them pioneers of a sort; they proselytized a new freedom within the boundaries of a committed relationship, thereby establishing their specialness and celebrating their spiritual bonding as something transcending any need for strictures on the flesh. Their excitement was in the continual joint reaffirmation of their worth vis-à-vis the external world.

Perhaps the most reliable and least problematic way to preserve excitement—and this judgment surely reflects my psychological bias—is by being able to share new perceptions and insights emanating from the unconscious. This kind of excitement does not depend on any kind of external drama, but on sensitivity to the stages of one's emotional development through the ordinary cycles of life. In short, the lovers undertake a joint emotional and psychological voyage, and for those who are psychologically attuned (I mean *attuned*, not trained), there is novelty and wonder enough to preserve the pitch of excitement. For them, the excitement of a joint voyage of discovery replaces that of the amorous quest.

Even without special psychological aptitude, passionate intensity can be kept alive by access to the unconscious and to the "primitive." Writers on love sometimes seem so committed to promoting "maturity" that they tend to overlook the importance of continuing access to the regressive within us all. One of love's sources and great strengths, part of its very nature, is that it normalizes and harmonizes the expression of infantile and forbidden wishes. But strangely enough, for fear of appearing childish, many lovers are inclined to permit regression only within the sexual sphere—perhaps because people are conditioned to think of sex as grown-up and mature by definition, no matter what form it takes, whereas other behaviors are not accorded the same imprimatur.

For many lovers, the freedom to use baby talk, to baby and be babied, to play-act infantile hurt or anger perpetuate the creative pleasures of love. The distinguished academician who, in the privacy of his bedroom, clowns and acts out Charlie Chaplin's Little Tramp with his beloved, recaptures his youth and his verve. How much more liberty he experiences than those who feel compelled to conduct their intimate relationships with an air of weighty seriousness! Actually, one of the joys of real intimacy is the freedom it gives to shuck off all the layers of adulthood that may feel superimposed and much too heavy. And yet there is surely a prejudice against such "infantilisms." Take, for example, the complaint raised against the Duke of Windsor in a recent book review. Commenting on his love letters, the reviewer writes: "His are all that one could wish of a man in love—a great deal more than one would wish, actually, as he is given to indulging in baby talk"—as though passion and baby talk were incompatible.

Yet many distinguished voices, particularly those not weighed down with the burdens of the psychological literature on maturity, speak to the delights of regression within the freedom accorded by love. If baby talk offends—and it surely offends many—then at least playfulness and laughter may be defended. One must not forget that one of the greatest joys of love is release from the self, and one facet of release from self is the release from obligations, from seriousness, from the constraints of maturity and the world of considered judgment.

Playfulness, of course, demands a capacity for imagination. As already suggested this comes to some lovers most readily in bed. Here is C. S. Lewis on the subject: "Banish play and laughter from the bed of love and you may let in a false goddess. She will be even falser than the Aphrodite of the Greeks; for they, even while they worshipped her, knew that she was 'laughter-loving'. . . . We are under no obligation at all to sing all our love-duets in the throbbing, world-without-end, heart-breaking manner of Tristan and Isolde; let us often sing like Papegeno and Papagena instead." Lovers act out things in bed which they want no one else to know about; it is part of the trust and gift of love that in it we can enact fantasies that reflect part of us—the part that we reserve for soul mates, not for the everyday buzz. And, of course, this is one of the secrets of preserving lust in committed relationships. (This is the reason so many object to the Masters and Johnson approach to sexuality; by programming sex, any propensity to playfulness is effectively squashed. Some sex therapists try to overcome this innate problem by their advice to their clients to share fantasies—anything to save them from performing strictly by rote.)

Those who detest infantilisms, or feel constrained in playfulness, in bed and out, may still find alternate outlets that serve a similar function. For some, games are an alternative form of play. I know some lovers who find their release by inserting some playfulness, perhaps mock combat, into their ritual games of backgammon or gin rummy, tennis or chess (Such playfulness may find its way into friendship, too. I think, for example, of two very rich men, who have created a running joke about putting one over on the other. They alternate picking up dinner checks, and each of them is always trying to outwit the other by picking up the "deli" check rather than the expensive one.)

And there are those passionately loving couples who are "the great romantic sparring partners" and still others who have roaring fights that do not estrange. Such lovers are able to express their autonomy, often extremely vociferously, within the context of a loving commitment. Paradoxically, it is the juice of the unrestrained quarrels that conserves the authenticity of the *emotional* part of their coupling, saving them from lassitude. (Some "tough" guys seem to do best with combative women; the women's strength is an insurance policy against the harm they feel they might inadvertently inflict on submissive women.)

But love is indeed idiosyncratic. Quite the opposite from those who find excitement by plumbing the depths, some lovers maintain intensity by skimming the surface. They have no real taste for indepth intimacy; for them ignorance sometimes preserves mystery. A few lovers purposely avoid knowing too much about the beloved; the apparent superficiality is in part an almost conscious desire to preserve Otherness, and mystery. This reaction is similar to that of a man I know regarding dishes he loves to eat; he insists that his wife never tell him the ingredients and thereby spoil his pleasure. Because intensity thrives on novelty, mystery, and a certain elusiveness, some schizophrenics appear endlessly interesting. Paradoxically, it is their madness that mimics mystery and depth, and this quality sometimes inspires long-lasting fascination if not always love.

There is another kind of elusiveness that can keep passion alive for at least one of the lovers. I always thought that part of the reason my grandfather stayed so passionately in love with his adored second wife was that she remained in love with her dead husband. Thus the great love of her life stoked his love. Other couples seem to have their own mini-versions of *La Ronde*.

Because jealousy jogs intensity, one or the other of the lovers may intuitively bring some threat of triangulation into the relationship. And of course, the spurious threat of triangulation is a staple of the Hollywood romantic comedies. Even in the movie *Topper*, when Cary Grant and Constance Bennett are ghosts, a triangle plays a role. Bennett decides they will both go to hell unless they do a good deed and that their good deed will be to liberate their staid and stuffy banker. In the course of their "rescue" of him, she spends the night with him in a hotel room—chastely, of course, because she is after all a ghost. Even so, Cary Grant's reaction is remarkable; he is jealously agitated and excited.

In *Love in Bloomsbury,* Frances Partridge tells of her courtship, love affair, and eventual marriage (as it turns out a long and successful one despite its unconventional beginnings) with Ralph Partridge, and in the telling we are drawn into the drama of several interlocking love affairs. When Frances first met Ralph, he was established in a relatively stable menage à trois. He was married to Dora Carrington whom he loved, but she was in love with Lytton Strachey who in turn loved Ralph. Since Lytton was homosexual, Dora's love for him could never become what she wanted. However, since Ralph adored her, Dora had agreed to marry him, partly because he was so unhappy, and partly because she saw that the good friendship between Ralph and Lytton might actually consolidate her own position.

Dora wrote one of the most moving of her letters to Lytton on the eve of her marriage in 1921:

So now I shall never tell *you* I do care again. It goes after today somewhere deep inside of me, and I'll not resurrect it to hurt either you or Ralph. Never again. He knows I'm not in love with him. . . . I cried last night to think of a savage cynical fate which had made it impossible for my love ever to be used by you. You never knew, or never will know the very big and devastating love I had for you. . . . I shall be with you in two weeks, how lovely that will be. And this summer we shall all be happy together.

The three lived together in a rather stable menage until Ralph, despairing of any truly intimate relationship with Carrington, fell in love with Frances and eventually married her (over the strenuous objections of Lytton and Carrington!). Even then, the four continued to spend considerable time together until 1932 when Lytton died of stomach cancer and Carrington killed herself over the death of her great love. Of course, the relationship between Carrington and Lytton is an extremely unconventional story of a stable (love) relationship between a passionate lover and a fond one. Curiously (and happily) enough, the Partridges themselves went on to live a remarkably stable, deeply loving married life that endured until Ralph's death—a relationship apparently quite free of triangles after its tempestuous beginnings. Frances had persevered in a highly ambiguous love affair despite the warnings and admonitions of many friends and relatives, and she and Ralph thereby demonstrated that auspicious beginnings are not requisite to ultimately successful enduring, passionate love. In fact, the very uncertainty at the beginning may have served to make their eventual happiness so much the sweeter.

Some few lovers preserve intensity in still another way. They form a kind of twinship. For them, excitement is renewed at the interface of their boundary (as a "we") with the external world. They mirror each other's specialness and worth. Sometimes they are the "darlings" of their social world, sometimes the enfants terribles, sometimes the self-styled aesthetes in the crude and vulgar wasteland that surrounds them. They are more fundamentally closed to the external world than those other couples I have just described—and therefore they draw fire from observers, sometimes even from their own children who feel excluded—but their bonds are surely passionate and enduring. As an observer, I find this kind of love quite successful on one plane, ultimately extremely limiting on another. The lovers seem to me to recapitulate that time in life when young adolescents, feeling weak in and of themselves, bond with others just like them in order to muster the requisite strength to negotiate the world. This "narcissistic" measure, in adults, proffers no viable Other, no transcendence, only a mirror. This kind of relationship is sometimes observed among homosexual lovers who dress alike and look alike; it is just as common among heterosexuals, but harder to spot. In those instances, solipsism of the couple (the "we") sometimes appears to have replaced the individual propensity to solipsism.

It is not possible from what I have said to draw up any recipe for romance. The customary mental health prescription for love relies too much on psychic maturity, but maturity is hardly a guarantor of passion. Intensity is just as likely to come out of a good neurotic fit, perhaps with one person needing to be subordinate, the other dominant. The best one can hope for, short of finding a love potion, is an awareness of the major problems that inhere in love, and a willingness to experiment with strategies for averting them. Above all, in the midst of any romantic crisis we should remember that love waxes and wanes, that dying love can often be revived, and that by modifying our own behavior, we can exercise some small means of control over the outcome of our loves.

Unconventional Love

Love always elicits envy, and as a consequence frequently elicits disapproval as part of the attempt to discredit it. This disapproval is multiplied a hundredfold if the love in question is unusual or unconventional. Many observers of love, out of an exaggerated respect for conformity and conventionality, literally do not allow themselves to see (by which I mean register) certain enduring forms of love. If they do see them they devalue them, because such loves violate too many presumptions about what love "ought" to be. Our era is very self-congratulatory in the latitude it accords sexual practices, and to some degree those congratulations are justified. But we remain extremely judgmental of many of the less common variants of love, in deference to a hierarchy of values that pronounces love in its highest form to be that which occurs between a man and a woman (of roughly the same age and background) and expresses itself in holy matrimony. I wholeheartedly endorse this as one very valuable form of love (though perhaps the most difficult of all to perpetuate). I do not concur with those who judge other kinds of pairings as misguided if not downright deviant. Heterosexual love, home, hearth, and family will all survive without such repressive partisanship.

There are at least three kinds of love toward which observers of love are particularly harsh: adulterous love, heterosexual love across a significant age discrepancy, and homosexual love. Adulterous love affairs draw fire not only because of the envy all love evokes but because adulterous love poses some danger to the established order. It threatens the spouse, the children, and the family of one or both of the lovers. It may also be injurious to an unmarried lover because he may ultimately be denied the privilege of concretizing his love in the external world.

Moreover, even if they are not themselves hurt by the adulterous relationship, many married people feel adulterous love as a threat to their own marriages, raising the possibility that they, too, might be betrayed. One woman's response to a well-known divorce illustrates how one's "moral" judgments are sometimes linked to one's own situation. She reacted to Nelson Rockefeller's divorce and subsequent marriage to Margaretta Fitler Murphy ("Happy") with horror, automatically assuming, without any evidence one way or the other, that Rockefeller had misused his utterly innocent first wife. Once she herself embarked on an adulterous affair her attitude shifted dramatically. Suddenly she became a staunch advocate of the "follow your destiny wherever it leads" point of view. But her original response is common to many married people whose security is sufficiently at risk to cause them to throw up a wall of objections—many of them valid—to adultery.

A particularly popular critique would have it that adulterous lovers are the kind who can only love when love is forbidden or who are so immature as to flee the daily intimacy of committed love. As is usual with such critiques, one may say "yes and no." Sometimes, of course, adulterous love is shattering to both the lovers and the families. And it is surely true that it may thrive unnaturally because of the external restrictions that attach to it. Adulterous love may draw some of its intensity from the fact that the lovers' desire for merger is not so threatening to autonomy when they are of necessity parted. Their intensity is further fuelled by the uncertainty and risks of the adulterous situation. The result is that the passionate yearning stage of love, which is usually relatively brief, can be sustained for an uncharacteristically long time. Moreover, each lover remains insulated from full exposure to those subtle defects in character that are revealed only over an extended period of time in very close quarters.

Still it cannot be denied that some of the most transforming and positive love affairs are in fact adulterous. Some unhappily married people use the reassurance that they can derive from a happier, more ego-enhancing affair to enable them to leave what has become a stultifying marriage—even when they cannot marry the lover who makes such a passage possible. One woman, married at a very early age to a man who turned out to be alcoholic, nonetheless had a very interdependent relationship with him. Breaking away seemed unthinkable, but she felt progressively depressed and panicked in the relationship. As is quite common in such circumstances, her unconscious prompted a resolution. She slipped, almost unawares, into what evolved into a passionate relationship with a man with whom she worked. This relationship proved facilitating to her, though without offering a solution in and of itself since her married lover could not bring himself to leave his wife and children. Nonetheless, faced incontrovertibly with the evidence of what was possible in a relationship, she found the courage to end her problematic marriage. Her new insight about a broadening range of possibilities virtually mandated a divorce, and luckily for her, she had no children at that time to complicate her decision. While her affair proved time-limited, it was, nonetheless, life-saving. Her subsequent marriage, some years later, to a third man proved to be a much more fulfilling and happy one than her first, in part because she had herself developed sufficiently to need less neurotic dependency.

It's probably not generally known how many adulterous affairs continue for the long term. (This is one of the bits of information that comes more easily to therapists, since they often hear more of the truth than friends sometimes do.) It's commonly assumed that adulterous love either fails of its own internal dynamics, or succeeds only by breaking up the marriages of its participants. However, this is not always the case and one of the more "satisfactory" forms of adulterous love is sometimes that in which the adulterous relationship endures over a period of decades, forming a kind of stable triangle. This was surely a more prevalent occurrence in certain countries in Europe during a period when divorce was rare; take, for example, the life-long bond between Juliette Drouet and Victor Hugo I have referred to before. But long-lasting adulterous love is a variant that is with us even today, when divorce is much easier and lovers can no longer rationalize their adultery as tragic necessity. (*Unable* to divorce has always been a more acceptable explanation than *unwilling*.) However, there are still lovers who deplore divorce on religious and moral grounds—their beliefs sometimes bolstered by a psychologically sound wariness of *too* much togetherness—and they may maintain very long-lasting love affairs. (The longest one that I personally know about is of twenty-odd years' duration.) In some of these long-term adulterous loves, the lover's emotional center is located to a large degree in the world of the imagination—imaginative because it attaches to the secret adulterous relationship and must sustain itself without either everyday togetherness or external validation from the outside world. The "we" is often a completely private creation of two isolated beings shut off from the world around them. Everyday life can and usually must continue to be centered in the conventional world, but then everyday life must be lived without the fullness of emotional engagement. (Some, though, do make the effort to integrate their social lives into their intimate lives and consequently are together in the world, but not in any way that supplies external acknowledgment of their coupledom.)

While one may take exception to such relationships on religious or moral grounds, still and all, from the perspective of the participants rather than from that of the observers, these love affairs provide the sense of meaning, transcendence, immediacy of experience, and transformation that are the essence of any reciprocated love.

Love is a creative synthesis. Because it is synthesized in the realm of the imagination, sometimes it can, when necessary, survive and even thrive there. Writing of mystical love when lovers are separated by virtue of an external obstacle, Alberoni says:

Each of them lives in the other's heart, and their love becomes a constant longing for one another, a suffering, because they are not together, but also a constant source of the greatest joy in memories, in the wait or simply in thoughts of their love. Then everything that happens becomes incidental compared with this profound love that agitates and excites them. . . . Love becomes the internal place of regeneration, an island withdrawn from the incidental, the rose garden in the middle of the desert, in which the soul quenches its thirst and from which it can return to the world.

Whether this sort of imaginary love is ultimately enriching or depleting is, of course, a difficult question to answer in the abstract, the experience of the lovers varying according to their circumstances and psychological needs. For some lovers, it is surely the experience that offers the most immediacy and authenticity despite its apparant immateriality.

I have said that I agree with Simmel that passionate love can endure. But my views may be more heretical still. For while I would agree that "maturity" (however that may be defined) may be the usual prerequisite to love, I do not believe that this is always the case. Passion and intensity require certain other attributes that may or may not coexist with maturity, but surely do not depend upon it. What follows is a strange love story, one I find hauntingly moving. It may or may not be completely factual, though I have no doubt that at its core it is emotionally true. It was told to me by the daughter of one of the protagonists, an observer both friendly and romantic.

Tristan and Isolde has been described as the greatest paean to erotic love ever composed, and it is the opera that my father as an adolescent became enamored with. He was a pianist and played the score with its rich variations of themes of love, longing, death, night, and nirvana with all the passion of an exquisite adolescent sensibility.

Richard Wagner's opera is based on the myth that the truest passionate love can only exist in death, where the spirits of the lovers can break through to eternity and forever consummate their love.

The opera begins as Tristan is escorting Isolde, daughter of the Irish king, to be the bride of his uncle, the king of Cornwall. Isolde is in a rage with Tristan because he has killed her lover in knightly combat. Isolde instructs her nurse to brew a poisonous potion that she will drink with Tristan to kill them both. The nurse substitutes the ingredient of love in the place of death, and after they drink they find themselves alive and passionately and forever in love.

Instead of saying, "Hey, wait a minute—the situation has changed—we have to marry each other," they continue on their appointed course, and Tristan delivers Isolde to be his uncle's bride.

They do, however, arrange to meet under cover of the night and become adulterous lovers whereupon they longingly sing:

> "So starben wir, um ungetrennt
> Ewig, einig ohne end'."

> ["Thus we might die undivided
> One forever without end"].

Their union is betrayed by Tristan's best friend, who has also fallen in love with the beautiful queen, and their love-making is interrupted by the king himself.

Tristan, mortally wounded by a blow from his best friend's sword, is banished to an island in disgrace. There he anxiously waits for Isolde to come and nurse him. When she finally arrives he is dying, and they sing the most glorious moments in this deeply passionate score, the famous Liebestod (love in death). Tristan dies of his wounds, and Isolde, by force of will, follows him in death moments later.

My father was raised in a proper middle-class home with many young siblings, a weak father and a semi-invalid mother. The children were brought up by a lovely robust nurse, a woman twenty years my father's senior. During his *Tristan and Isolde* phase my father and his nurse fell helplessly in love, and I feel the course of their love was informed by my father's identification with that opera and the myth it embodies.

I never knew the details of their relationship. I draw this story from fragments I was told, my observations as a child and adolescent, and the fantasies of the adult woman I am now, longing to see my father's life in some magnificent romantic order.

Their love affair spanned a half a century, and if the myth is true it continues still—even after their deaths.

When I try to picture the beginning of this affair, this is how I envision it: He—my father—is a tall, thin, very handsome and profoundly haunted young man sitting at the piano, his soul pouring through his long graceful fingers, playing the exquisitely moving music of Wagner whose melodies and harmonies have no musical boundaries but are determined and propelled by passion. Standing by his side, watching, listening, and receiving the music is this glorious woman, a woman whose role in his life has been to love and nourish uncritically. The music is the love potion and it is drunk in by the soon-to-be lovers. Suddenly there it is—no reason, judgment, morality, or responsibility—just pure love.

Given the circumstances—*he* a student, the eldest of many children, *she* the mother-substitute—the nature of their relationship was kept a secret for many years. In the daytime they were just two members of a busy household where no one suspected that they met under cover of the night as lovers.

Once my father finished college he moved out of the family home. She stayed on to raise the younger children, and their love for each other became known. Shortly thereafter his mother died, and he carried around the burden that it was the revelation of his affair—breaking through the barrier from night to day—that precipitated her death.

They remained lovers on and off throughout the years of his young adulthood—periodically trying to break apart, not really being able to do so. When I asked my mother why they never married, she said my father was ashamed of her—he was a rising and prominent star, she an aging nurse. That is not my favorite part of this story, so I choose to go back to the *Tristan and Isolde* myth for my explanation. If they had married it would have altered the passionate nature of their love. It would have become mundane and they wished it to be eternal. Perhaps, too, he could not compromise the family and he felt too guilty about his own mother's death.

He did marry my mother, a beautiful and vibrant woman, ten years his junior, but his attachment to his nurse was not to be broken, though it seemed that physically they were no longer lovers.

When his first child was born, my father wanted his nurse to come into his household to care for her. My mother staunchly opposed this move but gave into the wish that the child be named after both his mother and his nurse.

The nurse never married but remained a member of the family's extended household in one way or another throughout her life. She moved into my father's sister's home and helped raise her children. Our families were very close and she became "Aunt" to all of us, and was one of the most dearly beloved members of the family. Always accepting, never scolding, she was the one whose lap we sought when we were wounded, who taught us to knit and bake apple pies and made banana pancakes for the whole clan on Sunday mornings.

When I was an adolescent, my father became ill with a disease that was progressive, and he died five years later. During his illness my mother, busy raising a bevy of adolescent kids and no longer in love with a man who had always reserved the totality of his love for someone else, gave over the care of my father to his beloved nurse.

The two of them went to live in our country house, and we visited on weekends. He was then a fragile and aging man of sixty, she a youthful, healthy, and still beautiful woman of eighty. There they recreated the world that inspired their original passion—he, a haunted, but still beautiful man needing her care and ministrations, enthralled her with his music, his wit, and his need, while she provided love, and nourishment.

When he died she rapidly deteriorated and became senile. She had to be taken care of in a nursing home (a nice one in the country) where her room was filled with photographs of my father and all the children. We visited her every week, and she, with rapture, would tell us of Daddy's visits to her.

I do believe she willed her death. Her physical body remained completely healthy until the day she died. She finally wanted to join her lover, and I wish to believe they are together now and forever in eternity.

I am sure that many people would not so readily agree with the daughter's judgment, and my own, that this is in some way a triumphant love story. In fact, some might argue that this story epitomizes everything that is wrong with love—the nurse sacrifices her life in an impossible affair, the wife is betrayed, the husband is unable to separate from his nurse! And it is true that the limitations—perhaps we might even call them the neurotic fixations—of the protagonists are readily apparent. But given such real personal limitations, can we not also appreciate the power, the sheer originality, of a love that allowed two people, despite their limitations, to give one another a deep emotional and spiritual sustenance that in its own idiosyncratic way lasted a lifetime?

The story is, of course, also tantalizing because it hints at the profound ways our perceptions of our parents' erotic commitments enter into our own imaginative lives. The magical couple with whom the child identifies—the couple that is the anlage of the "we" to which the child aspires—is not always the parental couple. The knowledge of her father's romantic life had some blatant, and many subtle, influences on the daughter, among them perhaps her own commitment to be nurturant and to be a healer.

Of course, the story just related is unconventional on more than one count—it is hardly a story of adulterous love at all. It is a story of love across an age barrier, perhaps also of love touched by more incestuous longing than is generally manifest. Most often such stories are reversed—the man being some decades older than the woman. This latter variant often elicits criticism from those who feel that older women suffer a serious liability in our culture, and they are, of course, right; older women are excluded from opportunities for love, while their male cohorts continue to enjoy the extended possibilities of renewed amorous life. Naturally, I am sympathetic to this point of view and understand that in one sense, a great injustice is done. On the other hand, one does not elect one's own passions, and is surely not in any position to legislate someone else's.

For the older man and the younger woman, their love may be liberating, though in different ways. Love is a synthesis in which one has the opportunity to relive certain past experiences and to resolve them in ways that are commensurate with renewed psychological growth; in other words, love serves as a corrective for experiences that have gone sour before. For a young woman to have a loving experience with an older man can be one of the great transforming experiences, one that allows an inner maturation and self-acceptance that might not otherwise be forthcoming. (Of course, this kind of relationship may often backfire too. In Eliot's *Middlemarch*, Dorothea throws her life and love away on a third-rate pedant masquerading as a scholarly genius. And, in the ordinary case, both lovers run the risk of longevity; if the man survives into extreme old age, the sustaining illusions of both partners will be sorely tried.)

Some men may be first empowered only in middle life to be giving, loving, and nurturing in a way that has been psychologically (internally) denied them in previous decades. Therefore, I find myself in the contradictory position of understanding and being moved by love across the generations, at the same time sorrowing for the narrowing window of opportunities most women face as they get older.

Finally, among those loves commonly disapproved of, we come to homosexual love. I personally have no doubt that homosexual love—or, as I should say, love between homosexuals—is experienced in exactly the same way as it is experienced between heterosexuals. The point has been made many times that love poetry written by homosexuals is fully accessible in terms of its feeling, tone, and range to heterosexuals, and vice versa. Nor are the subjective disruptions of love different as recounted by heterosexuals or homosexuals. And, of course, there are a number of well-known, and celebrated, homosexual pairs: for example, Gertrude Stein and Alice B. Toklas; Janet Flanner (Genêt) and Natalia Danesi Murray. In his recent book *French Lovers*, Joseph Barry writes quite movingly, first of Jean Cocteau's love affair with Radiguet, author of *The Devil in the Flesh* who died at the age of twenty (of whom Cocteau had said "Working together is a permanent way of making love," and then of his long love affair with the actor Jean Marais. Though they were not to stay romantically intertwined, Cocteau and Marais did form a deep and enduring friendship. At the peak of their love, Cocteau had written, "My heart has found the answer to the eternal problem / You are I—I am you—We are we—They are they." But long after their *romantic* separation, he was still able to say "Our destinies continue side by side."

Homosexual love draws fire for much the same reason as adulterous love, it appears to be a threat to the social order. Homosexual love is disapproved of for its unconventionality, its threat to social role, and, perhaps, its threat to people's own security about their sexual identities. However, none of these fears ought blind others to the experience of the participants themselves, which seems identical to the experience of heterosexuals in love. In fact, some of the most telling critiques of the power biases that so often contaminate heterosexual love have come out of the perspective of homosexual love.

Theodor Reik, in some ways the wisest of the psychologists writing on love, says, "Wise men warn us again and again not to expect permanent and serene happiness from love, to remember that it brings misery, makes one dependent on an object, has downs as well as ups, like any human creation. It is not love's fault that we demand too much of it, putting all our eggs in one basket. We should know that there is no heaven on earth. It is even doubtful if there is heaven in heaven." His grasp of our extraor-

dinary and unrealistic expectations of love makes self-evident the real
reason we are so often unappreciative of what we have: love awakens in
us the hope of a *perfect* ecstatic union. It is precisely because love touches
the magical, wishful fantasies of earliest life that it has so much power over
us, but concomitantly demands so much perfection as to invite frustration
and sometimes defeat. Perhaps the underlying requisite for enduring love
is that the lover possess enough wisdom to acknowledge and appreciate
love's deep gratifications even within the context of its inescapable frustrations and the beloved's inevitable flaws.

> The honey of heaven may or may not come,
> But that of earth both comes and goes at once.

It is in this sense, in this realization, that I believe a certain kind of
"maturity" leavens love and enables it to endure with great pleasure.

Final Thoughts: Romantic Love as an Agent of Change

F ORWARD motion in our lives is not always linear. Though we think of progress as occurring in small incremental steps, movement in an individual's life can also be characterized by long periods of stasis followed by what appear to be leaps, abrupt discontinuities, and new beginnings. So it is with the internal changes that often accompany deep love and other profound commitments and conversions: they seem (whether they are or not) to be unconnected with anything that precedes them. Such transformations are so unpredictable that we must conclude that the evolution of personality is more than an orderly unfolding of psychological events preordained by biological and historical episodes in one's past; it depends on chance, choice, will, context, and opportunity as well.

We cannot understand ourselves as completely or reductively as we sometimes claim. Imagination and creativity—qualities of mind that defy quantification, though we may attempt to reduce their workings to a causal chain—shape those choices that make our paths and fates uncertain, unpredictable. At various times in our lives we feel some insufficiency or stasis and long for something else, though often the longing is not fully conscious. What that something else might be is generally unspecified, and what we find is by no means always what we thought we were looking for. But it is in the search for something else, something new and Other, that we come to find renewed meaning and hope in life.

Our pursuit cannot be understood as merely a search for diversion and novelty: we seek the absolute, the infinite, the transcendent. In so doing, we reinvoke archaic wishes for (and beliefs in) our own omnipotence. This will lead a few of us to commit ourselves to causes or creations of our own devising. But more of us are likely to find an outlet for our yearnings through that creative synthesis we call passionate love.

Affectionate bonding and passionate love overlap and have many qualities in common. Both offer tender nurturance, an opportunity for sexual satisfaction, and a variety of other gratifications that seem closely related to our earliest needs and pleasures. But passionate love appears to be characterized, in addition, by two emotional states that are experienced as discontinuous with everything that has preceded them; first, the state of heightened drama and self-awareness that accompanies falling in love and the idyllic phase of love; second, the state of transcendence and merger that, intermittently, characterizes the course of passionate love. These states of feeling, during which passionate love is experienced most intensely, not only seem to be radically discontinuous with the rest of our lives, but as a consequence, are the most conducive to significant internal change.

As much as we can say about the conditions leading up to change and the circumstances making it possible, the fundamental mechanism of change remains partly mysterious. Analysts and psychotherapists disagree about what propels change in the consulting room; the memoirs of a Thomas Merton or a Simone Weil stop short of enabling us to understand the leap of faith that constitutes a religious calling, and it is equally difficult to fully comprehend the comparable leap that lovers make in falling in love.

Still, although love in the end defies complete analysis, there is much that can be said about its role as one of life's pre-eminent crucibles for change. Because of the identification with the beloved that always occurs in passionate love, love often demands a significant reordering of values and priorities. In love the self is exposed to new risks that may result in enlarged possibilities. We are emboldened to cross internal psychological boundaries and defy taboos both internal and external, liberating us from ourselves and the strictures of habit and defense, the deformities of earlier unhappy experience and inhibitions. Under the sway of love, we may feel the impetus to begin new phases of life, initiate new projects and under-take new responsibilities. We may even feel born again, as love rewrites the narrative of our lives through its own compelling force. Love can thus be seen as a paradigm for any profound realignment of personality and values, such as those that occur in the great religious conversion experi-ences and in the process of psychoanalytic therapy.

Romantic love enacts its role as change-agent in part by giving us a chance to remake the past. It is not possible to be in love without reinvok-ing old conflicts, and as they are enacted once again, in a new context, we are provided with another opportunity to resolve them. Most signifi-cantly it is the conflicts of the Oedipal period which are revived in love, this time with the possibility of a happy ending. Just as adolescence is the

time of a second individuation, recapitulating some of the residual conflicts inherent in the original separation-individuation of childhood and
offering a better chance of successfully resolving them, so love offers us
yet another chance at completing psychological work which was left
unfinished. Love makes possible successful separation from the past (most
notably from our parents and our overdependence on them) but also and
simultaneously it affords us new opportunities for feelings of transcendence and union reminiscent of those feelings of oceanic oneness first
experienced in infancy. Love is thus a wonderfully elegant and efficient
means of tying up many of the unresolved issues and loose ends of our
lives and devising new and more vital syntheses. Love always gives us one
more chance.

Love also acts to change the boundaries of the self. In the falling-in-
love and idyllic-love phases, change is mediated through the many new
identifications that are formed, particularly through the sense of ourselves
as part of a "we." Change is also propelled by the feelings of hopefulness
and self-affirmation that accompany falling in love and that encourage us
to take new risks, hence to gain new knowledge of the self. By opening
new paths to us, love liberates us from the constricted possibilities of our
past. In moments of transcendence, the liberation from self and the union
with the Other seem equally to serve as impetus to change, particularly
because such epiphanic interludes reinforce the subjective sense of having
escaped the customary boundaries of the self.

In part, love acts as change-agent because it is an explorative, imaginative transaction between two people, a partial escape from our own unremitting subjectivity into another's. And in this it resembles, though it
exceeds by far, the liberation we sometimes experience reading great
literature. Perhaps the reason that fiction has so successfully claimed love
as its province is that fiction and love—at their respective bests—do
something similar: they enable their adherents (readers and lovers) to
enter into another consciousness. In the case of fiction, the consciousness
entered is, most immediately, that of the character through whose eyes
we are seeing events, but ultimately it is that of the author. In love the
consciousness we share is that of our beloved.

At its most sublime, then, love offers us the rare opportunity to liberate
ourselves from our own subjectivity. The state of mind that enables this
to occur is empathy, not complete identification. One feels *with* one's
beloved, one does not become one's beloved. Imagination—the act of
mind and spirit that love and literature have in common—may be so
pleasurable precisely because of the fine line it lives on, the line between

identifying with and submerging one's identity in an Other. In love the
balancing act required to remain on that line creates a tension that is both
intensely pleasurable and potentially problematic.

The exploration of and identification with another's subjectivity which
characterizes passionate love makes the self terribly vulnerable, because
it grants the self of the Other equal importance. The self's vulnerability
is greatest precisely at that time when the potential for expansiveness and
change is at its peak. But for the lover who assents to the opening up and
letting go demanded by passionate love, the rewards may be as great as
the risks. One of the profound insights of religion is that only he who loses
himself may find himself. This is surely as true in love as it is in religion,
though its application to secular matters is rarely perceived.

There are those who seek safety in love, who regard it primarily as
providing a safe haven from the indifference or hostility of the world.
They are making a twofold error. The first, obviously, is that love so often
proves unstable, hence no haven at all. But a second more subtle error lies
in the very concept of safety, which implies for most of us not simply
being safe to express or entertain our feelings but rather safe to remain
what we already are, to avoid the risks attendant upon the adventure of
becoming through love—or any other transformational means—the person we have not yet discovered.

"Oh Lord, we know what we are, but know not what we may be."
However well or ill we already know ourselves, we remain, as long as we
live, capable of fresh insight, fresh response, capable, that is, of new
knowledge. As Socrates said long ago, the right life for a human being is
the examined life, and as he by his own example made clear that is not
a life in which truth is arrived at, as at a destination or place of rest. Truth
resides, rather, in the process of searching for it, and the search is, ideally,
coextensive with our breath.

Love is, by turns, and in varying degrees, both the safe harbor and the
storm. But what it is most profoundly is a voyage, the destination of which
is largely unknown. For most of us today more than ever, love is the
primary mode of risk-taking, of the venture without which there can be
no sense of self-realization. The danger of suffering in love is nothing
compared to the danger of feeling that one has never lived, that one has
never taken the risk of feeling wholly vulnerable and alive. It is this that
Henry James portrays in his story "The Beast in the Jungle," and that
Coleridge's "Rime of the Ancient Mariner" dramatizes with its theme of
death-in-life. Suffering is less an agony than to live without affect. We are
all ruled by a horror vacui, and as long as suffering is not beyond our

powers of endurance or without hope of termination, it is a reminder that we are alive, while affectlessness is a reminder that we are failing to live. Our secret fear is that nothing can move us, and our ambition to be safe and secure is at odds with this other basic drive towards realization through feeling. Indeed, we know that our pains and sorrows are a source of endless self-interest; not simply, I think, from innate egotism or self-absorption, but as tangible proofs of our engagement in the ongoing process of living.

Love then is not only a major route to self-transcendence, but to self-realization and self-transformation as well. In an age when the other risks that commonly beset human beings have been disguised or diminished, the adventure of self grows in importance, and surely that is one of the reasons for the increasing significance of psychotherapy in people's lives. Psychoanalysis sees individuation as a never-ending process; a voyage of self-discovery. One of its fundamental insights is to have assimilated unto itself, for purposes of exemplifying humanity's key psychological dramas, the imagery of the great imaginative journeys (as for example, Freud's use of the Oedipus myth to illuminate one of the fundamental dilemmas of childhood).

Love, like other psychological and spiritual odysseys, is never final but holds forth the promise of continual unfolding, if we will only keep ourselves open to its challenge. Love is not an ultimate solution to our problems but a continual reaffirmation of process, a continual restatement within which we find no answer other than the ongoing attempt to achieve completeness and goodness. To turn back from the journey perpetuates our narrowness and incompleteness. As a Greek critic said of "nothingness," it "might save or destroy those who face it, but those who ignore it are condemned to unreality. They cannot pretend to a real life, which, if it is full of real risks, is also full of real promises."

In our personal evolution, we each must go out into the world and choose from what—and whom—we find there. The man who seeks sustenance from himself alone will starve. By no means preordained or out of our hands, the process of self-formation occurs in this interplay between the self and the world. It is in this sense that our choice of whom to love is life-altering. Each of us comes to know ourselves, and to be ourselves, through these choices and through the resulting encounters with the Other.

For us in our culture, perhaps the most important of our cultivated freedoms is the freedom to love, the most important of our choices whom we will love and what we will value. Love is also the predominant creative experience available to most of us. As a creative act, love has much in common with creative work in general and is thus well described in the works of Silvano Arieti, who described creativity as having a dual role: "at the same time as it enlarges the universe by adding or uncovering new dimensions, it also enriches and expands man, who will be able to experience these new dimensions inwardly." And so it is with love, perhaps in our time the primary vehicle for self-realization, transformation, and transcendence.

Notes

Page and line references refer to the ends of annotated passages. (Line counts include chapter headings and subheadings.)

INTRODUCTION

page/line

11/11   Scott Spencer, *Endless Love* (New York: Alfred A. Knopf, 1979), 162.

12/8   James makes this point a number of times in Lectures I and II of *The Varieties of Religious Experience: A Study in Human Nature* [1902] (New York: New American Library, 1958).

14/15   William James, *The Principles of Psychology* [1891], Chap. 9, reprinted in Vol. 53 of *The Great Books* (Chicago: Encyclopaedia Britannica, 1952), 147.

14/25   Milan Kundera, *The Unbearable Lightness of Being* (New York: Harper & Row, Colophon Books, 1985), 20.

16/1   Christopher Lasch, *Haven in a Heartless World: The Family Beseiged* (New York: Basic Books, 1977), 11–12. As Lasch points out, romantic love is attacked both by radicals and conservatives either as part of a defense of marriage or a criticism of it.

16/17   See Philip Thody, *Roland Barthes: A Conservative Estimate*, paperback ed. (Chicago: University of Chicago Press, 1983), 152.

16/40   Ralph Waldo Emerson, "Love," in *Emerson's Essays* (New York: Harper & Row, Colophon Books, 1951), 123.

17/4   Morton Hunt quoted in Dorothy Tennov, *Love and Limerence* (New York: Stein & Day, 1979), 167.

17/17   The rationale for this point of view is to be found in the work of Philip Slater, *The Pursuit of Loneliness: American Culture at the Breaking Point* (Boston: Beacon Press, 1976) and Erich Fromm, *Escape from Freedom* (New York: Avon Press, 1967) among others.

18/6   James Salter, *Light Years* (San Francisco: North Point Press, 1982), 300–301.

18/13   Viginia Woolf, *To the Lighthouse* [c. 1927], paperback ed. (New York: Harcourt Brace Jovanovich, Harvest Books, 1964), 155.

18/25   Through the myth Aristophanes tells in *The Symposium*, in Vol. 4 of *The Works of Plato*, translated by Benjamin Jowett (New York: Dial Press, ND).

18/27   *Phaedrus*, in *The Works of Plato*, Vol. 3, p. 397. Socrates says to Phaedrus: "Consider this, fair youth, and know that in the friendship of the lover there is no real kindness, he has an appetite and wants to feed upon you. As wolves love lambs so lovers love their loves."

19/8   This is one of the main themes of Rollo May's book, *Love and Will* (New York: W. W. Norton, 1969).

19/24   T. S. Eliot, *Four Quartets*, in *Complete Poems and Plays* (New York: Harcourt, Brace, 1952), 118.

20/12   Quoted in Matthew Josephson, *Victor Hugo* (Garden City, N.Y.: Doubleday Doran, 1942), 205.

20/24   In a letter written to Benjamin Bailey, November 22, 1817, *The Norton Anthology of English Literature*, 5th ed., Vol. 2, edited by M. H. Abrams (New York: W. W. Norton, 1986), 861.

22/5   To borrow Sulloway's designation for Freud in *Freud, Biologist of the Mind: Beyond the Psychoanalytic Legend* (New York: Basic Books, 1979).

23/17   Robert Waelder, "The Principle of Multiple Function: Observations on Over-Determination," *Psychoanalytic Quarterly* 5(1936):45–62, p. 50. Though Waelder sees love as an integrated act that is quite complex, he seems to miss its transformational and transcendent aspects.

23/35   Otto Kernberg has written about crossing the boundaries of the self as a "basis for the subjective experience of transcendence." See "Boundaries and Structures in Love Relations," in *Internal World and External Reality: Object Relations Theory Applied* (New York: Jason Aronson, 1985). The way in which I am using the term "break-through of internal psychological barriers" is related but broader and will be discussed more fully in Chap. 5.

25/26   Roland Barthes is instructive on this point: "Language (vocabulary) has long since posited the equivalence of love and war: in both cases, it is a matter of *conquering, ravishing, capturing*, etc. . . . However, there is an odd turnabout here: in the ancient myth, the ravisher is active, he wants to seize his prey, he is the subject of the rape (of which the object is a Woman, as we know, invariably passive); in the modern myth (that of love-as-passion), the contrary is the case: the ravisher wants nothing, does nothing; he is motionless (as any image), and it is the ravished object who is the real subject of the rape; the *object* of capture becomes the *subject* of love; and the *subject* of the conquest moves into the class of loved *object*. (There nonetheless remains a public vestige of the archaic model: the lover—the one who has been ravished—is always implicitly feminized.)" *A Lover's Discourse: Fragments*, translated by Richard Howard (New York: Hill & Wang, 1978), 188, 189.

CHAPTER ONE

29/22   Spencer, *Endless Love*, 119.

29/28   Helene Deutsch, *Confrontations with Myself* (New York: W. W. Norton, 1973).

30/27   *Romeo and Juliet*, I:iii, in *The Complete Works of Shakespeare* (New York: Books, 1947), 1014.

30/40   Lillian Hellman, *Pentimento* (Boston: Little, Brown, 1973), 237.

31/37   *Romeo and Juliet*, I:v, in *The Complete Works of Shakespeare*, 1018.

33/24   Dorothy J. Farnan, *Auden in Love: The Intimate Story of a Lifelong Love Affair* (New York: New American Library, 1984), 17–18.

33/26   Ibid., 17.

33/34   Ibid., 17.

33/38   Ibid., 19.

34/6   Ibid., 20.

34/26   *H. G. Wells in Love: Postscript to an Experiment in Autobiography*, edited by G. P. Wells (Boston: Little, Brown, 1984), 53–55.

35/27   Sybille Bedford, *Aldous Huxley: A Biography* [c. 1973] paperback ed. (New York: Carroll & Graf, 1985), 599.

36/25   Carson McCullers, *The Ballad of the Sad Café* (New York: Bantam Books, 1971), 26–27.

37/20   Sybille Bedford, *Aldous Huxley*, 136. Presumably, Nancy Cunard served as the model for Mrs. Vivash in *Antic Hay*.

37/27   Michel de Montaigne, "On Friendship," in *Essays*, translated and with an Introduction by J. M. Cohen (New York: Penguin Books, 1958), 97.

39/3   *As You Like It*, III:ii, in *The Complete Works of Shakespeare*, 242.

39/27   John Donne, "Batter my heart, three-personed God," in *The Norton Anthology of English Literature*, 5th ed., Vol. 1, edited by M. H. Abrams (New York: W. W. Norton, 1986), 1100.

40/7   This section draws upon Stendhal's *On Love* (New York: Liveright, 1947); Matthew Josephson, *Stendhal* (New York: Doubleday, 1946); and Michael Wood, *Stendhal* (Ithaca, N.Y.: Cornell University Press, 1971).

40/8   The allusion is to Paul Robinson's description of various sex researchers as sex enthusiasts in *The Modernization of Sex* (New York: Harper & Row, 1976).

40/14   Stendhal, *On Love*, xv.

40/20   Ibid., xv.

40/27   Ibid., xv.

42/16   *A Midsummer Night's Dream*, V:i, in *The Complete Works of Shakespeare*, 169.

page/line

43/9   Jorge Luis Borges, *Labyrinths* (New York: New Directions, 1964).

44/11   Simone Weil, *First and Last Notebooks*, translated by Richard Rees (Oxford University Press, 1970), 284.

46/8   Clement Greenberg cited in Laurence Bergreen, *James Agee: A Life* (New York: Penguin Books, 1984), 272.

47/24   Dominick Dunne, *The Two Mrs. Grenvilles* (New York: Bantam Books, 1986), 62.

48/17   Isadora Duncan, *My Life* [c. 1927] (New York: Liveright, 1955), 5.

48/24   Ibid., 5.

CHAPTER TWO

50/22   Stendhal was the first to attempt a classification of romantic love. Though not exhaustive, his classification is still useful, admirably describing most of the variants with which we are familiar. Although he claimed that he could distinguish a thousand variations of love, Stendhal described only four categories: passion-love, vanity-love, physical love, and mannered love. The first, passion-love, what I have called mutual love, is the type Stendhal viewed as authentic and valued most highly. See, *On Love*.

51/9   James Salter, *A Sport and a Pastime* [c. 1967] (San Francisco: North Point Press, 1985), 65.

52/18   Stendhal, *On Love*, 2.

53/27   Edith Wharton, *The House of Mirth* [c. 1905] (New York: Berkley, 1984), 65.

54/8   Anthony Trollope, *Phineas Finn* (New York: Penguin Books, 1985), 132.

54/31   Mary McCarthy, *The Company She Keeps* (New York: Avon Books, 1981), 222.

57/5   *Antony and Cleopatra*, I:v, in *The Complete Works of Shakespeare*, 846.

57/20   Franz Kafka, *Letters to Milena*, edited by Willi Hoas, translated by Tania and James Stern (New York: Schocken Books, 1962), 67.

58/7   Harold Brodkey, "Sentimental Education," in *First Love and Other Sorrows* (New York: Dial Press, 1957), 145.

58/34   Axel Madsen, *Hearts and Minds* (New York: William Morrow, 1977), 99.

59/10   André Malraux, *Man's Fate* [c. 1934] (New York: Vintage Books, 1969), 53.

61/9   Quoted in Madsen, *Hearts and Minds*, 51.

61/38   Woolf, *To the Lighthouse*, 150–51.

63/30   Salter, *Light Years*, 52.

63/33   Quoted in C. S. Lewis, *The Four Loves* (New York: Harcourt Brace Jovanovich, Harvest Books, 1960), 136.

63/34   Emily Brontë, *Wuthering Heights* (New York: Penguin Books, 1984), 122.

66/30   Ralph Waldo Emerson, "Love," in *Emerson's Essays*, 121.

68/33   Alice Walker, *The Color Purple* (New York: Washington Square Press, 1983), 109.

69/6   Sue Miller, *The Good Mother* (New York: Harper & Row, 1986), 116.

69/21   Ibid., 95.

70/2   Josephson, *Victor Hugo*, 204.

70/12   Arianna Stassinopoulous, *Maria Callas: The Woman Behind the Legend* (New York: Ballantine, 1982), 206.

70/23   Kundera, *The Unbearable Lightness of Being*, 120.

71/4   Francesca Stanfill, *Shadows and Light* (New York: Simon & Schuster, 1984), 169.

71/14   Ibid., 175, 176.

CHAPTER THREE

73/5   Jean Jacques Rousseau quoted in Irving Singer, *The Nature of Love*, Vol. 2 (Chicago: University of Chicago Press, 1984), 340.

74/32   Henry Purcell, *The Fairy Queen* [c. 1692], the drama adapted from *A Midsummer Night's Dream* by Shakespeare, edited by Anthony Lewis (Sevenoaks, Kent, Eng.: Novello, ND), 59–60. There is, of course, also a sexual meaning in this verse.

74/37   Emerson, "Love," in *Emerson's Essays*, 126.

page/line

75/12   Jonathan Swift, "Cadenus and Vanessa" [1727], in *Poetical Works* (London: Oxford University Press, 1967), 134.

75/27   Scott Spencer, *Endless Love*, 20.

76/14   Denis de Rougement, *Love in the Western World* (New York: Pantheon Books, 1956).

76/37   Although Freud formulates the libido theory in "The Three Essays on the Theory of Sexuality" [1905], in *S.E.*, Vol. 7, the first mention of the "pleasure principle" as such is to be found in "Formulations on the Two Principles of Mental Functioning" [1911], in *S.E.*, Vol. 12 (see p. 219, n. 1).
        Bibliographic note. *S.E.: The Standard Edition of the Complete Psychological Works of Sigmund Freud*, edited and translated by James Strachey (London: Hogarth Press, 1981; New York: W. W. Norton, 1981).

77/6   C. S. Lewis, *Four Loves*.

77/16   Ibid., 26.

77/39   Freud, "Inhibitions, Symptoms and Anxiety" [1926], in *S.E.*, Vol. 20, pp. 154–55.

78/16   Pascal, *Pensées*, with an Introduction by T. S. Eliot (New York: E. P. Dutton, Everyman, 1958), 47.

78/26   Marilyn French, *Beyond Power: On Women, Men, and Morals* (New York: Ballantine Books, 1985), 541.

79/20   This point has been made by a number of different theorists, among them Marilyn French in *Beyond Power*. Willard Gaylin also discusses some of the same complexities of the concept of pleasure in *Rediscovering Love* (New York: Viking Press, 1986).

79/25   Lewis, *Four Loves*, 144.

80/28   W. H. Auden, "Dichtung und Wahrheit (An Unwritten Poem)," Canto XVI, in *Collected Poetry*, edited by Edward Mendelson (New York: Random House, 1976), 493.

80/37   Kundera, *The Unbearable Lightness of Being*, 15.

81/10   Ibid., 58.

81/21   John Donne, "The Ecstasy," in *The Norton Anthology of English Literature*, 5th ed., Vol. 1, p. 1078.

81/38   Montaigne, "On Friendship," in *Essays*, 92.

82/9   Simone Weil, *First and Last Notebooks* (London: Oxford University Press, 1970), 73.

83/1   Freud, "Group Psychology and the Analysis of the Ego" [1921], in *S.E.*, Vol. 18, p. 91.

83/7   Freud, "Beyond the Pleasure Principle" [1920], in *S.E.*, Vol. 18, p. 50.

83/7   Ibid., 52.

83/10   Freud, "An Outline of Psycho-Analysis" [1940 (1938)], in *S.E.*, Vol. 23, p. 148.

83/15   Freud, "Group Psychology and the Analysis of the Ego" [1921], in *S.E.*, Vol. 18, p. 90.

83/20   See William Graham Cole, *Sex and Love in the Bible* (New York: Association Press, 1958).

83/32   *Symposium* in *The Works of Plato*, Vol. 4.

84/3   Ibid., 318.

84/11   Ibid., 158.

84/15   Ibid., 158.

84/37   Francesco Alberoni, *Falling in Love*, translated by Lawrence Venuti (New York: Random House, 1983), 69.

86/18   Hans Morgenthau, "Love and Power," in *The Restoration of American Politics* (Chicago: University of Chicago Press, 1962), 7–8.

86/28   Malraux, *Man's Fate*, 228.

86/34   Aldous Huxley, *The Devils of Loudun* [c. 1952] (New York: Carroll & Graf, 1986).

87/5   Malraux, *Man's Fate*, 227.

87/34   McCullers, *The Ballad of the Sad Café*, 26.

CHAPTER FOUR

92/33   Kundera, *The Unbearable Lightness of Being*, 88–89.

92/37   Ibid., 89.

93/22   The phrase is Louise Kaplan's, in *Adolescence: The Farewell to Childhood* (New York: Simon & Schuster, 1984), 115.

page/line

95/21   Freud, "Family Romances" [1909 (1908)], in *S.E.*, Vol. 9, pp. 240–41.

101/34   Isaac Babel, "First Love," in *The Collected Stories*, edited and translated by Walter Morison (New York: Criterion Books, 1955), 266.

102/21   Aldous Huxley, *The Genius and the Goddess*, in *Crome Yellow and Other Works* (New York: Harper & Row, Colophon Books, 1983), 301.

102/25   Ibid., 305.

107/14   Ivan Turgenev, *Spring Torrents* (New York: Penguin Books, 1986), 100.

107/37   For a good account of the theme of separation in *Romeo and Juliet*, see Katherine Dalsimer, *Female Adolescence: Psychoanalytic Reflections on Literature* (New Haven, Conn.: Yale University Press, 1986.)

108/20   Liv Ullmann, *Changing* (New York: Alfred A. Knopf, 1977), 89.

109/12   Peter Bayley, "From Master to Colleague," in *C. S. Lewis: At the Breakfast Table and Other Reminiscences*, edited by James T. Como (New York: Macmillan, Collier Books, 1979), 86.

109/15   This account of Lewis is also drawn from William Griffin, *Clive Staples Lewis: A Dramatic Life* (New York: Harper & Row, 1986).

110/5   A coproduction of the BBC and Episcopal Radio-TV Foundation, shown on Channel 13 on October 29, 1986.

111/14   See Roy Jenkins, *Asquith* [c. 1964], paperback ed. (New York: E. P. Dutton, 1966); and Michael Brock and Eleanor Brock, eds., *Asquith: Letters to Venetia Stanley* (Oxford, Eng.: Oxford University Press, 1985).

111/25   Brock and Brock, *Asquith: Letters to Venetia Stanley*, 466–67.

111/39   Ibid., 10.

CHAPTER FIVE

114/18   Alberoni, *Falling in Love*, 12–13.

114/22   *Symposium*, in *The Works of Plato*, Vol. 4, p. 318.

115/5   Freud, "Creative Writers and Day-Dreaming" [1908 (1907)], in *S.E.*, Vol. 9, p. 146.

115/19   Theodor Reik, *Of Love and Lust* (New York: Jason Aronson, 1984), 111.

115/37   Freud, "On the Universal Tendency to Debasement in the Sphere of Love (Contributions to the Psychology of Love II) [1912], in *S.E.*, Vol. 11, p. 181.

115/40   Martin Bergmann, "On the Intrapsychic Function of Falling in Love," *Psychoanalytic Quarterly*, 1980, 60. (My italics.)

118/8   Spencer, *Endless Love*, 313.

119/9   Charles Dickens, *A Tale of Two Cities* [c. 1859] (New York: New American Library, Signet Classics, 1980), 367.

123/13   Hyde, *The Gift: Imagination in the Erotic Life of Property*, 16.

125/24   Singer, *The Nature of Love*, Vol. 2, pp. 5, 6.

125/30   Spencer, *Endless Love*, 27.

126/4   Percy Bysshe Shelley, "Epipsychidion," in *The Complete Poems of Keats and Shelley* (New York: Modern Library, ND), 465.

126/16   Emily Brontë, *Wuthering Heights*, 121, 122.

126/21   Ernest Hemingway, *For Whom the Bell Tolls* (New York: Charles Scribner's Sons, 1983), 262–63. The lovers do *know* there is a difference, but they *feel* otherwise.
  ". . . Since we are different I am glad that thou art Roberto and I Maria. But if thou should ever wish to change I would be glad to change. I would be thee because I love thee so."
  "I do not wish to change. It is better to be one and each one to be the one he is."
  "But we will be one now and there will never be a separate one." Then she said, "I will be thee when thou art not here. Oh, I love thee so and I must care well for thee."

126/33   Montaigne, *Essays*, 99.

127/29   Barthes, *A Lover's Discourse*, 104.

128/13   William Wordsworth, "Intimations of Immortality from Recollections of Early Childhood," in *The Norton Anthology of English Literature*, 5th ed., Vol. 2, p. 209.

128/18   See note for p. 23, l. 35, above.

page/line

129/3   Martin Bergmann, "On The Intrapsychic Function of Falling in Love," 70.

130/17 *As You Like It,* IV:i, *The Complete Works of Shakespeare,* 248.

130/20 Ibid., II:iv, 237.

130/29 Quoted in Virginia Spencer Carr, *The Lonely Hunter: A Biography of Carson McCullers* (New York: Carroll & Graf, 1975), 228.

130/33 W. H. Auden, "The More Loving One," in *Collected Poems,* 445.

130/35 Duc de la Rochefoucauld, *Maximes,* quoted in Theodor Reik, *Of Love and Lust,* 103.

130/37 Goethe, *Wilhelm Meisters Lehrjahre,* quoted in Reik, *Of Love and Lust,* 103.

131/4   *As You Like It,* I:ii, *The Complete Works of Shakespeare,* 231.

132/6   Donald Keene, *World Within Walls* (New York: Grove Press, 1978), 253ff.

CHAPTER SIX

137/30 Hans Morgenthau, "Love and Power," in *The Restoration of American Politics,* 10.

139/13 Aldous Huxley, *The Devils of Loudun,* 67.

140/9   Simone de Beauvoir, *The Second Sex,* translated and edited by H. M. Parshley (New York: Vintage Books, 1974), 724.

141/12 Lesley Blanch, *The Wilder Shores of Love* (New York: Simon & Schuster, 1954), 7.

141/21 Ibid., 8.

141/27 Ibid., 40.

141/29 Ibid., 22.

141/34 Ibid., 22.

142/7   For an account of Drouet and Hugo's relationship see Matthew Josephson's *Victor Hugo* or André Maurois's *Olympio: The Turbulent Life of Victor Hugo* [c. 1956] (New York: Pyramid Books, 1968).

142/37 Virginia Haggard, *My Life with Chagall: Seven Years of Plenty with the Master as Told by the Woman Who Shared Them.* (New York: Donald I. Fine, 1986.)

143/27 Alma Mahler, *Gustav Mahler: Memories and Letters,* translated by Basil Creighton (Seattle: University of Washington Press, 1968), 21.

143/40 Anton Chekhov, "The Darling," in *The Tales of Chekhov,* Vol. 1 (New York: Ecco Press, 1984), 4.

144/34 Leo Tolstoy, "Criticism in 'The Darling,'" reprinted from "Readings for Every Day of the Year," in *The Tales of Chekhov,* 24.

144/38 Ibid., 25.

146/6   Kundera, *The Unbearable Lightness of Being,* 17.

149/21 Salter, *Light Years,* 50.

150/35 André Maurois, *Lélia: The Life of George Sand* (New York: Penguin Books, 1977.)

151/7   Ibid., 182–83.

151/11 Ibid., 189.

151/16 Ibid., 189.

151/23 Ibid., 191.

156/19 W. Somerset Maugham, *Of Human Bondage* [1915] (New York: Penguin Books, 1985), 278.

157/2   Ibid., 7.

157/22 Leslie Fiedler, *Love and Death in the American Novel,* [c. 1960] revised ed. (New York: Stein & Day, 1966).

157/34 Ibid., 313.

157/37 F. Scott Fitzgerald quoted in Elizabeth Hardwick, *Seduction and Betrayal: Women and Literature* (New York: Vintage Books, 1974), 91.

159/35 Aldous Huxley, *The Gioconda Smile,* [c. 1920] in *Crome Yellow and Other Works* (New York: Harper & Row, Colophon Books, 1983), 159–60.

159/39 Benjamin Constant, quoted in de Beauvoir, *The Second Sex,* 728.

161/22 This will be discussed at greater length in Chap. 11.

CHAPTER SEVEN

page/line

163/37   *Phaedrus,* in *The Works of Plato,* Vol. 3, p. 397.

164/29   The phrase is to be found in Roberto Mangabeira Unger, *Passion: An Essay on Personality*
         (New York: Free Press, 1984), 151.

164/39   Morgenthau, "Love and Power," in *The Restoration of American Politics,* 10.

165/16   W. H. Auden, "September 1, 1939," quoted in Philip Thody, *Roland Barthes:* 150.

165/37   Malraux, *Man's Fate,* 45.

166/12   Ibid., 50.

166/36   Henry James, *The Portrait of a Lady* [c. 1881], edited with an Introduction by Geoffrey
         Moore (New York: Penguin Books, 1984), 481.

168/13   Josephson, *Victor Hugo,* 205, 206.

168/26   Ibid., 219.

168/33   Ibid., 258.

169/5   Françoise Gilot and Carlton Lake, *Life with Picasso* (New York: New American Library,
         Signet Books, 1965), 80.

169/10   Ibid., 76.

170/23   Donald Spoto, *Falling in Love Again: Marlene Dietrich* (Boston: Little, Brown, 1985), 21.
         My account of Dietrich and von Sternberg is largely drawn from Spoto and from Charles
         Higham, *Marlene: The Life of Marlene Dietrich* (New York: W. W. Norton, 1977).

170/32   Higham, p. 89.

170/36   Ibid., 89.

171/13   Quoted in ibid., 103.

171/24   Spoto, *Falling in Love Again,* 31.

177/17   F. Scott Fitzgerald, *Tender Is the Night* (New York: Charles Scribner & Sons, 1934), 272.

177/25   Ibid., 276.

177/29   Ibid., 308.

177/34   Ibid., 277–78.

178/17   Edith Wharton, *Ethan Frome* [c. 1911], (New York: Charles Scribner's Sons, 1970), 70.

178/31   Ibid., 117–18.

182/13   Morgenthau, "Love and Power," in *The Restoration of American Politics,* 8.

182/22   Ibid., 11–12.

182/35   Philip Rieff, *Freud: The Mind of the Moralist* (New York: Doubleday, Anchor Books,
         1961), 168.

182/37   Ibid., 168.

184/24   "The Wife of Bath," in *The Canterbury Tales,* edited and translated by A. Kent Hieatt
         and Constance Hieatt (New York: Bantam Books, 1985), 239.

CHAPTER EIGHT

186/31   Stassinopoulous, *Maria Callas,* 313.

187/26   F. Scott Fitzgerald, *The Great Gatsby* (New York: Charles Scribner's Sons, 1925), 94.

188/17   Salter, *A Sport and a Pastime,* 72–73.

189/6   Stassinopoulous, *Maria Callas,* 304.

189/9   Ibid., 304.

190/25   The idealization and de-idealization as portrayed in this novel are the subject of an excellent
         paper by David Werman and Theodore Jacobs, "Thomas Hardy's 'The Well-Beloved' and
         the Nature of Infatuation," *International Review of Psycho-Analysis* 10(1983): 447–57.

192/39   Wells, *H. G. Wells in Love,* 56.

193/2   Ibid., 99.

193/38   Evelyn Keyes, *Scarlett O'Hara's Younger Sister, My Lively Life In and Out of Hollywood*
         (Secaucus, N.J.: Lyle Stuart, 1977), 185.

194/4   Ibid., 185–86.

194/10   Ibid., 187.

194/14   Ibid., 237.

362 Notes

page/line

197/16   Henri Troyat, *Tolstoy* (New York: Harmony Books, 1980), 382.

197/29   Wells, *H. G. Wells in Love*, 64.

199/26   Swift, "Cassinus and Peter" [1734], in *Poetical Works*, 531.

199/34   Ernest Becker, *The Denial of Death*, paperback ed. (New York: Free Press, 1973), 26.

200/29   Grace Paley, "A Woman, Young and Old," in *The Little Disturbances of Man* (New York: Penguin Books, 1985), 26.

200/36   Grace Paley, "An Interest in Life," in *The Little Disturbances of Man*, 95.

201/37   Judith Rossner, *August* (Boston: Houghton Mifflin, 1983), 90.

202/1   Ibid., 123.

202/8   Ibid., 123.

203/8   Mary Jane Moffat and Charlotte Painter, eds., *Revelations: Diaries of Women* (New York: Vintage Books, 1975), 155.

203/24   Ibid., 159–60.

206/6   Tolstoy, *Anna Karenina* (New York: Modern Library, n.d.), 769.

207/12   Miller, *The Good Mother*, 95.

208/29   Kernberg, *Internal World and External Reality*, 288.

208/35   Ibid., 288.

210/40   Katherine Mansfield, "A Dill Pickle," in *The Short Stories of Katherine Mansfield* (New York: Alfred A. Knopf, 1945), 334–35.

CHAPTER NINE

213/36   *The Inferno*, Canto V, in *The Divine Comedy*, translated by John Ciardi (New York: W. W. Norton, 1977), 28.

214/39   Leo Tolstoy, *Anna Karenina* (New York: Modern Library, ND), 137.

216/19   Fitzgerald, *Tender Is the Night*, 88.

216/24   Ibid., 88.

217/6   Tony Tanner, *Adultery in the Novel: Contract and Transgression* (Baltimore: Johns Hopkins University Press, 1979), 12. This section relies on the insights of Tanner and Leslie Fiedler (see note for p. 217, l. 13, below).

217/13   Leslie Fiedler, *Love and Death in the American Novel*, 1966.

217/24   De Rougemont, *Love in the Western World*, 16.

217/26   Alberoni, *Falling in Love*, 19.

217/30   Tanner, *Adultery in the Novel*, 12.

217/35   Ibid. This is a major theme in Tanner's Chap. 1.

218/8   The word *triangulation* used in this sense is Otto Kernberg's.

220/4   Otto Kernberg used the term "reverse triangulation" in a paper, "Between Conventionality and Aggression: The Boundaries of Passion," delivered at a conference, "Passionate Attachments: The Essential but Fragile Nature of Love," given Nov. 10, 1984. Others, including J. Chasseguet-Smirgel and myself, have also described the psychodynamics of this kind of triangle.

221/37   Arthur Miller, *After the Fall* (New York: Dramatists Play Service, c. 1964).

225/7   This point is eloquently made in Leonard Schapiro, "Critical Essay and Spring Torrents— Its Place and Significance in the Life and Works of Ivan Sergeyevich Turgenev," the Introduction to Ivan Turgenev, *Spring Torrents* (New York: Penguin Books, 1986).

225/12   Ibid., 197.

225/24   Ibid., 197.

225/30   Turgenev, *Spring Torrents*, 137.

225/38   As Schapiro has pointed out, while the wife, the lover, and the complaisant husband are a favorite triangle in Turgenev's fiction, there is another triangle hidden behind it, one which comes to light in Tugenev's autobiographical short story "First Love." The story describes a young boy's passionate love for the beautiful, uneducated Princess Zinaida, who rents the summer cottage next door. She is commanding and imperious to the suitors who flock around her, but the boy divines that she is herself in love. He follows her and much to his surprise discovers that her lover is none other than his father; he witnesses an exchange in which his father strikes Zinaida with a riding crop—because Zinaida, who is pregnant, demands that he leave his wife—and the boy sees Zinaida kiss the welt on her

page/line

arm. One can only speculate that Turgenev's admiration for his charming, strong-willed father may have found its way into his admiration for similarly strong-willed women. "First Love" can be found in Ivan Turgenev, *First Love and Other Tales*, translated with an Introduction by David Magarshack (New York: W. W. Norton, 1968), 142–218.

232/10   Gilot and Lake, *My Life with Picasso*.

235/25   Kundera, *The Unbearable Lightness of Being*, 16.

235/32   Ibid., 62.

236/21   Quoted in Carr, *The Lonely Hunter*, 147.

236/25   Ibid., 148.

236/38   Ibid., 171.

237/1   Ibid., 371.

237/4   Ibid., 171.

CHAPTER TEN

242/22   Freud (in "Fragment of an Analysis of a Case of Hysteria" [1905 (1901)], in *S.E.*, Vol. 7, pp. 3–122) made the further distinction that some transference feelings are "mere reprints" while others have undergone sublimation and are therefore revised editions of the original feelings.

242/39   Freud, "The Future of an Illusion" [1927], in *S.E.*, Vol. 11, p. 24.

243/2   Ernest Becker uses the phrase "taming terror." "This is how we can understand the essence of transference: as a taming of terror." My discussion on the nature of transference in everyday life closely follows Becker's. *The Denial of Death*, 145.

243/19   Ibid., 146.

245/4   Freud, "Observations on Transference-Love (Further Recommendations in the Technique of Psycho-Analysis III)" [1915], in *S.E.*, Vol. 12.

245/27   Ernest Jones, *The Life and Work of Sigmund Freud*, Vol. 1 (London: Hogarth Press, 1953), 225.

245/38   Ernest Jones revealed her identity in his biographical study of Freud, *The Life and Work of Sigmund Freud*, Vol. 1. George Pollock has written extensively on Anna O (Bertha Pappenheim). See "Glückel von Hameln: Bertha Pappenheim's Idealized Ancestor," *American Imago* 20(1978); and "Anna O: Insight, Hindsight, and Foresight," in *Anna O: Fourteen Contemporary Reinterpretations*, edited by Max Rosenbaum and Melvin Muroff (New York: Free Press, 1984).

246/4   Thomas Szasz, "The Concept of Transference," *International Journal of Psycho-Analysis* 44(1963):432–43.

246/16   Freud, "Fragment of an Analysis of a Case of Hysteria," 116.

246/22   Roy Schafer, citing a personal communication from Charles Rycroft, "The Interpretation of Transference and the Conditions of Loving," *Journal of the American Psychoanalytic Association* 25(1977):335–62, 340.

246/36   Szasz, "The Concept of Transference," 432–43.

247/1   Martin Bergmann has chronicled the changes in Freud's thinking about transference, transference love, and love in three very rich papers on love: "On the Intrapsychic Function of Falling in Love," *Psychoanalytic Quarterly* 49(1980):56–77; "Platonic Love, Transference Love, and Love in Real Life," *Journal of the American Psychoanalytic Association* 30(1982):87–111; and "Psychoanalytic Observations on the Capacity to Love," in *Separation-Individuation: Essays in Honor of Margaret S. Mahler*, edited by J. P. McDevitt and C. F. Settlage (New York: IUP, 1971). My abbreviated account of Freud's changes in conceptualizing transference love largely follows Bergmann's account.

247/21   Freud, "Observations on Transference-Love" [1915], in *S.E.*, Vol. 12, p. 168.

247/32   Bergmann, "Platonic Love, Transference Love, and Love in Real Life."

249/8   Roy Schafer, "The Interpretation of Transference and the Conditions of Loving," 340.

249/12   Bergmann, "Platonic Love, Transference Love, and Love in Real Life," 106–7.

249/30   Ibid., 109.

250/10   Aldo Carotenuto, *A Secret Symmetry: Sabina Spielrein Between Jung and Freud*, Commentary and Introduction by Bruno Bettelheim (New York: Pantheon Books, 1982).

250/20   Quoted in ibid., 154.

250/38   Quoted in ibid., 159.

364 Notes

page/line

251/17 Ibid., 94.

251/22 Ibid., 12.

251/31 Quoted by Bettelheim in ibid., xix.

252/7 Quoted by Bettelheim in ibid.

252/10 Ibid., 48.

253/5 Ibid., xxxviii. The love affair turns out to be unusually well documented not only because of Spielrein's diary and the letters but because both Jung and Spielrein implicated Freud at different points in their relationship and for different reasons. From almost the very beginning of the Freud-Jung correspondence—as early as Jung's second letter to Freud, written in 1906—Jung is drawing Freud into the complicities of his involvement with Spielrein. In the letter, he makes mention of a difficult case and then describes Spielrein's case history. In other words, Jung's involvement with Spielrein was the issue he used to initiate a personal relationship with Freud. And I have already quoted the letter he wrote to Freud in the traumatic aftermath of this affair. In the meantime, Spielrein, too, wrote to Freud asking him for an interview, but Freud proved evasive. Nonetheless, Spielrein eventually moved to Vienna and became part of Freud's psychoanalytic circle.

    The story of this amazing love affair and what evolved into an intellectual triangle has been unearthed so recently that it has not yet entered into the immense scholarship on the evolution of Freud's thinking. However it is of some interest that these events became known to Freud in those years when he would still have been working out his theories about the erotic transference. Bettelheim believes that Freud's discovery of Jung's relationship with Spielrein affected him very deeply. Freud was known to have fainted twice in his life—both times during meetings with Jung—and a number of people including Jung himself have tried to explain what the causes of those episodes might have been. Bettelheim raises a new possibility altogether by suggesting that the first faint was in the context of Freud's first meeting with Jung after he had learned about Spielrein.

253/18 J. G. Gaarlandt, *An Interrupted Life: The Diaries of Etty Hillesum (New York: Pantheon Books, 1984).*

254/20 For a fuller discussion see Ethel S. Person, "The Erotic Transference in Women and in Men: Differences and Consequences," *Journal of The American Academy of Psychoanalysis* 13(1985):159–80.

    The erotic transference, heterosexual or homosexual, may be unmanageably intense, leading to a stalled treatment or a reactively hostile one. It may be complicated by sexual or romantic acting out either in or out of the analytic situation. Or it may be so frightening to some patients that they break off treatment. Sometimes the patient remains in treatment but the erotic transference proves difficult to analyze.

    The dangers of successfully suppressing or repressing the experience of the erotic transference are less dramatic than the dangers attendant to the erotic transference used as resistance, but they are nonetheless substantial. The inability to merge sexual and dependency yearnings perpetuates instability in the capacity to form enduring love relationships. And this latter problem appears to be more common among men—in the therapy situation and in life—than among women.

255/1 Eva Lester, "The Female Analyst and the Eroticized Transference," *International Journal of Psycho-Analysis* 66(1985):283–93.

255/5 Grete Bibring reported one case sometimes cited as the single exception in the literature in which her male patient developed a florid transference to her, but it was so infused with primitive elements, that it cannot be properly considered an erotic transference. See Bibring, "A Contribution to the Subject of Transference," *International Journal of Psycho-Analysis* 17(1936):181–89.

255/6 Laila Karme, "The Analysis of a Male Patient by a Female Analyst: The Problem of the Negative Oedipal Transference," *International Journal of Psycho-Analysis* 60(1979):253–61.

255/21 However, there are some exceptions and one may occasionally see well-developed and sustained erotic transferences in male patients to their female doctors. One sometimes sees them among older men in relation to younger women. This constellation is most often seen in the training situation, very often in low-cost clinics. For a variety of reasons, including the youth and inexperience of the analyst, these have not been reported in the literature. They also appear to occur more frequently either in men with a strong bisexual identification or homosexual conflict, *not* in homosexual men. In these casees the erotic transference experienced towards the female analyst may serve as a defense against the more threatening homosexual longing, that is, the positive Oedipal constellation serves as a defense against the negative one. For a fuller discussion of the exceptions, see Person, "The Erotic Transference in Women and in Men: Differences and Consequences."

255/23   Some sexual fantasies betray pre-Oedipal components, sometimes aggressive in nature, as a defense against affectionate longings. See ibid.

255/27   See Ethel Person, "The Omni-Available Woman and Lesbian Sex: Two Fantasy Themes and Their Relationship to the Male Developmental Experience," in *The Psychology of Men: New Psychoanalytic Perspectives*, edited by Gerald I. Fogel, Frederick Lane, and Robert Liebert (New York: Basic Books, 1986), 71–94; and Ethel Person, "Male Sexuality and Power," *Psychoanalytic Inquiry* 6(1986):3–25.

256/13   My account is drawn from Paul Stern's biography, *C. G. Jung: The Haunted Prophet* (New York: George Braziller, 1976); and Vincent Brome's *Jung: Man and Myth* (New York: Atheneum, 1978).

256/16   Stern, *C. G. Jung*, 131. The relationship between Wolff and Jung underwent many changes. At one point, Wolff tried to insist that Jung divorce Emma and marry her, something he was averse to doing. In 1920, Jung began still another relationship with a woman, Ruth Bailey, that continued until the end of his life, but nonetheless occasionally spent weekends with Wolff. By 1946, Bailey wrote, "As I came more and more into the picture, Toni seemed to be fading. She was unlucky. She had very bad arthritis. It made her fingers fat. She was getting on for 60. There were times when Jung deliberately avoided her. He would say, 'Toni is coming today. I hope she doesn't stay very long.' " (Brome, *Jung*, 257). Toni died in 1952. Jung did not go to her funeral.

256/27   E. James Lieberman, *Acts of Will: The Life and Work of Otto Rank*. (New York: Free Press, 1985.)

257/3   Ibid., 344.

257/18   Ibid., 350.

257/36   Lucia Tower, "Countertransference," *Journal of the American Psychanalytic Association* 4(1936):224–55.

258/3   Phyllis Greenacre, "The Role of Transference: Practical Considerations in Relation to Psychoanalytic Theory," *Journal of the American Psychanalytic Association* 2(1954):671–84.

258/18   S. H. Kardener, M. Fuller, and I. N. Mensh, "A Survey of Physician's Attitudes and Practices Regarding Erotic and Nonerotic Contact with Patients," *American Journal of Psychiatry* 130(1973):1077–81; Nanette Gartrell, J. Herman, S. Olarte, M. Feldstein, and R. Localio, "Psychiatrist-Patient Sexual Contact: Results of a National Survey, I: Prevalence," *American Journal of Psychiatry*, 143(1986):1126–31.

258/23   If a woman therapist does have either sexual or erotic fantasies, or both, about male patients, she is less likely to dwell upon or openly acknowledge them because of cultural prohibitions. Her own inhibitions about such fantasies subtly inhibit inquiries into the patients' defenses against his erotic feelings toward her. Her embarrassment at presuming to be found "sexual" and erotically desirable, in the face of the patients' disclaimers, also serves as an impediment to interpreting the resistance to the erotic transference.

258/40   The difference in the manifestation of the erotic transference that I have described ought not to be taken as an argument in favor of either same-sex or cross-sex patient-therapist dyads. Therapeutic outcome has, by and large, not been tied to the therapist gender, and there are always problems and opportunities specific to any given dyad.

259/37   Freud, "On Narcissism: An Introduction" [1914], in *S.E.*, Vol. 14, pp. 67–102. Quotation on p. 94.

260/10   Now it may be that the helpless infant never truly felt omnipotent—perhaps had little sense of self at all. But the idea of perfect satiety and the power to command it surely enters the imagination at some point in the form of the fantasy of the perfect child who commands perfect attention; this may be part of the fantasy informing the power of the image of Madonna and child. Whether or not the infant actually feels omnipotent, the image of infantile omnipotence becomes one of our inner ideals.

261/31   Bergmann, "Platonic Love, Transference Love, and Love in Real Life," 107.

263/15   Elmore Leonard, *Unknown Man, No. 89* (New York: Avon Books, 1984), 111.

263/24   Ibid., 123.

CHAPTER ELEVEN

page/line

266/6   Quoted by de Beauvoir in *The Second Sex*, 712.

266/9   Ibid. 712.

267/26   Malraux, *Man's Fate*, 227, 228.

268/9   See, for example, Carol Gilligan, who is one of the major researchers and theorists to
         demonstrate the female tendency to relatedness, the male tendency to separation. *In a
         Different Voice: Psychological Theory and Women's Development* (Cambridge, Mass.:
         Harvard University Press), 1982.

269/19   Nancy Chodorow, *The Reproduction of Mothering: Psychoanalysis and the Sociology of
         Gender* (Los Angeles: University of California Press, 1978); Dorothy Dinnerstein, *The
         Mermaid and the Minotaur* (New York: Harper & Row, 1976); Ethel Person, "Women
         Working: Fears of Failure, Deviance and Success," *Journal of the American Academy of
         Psychoanalysis* 10(1982):67–84.

270/16   Rachel Brownstein, *Becoming a Heroine: Reading About Women in Novels* (New York:
         Viking Press, 1982), xv.

270/25   My discussion of the romance novel is informed by two important studies: Ann Barr
         Snitow's "Mass Market Romance: Pornography for Women Is Different," *Radical History
         Review* 20(1979):141–61; and Janice A. Radway's *Reading the Romance: Women, Pa-
         triarchy, and Popular Literature* (Chapel Hill: University of North Carolina Press, 1984).

270/33   Radway, *Reading the Romance*, 123. Radway has done a statisical analysis of the traits most
         frequently associated with both the male and female protagonists of romance novels, and
         she describes "the ideal heroine" as characterized "by unusual intelligence or by an extraor-
         dinarily fiery disposition."

271/19   Radway is able to identify specific female dynamics portrayed in specific conventions of
         the romance novel. See *Reading the Romance*, Chap. 4.

271/28   Further, a woman's satisfaction may be vicarious in another important way. Her lover's
         desire of her, sometimes confirmed through her seeing his erection, assuages her. Her desire
         is sometimes triggered by her seeing him look at her breast with desire; from the beginning
         her identification with his desire is used to validate her own worth, and may sometimes
         come to substitute for her own desire.

273/2   Radway, *Reading the Romance*, 31.

273/19   Bruno Bettelheim, *The Uses of Enchantment: The Meaning and Importance of Fairy Tales*
         (New York: Vintage Books, 1977), 112.

275/33   Ethel Person, "Women Working."

276/2   Ibid.

276/29   Ethel Person, "Male Sexuality and Power," *Psychoanalytic Inquiry* 6(1986):3–25.

278/10   Ethel Person, "The Omni-Available Woman and Lesbian Sex," in *The Psychology of Men*.

279/12   Freud, "Beyond the Pleasure Principle" [1920], in *S. E.*, Vol. 18, p. 50. Karen Horney,
         "The Dread of Woman: Observations on a Specific Difference in the Dread Felt by Men
         and Women Respectively for the Opposite Sex," *International Journal of Psychoanalysis*
         13(1932):348–60; Janine Chasseguet-Smirgel, *Creativity and Perversion* (New York: W.
         W. Norton, 1984); and Joyce McDougall, *Plea for a Measure of Abnormality* (New York:
         IUP, 1980).

279/34   Horney, "The Dread of Women," 356.

280/5   Ibid., 357.

280/21   The boy's original narcissistic wound is aggravated in adolescence by the hypersexuality of
         the adolescent male, whose female counterpart is generally not tormented by a comparable
         hormonal surge. The typical male adolescent experience is one of perpetual sexual arousal
         without an adequate outlet. This recapitulates the intensely non-gratifying situation of the
         Oedipal period and his feelings of inferiority vis-à-vis other men. Throughout life, he can
         never be certain of a woman's sexual desire; her sexual desire is not so evident as his own
         erection. This sexual difference simply intensifies his doubts about the woman's feelings
         for him, thus constituting another reason for him to try and control her body and soul.
               For a fuller account of these psychodynamics in male development, see Person, "Male
         Sexuality and Power"; and Person, "The Omni-Available Woman and Lesbian Sex."

282/4   Shulamith Firestone, *The Dialectic of Sex: The Case for Feminist Revolution* (New York:
         Bantam Books, 1970), Chap. 6–7.

282/9   Phyllis Rose, *Parallel Lives* (New York: Alfred A. Knopf, 1983), 8.

283/3   Person, "Women Working."

Notes

page/line

283/9   Gertrude Ticho, "Female Autonomy and Young Adult Women," *Journal of the American Psychoanalytic Association* 24(1976):153.

284/18   Edmund Wilson, *The Fifties*, edited and with an Introduction by Leon Edel (New York: Farrar, Straus and Giroux, 1986), 303.

284/22   Susan Sontag, "The Double Standard of Aging," in *Psychology of Women: Selected Readings*, edited by Juanita H. Williams (New York: W. W. Norton, 1979), 462–78.

286/5   Francesca M. Cancian, "The Feminization of Love," *Signs* 4(1986):692–709.

CHAPTER TWELVE

292/36   Troyat, *Tolstoy*, 377–78.

294/13   Quoted in Patricia Beer, *Reader, I Married Him* (New York: Harper & Row, 1974), 6.

294/17   Ibid., 7.

294/34   Quoted in Hardwick, *Seduction and Betrayal*, 27.

295/24   My account of Adèle H. is taken largely from Josephson's *Victor Hugo*.

296/30   Robert C. Bak, "Being in Love and Object Loss," *International Journal of Psycho-Analysis* 54(1973):1–8.

296/32   Ibid., 3.

297/23   Ibid., 7.

298/15   *Anna Karenina*, Part 2, Chap. 9, 154.

298/27   Ibid., Part 2, Chap. 9, 154–55.

299/19   Ibid., Part 2, Chap. 28, 220.

300/5   De Beauvoir, *The Second Sex*, 732.

301/40   Max Frisch, *Montauk*, translated by Geoffrey Skelton (New York: Harcourt Brace Jovanovich, Harvest Books, 1976), 83.

302/5   Ibid., 85.

306/31   Edna O'Brien, "The Love Object," in *A Fanatic Heart* (New York: Farrar, Straus & Giroux, 1984), 171, 172.

308/5   Marcel Proust, *Swann's Way*, translated by C. K. Scott-Moncrieff (New York: Modern Library, 1956).

308/11   Ibid., 549.

313/14   De Beauvoir, *The Second Sex*, 526.

314/28   Ibid., 523.

315/12   The term is Ellenberger's. See *The Discovery of the Unconscious* (New York: Basic Books, 1970).

315/17   Quoted in Robert Craft, *Stravinsky: The Chronicle of a Friendship* (London: Victor Gollancz, 1972), 301.

315/29   I am grateful to Nancy Wexler, who gave me her sister's biography of Emma Goldman and thereby piqued my interest in this extraordinary woman. See Alice Wexler, *Emma Goldman* (New York: Pantheon Books, 1984). See also Candace Falk's *Love, Anarchy, and Emma Goldman* (New York: Holt, Rinehart & Winston, 1984).

315/30   Wexler, Ibid., 147.

316/3   Ibid., 143.

317/9   Margeurite Duras, *The War: A Memoir*, translated by Barbara Bray (New York: Pantheon Books, 1986).

317/24   Ibid., 62.

317/30   Ibid., 63–64.

318/24   Something comparable to this may be observed in the late work of Van Gogh, (to move from the movies to the museum). It has been said that part of the emotional force of his last paintings—those done in the months before he committed suicide—may depend upon secondary imagery. There appear in his landscapes, in the trees and the clouds, what seem to be faces and human figures. Though these may easily be overlooked by the casual observer, the viewer's overall response to Van Gogh's paintings may well depend on his processing that hidden world, whether consciously or otherwise. Something analogous seems to go on in the great movies.

318/38   Spencer, *Endless Love*, 162.

page/line

321/1   Otto Kernberg has addressed the question of the psychopathology of love, distinguishing those that generally derive from personality disorders from those that derive from neurotic conflicts. See particularly "Barriers to Falling and Remaining in Love" in *Object Relations Theory and Clinical Psychoanalysis.*

CHAPTER THIRTEEN

322/9   Reik, *Of Love and Lust*, 81.

322/11 W. H. Auden, "Lullaby," in *Collected Poems*, 131.

323/23 Auden, "Dichtung und Wahrheit," Canto XLII, *Collected Poems*, 498.

324/16 Salter, *A Sport and a Pastime*, 64, 65.

326/15 Nigel Nicolson, *Portrait of a Marriage* (New York: Atheneum, 1973), ix.

326/24 Ibid., 231.

329/14 Georg Simmel, *On Women, Sexuality and Love*, translated and with an Introduction by Guy Oakes (New Haven, Conn.: Yale University Press, 1984), 133.

330/17 Quoted in Maurois, *Lelia*, 355.

331/20 Quoted in Linda Schierse Leonard, *On the Way to the Wedding: Transforming the Love Relationship* (Boston: Shambhala, 1986), 133.

332/15 Michiko Kakutani, "Mia Farrow and Her Director on Their Film Collaboration, *New York Times* (22 January 1984).

333/6   Wilfred Sheed, *Frank and Maisie: A Memoir with Parents* (New York: Simon & Schuster, 1985), 255.

333/29 Ibid., 59, 60.

333/30 Ibid., 262.

334/1   Ibid., 257.

334/6   Ibid., 255.

334/7   The phrase is Elizabeth Hardwick's, in *A View of My Own* (New York: Noonday Press, 1963), 88.

334/17 This point is emphasized by Phyllis Rose in *Parallel Lives.*

334/27 Quoted in Patricia Beer, *Reader, I Married Him*, 14–15.

335/1   Ibid., 15, 16.

336/11 Judith Martin's review of *Wallis and Edward: Letters, 1931–1937, The New York Times Book Review*, June 29, 1986, 12.

336/28 Lewis, *The Four Loves*, 140–41.

338/5   Frances Partridge, *Love in Bloomsbury* (Boston: Little, Brown, 1981).

338/25 Ibid. 94.

343/2   Alberoni, *Falling in Love*, 123.

347/17 Joseph Barry, *French Lovers: From Heloise and Abelard to Beauvoir and Sartre* (New York: Arbor House, 1987), 272.

347/22 Ibid., 269.

347/23 Ibid., 281.

347/39 Reik, *Of Love and Lust*, 194.

348/11 Wallace Stevens, "Le Monocle de Mon Oncle," in *The Collected Poems of Wallace Stevens* (New York: Alfred A. Knopf, 1954), 15.

FINAL THOUGHTS

349/26 According to Giambattista Vico, "a finitude which tends toward infinity." Quoted in Silvano Arieti, *Creativity: The Magic Synthesis* (New York: Basic Books, 1976), 30.

352/22 *Hamlet*, IV:v, in *The Complete Works of Shakespeare.*

352/26 *Apology*, in *The Works of Plato*, 1100.

353/29 Demetrios Capetenakis, *A Greek Poet in England* (London: John Lehmann, 1947), 71.

354/6   Arieti, *Creativity*, 5.

References

BOOKS AND ARTICLES

Alberoni, Francesco. *Falling in Love*. Translated by Lawrence Venuti. New York: Random House, 1983.

Arieti, Silvano. *Creativity: The Magic Synthesis*. New York: Basic Books, 1976.

Arlow, Jacob A. "Object Concept and Object Choice." *Psychoanalytic Quarterly* XLIX(1980): 109–33.

Auden, W. H. *Collected Poems*. Edited by Edward Mendelson. New York: Random House, 1976.

Babel, Isaac. *The Collected Stories*. Edited and translated by Walter Morison. New York: Criterion Books, 1955.

Bak, Robert C. "Being in Love and Object Loss." *International Journal of Psycho-Analysis* 54(1973): 1–8.

Barry, Joseph. *French Lovers: From Heloise and Abelard to Beauvoir and Sartre*. New York: Arbor House, 1987.

Barthes, Roland. *A Lover's Discourse: Fragments*. Paperback ed. Translated by Richard Howard. New York: Hill and Wang, 1978.

Becker, Ernest. *The Denial of Death*. Paperback ed. New York: The Free Press, 1973.

Bedford, Sybille. *Aldous Huxley: A Biography*. [c. 1973.] Paperback ed. New York: Carroll and Graf, 1985.

Beer, Patricia. *Reader, I Married Him*. New York: Harper and Row, 1974.

Bergmann, Martin S. "On the Intrapsychic Function of Falling in Love." *Psychoanalytic Quarterly* XLIX (1980): 56–77.

———. "Platonic Love, Transference Love, and Love in Real Life." *Journal of the American Psychoanalytic Association* 30(1982): 87–111.

———. "Psychoanalytic Observations on the Capacity to Love." In *Separation-Individuation: Essays in Honor of Margaret S. Mahler*. Edited by J. P. McDevitt, and C. F. Settlage. New York: IUP, 1971.

Bergreen, Laurence. *James Agee: A Life*. New York: Penguin Books, 1984.

Bettelheim, Bruno. *The Uses of Enchantment: The Meaning and Importance of Fairy Tales*. New York: Vintage Books, 1977.

Bibring-Lehner, Grete. "A Contribution to the Subject of Transference" *International Journal of Psycho-Analysis* 17(1936): 181–89.

Blanch, Lesley. *The Wilder Shores of Love*. New York: Simon and Schuster, 1954.

Borges, Jorge Luis. *Labyrinths*. Paperback ed. Edited by Donald A. Yates and James E. Irby. New York: New Directions Books, 1964.

Brock, Michael and Eleanor, eds. *H. H. Asquith: Letters to Venetia Stanley*. Paperback ed. Oxford: Oxford University Press, 1985.

Brodkey, Harold. *First Love and Other Sorrows*. New York: The Dial Press, 1957.

Brome, Vincent. *Jung: Man and Myth*. New York: Atheneum, 1978.

Brontë, Emily. *Wuthering Heights*. New York: Penguin English Library, 1984.

Brownstein, Rachel M.. *Becoming a Heroine: Reading About Women in Novels*. New York: Viking Press, 1982.

Cancian, Francesca M. "The Feminization of Love" *Signs* 4(1986): 629–709.

Capetanakis, Demetrios. *A Greek Poet in England*. London: John Lehman, 1947.

Carotenuto, Aldo. *A Secret Symmetry: Sabina Spielrein between Jung and Freud: The Untold Story of the Woman Who Changed the Early History of Psychoanalysis.* Paperback ed. Commentary by Bruno Bettelheim. New York: Pantheon, 1982.

Carr, Virginia Spencer. *The Lonely Hunter: A Biography of Carson McCullers.* Paperback ed. New York: Carroll and Graf, 1975.

Chasseguet-Smirgel, Janine. *Creativity and Perversion.* New York: W. W. Norton, 1984.

Chaucer, Geoffrey. "The Wife of Bath" in *The Canterbury Tales.* Edited by A. Kent Hieatt and Constance Hieatt. Toronto and New York: Bantam Books, 1984.

Chekhov, Anton. *The Tales of Chekhov, Vol. I: The Darling and Other Stories.* Paperback ed. Translated by Constance Garnett. New York: Ecco Press, 1984.

Chodorow, Nancy. *The Reproduction of Mothering: Psychoanalysis and the Sociology of Gender.* Los Angeles: University of California Press, 1978.

Cole, William Graham. *Sex and Love in the Bible,* New York: Association Press, 1958.

Como, James T., ed. *C. S. Lewis at the Breakfast Table and Other Reminiscences.* New York: Collier Books, 1979.

Craft, Robert. *Stravinsky: The Chronicle of a Friendship 1948–1971.* London: Victor Gollancz, Ltd., 1972.

Dalsimer, Katherine. *Female Adolescence: Psychoanalytic Reflections on Works of Literature.* New Haven, Conn.: Yale University Press, 1986.

Dante. *Inferno.* Canto V in *The Divine Comedy.* Translated by John Ciardi. New York: W. W. Norton, 1977.

de Beauvoir, Simone. *The Second Sex.* [c. 1952.] Translated and Edited by H. M. Parshley. New York: Vintage Books, 1974.

de Rougemont, Denis. *Love in the Western World.* New York: Pantheon Books, 1956.

Deutsch, Helene. *Confrontations with Myself.* New York: W. W. Norton, 1973.

Dickens, Charles. *A Tale of Two Cities.* [c. 1859.] New York: New American Library, Signet Books, 1980.

Dinnerstein, Dorothy. *The Mermaid and the Minotaur: Sexual Arrangements and Human Malaise.* New York: Harper and Row, 1976.

Donne, John. "The Ecstasy." In *The Norton Anthology of English Literature,* Fifth ed., Vol. 1. Edited by M. H. Abrams. New York, W. W. Norton, 1986.

Du Maurier, Daphne. *Jamaica Inn.* New York: Doubleday, 1936.

Du Maurier, Daphne. *Rebecca.* New York, Avon Books, 1971.

Duncan, Isadora. *My Life.* [c. 1927.] Paperback ed. New York: Liveright, 1955.

Dunne, Dominick. *The Two Mrs. Grenvilles.* New York: Bantam Books, 1986.

Duras, Marguerite. *The War: A Memoir.* Translated by Barbara Bray. New York: Pantheon, 1986.

Eliot, T. S. *Four Quartets.* In *The Complete Poems and Plays.* New York: Harcourt, Brace, 1952.

Ellenberger, Henri F. *The Discovery of the Unconscious.* New York: Basic Books, 1970.

Emerson, Ralph Waldo. *Emerson's Essays.* [c. 1926.] Paperback ed. Introduction by Irwin Edman. New York: Harper and Row, Colophon Books, 1951.

Falk, Candace. *Love, Anarchy and Emma Goldman.* New York: Holt, Rinehart and Winston, 1984.

Farnan, Dorothy J. *Auden in Love: The Intimate Story of a Lifelong Love Affair.* New York: New American Library, Meridian Books, 1984.

Fiedler, Leslie A. *Love and Death in the American Novel.* [c. 1960.] Revised ed. New York: Stein and Day, 1966.

Firestone, Shulamith. *The Dialectic of Sex: The Case for Feminist Revolution.* New York: Bantam Books, 1970.

Fitzgerald, F. Scott. *The Great Gatsby.* [c. 1925.] Paperback ed. New York: Charles Scribner's Sons, (ND).

——. *Tender Is the Night.* [c. 1933.] Paperback ed. New York: Charles Scribner's Sons, (ND).

French, Marilyn. *Beyond Power: On Women, Men, and Morals.* New York: Ballantine Books, 1985.

Freud, Sigmund. *The Standard Edition of the Complete Psychological Works* Edited and Translated by James Strachey. London: Hogarth Press; New York: W. W. Norton, 1981.

(1905 [1901†].) "Fragment of an Analysis of a Case of Hysteria." Vol. 7:3–122.

(1905.) "Three Essays on the Theory of Sexuality." Vol. 7:123–245.

(1908 [1907].) "Creative Writers and Day-Dreaming." Vol. 9:141–53.

† Published in 1905 though written in 1901.

(1909 [1908].) "Family Romances." Vol. 9:235–41.

(1910.) "A Special Type of Choice of Object Made by Men (Contributions to the Psychology of Love I)." Vol. 11:163–75.

(1911.) "Formulations on the Two Principles of Mental Functioning." Vol. 12:213–26.

(1912.) "On the Universal Tendency to Debasement in the Sphere of Love (Contributions to the Psychology of Love II)." Vol. 11:177–90.

(1915 [1914].) "Observations on Transference-Love (Further Recommendations on the Technique of Psycho-Analysis III)." Vol. 12: 157–73.

(1914.) "On Narcissism: An Introduction." Vol. 14:67–102.

(1920.) "Beyond the Pleasure Principle." Vol. 18:1–64.

(1921.) "Group Psychology and the Analysis of the Ego." Vol. 18:65–143.

(1926.) "Inhibitions, Symptoms, and Anxiety." Vol. 20:75–175.

(1927.) "The Future of an Illusion." Vol. 21:3–56.

(1940 [1938].) "An Outline of Psycho-Analysis." Vol. 23:139–207.

Frisch, Max: *Montauk*. Paperback ed. Translated by Geoffrey Skelton. New York: Harcourt Brace Jovanovich, Harvest Books, 1976.

Fromm, Erich. [c. 1941.] *Escape from Freedom*. New York: Avon Press, 1967.

Gaarlandt, J. G. *An Interrupted Life: The Diaries of Etty Hillesum 1941–43*. New York: Pantheon Books, 1984.

Gartrell, Nanette; J. Herman; S. Olarte; M. Feldstein; and R. Localio. "Psychiatrist-Patient Sexual Contact: Results of a National Survey, I: Prevalence." *American Journal of Psychiatry* 143(1986): 1126–31.

Gaylin, Willard. *Rediscovering Love*. New York: Viking, 1986.

Gilligan, Carol. *In a Different Voice: Psychological Theory and Women's Development*. Cambridge, Mass.: Harvard University Press, 1982.

Gilot, Françoise and Carlton Lake. *Life with Picasso*. New York: Signet Books, 1965.

Greenacre, Phyllis. "The Role of Transference: Practical Considerations in Relation to Psychoanalytic Theory." *Journal of the American Psychoanalytic Association* 2(1954): 671–84.

Griffin, William. *Clive Staples Lewis: A Dramatic Life*. New York: Harper and Row, 1986.

Haggard, Virginia. *My Life with Chagall: Seven Years of Plenty with the Master as Told by the Woman Who Shared Them*. New York: Donald I. Fine, 1986.

Hardwick, Elizabeth. *A View of My Own*. [c. 1951.] New York: The Noonday Press, 1963.

———. *Seduction and Betrayal: Women and Literature*. Paperback ed. New York: Vintage Books, 1974.

Hardy, Thomas. *Tess of the D'Urbervilles*. [c. 1891.] New York: Bantam Books, 1984.

———. *The Well-Beloved*. [c. 1897.] New York: Macmillan, 1975.

Hellman, Lillian. *Pentimento*. Boston: Little, Brown, 1973.

Hemingway, Ernest. *For Whom the Bell Tolls*. [c. 1940.] Paperback ed. New York: Charles Scribner's Sons, (ND).

Higham, Charles. *Marlene: The Life of Marlene Dietrich*. New York: W. W. Norton, 1977.

Horney, Karen. "The Dread of Woman: Observations on a Specific Difference in the Dread Felt by Men and by Women Respectively for the Opposite Sex." *International Journal of Pscyho-Analysis* 13(1932): 348–60.

Huxley, Aldous. *The Devils of Loudun*. [c. 1952.] Paperback ed. New York: Carroll and Graf, 1986.

———. *The Genius and the Goddess*. [c. 1955.] In *Crome Yellow and Other Works*. New York: Harper and Row, Colophon Books, 1983.

———. *The Gioconda Smile*. [c. 1920.], in *Crome Yellow and Other Works*. New York: Harper and Row, Colophon Books, 1983.

Hyde, Lewis. *The Gift: Imagination in the Erotic Life of Property*. Paperback ed. New York: Vintage Books, 1983.

James, Henry. *The Portrait of a Lady*. [c. 1881.] Edited with an Introduction by Geoffrey Moore. New York: Penguin Books, 1984.

James, William. *The Principles of Psychology*. [c. 1891.] Reprinted in *The Great Books*. Chicago: Encyclopedia Britannica, 1952.

———. *The Varieties of Religious Experience*. New York: New American Library, Mentor Books, 1958.

Jenkins, Roy. *Asquith.* [c. 1964.] Paperback ed. New York: E. P. Dutton, 1966.

Jones, Ernest. *The Life and Work of Sigmund Freud.* Vol. I. London: Hogarth Press, 1953.

Josephson, Matthew. *Stendhal.* New York: Doubleday, 1946.

————. *Victor Hugo.* Garden City, New York: Doubleday Doran & Co., 1942.

Kafka, Franz. *Letters to Milena.* [c. 1953.] New York: Schocken Books, 1962.

Kakutani, Michiko. "Mia Farrow and Her Director on Their Film Collaboration." *The New York Times,* 22 January 1984.

Kaplan, Louise J. *Adolescence: The Farewell to Childhood.* New York: Simon and Schuster, 1984.

Kardener, Sheldon H.; Marielle Fuller; and Ivan N. Mensh. "A Survey of Physician's Attitudes and Practices Regarding Erotic and Nonerotic Contact With Patients." *American Journal of Psychiatry* 130(1973): 1077–81.

Karme, Laila. "The Analysis of a Male Patient by a Female Analyst: The Problem of the Negative Oedipal Transference." *International Journal of Psycho-Analysis* 60(1979): 253–61.

Keats, John. *The Complete Poetical Works and Letters of John Keats.* Edited by Horace E. Scudder. Cambridge ed. Boston and New York: Houghton Mifflin, 1899.

Keene, Donald. *World Within Walls.* New York: Grove Press, 1978.

Kernberg, Otto. *Internal World and External Reality.* New York: Jason Aronson, 1985.

————. *Object-Relations Theory and Clinical Psychoanalysis.* New York: Jason Aronson, 1976.

Keyes, Evelyn. *Scarlett O'Hara's Younger Sister, My Lively Life In and Out of Hollywood.* Secaucus, N.J.: Lyle Stuart, 1977.

Krantz, Judith. *Mistral's Daughter.* [c. 1982.] New York: Bantam Books, 1983.

————. *Princess Daisy.* New York: Bantam Books, 1981.

Kundera, Milan. *The Unbearable Lightness of Being.* New York: Harper and Row, Colophon Books, 1985.

Lasch, Christopher. *Haven in a Heartless World: The Family Besieged.* New York: Basic Books, 1977.

Leonard, Elmore. *Unknown Man, No. 89.* [c. 1977.] New York: Avon Books, 1984.

Leonard, Linda Schierse. *On the Way to the Wedding: Transforming the Love Relationship.* Boston: Shambhala, 1986.

Lester, Eva. "The Female Analyst and the Eroticized Transference." *International Journal of Psycho-Analysis* 66(1985): 283–93.

Lewis, C. S. *The Four Loves.* Paperback ed. New York: Harcourt Brace Jovanovich, Harvest Books, 1960.

Lieberman, E. James. *Acts of Will: The Life and Work of Otto Rank.* New York: Free Press, 1985.

McCarthy, Mary. *The Company She Keeps.* New York: Avon Books, 1981.

McCullers, Carson. *The Ballad of the Sad Café.* New York: Bantam Books, 1971.

McDougall, Joyce. *Plea for a Measure of Abnormality.* New York: IUP, 1980.

Madsen, Axel. *Hearts and Minds.* New York: William Morrow, 1977.

Mahler, Alma. *Gustav Mahler: Memories and Letters* Translated by Basil Creighton. Seattle, University of Washington Press, 1968.

Malraux, André. *Man's Fate.* [c. 1934.] New York: Vintage Books, 1969.

Mansfield, Katherine. *The Short Stories of Katherine Mansfield.* New York: Alfred A. Knopf. 1945.

Martin, Judith. "The Intimate Correspondence of the Duke and Duchess of Windsor." *The New York Times Book Review,* 29 June 1986.

Maugham, W. Somerset. *Of Human Bondage.* [c. 1915.] New York: Penguin Books, 1985.

May, Rollo. *Love and Will.* New York: W. W. Norton, 1969.

Maurois, André. *Lélia: Life of George Sand.* Translated by Gerard Hopkins. New York: Penguin Books, 1977.

————. *Olympio: The Turbulent Life of Victor Hugo.* [c. 1956.] Paperback ed. New York: Pyramid Books, 1968.

Miller, Arthur. *After the Fall.* [c. 1964.] New York: Dramatists Play Service, Inc., (ND).

Miller, Sue. *The Good Mother.* New York: Harper and Row, 1986.

Moffat, Mary Jane; and Painter, Charlotte, Eds. *Revelations: Diaries of Women.* New York: Vintage Books, 1975.

Montaigne, Michel de. *Essays.* [c. 1958.] Translated and with an Introduction by J. M. Cohen. New York: Penguin Books, 1983.

Morgenthau, Hans J. "Love and Power," in *The Restoration of American Politics.* Chicago: University of Chicago Press, 1962.

Nicolson, Nigel. *Portrait of a Marriage: V. Sackville-West and Harold Nicolson.* New York: Atheneum, 1973.

O'Brien, Edna. *A Fanatic Heart.* New York: Farrar Straus Giroux, 1984.

Paley, Grace. *The Little Disturbances of Man.* [c. 1956.] New York: Penguin Books. 1985.

Partridge, Frances. *Love in Bloomsbury: Memories.* Boston: Little, Brown, 1981.

Pascal, Blaise. *Pensées* with an Introduction by T. S. Eliot. Paperback ed. New York: E. P. Dutton, 1958.

Person, Ethel S. "The Erotic Transference in Women and in Men: Differences and Consequences." *Journal of the American Academy of Psychoanalysis* 13(1985): 159–80.

———."Male Sexuality and Power." *Psychoanalytic Inquiry* 6(1986): 3–25.

———."The Omni-Available Woman and Lesbian Sex: Two Fantasy Themes and their Relationship to the Male Developmental Experience." *The Psychology of Men: New Psychoanalytic Perspectives.* Edited by G. I. Fogel; F. M. Lane; R. S. Liebert. New York: Basic Books, 71–94, 1986.

———."Women Working: Fears of Failure, Deviance and Success." *Journal of the American Academy of Psychoanalysis* 10(1982): 67–84.

Person, Ethel S., and Lionel Ovesey. "Psychoanalytic Theories of Gender Identity." *Journal of the American Academy of Psychoanalysis* 11(1983): 203–26.

Plato. *Apology.* Translated by Benjamin Jowett. In *The Works of Plato.* New York: Dial Press, (ND).

———.*Phaedrus.* Translated by Benjamin Jowett. In *The Works of Plato.* New York: Dial Press, (ND).

———.*Symposium.* Translated by Benjamin Jowett. In *The Works of Plato.* New York: Dial Press, (ND).

Pollock, George H. "Anna O: Insight, Hindsight, and Foresight." In *Anna O: Fourteen Contemporary Reinterpretations.* Edited by Max Rosenbaum and Melvin Muroff. New York: Free Press, 1984.

———."Glückel von Hameln: Bertha Pappenheim's Idealized Ancestor." *American Imago* 28(1971): 216–27.

Proust, Marcel. *Swann In Love.* Translated by C. K. Scott Moncrieff and Terence Kilmartin. New York: Modern Library, 1956.

Purcell, Henry. *The Fairy Queen.* [c. 1692.] The drama adapted from *A Midsummer Night's Dream* by Shakespeare. Edited by Anthony Lewis. Sevenoakes, Kent, Eng.: Novello (ND).

Radway, Janice A. *Reading the Romance: Women, Patriarchy, and Popular Literature.* Paperback ed. Chapel Hill: University of North Carolina Press, 1984.

Reik, Theodor. *Of Love and Lust.* [c. 1941.] Introduction by Murray H. Sherman. New York: Jason Aronson, 1984.

Rieff, Phillip. *Freud: The Mind of the Moralist.* New York: Anchor Books, 1961.

Robinson, Paul. *The Modernization of Sex.* New York: Harper and Row, 1976.

Rose, Phyllis. *Parallel Lives: Five Victorian Marriages.* New York: Random House, 1983.

Rossner, Judith. *August.* Boston: Houghton Mifflin Co., 1983.

Salter, James. *Light Years.* [c. 1975.] Paperback ed. San Francisco: North Point Press, 1982.

———. *A Sport and a Pastime.* [c. 1967.] San Francisco: North Point Press, 1985.

Sartre, Jean-Paul. *Being and Nothingness.* New York: Washington Square Press, 1966.

Schafer, Roy. "The Interpretation of Transference and the Conditions of Loving." *Journal of the American Psychoanalytic Association* 25(1977): 335–62.

Shakespeare, William. *Antony and Cleopatra.* In *The Complete Works of Shakespeare.* New York: Books, 1947.

———. *As You Like It.* In *The Complete Works of Shakespeare.* New York: Books, 1947.

———.*Hamlet.* In *The Complete Works of Shakespeare.* New York: Books, 1947.

———. *A Midsummer Night's Dream.* In *The Complete Works of Shakespeare.* New York: Books, 1947.

———. *Romeo and Juliet.* In *The Complete Works of Shakespeare.* New York: Books, 1947.

Sheed, Wilfred. *Frank and Maisie: A Memoir with Parents.* New York: Simon and Shuster, 1985.

Shelley, Percy B. "Epipsychidion." In *The Complete Poems of Keats and Shelley.* New York: Modern Library (ND). 464–77.

Simmel, Georg. *Georg Simmel: On Women, Sexuality, and Love.* Translated and with an Introduction by Guy Oakes. New Haven, Conn.: Yale University Press, 1984.

Singer, Irving. *The Nature of Love. Vol. 1: Plato to Luther.* Chicago: University of Chicago Press, 2d ed., 1985.

———. *The Nature of Love. Vol. II: Courtly and Romantic.* Chicago: University of Chicago Press, 1985.

Singer, Isaac Bashevis. *Enemies, A Love Story.* New York: Farrar, Straus and Giroux, 1972.

Slater, Philip. *The Pursuit of Loneliness: American Culture at the Breaking Point.* Revised ed. Boston: Beacon Press, 1976.

Snitow, Ann Barr. "Mass Market Romance: Pornography for Women is Different." *Radical History Review* 20(1979): 141–61.

Sontag, Susan. *A Barthes Reader.* Edited and with an Introduction by Susan Sontag. New York: Hill and Wang, 1982.

———. "The Double Standard of Aging." *Psychology of Women: Selected Readings.* Edited by Juanita H. Williams. New York: W. W. Norton, 1979, 462–78.

Spencer, Scott. *Endless Love.* New York: Alfred A. Knopf, 1979.

Spoto, Donald. *Falling in Love Again: Marlene Dietrich.* Boston, Toronto: Little, Brown, 1985.

Stanfill, Francesca. *Shadows and Light.* New York: Simon & Schuster, 1984.

Stassinopoulos, Arianna. *Maria Callas: The Woman Behind the Legend.* New York, Ballantine Books, 1982.

Stendhal. *On Love.* Translated by H. B. V. under the direction of C. K. Scott-Moncrieff. New York: Liveright, 1947.

Stern, Paul. *G. G. Jung: The Haunted Prophet.* New York: George Braziller, 1976.

Stevens, Wallace. *The Collected Poems of Wallace Stevens.* New York: Alfred A. Knopf, 1954.

Sulloway, Frank J. *Freud, Biologist of the Mind: Beyond the Psychoanalytic Legend.* New York: Basic Books, 1979.

Swift, Jonathan. *Poetical Works.* New York: Oxford University Press, 1967.

Szasz, Thomas. "The Concept of Transference." *International Journal of Psycho-Analysis* 44(1963): 432–43.

Tanner, Tony. *Adultery in the Novel: Contract and Transgression.* Paperback ed. Baltimore: Johns Hopkins University Press, 1979.

Tennov, Dorothy. *Love and Limerence.* New York: Stein and Day, 1979.

Thody, Philip. *Roland Barthes: A Conservative Estimate.* Paperback ed. Chicago: The University of Chicago Press, 1983.

Ticho, Gertrude. "Female Autonomy and Young Adult Women." *Journal of the American Psychoanalytic Association* 24(1976): 139–55.

Tolstoy, Leo. *Anna Karenina.* New York: Modern Library, ND.

Tower, Lucia. "Countertransference." *Journal of the American Psychoanalytic Association* 4(1936): 224–55.

Trollope, Anthony. *Phineas Finn.* New York: Penguin Books, 1985.

Troyat, Henri. *Tolstoy.* [c. 1967.] Translated by Nancy Amphoux. New York: Harmony Books. 1980.

Turgenev, Ivan. *First Love and Other Tales.* Translated and with an Introduction by David Magarshack. New York: W. W. Norton, 1968.

———. *Spring Torrents.* Translated by Leonard Schapiro, with Notes and a Critical Essay. New York: Penguin Books, 1986.

Ullmann, Liv. *Changing.* New York: Alfred A. Knopf, 1977.

Unger, Roberto Mangabeira. *Passion: An Essay on Personality.* New York: Free Press, 1984.

Waelder, Robert: "The Principle of Multiple Function: Observations on Over-Determination." *Psychoanalytic Quarterly* 5(1936): 45–62.

Walker, Alice. *The Color Purple.* New York: Washington Square Press, 1983.

Weil, Simone. *First and Last Notebooks.* London: Oxford University Press, 1970.

Wells, G. P. (Ed.). *H. G. Wells in Love: Postscript to an Experiment in Autobiography.* Boston: Little, Brown, 1984.

Werman, David S.; and Jacobs, Theodore J. "Thomas Hardy's 'The Well-Beloved' and the Nature of Infatuation." *International Review of Psycho-Analysis* 10(1983): 447–57.

Wexler, Alice. *Emma Goldman: An Intimate Life.* New York: Pantheon, 1984.

Wharton, Edith. *Ethan Frome.* [c. 1911.] Paperback ed. New York: Charles Scribner's Sons, 1970.

———. *The House of Mirth.* [c. 1905.] With an Introduction by Marilyn French. New York: Berkley Books, 1984.

References

Wilson, Edmund. *The Fifties.* Edited and with an Introduction by Leon Edel. New York: Farrar, Straus and Giroux, 1986.

Wood, Michael. *Stendhal.* Ithaca, N.Y.: Cornell University Press, 1971.

Woolf, Virginia. *To the Lighthouse.* [c. 1927.] Paperback ed. New York: Harcourt Brace Jovanovich, Harvest Books, 1964.

Wordsworth, William. "Intimations of Immortality from Recollections of Early Childhood." In the *Norton Anthology of English Literature,* 5th ed. vol. 2.

MOVIES

All About Eve, U.S., 1950. TCF (Darryl F. Zanuck), w d Joseph L. Mankiewicz, starring Bette Davis, George Sanders, Gary Merrill, Anne Baxter.

An Officer and a Gentleman, U.S., 1982. Paramount (Martin Elsand) w Douglas Day Stewart, d Taylor Hackford, starring Richard Gere, Debra Winger, Lou Gossett, Jr., Robert Loggia.

The Blue Angel, Germany, 1930. UFA (Erich Pommer), w Robert Liebmann, Karl Zuckmayer, Karl Vollmoeller, from novel *Professor Unrath* by Heinrich Mann, d Josef von Sternberg, starring Marlene Dietrich, Emil Jannings.

Casablanca, U.S., 1942. Warner (Hal B. Wallis), w Julius J. Epstein, Philip G. Epstein, Howard Koch, from unproduced play *Everybody Comes to Rick's* by Murray Burnett and Joan Alison, d Michael Curtiz, starring Humphrey Bogart, Ingrid Bergman, Claude Rains, Paul Henreid.

City Lights, U.S., 1931. UA (Charles Chaplin), w d Charles Chaplin, starring Charles Chaplin, Virginia Cherrill, Harry Myers.

Dark Victory, U.S., 1939. Warner (David Lewis), w Casey Robinson, from the play by George Brewer Jnr, Bertram Bloch, d Edmund Goulding, starring Bette Davis, George Brent, Humphrey Bogart, Ronald Reagan, Geraldine Fitzgerald, Henry Travers, Cora Witherspoon, Dorothy Peterson.

The Enchanted Cottage, U.S., 1945. RKO, w De Witt Bodeen, Herman J. Mankiewicz, from the play *The Enchanted Cottage* by Sir Arthur Wing Pinero, d John Cromwell, starring Dorothy McGuire, Robert Young, Herbert Marshall, Mildred Natwick.

The Godfather, U.S., 1971. Paramount/Alfran (Albert S. Ruddy), w Francis Ford Coppola, Mario Puzo from Puzo's novel *The Godfather,* d Francis Ford Coppola, starring Al Pacino, Marlon Brando, Robert Duvall, James Caan, Diane Keaton.

Gone With the Wind, U.S., 1939. MGM (David O. Selznick), w Sidney Howard from the novel *Gone With the Wind* by Margaret Mitchell, d Victor Fleming, George Cukor, Sam Wood, starring Clark Gable, Vivien Leigh, Olivia de Havilland, Leslie Howard, Thomas Mitchell, Hattie McDaniel.

The Graduate, U.S., 1967. UA/Embassy (Lawrence Turman), w Calder Willingham, Buck Henry, from novel *The Graduate* by Charles Webb, d Mike Nichols, starring Dustin Hoffman, Anne Bancroft, Katharine Ross.

Hannah and Her Sisters, U.S., 1986. Orion (Robert Greenhut), d w Woody Allen, starring Woody Allen, Mia Farrow, Michael Caine, Barbara Hershey, Dianne Wiest.

Last Tango in Paris, France/Italy/U.S., 1972. Les Artistes Associes/PEA/UA (Alberto Grimaldi), w Bernardo Bertolucci, Franco Arcalli, d Bernardo Bertolucci, starring Marlon Brando, Maria Schneider, Jean-Pierre Leaud.

Laura, U.S., 1944. TCF (Otto Preminger), w Jay Dratler, Samuel Hoffenstein, Betty Reinhardt, from novel *Laura* by Vera Caspary, d Otto Preminger, starring Gene Tierney, Dana Andrews, Clifton Webb, Judith Anderson, Vincent Price.

Lilith, U.S., 1964. Columbia/Centaur (Robert Rossen), w d Robert Rossen from novel *Lilith* by J. R. Salamanca, starring Warren Beatty, Jean Seberg, Kim Hunter.

Menage, France, 1986. Hachette Premiere/DD Productions/Cine Valse/Philippe Dussart Sarl (Rene Cleitman) w d Bertrand Blier, starring Gerard Depardieu, Michel Blanc, Miou-Miou.

Mr. Skeffington, U.S., 1944. Warner Brothers (Julius J. & Philip G. Epstein) w Julius J. Epstein and Philip G. Epstein from novel *Elizabeth,* d Vincent Sherman, starring Bette Davis, Claude Rains.

Morocco, U.S., 1930. Paramount, w Jules Furthman, from novel *Amy Jolly* by Benno Vigny, d Josef
    von Sternberg, starring Marlene Dietrich, Gary Cooper, Adolphe Menjou.

Ninotchka, U.S., 1939. MGM (Ernst Lubitsch) w Charles Brackett, Billy Wilder, Walter Reisch,
    Smelchior Lengyel, d Ernst Lubitsch, starring Greta Garbo, Melvyn Douglas.

Now, Voyager, U.S., 1942. Warner Brothers (Hal B. Wallis) w Casey Robinson from novel *Now,
    Voyager* by Olive Higgins Prouty, d Irving Rapper, starring Bette Davis, Claude Rains, Paul
    Henreid, Gladys Cooper.

The Philadelphia Story, U.S., 1940. MGM (Joseph L. Mankiewicz) w Donald Ogden Stewart, from
    the play by Philip Barry, d George Cukor, starring Katharine Hepburn, Cary Grant, James
    Stewart, Ruth Hussey.

The Postman Always Rings Twice, U.S., 1946. MGM (Carey Wilson) w Harry Ruskin, Niven Busch,
    from novel *The Postman Always Rings Twice* by James M. Cain, d Tay Garnett, starring
    Lana Turner, John Garfield.

Radio Days, U.S., 1987. Orion (Robert Greenhut) w d Woody Allen, starring Mia Farrow, Seth
    Green, Julie Kavner, Josh Mostel.

Shanghai Express, U.S. 1932. Paramount, w Jules Furthman, d Josef von Sternberg, starring Marlene
    Dietrich, Clive Brook, Warner Oland, Anna May Wong.

Somewhere in Time, U.S., 1980. Universal (Steven Deutsch) w Richard Matheson from his novel,
    d Jeannot Szwarc, starring Christopher Reeve, Jane Seymour, Christopher Plummer,
    Teresa Wright.

Sophie's Choice, U.S., 1983. Universal (Alan J. Pakula/Keith Barish) w d Alan J. Pakula from the
    novel by William Styron, starring Kevin Kline, Meryl Streep.

The Story of Adèle H., France, 1975. Films du Carrosse/Artistes Associes (Marcel Berbert, Claude
    Miller), w d Francois Truffaut, Jean Gruault, Suzanne Schiffman, starring Isabelle Adjani,
    Bruce Robinson, Sylvia Marriott.

Swept Away, Italy, 1975. d Lina Wertmuller, starring Giancarlo Giannini, Mariangela Melato.

The Way We Were, U.S., 1973. Columbia/Rastar (Ray Stark), w Arthur Laurents from his novel,
    d Sydney Pollack, starring Barbra Streisand, Robert Redford.

The Women, U.S., 1939. MGM (Hunt Stromberg), w Anita Loos, Jane Murfin from the play by
    Clare Boothe Luce, d George Cukor, starring Norma Shearer, Joan Crawford, Rosalind
    Russell, Mary Boland, Paulette Goddard, Joan Fontaine, Ruth Hussey.

Topper, U.S., 1937. Hal Roach, w Jack Jevne, Eric Hatch, Eddie Moran, and Norman Z. McLeod,
    from the novel by Thorne Smith starring Cary Grant, Constance Bennett, Roland Young,
    Billie Burke.

Index

Index

Index